Irene,
we've had a great
ride at the bookstore.
I'll miss you terribly.
Love, Sandy

I won't say
good-bye — I know I'll
see you in D.C. — but, it
won't be the same without
you here —
Fondly,
Cathie

I will miss you!
Fondly, Peggy
P.S. Keep in touch!!

My bookstore dream
wouldn't have happened
if you hadn't jumped
on board with enthusiasm
and an organized
scheduling calendar!
Much appreciation,
Anne

Irene,
It has been
nice getting
to know you.
You will be
remembered.
Sincerely,
Marge

Irene,
We have our own "Tales" don't we Irene!
Don't forget ME —
Love,
Lynne

Dear Irene, you're a
you're a local.
national + looking.
Treasure! Looking
forward to seeing
you in D.C.
Fondly,
Mary

Irene! We've shared and been
through so much together
over the past few years.
I'll miss you terribly
my dear friend,
but I know we'll
see each other
again in DC
+ elsewhere
Susan

TALES
of the
NEW ENGLAND
COAST

COMPILED BY FRANK OPPEL

CASTLE

ISBN: 0-89009-873-5

8th Printing

TABLE
OF
CONTENTS

1
Martha's Vineyard

Martha's Vineyard.

By William A. Mowry.

ALL honor to Bartholomew Gosnold. He discovered Martha's
Vineyard. He made the first
English settlement in New England.
His foot first pressed the shores of
Maine. He, first of all Englishmen,
traversed the sands of Cape Cod.
He and his twenty men first sailed
along the southern shores of Nantucket and Martha's Vineyard. On
the 21st of May, 1602, he anchored his
little vessel and went ashore on No-
Man's-Land. He named it Martha's
Vineyard, but afterwards transferred
the name to the larger island north of
it. On May 24th, he sailed past Gay
Head, and from its resemblance to
the cliffs of Old Dover, England, he
called it "Dover Cliff." The next
day, Gosnold sailed across the entrance of Vineyard Sound and came
to anchor at a "rocky ilet." This little island he named Elizabeth Isle, in
honor of his queen. Subsequently he
named the entire line of islands the
Elizabeth Islands. Beginning upon
the west, the eight largest islands bear
the euphonious names of Cuttyhunk,
Penikese, Nashawena, Pasque, Naushon (the largest), Weepecket, Unca-
tena, Nonamesset.

At Cuttyhunk, which Gosnold
called Elizabeth Isle, he made the
first settlement of Englishmen in New
England. Here he built a house and
a fort, intending to remain there with
"eleven men who promised to tarry
with him" and establish a permanent
plantation. From this point Gosnold
made several visits to the adjacent
islands and to the mainland. He
first of all sailed through that wonderful Vineyard Sound, through which
strait at the present time more vessels
pass in one year than through any
other channel of water in the whole

VINEYARD HAVEN.

world, excepting only from the Straits of Dover to London. As Gosnold visited these islands and the mainland, as he looked out upon the great forests of "beeches and cedars," as he saw large tracts of "low, bushy trees, three or four feet in height, which bear some kind of fruit as appears by their blossoms," as he saw quantities of "strawberries, as sweet and much bigger than ours in England, raspberries, gooseberries, whortleberries, and such an incredible store of vines, as well in the woody part of the island, where they run upon every tree, as on

velvet,"—we may well believe that Gosnold attributed to these islands such appellations as "fair fields," "fertile meadows," "stately groves," "pleasant brooks," "beauteous rivers" and "fragrant flowers."

Three weeks Gosnold and his men spent in erecting his house and fort. Many disputes and controversies arose, however, until it was decided that they should abandon their enterprise and return to England. They left the island with "many true, sorrowful eyes," and after a short passage of only five weeks they came to

the outward parts," and again when he looked out upon an island "full of high-timbered oaks, their leaves twice as broad as ours, cedars straight and tall, beech, elm, holly, walnut trees in abundance, hazelnut trees, cherry trees, the leaf, bark and bigness not different from ours in England, but the stalk beareth the blossom or fruit at the end thereof like a cluster of grapes, forty or fifty in a bunch, sassafras trees, great plenty all the island over, a tree of high price and profit, also divers other fruit trees, some of them with strange barks of an orange color, in feeling soft and smooth like

anchor before Exmouth, "all being in good health, having had no sickness in their company during their entire voyage, but on the contrary," as the scribe of the party wrote, "being much fatter and in better health than when we went out."

Gosnold's house was the first habitation built by the English on the shores of New England. One cannot sail through that famous Vineyard Sound or ramble upon the shores of Martha's Vineyard, either at Old Town or Great Harbor (Edgartown), New Town (West Tisbury) or Dover Cliff (Gay Head), without one's

IN COTTAGE CITY.

thought running back to the time of Gosnold and the Indians and this first attempted settlement upon these shores. At first the Vineyard, Nantucket and the Elizabeth Island were not included in any of the colonial governments of New England. Under a grant from the king, William, Earl of Sterling, claimed all the islands between Cape Cod and the Hudson River. His agent, James Forcett, as early as 1641, granted to Thomas Mayhew and his son Thomas, of Watertown, all these islands, the Elizabeth Islands, the Vineyard and Nantucket, with the same powers of government which the people of Massachusetts received from their charter.

The first settlement in Martha's Vineyard was made in 1642 by Thomas Mayhew, the son, and a few persons with him, who established themselves at Edgartown. For a long time this place was called Old Town. The father soon after came to the settlement and became the governor of the colony. In 1644, however, these islands were annexed to the jurisdiction of Massachusetts, probably at the request of the inhabitants. Twenty years later, they came under the control of New York, and while connected with that colony were formed into a county. Martha's Vineyard has ever since remained as Duke's County. The charter of Massachusetts from William and Mary, which reached New England in 1692, reconveyed these islands

STEAMERS AT COTTAGE CITY.

CROQUET AND TENNIS COURTS AT COTTAGE CITY.

from New York to Massachusetts. In 1695 Nantucket became a county by itself.

Thomas Mayhew was the progenitor of a large family, some of whom are still found among the residents of Martha's Vineyard. Thomas Mayhew, Jr., became a minister, pastor of the church here established, and missionary to the Indians. Through his instrumentality, "many of the natives were induced to embrace the Christian faith."

At the time of the first settlement upon this island, at Great Harbor, as it was then called, the Indians were very numerous. The original settlement was half a mile or more south of the present courthouse. The spot where the village of Edgartown stands to-day was at that time an ancient Indian burying ground. In later years, when cellars have been dug, human bones were found in great quantities. Occasionally the skeleton of a giant would be exhumed. In one case, a huge jawbone of a man

was dug out from the ground, larger than that of any man at the present time, so large that it could be placed against the face of an ordinary man and entirely surround his jaw. Directly south of the village, in early times, was what was termed a "kitchen midden." This term signifies a shell heap, a dumping ground. It had a rich black mold two feet deep, in which were found deer's horns and various specimens of shells, some of which seem to be of species extinct at the present day. This "kitchen midden" certainly indicates that the Indians had had a settlement there for ages. The ancient Indians of Martha's Vineyard were a hospitable race and more friendly and peaceful than those upon the mainland.

Rev. Thomas Mayhew was the first missionary to the aborigines. His labors antedated those of the Apostle Eliot. After his death his father assumed the work, and a few years later his son, and this laudable missionary enterprise to the Indians was carried on by some member of the family till the beginning of the present century. In the early days of the settlement, nearly all the Indians upon the island became professed Christians. They were formed into a church in 1659, and another Indian church was established in 1670. Full-blooded Indians lived in this locality as late as the early part of the present century, but none can be found to-day on the island. The last one of the pure bloods was Simon Johnson, a deacon in the Baptist Church at Gay Head, who died about twenty-five years ago.

At the time of King Philip's War, all the Indians upon the mainland and Martha's Vineyard suffered severely from the invasion of the British, who were as cruel and brutal here as upon the coast of Connecticut and Rhode Island. Subsequent to the Revolution the islanders turned their attention to the whale fishery, which in due time came to be the source of the principal wealth of the island. Both Nantucket and Martha's Vineyard at first carried on whale fishery after the most primitive style, pursuing these monsters of the deep in rowboats from the shore. Even in this fashion they found the business profitable. A little later small vessels were fitted out for the whale fishery, which in turn were successful in bringing

COTTAGES AT COTTAGE CITY.

were confederated against the English; but Mayhew had such confidence in his Indians that he employed them as a guard for the island, furnished them with ammunition, instructed them in military tactics and in rules for the safety of the people should the danger become imminent. These converted Indians proved reliable, so that the terrible storm which raged within Massachusetts and Rhode Island was entirely averted from these islands. The islanders escaped all harm during the sanguinary struggle.

In the Revolutionary War they were not so fortunate. Nantucket wealth to the hardy islanders. In due time Edgartown and Nantucket vied with New Bedford for the prize of leadership in this hazardous industry. Large ships were built, manned and commanded by hardy sons of Martha's Vineyard, and these vessels sailed every sea where whales were known to exist, in both latitudes, from the equator to the Arctic and Antarctic icebergs. Many a man is now living on Martha's Vineyard who in his younger days followed the seas and threw a harpoon. How often have I sat hour after hour and listened to the tales of their adventurous exploits. Here is a story which one of these men told me only a few weeks ago:

"How long did I follow the seas? Well, something over thirty year. Whaling all that time? Oh, no, I was on a whaler the first part of the time, but in a merchantman the latter part. I first went to sea when I was a youngster, fifty year ago. I've never bunked in the fo'c's'le. I went out as cabin-boy at first, and I've been in the cabin ever since. I've held various positions as ship's officer. Where have I sailed? Well, in all

that to the rajah and no man in the village would dare to touch you. All you got to do is to get on the right side of the guv'nor and you're all right. Then I've been all round Australia and New Zealand. But I've had a good time over and over again at Norfolk Island. One time we anchored there, and some of us fellows attempted to go ashore in a row-boat. It's pretty bad making a landing. The surf ran high and we were laboring hard at the oars when I see a native swing off into the water and

latitudes pretty much, and all longitudes. I've been around the world again and again. I've been whaling up on the Northwest coast beyond Bering Straits; I've found them in the Ar'tic and in the Antar'tic. When I was on a merchantman at one time I went all through the Malay Islands. They told us we mus'n't go ashore, any of us, for the natives were hostile. We went ashore just the same. All you had to do was to carry a couple of yards of calico for an apun, or a cheap pocket-knife, or a dirk, or a string of beads,—and jest you give

swim for the boat. He got to us and we pulled him in. He says: 'Here, you fellows, give me the steering oar, and I'll land you.' So we gave him the steering oar, and he says: 'Now, you do jest as I tell you'; and we watched until by and by he sung out: 'Now, all pull for your lives'; and we pulled, just as a big wave struck us and pushed us away up on to the sand. Before the wave could carry us back, a dozen men seized hold of the boat and pulled her ashore. Well, we were lying round there on the dock, when one of the natives came

MARTHA'S VINEYARD SUMMER INSTITUTE.

up to me and says: 'I know who you are, you're Bowers from Nantucket or Martha's Vineyard, United States.' He called my name right out, and he called it straight too. Well, I looked at him and I said: 'Where did you ever see me?' 'I never saw you before.' 'How did you know who I was then?—for you've told it right.' 'Well, you come up to the house, and I'll tell you.' So I started off with him, and we went about a mile through the woods, by a little narrow crooked path, thick bush on either side, so that we couldn't see ten feet ahead of us. We got up to the house, a large square house with big rooms. Then he brought out a photograph and showed me. Well, sure's you live, that was a photograph

of my friend Mather and myself taken together. Now Mather was an old messmate of mine, and one time in a foreign port we had this picture taken. And I said: 'Well, well, how did you come by that?' 'Oh, Mather gave that to me; he told me all about you; he thought the world of you. And if you are Mather's friend you are my friend.' And then he took me upstairs and showed me a good nice room with a fine bed and everything well furnished, and says: 'There,

STUDENTS AT THE INSTITUTE.

Photograph by Baldwin Coolidge.

GAY HEAD.

that's your room. You come here whenever you like, and this room is at your service; now make yourself at home.' So I went up there to see him frequently, and one day,—what do you think? As I was going back down to the harbor,—for you see there was but one real harbor to that island, and that was Sydney Bay,—going back to that harbor, right in the middle of the woods, in that little, narrow, crooked path, I come right up face to face with a man I knew. He was from the Vineyard, and we both stopped and stood there and looked at each other. And if that wasn't strange;—in that little, narrow, crooked path, there I met my old shipmate, Tyler, that I hadn't seen for years and years! Well, I guess 'twas two minutes before either of us spoke, and then Tyler says: 'Well, old shipmate, what are you doing here?' And I said, 'Well, old shipmate, what are *you* doing here?' And then we both said, 'I am glad to see you,' and shook hands and laughed and had a good time. Well, when you meet an old friend and countryman away off at the ends of the earth like that, under such circumstances, you have a good many questions to ask him, and when he answers them all he pays you back by asking just as many more."

I tell this because it is representative of the lives and experiences of many of the men still living in Martha's Vineyard. This man is a most intelligent man, proud of his voyages. He kept a diary, writing in

GAY HEAD LIGHTHOUSE.

it every day. I fancy that that old diary would give men and women, not to say schoolboys and girls, many an important lesson in geography. The whaling business has passed by, and scarcely a whaling vessel can be found belonging to any of those ports along the coast. Edgartown has very few vessels traversing the high seas, and those mostly fishing smacks.

The Martha's Vineyard of to-day is very different from the Martha's Vineyard of the early time. Oldtown is a quiet summer watering place. Newtown or West Tisbury comprises a community of farms. Gay Head, with its famous lighthouse near the spot where the *Columbus* was wrecked, has its few half-breed Indians and its wonderful Dover Cliffs of colored clay. Chilmark is the largest of the five townships, with a variety of interests, and it includes Vineyard Haven and West Chop. But Cottage City surpasses all in population and as a summer resort. The chief interest in the island to-day is found in its great attractions for summer residents. Its growth in this respect has been phenomenal. This beautiful island has charms for all sorts of visitors. The naturalist finds here specimens of vegetable and animal life which are either rare or unknown in other parts of the world. Although the island as a whole is composed of sand, the great variety which nature shows in vegetation is little less than marvelous. Professor Burgess, who has

THE PARK AT COTTAGE CITY.

taught the classes in botany in the Martha's Vineyard Summer Institute for fourteen years, has analyzed and classified over seven hundred species of plant life found upon the island. The algæ show almost an infinite variety of exquisite beauty. "Here are ribbons, green, purple, orange, crimson, red; and here are ruffles and laces of richer hue and more delicate tracery than any that grace the robe of a queen."

The climate during the summer months makes Martha's Vineyard most attractive and restful. The eastern end of the island has now become one large watering place, with summer visitors from various parts of the country. The causes which have brought this about are worth noticing. First of all should be mentioned the Methodist Camp-meeting. In August, 1835, in a beautiful secluded grove of oak trees, a few far-seeing Methodists held a camp-meeting. The experiment was repeated the next year; and out of that humble beginning important results have grown. Those early camp-meetings were primitive and unique. The worshipers stretched a large tent for the meeting, and each family erected a rude tent for its own habitation. The first year there were nine of these tents; but soon the number in attendance increased, until the Martha's Vineyard camp-meeting became the largest of the kind in the country. Cottages soon took the place of tents, —at first cottages of humble proportions and so huddled together as to occupy but small space; later men of wealth from various parts of the country, particularly from New York, built large cottages and laid out beautiful grounds. In due time an association was formed and incorporated, which now owns the large tract called the Camp Grounds, with its hundreds of cottages and its great iron taber-

nacle for the camp-meetings and worship on Sundays through the season. This tabernacle is located in the centre of a circular ground finely laid out with trees and shrubbery, grass plots and concrete walks. It will seat five thousand people, and has the finest acoustic properties. Within the camp grounds everything is kept in the most excellent order, with due regard to beauty, health and comfort. In the old times, forty years ago, when tents predominated and cottages were scarce, at camp-meeting time the tents of all kinds and sizes

with house lots and ample parks and drives, and the place is now known as the Vineyard Highlands. From the high bluffs on these Highlands are charming views of the sound, the constant line of sailing vessels, the steamers arriving and departing, the shores of the mainland opposite, Lake Anthony, the camp gronuds, and Oak Bluffs. Within the lands of this Vineyard Grove Company, in 1875, the Baptists established a camp-meeting, and in a beautiful grove of oak trees they erected the Baptist Temple, a fine circular building with open

WHERE COTTAGE CITY GETS ITS WATER.

numbered two hundred and fifty, one year three hundred and twenty. To-day the tent is a rarity, but within the limits of the town of Cottage City there are eleven hundred cottages of all sorts, sizes and dimensions.

Just across Lake Anthony from the camp grounds are the Highlands, a beautiful location and admirably adapted for attractive summer residences. Here some gentlemen purchased two hundred acres or more of land, and were incorporated in 1870 as the Vineyard Grove Company. They laid out the land artistically,

sides, where religious services are held on Sundays in summer, and camp-meeting or, as they call it, "Religious Gathering," annually, in the month of August.

Cottage City is admirably located for a summer watering place. On the one side are Oak Bluffs and the Camp Grounds, with the Oak Bluffs wharf; and on the other side are the Vineyard Highlands and the Highland wharf. Lake Anthony, a beautiful sheet of water, lies between, with Sunset Lake farther to the west. This is a charming sheet of fresh water emptying into the salt water at the Causeway, which is the town road from one side to the other.

Lying as it does out in the Atlantic Ocean, Martha's Vineyard enjoys sea breezes every day and at all hours. No matter which way the wind is, it blows from across the sea. The temperature during all the summer months averages about ten degrees lower than upon the mainland. Cottage City is supplied with pure water of the best quality from an inland lake. The soil is sandy, and the surface is so undulating that drainage is of the very best. As to the healthfulness of

tween the ages of eighty and ninety than between seventy and eighty.

Cottage City has a permanent population of more than one thousand; and sometimes, during the height of the season, the summer residents number twenty-five thousand. It has two excellent beaches, with hundreds of bathing houses, and the bathing is the most delightful on the entire Atlantic coast. The water is from fifteen to twenty degrees warmer than at Nantasket Beach, and the tide ebbs and flows only about two feet, so that bathing is good at any hour of the day. The beaches are perfectly safe,

the island, it has been said that a physician could not find sufficient support unless he was at the same time a surgeon. An aged Methodist minister told the writer that, during a year and a half of his pastorate at Edgartown, he attended the funerals of eleven members of the church, only one of whom was under seventy years of age; and during one year's pastorate at Vineyard Haven, he buried seven members of the church, whose combined ages made five hundred and fifty years. Thirty-four per cent of the population reach the age of sixty years, and more persons die be-

free from dangerous surf and undertow. It is no unusual sight to see five hundred persons bathing at one beach at one time. The streets and sidewalks of the entire village are concreted, the place having between thirty and forty miles of concrete pavement. It is therefore the paradise of bicyclists. The L. A. W. has for many years held its annual meet here. At Martha's Vineyard, too, the New York Yacht Club has headquarters; and every summer, in August, the yacht race presents one of the most beautiful sights to be found anywhere.

SUNSET LAKE.

The old nautical proverb, "If you are in a safe harbor, do not put to sea in a storm," has its counterpart at Martha's Vineyard: "If you are at sea in a storm, put into the nearest safe harbor." Vineyard Haven and Edgartown Bay furnish safe harbors to thousands of vessels in time of storm. It is no unusual thing, during the summer, to see in Vineyard Haven one hundred, two hundred, or even three hundred vessels of various kinds at anchor. When the storm is over and these vessels have weighed anchor, you may sometimes see a hundred or a hundred and fifty of them starting out in a straight line, in the direction of Nantucket, to sail around Cape Cod to various eastern ports. The entire coastwise commerce of America, sailing between any port northeast of Martha's Vineyard and any port to the westward and southward, passes through Vineyard Sound. Trans-atlantic craft sail outside, but every coasting vessel passes directly by Cottage City, between it and the mainland, and within five miles. The number of vessels passing here is estimated to exceed fifty thousand annually.

As already stated, Vineyard Haven Bay furnishes the very best anchorage ground for vessels. This has occasioned the building up of the very beautiful village of Vineyard Haven,

which has many quaint and interesting features. The village is nestled cosily around the harbor, and the houses are built upon a declivity in quaint and picturesque style. Here is located a marine hospital and a "sailors' snug harbor." A mile or two eastward from Vineyard Haven is West Chop, with its lighthouse and fog horn. A few Boston men have lately purchased land at this point and built fine cottages, making in the summer a pleasant community of intelligent people.

Three miles south of Edgartown is Katama and the South Beach, connected with Edgartown and Cottage City by a railroad. The south beach is noted for its surf, especially after a southerly storm. On the

THE EPISCOPAL CHAPEL.

BEECH GROVE SPRING.

Vineyard Sound and the tide is setting strongly toward the west, it produces a rough sea, which is not favorable to pleasurable navigation.

Excursions from Cottage City during the summer months are numerous and delightful. Hundreds of people take the trip from Cottage City to the quaint old town of Nantucket. Short excursions are frequent from Cottage City to Wood's Holl, where is located the station of the United States Fish Commission. A visit to this establishment is of great interest. Weekly excursions are made during the season from Cottage City to Gay Head. This is a delightful trip of twenty-five miles, covering the entire length of Vineyard Sound between Martha's Vineyard and the Elizabeth Islands. Gay Head is famous for its lighthouse and its clay cliffs. The lighthouse is one of the most important on the entire Atlantic coast. It is a light of the first order. There are less than half a dozen lights of this order on the entire Atlantic coast. There are four lighthouses on the island—at Gay Head, at West Chop, at East Chop and at Cape Poge. The famous cliffs, which have made Gay Head known

north and east coasts the surf seldom runs high; but the south coast, with its shallow water, furnishes the very best conditions for high running surf. Katama Bay separates Martha's Vineyard from the island of Chappaquiddeck, which is easily reached by boats from Edgartown, and which has an interesting life of its own.

The entire island of Martha's Vineyard, as well as Nantucket, is of peculiar formation. The whole southern coast has a line of salt lakes, and the shore is very shoal. There can therefore be no harbors on the south side of Martha's Vineyard or of Nantucket, and vessels are obliged to keep off a long distance from the land. The tides, too, on the eastern end of Martha's Vineyard have some peculiarities; they flow east and west; they also run with considerable rapidity north and south along the coast past Cottage City. When the wind blows fresh from the west sweeping through

MARTHA'S VINEYARD CEDARS.

the world over, constitute a long, high bluff, running down to the sea. This bluff is about a hundred feet in height. The cliff is composed of red, yellow, blue, indigo, black and white clay. Pottery is made from this clay, with its variegated colors, which is sold to the summer visitors and carried all over the country as souvenirs of the island. Tisbury and West Tisbury comprise the central part of the island. Here the soil, which at Cottage City and at Edgartown is light and sandy, is heavy and strong, well adapted to good crops. Much of this part of the island is well wooded with pines and

shops for books, stationery, periodicals, shells, trinkets, island souvenirs and bric-a-brac, and photograph galleries. The place is lighted by gas and electricity. Street railroads carry passengers to various points of interest in the town and also to Vineyard Haven. The Board of Trade is vigorous and efficient. Here is a Grand Army post, a public library, telegraph and express offices, and a post office. Four steamboats daily transport the mail, passengers and freight to and from the island. These boats run to New Bedford, Woods Holl and Nantucket. The

EDGARTOWN.

oaks once large, but now of inferior size. Indeed all the trees upon this and the neighboring islands are smaller than formerly. It is customary to cut off the whole growth from the woodlands once in about thirty years.

Cottage City was set off as a township about seventeen years ago. The place is just what the name indicates. With a small winter population and a very large number of summer residents, most of whom live in small cottages nestled close together, the place really makes a city of cottages. Circuit Avenue is the principal business street. Here are stores and shops of all kinds, markets for meats and vegetables, grocery and dry-goods stores,

town maintains good schools and an efficient fire department.

At Vineyard Highlands is located the Martha's Vineyard Summer Institute. This school was first opened in the summer of 1878, with about seventy-five students and Col. Homer B. Sprague as president. It was incorporated in 1880. The present large building, called, in honor of the distinguished naturalist who established the first summer school in this country upon the neighboring island of Penikese, Agassiz Hall, was built and first occupied in 1882. Colonel Sprague had at that time been succeeded in the presidency of the Institute by Prof. William J. Rolfe, the well-known Shakespearian critic. He served from 1882 to 1887, when the present executive board was elected. The high standing and public appreciation of the school are shown by the increase in attendance. In 1878, seventy-five pupils were present; in 1887, one hundred and fifty; in 1894, '5 and '6, the number was over seven hundred. T h e r e are over forty instructors, who are specialists in their several departments. The Institute provides for its members and for the citizens generally a course of fine entertainments

THE WATERSPOUT OF 1896.

each summer, in the Union Chapel. Connected with the school is a dormitory and a café for the better accommodation of its members.

No country in the world has made more rapid progress in the education of the masses than America. No subject to-day receives a wider attention, a more patient hearing or a more earnest interest than the question of education. In no direction has greater advance been made during the last twenty years than in the new methods of instruction among the teachers in American schoolhouses. The American public is d e m a n d i n g a broader knowledge of the principles of psychology and pedagogy, on the part of

all teachers in schools of all grades, from kindergarten to university. the elevation of the public school- such as this at Martha's Vineyard for the elevation of the public school teachers of the country.

Martha's Vineyard stands in the forefront among summer resorts along the Atlantic coast, for boating and fishing and bathing. There is hardly a yacht upon the Atlantic coast which does not know the pleasure of a visit to the Vineyard. Every yachtsman, in planning for his summer cruise, takes pains to arrange an occasional run ashore at Cottage City. The island may be called the hub of the very best fishing ground upon the Atlantic coast. Blue-fishing combines the two great sports of fishing and sailing; and off the shores of

YACHTS AT VINEYARD HAVEN.

Martha's Vineyard is the perfection of this fine sport. Are there any better bluefish grounds anywhere upon the coast than within ten miles of Cottage City? Tell your skipper to run his boat into Muskegat Channel. This channel is filled with shoals, "grounds" and "rips," all excellent and available bluefish haunts. Here are miles in length and miles in breadth of the very best bluefishing grounds. If you are bent upon the very finest fishing, run the boat over "Shark Ground" or "Tom Shoal." Tell the skipper to sail along from Wasque Point to Skiff's Island, and you will certainly be successful in your fishing. For fine scup and rock-bass grounds, try the "Squash Meadow Shoal," only two miles out from Cottage City wharf. All along the north side of the island is good fishing ground for tautog and other varieties. For cod, cruise around Gay Head and No-Man's-Land.

Every place upon the seacoast at times experiences severe winds. Certain portions of the Atlantic coast are specially dangerous in storms. The sheltered positions of Edgartown Bay and Vineyard Haven render the section around the eastern extremity of Martha's Vineyard less dangerous than many other portions of the coast. But of course there are times when the wind blows with such fury as to snap cables, drag anchors and create danger, confusion and loss to the shipping. Vineyard Haven is less protected from a northeast storm than when the wind is in other quarters. There have been times when vessels have been piled up in confusion and much damage has been done.

On the 19th of last August, it was my good fortune to witness a remarkable waterspout a few miles to the eastward of Cottage City. Between twelve and one o'clock my attention was arrested by a singular black cloud directly in the east. Near the northern extremity of this cloud, which was very dense and very black,

there suddenly appeared a narrow whirlwind shooting downward. It rapidly extended until it reached the water. The appearance of this waterspout was very grand. Near the surface of the water the atmosphere was so agitated as to form a spray extending some distance. Above this mist, through which a vessel could be seen, the circular column extended upward a long distance to the black cloud. At the top this column was tunnel-shaped, being larger at the cloud and diminishing in size downward. For nearly fifteen minutes the position and size and shape of the waterspout scarcely changed; then the middle section gradually diminished in size until the lower part disappeared entirely, leaving a tunnel-shaped appearance extending downward from the cloud about half way to the water and ending in what appeared like a sharp point. Very soon, however, it reformed, until the column was complete from the cloud to the water. This time the upper portion was bent, the weight of the cloud lying to the southward, this upper section bent southerly toward the cloud. This second formation lasted some ten minutes and then gradually disappeared.*

We are living in the time of summer outings, of restful vacations in seaside and mountain resorts. What multitudes from the cities spend more or less time in the summer at Fabyan's and Crawford's, in Jefferson and on Mt. Washington, at the Profile House, North Conway, Whitefield, around Lake Winnepesaukee, throughout the whole region of the White Mountains, and in many other sections of New Hampshire! What crowds spend a few weeks among the Green Mountains of Vermont, in the Adirondacks of New York, in the elevated regions of the Colorado Rockies! There are the swarms at Saratoga and Newport, Old Orchard and Mt. Desert. The

* A full description of this remarkable waterspout may be found in *The Scientific American* of September, 1896

islands of Maine are alive with pleasure seekers, hard-worked men and women hunting for rest. At Cape Cod and all along shore are found strangers, by families, by scores and by hundreds. Among the seaside resorts, Martha's Vineyard holds a high rank. Last summer even the seven hundred members of the Summer Institute included representatives from forty states and provinces. The number of summer visitors at the Vineyard is annually increasing. The mild climate, wholesome air, pure water, beautiful drives, excellent fishing and moderate prices, all serve to attract the many who are seeking rest and recreation.

The question annually arises: Which is preferable for summer rest, the seaside or the mountains? Some enjoy the mountain tops, the variety of scenery, the changing clouds, the sunshine and shadow. They cannot abide the seaside; to them it is flat, monotonous, uniform. Their enthusiasm is excited only by jagged peaks, high cliffs, deep chasms, ravines, mountain streams. Others, however, are charmed by the ever active, never ceasing restlessness of the waves. They see in old ocean the emblem of eternity, of infinity. They are exhilarated by the atmosphere at the sea level. The constant winds, purifying, energizing, invigorating, attract them; the ever changing kaleidoscope of the vessels with their white sails and their steady motion, the clouds over the sea, which have equal charms to them with the clouds around the mountain tops, the reflection of sunlight and shadow from the surface of the ocean,—all these present to their eyes an ever enchanting waterscape. The calm and the storm, the gentle zephyrs and old Boreas give variety to the scene. The lashing waves, the beating surf, and anon the placid calm,—these to multitudes of people make a visit at the seaside attractive, restful and invigorating. To the tired worker seeking rest the seaside especially appeals. The murmuring of the waves lulls him to sleep, the atmosphere gives him tone and body and strength. The variety of light and shade, of wind and wave, the sailing ships, the sportive boats, the stately steamer,—all attract his attention, without tiring his nerves.

Whether one turns to the seaside for rest and health, or for social delight, or for beauty, there are few places upon the Atlantic coast which offer more than this largest island upon the coast—Martha's Vineyard!

2

On the
Old Boston
Post Road

Drawn by Stanley M. Arthurs.

CHANGING HORSES.

Scribner's Magazine

NOVEMBER, 1908

On the Old Boston Post Road.

ON THE OLD BOSTON POST ROAD

By Stanley M. Arthurs

ILLUSTRATIONS BY THE AUTHOR

S far back as the year 1772 there was a stage running from Boston to New York, which if it had good luck and no serious break-downs in the wilderness, pulled in over the Bowery road in thirteen days with its weary, travel-sore passengers.

They could have gone by the slow, sailing packets in much shorter time and with greater comfort, but even then in unfavorable weather, they might beat around for more than a week before reaching their journey's end. If New Yorkers had relatives in Boston they were farther away than our English cousins are now, and consequently travel did not develop extensive proportions in the Colonies.

Business dealings were almost entirely with the Mother Country, partly because she demanded it, and largely because the Colonies had little that they could furnish each other and thus form a basis of trade. Such raw material as they could deal in had had first to be put through English mills.

These early coaches were not entrusted

23

with the mail. Long before that time a monthly service had been established between these two points by the colonial authorities, and the first postman to arrive from Boston had appeared on horseback in the little Dutch burgh of Haarlem in January, 1692, travelling two hundred and fifty miles or more through the intervening stretches of snow-locked forest and morass, with no better road to follow than an uncertain trail blazed with an axe. In 1704 Madame Sarah Knight, a plucky Boston school mistress, with more love for the land than the sea, journeyed with "the Post" to New York, and was probably the first woman to travel overland on the Boston Post Road. She not only endured the hardships, but kept a lively journal of her experiences, which well depicts the discomforts and dangers of travel in that day. In it there is a prevailing sense of humor that did not desert her, even when at times her courage faltered.

Coming to one stream whose turbulent waters proved too much for her faith in horse flesh to ford in the usual manner, she sought the assistance of "a ladd and canoo" and was ferried across, while the Post led her horse and rode his own. She must have been of rather portly dimensions for she recounts—"When we were in, the canoe seemed ready to take in water; which greatly terrified me. Sitting with my hands fast on each side, my eyes steady, not daring so much as to lodge my tongue a hair's breadth more on one side of my mouth than t'other, nor so much as to think on Lott's wife, for a wry thought would have oversett our wherey."

Her "wherey" was not "oversett" and she arrived safely in New York, and, moreover, chose to return over the same route a little later.

The good old coaching days cannot be said to have started with the pre-Revolutionary "stage wagons," as they were called, and our New England ancestors were prayerfully solicitous for their friends and relatives who ventured southward in them. The "rolling stock" of 1795 carried more passengers but were scarcely more comfortable. They were virtually springless cars, built to carry twelve persons. Their seats were merely boards, without either cushions or back-rests, with no accommodation for baggage except such as could be packed beneath the seats, and only fourteen pounds was allowed there. Light curtains at the sides furnished the only protection in bad weather.

In such a rig, and over roads that still twisted around charred tree-stumps and were filled with the oft-mentioned "quagmires," the learned President Quincy of Harvard came on a visit to New York toward the end of the century. He was always willing to climb out in the mud to assist the driver in rescuing their machine from ruts or bogs; each morning, whether it was fair or stormy, he was aroused at the dreary hour of three, and dressed by the sleepy light of a horn lantern and farthing candle; then, with more haste than their progress afterward warranted, he had a frugal breakfast with his fellow-passengers and rattled off again for another day's thumping and bumping until ten o'clock in the evening. When finally at his destination, he wondered "at the ease as well as the expedition, with which the journey had been effected."

I fancy he must have been more thankful that his journey was over, than impressed with its "ease and expedition."

The hardy drivers of these coaches not infrequently fortified their endurance by

Drawn by Stanley M. Arthurs.

The mail stage and the slow freight.

too numerous potations of courage-making flip or "kill devil rum"; and then in their exuberance of vigor, they brought coach and passengers with a crash against a tree trunk, or by too reckless manœuvring "over set" the whole in the roadway.

The traveller Melich speaks of seeing many such wrecked stage-coaches, and describes one experience of his own, when fagged out by a day's journey he had fallen asleep after nightfall:

"I heard a confused noise in my sleep and started up. I felt a motion, as if I had been flying, but I had not a moment to consider what it might be; the stage door fell down upon its side with a crash, and I found myself and eleven more floundering like so many fish in a net."

The accident, he says, was occasioned by the driver being drunk and, in his frolic, trying to pass, on too scant a margin, another

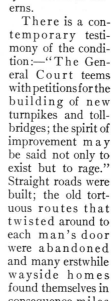

A tavern host.

stage. With some satisfaction he adds, that the driver paid dearly for his folly by being discharged on the spot by one of the proprietors who happened to be along; he was left to recover his scattered wits while the proprietor drove the stage to town.

In 1806 such progress had been made that daily stages left both New York and Boston, the more rapid mail coaches making the run in three days. The usual charge for passage on coaches running through Worcester, Hartford and Stamford was sixteen dollars. The demand for new and improved roads became imperative, far exceeding the slight pecuniary resources of the different states. This resulted in the roads being constructed largely by private individuals, or companies, under control of the Legislature. They financed their expensive undertakings by the sale of lottery tickets. It was a curious code of ethics that frowned upon gambling with cards, yet sanctioned with public approval this mode of gambling and licensed it by law.* For whatever purpose issued, whether for public or private gain, lottery tickets found always a ready sale, and the drawing of numbers was a lively occasion at taverns.

There is a contemporary testimony of the condition:—"The General Court teems with petitions for the building of new turnpikes and toll-bridges; the spirit of improvement may be said not only to exist but to rage." Straight roads were built; the old tortuous routes that twisted around to each man's door were abandoned and many erstwhile wayside homes found themselves in consequence miles off the beaten track. Toll-gates on the turnpikes were at intervals of about ten miles and the charge for a stage-coach was twenty-five cents, a levy for a two-horse carriage, and down to one cent each for foot passengers and cattle driven along the road. Persons going to church were given free use of the turnpike, as were those whose homes opened upon it.

The palmy days of the Boston stage began when, in conjunction with the early Sound steam-boats, it brought New York and Boston within less than thirty hours of each other. The country was then well

* Not only did lottery selling furnish the means for early road-building, but for church building as well, and for the establishment of schools and endowment of colleges; indeed, even state debts were paid in that manner. In the little state of Rhode Island alone, in the year 1826, the sale of lottery tickets exceeded the sum of one million six hundred thousand dollars.

established and prosperous and looking forward to a brighter future. In 1829 largely under the control of the Eastern Stage Company, seventy-seven lines radiated from Boston in different directions. Over sixteen hundred stages rolled in and out over its streets every week. In 1832, three years later, this number had increased to one hundred and six lines running regularly; and twenty-nine steam-boats were running from New York to near-by points. A trip from Boston to Savannah, Georgia, or even farther, could be timed and planned before starting through "Badger and Porter's Stage Register" a publication appearing monthly from the printing establishment of Jonathan Parmenter in Boston. It gave tables of all established stage, steam-boat and packet lines, and a record of all new ones; the fare and distances from point to point, with the names and rates at different taverns en route.

A stage driver.

In fact, Parmenter's publication was the Baedeker of stage travel. It was said "taverns were thick as fiddlers in hell." Commodious barns were built, countless blacksmith and farrier's forges glowed along the lines, keeping in repair and running order the vehicles of traffic. Lumbering "Conestogas," like ancient arks, dotted the highway, and at night could be seen anchored at the roadside near the village or tavern which formed their source of supply. Tethered to their wheels, or grazing along the road, were the horses, whose only protection from summer or winter's storms was the lee-side of the wagon and a covering of oilcloth or rough blanket, and the warmth of their own rugged bodies. The team drivers also carried their own accommodations, a straw mattress and blankets, in which they slept under the tunnel-like canvas tops.

During the War of 1812, when American shipping lay locked in port, the hapless victim of the Embargo Act, or of British blockade, these Conestogas furnished the only means of freight transportation, and crept over the highways from Maine to Georgia, in great caravans, scores at a time, often under military escort. Like treasure-laden ships from afar, they were enveloped in an enticing air of mystery. Their great canvas tops did not reveal their identity, whence they hailed, nor with what riches they came burdened; but the ponderous roll and creak of the wheels spoke of their bulk and weight, and an unsociable dog trotting beneath kept away the curious. With the light musical jingle of many bells and chains as an accompaniment, and each wagon drawn by eight or more horses encased in heavy harness, gayly decorated with many plumes and ribbons, these retinues passed through village and township.

"To eye entrancing as the glittering train
　Of some sun-smitten pageant of old Spain."

With what a dash and flourish did the fast mail coaches, well named "The Thoroughbred" or "The Thunderbolt," pass these freight trains of other days. For them a fair day's journey was twenty-five or thirty miles, while the mail coaches, with frequent relays, covered twelve miles or more an hour over the hard turnpikes.

The first steam-boats began to feel their way up the Sound early in the century, going first to New Haven in 1815, to New

Drawn by Stanley M. Arthurs.

A wayside passenger.

London and Norwich in 1818, and later they ventured into the open sea and around the troubled waters of "Pint Judy" to Providence. That was a risky trip for these early steam-boats, for their engines were none too well-trained and their light iron boilers encased in wood were not celebrated for safety, and frequently exploded, leaving what remained of boat and passengers to navigate by sail.

It was, therefore, to the conservative-travelling public that the promoters of the New London line appealed when they advertised that their passengers "avoid the dangers of a sea voyage around Point Judith," and that "their engine had copper boilers." The fare by that line to New York in 1827 was $7.50, and letter postage was 18¾ cents.

An early morning start from Boston was necessary in order to reach New London or Norwich in time for the night boats, and as the clock on old South Church pealed the hour of three, the coaches started from Marlboro Hotel, taking different routes through the city to collect the various passengers who had registered for the trip at the stage office or in the stage book at appointed hotels.

A call boy had previously been sent around to awaken them, and he sometimes was the innocent occasion of a scene of nocturnal discord, and brought muttered imprecations down upon his head by thumping the wrong knocker and awaking some home-keeping sleepy Bostonian.

Passengers and baggage would be waiting as the stage appeared, its empty body heaving and tossing "like a ship upon a raging sea," its enormous wheels rumbling like distant thunder. Woe to the tardy who were not in readiness when it drew up; for in a moment either the coach door closed with an occupant within or the impatient team started with the prospective passenger without. We can picture them a little later in their chaises galloping in the wake of the stage, hoping to overtake it at its stop for breakfast or before. With the last passenger aboard and baggage secured, the coach threaded its way through streets, vacant and silent as if locked under the magic wand of enchantment. In darkness, except for the dim glow of the stage lamps, the passengers without a clear idea of each others' identity uncomfortably endeavored to resume their morning's nap.

As the gray light tempered the darkness, the returning life of the country side was evidenced by twinkling lights, first in the second story or from an elm-sheltered attic window; then in the cosey glow of crackling hearth fires in the kitchens and curling strips of blue smoke from ample chimneys, and fleeting whiffs of cooking breakfasts.

In the early morning perhaps thirty coaches would pass, filled with way passengers and those bound for New York. The stops for breakfast were at appointed taverns, where for hours before the bustle of preparation had been going on. It might be at the famous Wayside Inn in Sudbury town or even as far away as Walpole, nineteen miles from Boston.

We need no better assurance as to the excellence of the feasts prepared in these hostelries than the enthusiastic laudations they drew from the epicures of France, or the rotund, beef-loving Englishman, who, if he found nothing else quite to his liking in America, could record his grateful appreciation of the tavern fare and the tavern host.

In glowing reminiscences they enumerate these early morning repasts of fish and fowl, mutton, steak, waffles, johnnie cakes and bread and butter, with abundant supplies of milk and cream, eggs and vegetables; and hotel dinners that included touches of completeness that both surprised and delighted them. Their breakfasts and teas in English taverns were meagre affairs, by comparison.

It may be said that a few hours' trouncing and jolting in the open air in these stage-coaches furnished all the necessary training for a proper frame of mind and body to appreciate this appeal to the "inner man." I think it is a French adage which offers to appease the hungry by means of sleep:

"He who sleeps feasts."

Such a proverb could not be applied to American stage-coach days. Sleep they did not much indulge in, but feast they certainly did, around bountifully laden tavern boards.

The surroundings and general appearance of these wayside abodes of hospitality were well fitted for inward appeal. The din of innumerable cackling hens announced the steady production of eggs for toddy, eggs for custard, eggs for pie and cake, and eggs for future broilers. Flocks of haughty complaining geese and contented ducks waddled around their borders. At their backs stood a forest of apple, pear, and plum trees, and rolling fields of wheat or tasselled corn and meadow land and cattle.

But even more was the Inn the centre of the business, social, and at one time even the civic life of the community, for Court once held its regular sessions there. It remained the head-quarters for all sales and "vandues," for the opponents of different political creeds to solve the intricacies of self-government, and it was often the post-office. Many taverns provided rooms with polished floors for dancing, and gay coaching parties came from Boston or Providence and mingled in the sinuous web of the quadrille and contra-dance. Gallant sparks came from town in broadcloth suits of purple and maroon, high-rolled collar and ruffled neckerchief and scant waistcoats of flowered silk with dangling fobs, and with them bewitching maids clad in trim gowns of white and buff, silken hose and slippers. Then the building glowed with light and cheer and the music of violin and piano-forte drifted from open windows and down the highway.

The tavern host was the gleaner of the world's news as recounted by his many guests. His advice was sought upon all matters, whether of private or public importance. They were men of prominence and personal worth, for it would have been difficult for any one else to have obtained a license. Sometimes, as with Lyman Howe, who presided at the Wayside Inn, a crest and coat of arms denoted a lineage from families opulent and distinguished in England. They perforce were genial and open-hearted and could entertain as well the obscure traveller as men of fame and prominence in affairs. Imposing personalities from both England and the Continent were at times their guests; such men as Baron von Humboldt, Louis Philippe, Lafayette, or the brilliant Prince Talleyrand, and such native political heroes as Webster, Clay, and Adams; and distinguished men of letters and business. Able to set for their guests a table "fit for a king," they were able, also, to preside with dignity and grace at that self-same table.

And these were lively days in the villages along the highway. Their coaching stables contained literally hundreds of restive,

well-fed horses. A keen rivalry existed at times between competing companies, and their rate wars offered very attractive inducements for travel, as well in England as in this country. There is a record of two lines running into Liverpool, which in their bids for public patronage reduced travelling expenses to a minimum. With a gradually reducing scale of rates, the proprietor of one line finally advertised the following fares:

> Inside—What you please.
> Outside—ditto ditto.

There would seem to be nothing to add to such terms, but the other party was not at all disheartened and revised his schedule as follows:

> Inside—Nothing at all and a bottle of wine.
> Outside—   ditto   ditto.

Yet even better terms than these were offered by a line running from Boston to Providence, for not only was free transportation advertised, and a bottle of wine, but a full-size dinner as well.

Coach-making developed into a thriving industry, employing hundreds of men. Each builder developed his own ideas of construction and many queer and varied types appeared upon the thoroughfare. A few picturesque examples are still stored in barns near the roadside recalling the past like stray pages from some old journal of the road. The rival stage companies introduced many pretentious coaches gay with bright-red and yellow bodies and striped blue or green wheels, with doors embellished with designs and named to accent their feats of speed. From the many types was evolved in 1827 the familiar Concord coach, which with very few alterations is being constructed to-day just as it was then. It soon superseded all other forms, representing the acme reached in the construction of public coaches. After serving its day in the East, this trustworthy vehicle, swung a little lower on the running gear, trundled westward to run the gauntlet on the prairie and mountain side under the hair-trigger driving of "Shot Gun Taylor" and "Indian Bill."

Rugged of outline, with comfortable homely furnishings, huge of wheel and broad of tire, with sturdy hub and axle, they carried all who could pile in or on the body and over any road that a cart could travel. At holiday season or at the ending

Drawn by Stanley M. Arthurs.

The steamboat landing at Norwich.

of a school or college term, these old rigs were well compared to the venerable Trojan horse, except that they swarmed with life outside as well as in. I have read of disappointed school-boys, who, unable to find a vacant spot upon the home-bound coach, were forced to spend a dreary Thanksgiving Day at college, tormented by visions of unattained good things at home.

These coaches carried readily nine passengers inside, three upon the back seat, three in front (facing the rear). Between them were three individual seats, which could be tilted backward to gain access to those in the front or rear. The occupants of these could rest their backs upon a broad leather strap hooked to either side of the coach. On top the driver occupied a slanting seat and was protected from being crowded by the passenger at his side by a light iron railing. On the coach, at their back, was a seat holding three others. A heavy boot at the rear held the trunks and heavier baggage; the lighter bundles and bandboxes were piled on top.

The fast mail stage was of lighter construction and carried fewer passengers. Night and day it could be heard passing along the highway, under the skilful "tooling" of as finished drivers as ever played the ribbons. There was a ring of distinction in the music of its horses' hoofs that separated it from every other sound of the turnpike, and a mutual knowledge and understanding existed between the master and beast. His team was not a selected, mated array, but constantly contained new and untrained material in its make-up that in other hands would have brought calamity and distress to the trusting maid, who was only too glad to ride perched high in the air at his elbow.

Kicking, vicious, otherwise unbreakable horses were welcome additions to his team as possessing a commendable spirit, capable of being turned to proper account. In all weather, notwithstanding the impediments offered by the tide of commerce upon the highway, skilfully and accurately, with scarce perceptible lessening of speed, he brought his coach safely and always on time to its destination. No wonder he typified the secret aspirations of growing youth in the village and farm-side, and held the constant admiration of both maid and matron.

Who could witness with indifference the gay dash of his approach to the changing station, the perfect curve with which his team swings before the tavern door, and then with fresh horses is off again before the coach ceases rocking.* These men were horsemen born. Stage drivers ran in families, *aviator nascitur non fit*, as it were; if that be so, many of their descent and family must have been among the drivers of the Deadwood coach and the stages running through the treacherous passes of the Rockies in a later day of coaching.

The canvas mail bags were carried beneath the driver's seat for safety and, while stage robberies were not frequent in New England, the current newspapers abounded with reports of the escapades of "The Knights of the Road," and we are left with the impression that these worthy horsemen had at their command a blunderbuss loaded with enough shot to annihilate a dozen "road agents" at one time.

A favorite haunt for plying their vocation lay in the pine-covered wilds between Baltimore and Washington. Robberies there were alarmingly frequent, and Congress finally provided a guard to protect the United States mail and the passengers from their ministrations.

A copy of the *Rhode Island American*, appearing in 1820, reports a robbery in that vicinity in which twenty-one thousand dollars peremptorily changed hands, and Mrs. Earle † describes another which occurred there two years before. The robbers were captured, and over ninety thousand dollars in bills and drafts were recovered.

New York could boast, in 1820, of 125,000 inhabitants. Boston, the third largest city, contained about 50,000 persons. Between them journeyed with some leisure the native Yankee on his own heath and soil, the Quaker gentleman from Pennsylvania, and the Southern planter, seeking a market for his products, and among the patrons of the coach and steam-boat lines were many critical Englishmen. Newspapers were not so common then, nor such active agents in moulding public opinion, as to do the thinking for the whole country. The individual Yankee thought for himself, in his own independent fashion, and the planter gen-

* This rapid change was effected by eight men, four to unharness, and four to attach the new team, and was accomplished in the short time of one minute.
† "Stage Coach and Tavern Days."

tleman introduced an entirely different life and experience within the confines of the rumbling coach. That animated and prolonged discussions were the result, we can gather from reading of that not very remote time. Frequent mention is made by the travellers of the entertaining companions they encountered, whose original talents for story-telling and singing were so thorough, and whose observations were so witty and shrewd as to make the time pass very merrily.

Sometimes, no doubt, the personalities were not conducive to such pleasant memories. There is a contemporary story of two Englishmen and a Bostonian journeying in the same coach. The visitors, much to the Yankee's discomfort, were indulging their patriotism by abusing everything American; the beef, the mutton, the bread, the fruit and milk, each in turn failed to equal the high standard of England. The laws were not satisfactory, nor were the people to their liking; the roads were unbearable, and the climate, even, failed to compare favorably with London fogs. The American was compelled to listen, annoyed both by their utter disregard for his presence and by their arraignment of his country. Finally, there came on a tremendous thunder storm, with alarming flashes of lightning and a heavy wind, which deluged the stage with water, but did not quiet the complaining Englishmen. Suddenly, with a blinding flash of light and with a reverberating crash of thunder that shook the coach, the lightning demolished a near-by tree. Unable longer to restrain himself, the American burst forth in rage, "There, damn you! I guess that thunder and lightning is as good as anything you have in England."

.   .   .   .

There were many routes over which the Boston stage rumbled en route to New York, all of them active channels of commerce. To-day parts of the same roads are almost untravelled—deserted except by the few farmers living near them. In its best days the thoroughfare was often changed, when improved or shorter routes could be made. Since then, it has continued to change, until nothing is left to indicate its past life and usefulness, except a few crumbling landmarks—the generous roomy taverns. One by one many of them have met their fate in fire and ashes, or have been otherwise destroyed; but the older residents can point out where they stood, and tell the name of their once-creaking sign-board, and of the wonderful picture that adorned its face, and give you the name of the tavern keeper who prospered so long as the stages ran.

On the road where once the stage horn blew, now in the distance can be heard the scream of the locomotive, or the grinding of trolley cars. Indeed, across the very face of the old highway their bands of iron have locked its past, and secured the present.

A little further back on the road, where neither the sound of the engine nor trolley has yet penetrated, one may still imagine the passing of the homely stage with its passengers, arriving perhaps at sunset before a village, and one can sense the joy, both of the travellers and the town folk, when the stage horn plays again,

"Polly put the kettle on, and we'll all have tea." For the passengers it meant, the good supper and the luxury of a soft bed and snow-white linen; for the others, the expected intelligence from an outside world.

Drawn by Stanley M. Arthurs.

The evening mail

3
Old York, a Forgotten Seaport

Old York, a Forgotten Seaport

By Pauline Carrington Bouvé

Illustrated from Photographs by W. N. Gough, and others

THERE is a picturesque and romantic element surrounding the earlier settlements along the Maine coast that is quite distinct from that which invests other places in New England with historic interest. Here religious zeal was not so primarily the keynote, as in the rising scale of progress in the Massachusetts Bay Colony, nor did social prestige continue so long a dominant factor as among the Cavaliers of Virginia. Nevertheless, religious predilection and social ambition were the motive springs that brought into existence that aristocratic little Episcopal settlement of Gorgeana, now York, in the Province of Maine, on the Atlantic seaboard, latitude 43° 10′ north, longitude 70° 40′ west.

Although the first settlement in Maine was at Kittery in 1623, the ancient town of Gorgeana has a more important claim upon the interest of the student of American history, a claim, indeed, which envelopes old-fashioned York with a dignity that cannot be shared by any other town, for an English city charter—the first grant of incorporation for city ever given in America—was made over to York by his Majesty King Charles I. in 1640. This fact establishes for York a priority right to some measure of national as well as local fame.

But there are hints of fair-faced foreigners along this rugged coast before the Spanish, French, Dutch, English came. Five hundred years before Columbus set sail to find a new world, the prows of Scandinavian vessels had breasted these tides, if one may believe the records of Thorlack of Iceland, in which are chronicles of Norse voyagers gale-driven to the coast of Labrador, who cruised southward, reaching the New England coast. In these records one reads the story of Gudrida, wife of a bold Northman navigator, who bore a fair-haired child on the new world's shores. How much of the romance of the Saga has crept into these ancient Icelandic chronicles, it is not easy to say, but certainly Sir Humphrey Gilbert and Captain Gosnold and Martin Pring and doughty Captain John Smith sailed along the coast in the vicinity of York, a long time before the town was in existence.

In the year 1622 the Plymouth Council granted a tract of land lying within the Province of Maine to two gentlemen, Sir Ferdinando Gorges and Captain John Mason. Some years

41

later, in 1629, the two divided their interests, Captain Mason taking the part that lay north of the Piscataqua River and Sir Ferdinando, that which lay south of it.   In 1635 the Plymouth Council gave up the old patent and took out a new one, under which the land comprised was divided into twelve portions.   The third and fourth divisions which lay between the Kennebec and Piscataqua rivers and extended one hundred and twenty miles from the sea, were granted to Gorges.   The charter to the Council was afterwards revoked, but Charles I. gave on the third of April, 1639, the same territory to Sir Ferdinando Gorges, whom he invested with almost royal authority and to whom he entrusted the establishment of Episcopal worship in a region where the power of Puritan dissent was already becoming more than ever obnoxious to the haughty Stuarts.   Sir Ferdinando, who had been a British naval officer and had held the important office of Governor of Plymouth, England, belonged to an ancient family whose fortunes had fallen from them, so he eagerly embraced the opportunity that

now seemed to be within his grasp, to better his worldly condition and restore the prestige of wealth to his name.

The colonies in America seemed to be an asylum for religious belief, a stage for the play of political ambition, and an Eldorado where destitute scions of noble houses might retrieve their fortunes, as the needs in each case might be. Such diverse elements made up one of the strangest social and political eras that the world has ever seen—an era in which sombre fanaticism, daring adventure, rapacious greed, and sinister intrigue mingled in a wild pageant.

Sir Ferdinando, who was past middle life, dreamed of founding on this strip of Maine coast a great seaport city from whose wharves armed vessels and ships of commerce should sail to all parts of the world, bearing the victorious arms of the King and bringing back merchandise of every description.   So it came about that the King gave his ambitious emissary, in 1640, the first English charter for a city that was ever issued in America, and so, with the dream of a Cathedral City in his brain, where the power

YORK HARBOR

YORK VILLAGE

of stole and mitre should be second only to that of crown and sceptre, Sir Ferdinando ordered a "Church Chapel" or "oratory," and "Governor's palace" to be built, and sent his young kinsman, William Gorges, as his deputy until he should come.

In 1639 he had sent to the "plantations" a band of skilled workmen with all of the necessary implements of toil, and the tools and machinery in use at that time for the building of houses and ships, together with oxen and the requisites for agriculture.

A year later, when his "cosen," nephew, or grandson (severally described by different histories), Thomas arrived from England with the deputy Lord Proprietor, William Gorges, he found the "Governor's palace" in dilapidation and everything in a state of demoralization. Yet despite this condition of affairs, Sir Ferdinando persevered in the project and secured the city charter, dated March 1, 1640,

The territory incorporated comprised twenty-one square miles, and the first city in America was named Gorgeana.

The citizens had authority to elect a mayor and eight aldermen each year, and could hold estate to any amount. Thomas Gorges was the first mayor, and the aldermen were, Bartholomew Barnett, Roger Garde, George Puddington, Edward Godfrey, Arthur Bragdon, Henry Simpson, Edward Johnson, and John Rogers. Roger Garde was also the recorder. The mayor and eight aldermen were *ex-officio* justices, and annually appointed four sergeants, whose badges of office were white rods.

In 1643, Thomas Gorges returned to England, leaving Roger Garde as mayor, and in 1647 the ambitious Sir Ferdinando, without ever having seen the embryo city of his dreams —for the great warship which was to convey him to the colonies was wrecked when she was launched—

43

OLD YORK GAOL

died in prison at the age of seventy-five, discouraged but not yet quite hopeless of the ultimate future of Gorgeana. Two years later, 1649, unhappy Charles I. laid his head upon the block. Meantime, after the proprietor's death, the people of Gorgeana, Kittery, Wells, and the Isles of Shoals (which latter were included in Sir Ferdinando's grant) met together and after much squabbling and turmoil formed themselves into a Confederacy for administration and protection.

After the King's execution, the rivalry that had always existed between the two colonies, Massachusetts and the Province of Maine, was no longer held in abeyance, and in 1652 the stronger colony of Massachusetts

made good her claim to the ownership of her weaker sister and assumed control of her. The city charter was revoked, a town charter was granted, and the name of Gorgeana was changed to that of York. At the same time, Roundhead influences were immediately set in motion to suppress the Royalist feeling that was very strong in the Episcopal settlement.

One of the first acts of the new rulers was the erection of the Gaol, which was in accordance with the act passed in 1647 that "Each County shall have a house of correction," and these persons committed to such houses of correction or prisons "shall first be whipped not exceeding ten stripes." There is a bit of genuine Puritanical spirit in this enactment, and in 1653

44

the famous old York Gaol was built, to stand, perhaps, as a silent menace to those who might be secretly in sympathy with the cause of young Charles Stuart, the exiled and fugitive heir to the throne of Great Britain.

The Civil War in England that raged between Charles I. and the British Parliament from 1641 to 1649 was a period of great inquietude to the inhabitants of York, who were at heart loyal to the Stuarts, and who detested Cromwell and their Roundhead neighbors, the "Bostonians," as the Massachusetts Colonists were now called by the French settlers in Canada. It was during the first year of this war that Cromwell gained a victory over a body of Scotch troops fighting under the Royal Standard in the north of England. In this engagement a number of Scotch royalists were taken prisoners, and among them were the Donalds or Donnells, the Maxwells and the McIntyres, all of whom were destined to play no inconsiderable part

in the history of loyal little York across the wide Atlantic.

Cromwell's officer ordered that the Scotch prisoners should be ranged in a row and that every tenth man should be shot and that the rest should be deported to the American Colonies. Micum McIntyre, one of the prisoners, counted and discovering that he was *a tenth man*, with one superhuman effort broke his bonds and attempted an escape. The daring of the venture pleased his captors, and though he was recaptured they commuted his sentence to exile. Packing all that was left of his individual belongings in a small oaken box, McIntyre with his fellow prisoners, the Maxwells and Donalds, set forth upon the voyage to New England. It was natural that upon hearing of Sir Ferdinando Gorges' Settlement at York, these young soldiers should make their way thither, and they took up their abode in what is now known as the second parish, a little settlement

45

which still bears the name of Scotland. But Micum McIntyre, "Gentleman," the most destitute one of the penniless Scotch troopers, met good luck in the

MICUM McINTYRE'S BOX

New World. His story was told the writer by his lineal descendant, Mr. John McIntyre, the richest man in York County today. "Micum had a neighbor, a sort of Scotch cousin, who was in failing health and who had taken a great liking to the young fellow. One day this man sent for him and said, 'Kinsman, I am dying, and I am grieved to have my wife alone without protection in this wild country. 'Tis no fit place for a woman without husband, father, or brother, so I will bequeath her and all my land and property to you, Kinsman, if you will take them both and do fairly by each. What say you?' And Micum agreed to the arrangement, so before many months passed he was the inheritor of an estate and a wife!"

It was this same Micum who built the old McIntyre Garrison House on York River, which is within a few rods of Mr. John McIntyre's dwelling. This landmark of a fearsome and tempestuous period is the only one left of the many block houses that were built by the early settlers of the region, and it is still in a state of comparatively good preservation. Like all such of that section, it faces south, for that way runs York River, down whose waters came the canoes of the hostile Indians. As frequent and sudden incursions of their savage neighbors might always be expected, it was of the greatest importance to have a clear river view. The old house with its rough-hewn timbers dove-tailed and trunnelled together, its caulked seams, and its loopholes for musketry, is one of the most interesting relics of the colonial period in New England. Up in the loft where the flooring is still intact there are "draws" from which watch could be

THE BEST ROOM

kept on an approaching enemy, while in the juttings of the second story that projects over the first all around, there are openings from which missiles could be thrown upon the heads of the invaders, or from which water might be poured if the enemy should set fire to the house. The stout wooden bar that was held in place across the heavy oaken door by another of like dimensions, the latter one being propped against it and made fast by the first step of the stairway, did good service two hundred and sixty years ago, before the day of locks in York.

Up at the new McIntyre mansion, the daughter of the house shows visitors a smooth, round stone that is known in the neighborhood as the "pound stone." When Micum's "inherited wife," Hannah Pierce, was preparing to emigrate to the Colonies, she was walking along the shore one day, and picked it up. "This, perchance, weighs about a pound," she said as she balanced it in her palm. "I'll see if it does," and finding that it really did, and exactly to a dot, the thrifty housewife put it in her pocket and brought it all the way across the broad ocean. "For," said she, "it may chance there be no such thing as

THE POUND STONE

scales and weights for the fair measure of cheese and butter in those savage lands."

Here, too, young Malcolm McIn-

TABLE CHAIR IN THE GARRISON HOUSE

tyre, after a good deal of persuasion, arrayed himself in an ancestor's suit of clothes, and, holding an old sword taken from the Junkin Garrison in his hand, posed for an illustration of "Ye olden time." There was a bit of inspiration in the boyish freak, for his family's arms show a hand holding a drawn sword, with the prophetic motto, *"Through Difficulties."*

From the time of its earliest settlement, the location of Maine made it an easy prey to the incursions of the savage tribes that roamed from its boundaries northward to the French settlements of Acadia and Canada. Acadia, as the French understood it, consisted of Nova Scotia, New Brunswick, and a very large part of Maine. In these wilds, the Abenakis, who were converts to Romanism and strong allies of France, hunted, fished, and harassed the English trading settlements of Maine. In 1689 they entirely destroyed the outpost of Pemaquid. In 1690 they and their French friends had made so many attacks upon the New England ports and villages that nothing was left on the eastern side of the Piscataqua River except the towns of Wells, York, and Kittery. Sir William Phips's easy conquest of Port Royal had, however, somewhat changed the attitude of the Abenakis toward the English settlers, whom they began to fear and whose trade was attractive. Five chiefs of the nation signed a truce with the Massachusetts commissioners which filled the French with alarm. If these Abenakis made terms with the "Bostonians," the settlements on the St. Lawrence would be in danger of attack, a thing not to be feared so long as the savages remained loyal to France. It was French policy, therefore, to arouse the antagonism of the Abenakis against the English. Some of the tribes had no part in the truce and were still thirsty for English blood. To them the French addressed themselves to such effect that the village of York was attacked and almost destroyed by a band of savages led by French, on the night of February 5, 1692. The enemy had made their way along the frozen streams and trackless forests on snow-shoes, journeying for nearly a month toward hapless little York. Arriving at Mount Agamenticus on the afternoon of the fourth, they could see plainly from its summit the group of scattered houses of the settlement along the banks of the Agamenticus or York River. The attack was successful and before dawn one hundred and fifty of the inhabitants had been killed or taken captive, and every house on the northeast side of the river burned, with the exception of the garrison house, the meeting-house, and the old gaol. Among the captives was a child of four, whose sturdy efforts to get away so amused his captors that he was allowed to escape. This was the first Indian adventure of Jeremiah Moulton, whose name afterwards became a terror to the red man, who was a distinguished officer in the French War, holding the rank of Colonel at the capture of Louisburg and marching all the way from York to Quebec with a company of soldiers. He was also an official resident of the Gaol years afterwards, while serving as sheriff of the Province of Maine. His son, Jeremiah junior, was an officer in the Revolutionary War and died of "army fever" in 1777, while his grandson, Jotham, was commissioned Brigadier-General February 8, 1776. The three daughters of the second Colonel Jeremiah, Abegail, Hannah, and Lucy, were married to Dr. Job Lyman, Captain Samuel Sewall, and Mr. Storer Sewall, respectively, and the ancestral home of the Moultons and of the original Colonel Jeremiah is now the residence of Judge Putnam, who inherited it from his mother, a daughter of Captain Samuel Sewall and Hannah (Moulton) Sewall.

Although Sir Ferdinando Gorges had dreamed of establishing an Episcopal form of worship in York, there was no clergyman there during his government. In 1660, one Burdet had, indeed, gathered a congregation about him, but he was found guilty of improper conduct by the civil authority and soon after gave up the rôle of teacher and preacher. Due, perhaps, to this lack of spiritual instruction, one may read an extraordinary record

PUTNAM COAT OF ARMS

of "an humble petition to the Court" presented by Richard Cutts and John Cutting, stating "that contrary to the act or order of the court which says 'no woman shall live on the Isle of Shoals' John Reynolds has brought his wife thither, also a stock of goats and swine. . . . Your Petitioners therefore pray that the act of court may be put in execution of the removal of all women, also the goats and swine." The Court had the obnoxious swine removed, but Goodie Reynolds was allowed to enjoy the company of her husband "if no further complaint come against her." Two decades later, however, the order of things was changed, for at a court held Dec. 24, 1665, "Joane Ford of the Isles of Shoals was sentenced to receive" nine stripes at the post for "calling the Constable a horn-headed and cow-headed rogue."

After the death of Charles I. the Episcopal element seems to have been eliminated almost utterly from the town of York, and the stricter religious principles of the Puritans began to thrive on that soil that was intended to nurture Episcopacy.

The restoration of royal government in England brought unpleasant changes to the people in the Province of Maine, who had found under the administration of Cromwell's Protectorate more freedom of thought and action than they had before enjoyed, for dissolute Charles II. was growing jealous of the Colonies. In 1676 he confirmed the rights of the heirs of Sir Ferdinando Gorges "both as to soil and government." All of these rights and titles to the Province of Maine the people relinquished to Massachusetts in 1676 for the sum of one thousand two hundred and fifty pounds. This proceeding the king bitterly resented. Massachusetts declined to give up what she had bought and at once assumed absolute jurisdiction.

Sir William Phips, the hero of Port

SEWALL COAT OF ARMS

Royal, and the new Royal Governor, brought the William and Mary charter from England. This was dated October 7, 1691, and went into effect May 14, 1692. As Parkman remarks, two giant intellects within two invalid bodies were now struggling for supremacy in Acadia—the genius of Richelieu and the genius of William of Orange—and the Province of Maine was the scene of many conflicts.

It was the June following the terrible massacre at York that the French and Abenakis crossed Penobscot Bay and marched upon Wells, one of the villages of the early York Confederacy. This village had been, during the winter, crowded with refugees from pillaged farmhouses, but famine and misery had driven most of them beyond the Piscataqua, and the few left had taken refuge in the five fortified houses. Of these that belonging to Joseph Storer was the largest and safest, as it was surrounded by a palisade. It was occupied by fifteen armed men under a militia officer, Captain Convers. Two sloops and a sail boat ran up the neighboring creek, bringing fourteen more men and food for the half starved garrison. This was fortunate, for the next morning one of Storer's men, John Diamond, while on his way from the garrison house to the sloops was seized by the Indians "and dragged off by the hair." With yells and warwhoops some of the Indians rushed upon the garrison, demanding their surrender, while others attacked the sloops, but were repulsed by the handful of men on board. The ebbing tide had stranded the vessels and the Canadians constructed a shield of planks which they fastened to a cart

and attempted to shove toward the sloops in the mud; then the tide began to rise, and, the chief of the attacking party being killed, the rest broke and ran, many falling under the fire of the sailors. Then the whole body, nearly four hundred in all, fell upon the garrison house. The disparity in numbers was appalling. An Englishman suggested surrender. "If you say that again," answered Convers, "you are a dead man." "Had the allies made a bold assault," remarks Parkman, "he and his followers must have been overpowered; but this mode of attack was contrary to Indian maxims." When the assailants offered terms brave Convers replied, "I want nothing but men to fight with!" The women in the garrison passed ammunition to the men, and sometimes they fired themselves upon the enemy. Thirty resolute men had withstood four hundred and foiled one of the fiercest and most formidable bands that ever attacked the settlers in Acadia. Poor John Diamond, the prisoner, was tortured to death. There is an archaic simplicity, an antique heroism, an imperishable glory in this story of Captain Convers and his dauntless band of thirty!

The William and Mary Charter embraced the whole territory of the State of Maine, in two divisions: that extending from the Piscataqua to the Kennebec was called the Province of Maine; that between the Kennebec and St. Croix River was called Sagadahoc. Legislative power was vested in two branches. The Council, or Board of Assistants, consisted of twenty-eight members, and formed the upper house, while the other was called the House of Representatives.

COL. JEREMIAH MOULTON'S WAISTCOAT AND
TANKARD

The ecclesiastical history of York dates from the organization of the first Congregational Church by the Reverend Shubael Dummer, about 1662. This man of God, who was a native of Newbury, Massachusetts, a graduate of Harvard, and greatly respected, was killed by the Indians in the York massacre. He married a daughter of the celebrated Edward R. Rishworth, the first chosen "recorder of writts." Six years later a remarkable man, also from Newbury, came to York, where he preached until his ordination in 1700. This was the eccentric Samuel, familiarly known as "Father" Moody, who declined a stipulated salary and chose to live upon the voluntary contributions of the people. This does not appear to have been an altogether successful arrangement, for more than once his family came very near to starvation. In fact, Mr. Moody had to appeal to the General Court of Massachusetts for "such allowance as your wisdom and justice shall see fit." The Court "saw fit" to allow twelve pounds sterling. Father Moody appears to have exercised the privilege of making personal remarks from the vantage ground of his pulpit with appalling frankness. It was the Sunday after Judge Sewall's marriage, that that stately gentleman in small-clothes, silver shoe buckles, powder and ruffles, repaired to the house of worship accompanied by his bride in her wedding slippers and arrayed in one of her bridal gowns. Father Moody paused in his discourse, and pointing to the pair said rebukingly, *"Here comes Judge Sewall with his lady and his ungodly strut."* How the poor bride must have felt! The memory of her gracious and dignified bearing is still cherished in York where they point out the old Sewall Mansion to strangers with pride, and those historic wedding slippers are

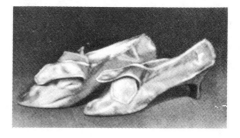

kept under a glass case in the loan collection of local curios.

For half a century York's leading man was David Sewall. He was graduated from Harvard in 1755, and was classmate and life-long friend of John Adams. Admitted an attorney in 1760 he was for sixty-four years identified with the town's history. It was during Washington's administration that the beautiful and stately residence now known as Coventry Hall, the summer home of Rev. Frank Sewall of Washington, was built. Here Judge Sewall entertained President Monroe on

COVENTRY HALL

his "progress" eastward, horses for the President's private coach being furnished along the road, and the officers of the York County Regiment of Militia acting as mounted escort from the Maine line.

David Sewall's stone in the Old Burying Ground bears the following well deserved inscription:

"Concecrated to the memory of the Hon. David Sewall, L. L. D. An elevated benevolence was happily directed by an enlightened intellect. Conscientious in duty he was ever faithful in its discharge. Piety with patriarchal simplicity of manners conspired to secure him universal esteem.

"Having occupied the Bench of the Supreme Court of the State and District Court of the U. States with dignified uprightness for forty years without one failure of attendance, he retired from public life in 1818 and died Oct. 22, 1825, aged XC years.

> Death but entombs the body,
> Life the Soul."

It was during the ministry of Father Moody that the "Parish Society" of York was organized under a warrant issued by William Pepperell, dated March 5, 1731. It was also during his pastorate, in 1747, that the old meeting-house was burned and the present one was erected, such of the timbers as were sound of the old building being incorporated in the new. Father Moody married Hannah Sewall, and left a son and daughter, The Reverend Joseph Moody and Mrs. Emerson of Malden, great aunt of Ralph Waldo Emerson.

The son's life story makes one of the strangest, saddest pages of York history. Born in 1700, he graduated from Harvard at eighteen and soon afterwards was made Register of Deeds of York County. In 1730 he was Judge of the County Court. Father Moody, however, was anxious to have his son enter the ministry, and with filial obedience but poor judgment, Joseph resigned his civil office

52

HANNAH SEWALL MOODY

and was ordained pastor of the Congregational Church of the Second Parish of York in 1732, his father assisting in the ceremony. The eccentric disposition of the father was accentuated in the sensitive, dreamy, morbid temperament of the son. Perhaps the young minister regretted having given up a profession which promised a brilliant career. Perhaps overwork destroyed the equilibrium of a peculiarly delicately balanced brain, or it may have been that the morbid New England conscience made him brood overmuch upon the unfortunate accident of his boyhood when he had accidentally shot his hunting companion, young Preble, when they were out together one day. At all events, the brilliant young minister's mind became impaired. He resigned his pastorate, declaring that the weight of an unpardonable sin was upon his guilty soul and that he was unfit to enjoy the fellowship of men. Retiring from the society of friend and neighbor, he covered his face with a black handkerchief. This he never removed, and he became known far and near as "Handkerchief Moody." One can imagine the awe of the villagers, the fear of the children as they scudded down lanes and around corners, the hush of feminine chatter when that ghost-like figure with the veiled face was seen about the streets of the quaint old town—a figure of mystery and tragedy. The old moth-eaten table upon which he took his solitary meals is one of the most interesting relics preserved in the Gaol, now used as a museum.

One day the black-veiled minister, who had not for many years lifted his beautiful voice in song, suddenly began to sing. Through the closed door of his room came in clear melodious notes, the hymn,

"Oh for an overcoming faith
To cheer my dying hours!"

The next morning they found him dead in his bed. Let us hope that the "overwhelming faith" was given to cheer the lonely end of a lonelier life.

There were other strange personages who used to wander about old York. The mysterious St. Aspinquid, the In-

HANDKERCHIEF MOODY'S TABLE

dian missionary whose grave lies on the heights of Mount Agamenticus, was once a familiar figure in the vicinity. Tradition says he was a native of York, England, who came to Maine, and dwelt among the Indians, who grew to know and love him, and to whom he was somewhat a father as well as a teacher. None knew his name. From the date of his advent in York it might very reasonably be assumed that he was one of the English Jesuit priests, exiled by the destruction of the monasteries by Cromwell's Puritans, and that as was the fashion of that Order, he adopted the dress and manner of life of the savages he came to Christianize. How else could the title St. Aspinqu have originated? It would have been natural for the children of the forest to have learned stories of angel, martyr and saint from his life and to have called their benefactor by that name he had taught them to revere. At his death his faithful followers brought a sacrifice of six thousand five hundred and eleven votive animals.

"Old Tricky," a piratical fisherman who lived at Bra'boat Harbor, was very much feared along the coast as a malevolent creature who "laid curses" on those he disliked. These curses, however, could not take effect until he had bound a certain amount of sand with a rope. According to tradition, before a storm he used to be heard muttering, "More rope, more rope," and even now superstitious folk say the figure of an old man with shaggy locks flying in the wind and bearing a bag of sand on his back may be seen hurrying along the gray sands, and between the sobbing of the wind and sea, the cry "more rope, more rope," may be heard now and

then. His bible, which is supposed to be haunted, is one of York's most cherished treasures.

Still later, before 1832, Mistress Betty Potter and her familiar friend, Mistress Esther Brooks, were awe-inspiring citizens of York. These spinsters lived on the dividing line between York and Kittery, by which device they escaped paying taxes in either town. When, however, President Jackson had the nation's "surplus revenue" divided among the inhabitants of the United States, Betty and Esther, not living in either place, were the only people in America who failed to receive their respective shares, the just reward of iniquity!

Mrs. Emma L. Paul, the great-granddaughter of Elder John Brad-

HANDKERCHIEF MOODY'S CRADLE

OLD BRADBURY HOUSE

bury, who was a staunch adherent of the King, owns and resides in the old Bradbury house in York. Elder John was a grandson of Thomas Bradbury who came to York in 1639 as the agent of Sir Ferdinando Gorges, and who afterwards settled in Salisbury, Massachusetts. It was Mary Perkins, the wife of this Thomas Bradbury, who at the age of ninety years was tried and condemned for "witchcraft." The good lady's escape is a strange story, belonging to Salisbury rather than to York history.

The loan collection of curios in the Gaol Museum owes its existence to the energy and good judgment of the ladies of York village, who three years ago saved the historic old building from the ravages of time, rats, and tramps. The suggestion came from William Dean Howells, the novelist, who, passing the dilapidated house one day and observing the door swinging open over the rotting sills, remarked: "Why can't you save the old house? It is worth saving." This was the seed of the idea. Not only the old Gaol was preserved, but colonial relics, some of much more than local interest and value, were collected by the ladies of the town, who established a museum of York antiquities within the walls that once grimly guarded evil doers. Mrs. Newton Perkins, who owns the ancient Pell House, just above Sewall's Bridge, gave a lawn party to inaugurate "doing something to get funds for the project." Thomas Nelson Page, John Fox, and Mr. Howells read on the occasion. The idea was popular and the "Village Historical and Improvement Society" began its work of preservation and rejuvenation.

The Pell house stands not far from the famous old "Sewall's Bridge," said to be the first pile bridge in the United States, built in 1761 by Major Samuel Sewall, a great architect in his day. He was engaged soon after to build a similar bridge between Boston and

THE PELL HOUSE

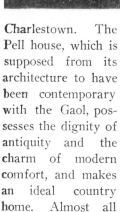

Charlestown. The Pell house, which is supposed from its architecture to have been contemporary with the Gaol, possesses the dignity of antiquity and the charm of modern comfort, and makes an ideal country home. Almost all of the distinguished old Colonial families that helped to make York honored of old are represented in name and in blood today,—Moulton, Bradbury, Sewall, McIntyre, Dennett, Moody, Barrell, Varrell, Donnell, Bragdon, Dummer, Stacey, Jenkins, and many others of note.

But this old town with the fragrance

of old laces and brocade still hanging about it—aristocratic York with its legends, its traditions, its historic associations—is no longer isolated and remote; although it is in truth a forgotten seaport, for its wharves are almost deserted and sea-traffic has passed it by, it has become a Mecca for artists, literary folk, and summer visitors.

The first summer hotel was built early in the seventies and when the steam railroad came in 1887, to take the place of the dusty stage coach

THE BARRELL MANSION

from Portsmouth, hotels and boarding houses grew in number and improved in quality and handsome cottages for summer residents began to dot the shores. The growth of the town as a summer resort has been very fast during the last few years and has developed within its limits four quite distinct summer villages,—York

Harbor, York Beach, York Cliffs, and Long Beach. Even York Village, always the town's centre for business and public and church affairs, gains by the summer invasion so that frequently the resident population of about three thousand becomes between the months of June and September a community of ten thousand, and much has been done to make life pleasant for the strangers and those who come back to their birth-

SEWALL'S BRIDGE

GOLF CLUB

place. The handsome new Golf Club House is a good example.

The historic houses of this quaint town draw visitors from the surround-

THOMAS NELSON PAGE'S COTTAGE

ing neighborhoods, and the witch's grave in the old burying ground, where the dead of many generations sleep, arouses a great deal of speculation. As witches, by an unwritten law, were almost never married, and as they were usually buried either at low-water mark or at the junction of three roads, this grave of "Mary Nason, wife of Samuel Nason, died August 28, 1772, aged 29 years," does not seem to fit the requirements of a *bona fide* witch. In spite, however, of these discrepancies, this wide tablet slab lying between two upright head and foot-stones possesses a weird interest to those who are inclined to superstition.

Stage Neck, where the Marshall House stands, is the historic ground where the people from the Isles of Shoals were ordered to remove during the Revolution. The view from here is one of the finest in the neighborhood, surpassed only perhaps by that from Mount Agamenticus, the highest point along this part of the Maine coast. Northward stretches the rocky coast with a background of woodland, while to the east lies the blue ocean with Boon Island Lighthouse clearly visible nine miles away. One of the early lighthouse keepers, Captain Eliphalet Grover, spent his time in making bass viols, one of which he presented to the first Congregational Church in York,

June 4, 1834. His successor was also a musician and played upon it for many years.

The old town celebrates, this summer, its two-hundred-and-fiftieth birthday since Massachusetts bought out the right of the Province of Maine in 1652, and it will wear holiday garb during the pageant: but to enjoy the unique charm of the place, one must visit it when the hush of a drowsy summer afternoon lies over the town; when the shady streets are quiet and the grim old Gaol, the haunted witch's house, and the ancient head-stones in the cemetery are bathed in the sunshine and, like the land of the Lotos Eaters, it seems a place where it is "always afternoon."

Then indeed the magic thrall of history, poetry, and tradition falls upon the visitor, and invests with a halo of romance this quaint old York—a forgotten seaport.

THE WITCH'S GRAVE

4
The Great Shell Mounds of Damariscotta

THE GREAT SHELL MOUNDS OF DAMARISCOTTA.

By George Stillman Berry.

ON numerous river banks and other water shores all over the globe are found large deposits of shells, both of the oyster and other bivalves. These collections usually take the form of banks or mounds, and in many instances are covered with soil and vegetation to so great an extent that their discovery has been made only by accident. Often, however, by the encroachment of water upon land the shell banks have been eroded so that large sections are exposed to view. There are thousands of these small heaps on every continent, ranging in quantity from a few bushels to a mass whose huge dimensions form a feature of the landscape. Some of the greatest of these mounds are widely known, having for years received the investigations of scientists and the pilgrimages of the curious. Among them may be mentioned the ones on the peninsula of Denmark, in Japan, in Florida and in British Columbia. These and similar deposits of shell were formerly thought to be natural beds of bivalves, raised by elevation of the land from their former position underneath the waters of bays and inlets. But investigation has established the fact that these are not natural beds, but are heaps of the cast off valves of those animals whose succulent parts were consumed by a human population. New England is by no means destitute of these relics, as numerous shell banks on the coast of Maine and Massachusetts testify. It is the purpose of this article to confine attention to the immense oyster shell deposits on the Damariscotta river in Maine, not only because they are nearly, if not quite, the largest oyster shell mounds in the world, but also because a description of them would apply very closely to all other artificial clam and oyster heaps.

The Damariscotta is a short but broad tide-water river, lying midway between the Kennebec and the Penobscot. Fifteen miles from its mouth, at the bridge connecting the towns of Damariscotta and Newcastle, the river narrows perceptibly and runs between hilly banks in a channel not more than a hundred yards wide. A little over a mile above the bridge the river bends at right angles towards the west, and a hundred rods further enlarges into a bay nearly two miles long and half a mile wide. This bay receives the waters of a lake, which rests upon the higher land terminating at this point the upper course of the river. The deposit of oyster shells, in continuous or solitary heaps, lie on both sides of the river for a few hundred yards below and above the bend. There are five mounds of large size, besides numerous other deposits containing from a few bushels to many tons.

The existence of these mounds has been known to white men from the time when George Popham, cruising off the coast of Maine in the early part of the seventeenth century, was informed by the Indians of immense deposits of oyster shells in the interior. The conspicuous position of the mounds, particularly the one lying on the western shore just below the bend in the river, could not fail to attract marked attention. This great mound on the peninsula extends in the form of a bluff four hundred feet along the shore and is exposed on the side towards the river throughout its whole extent. The northern portion has a thickness of only a few feet, its position on higher ground making it rise to nearly the same level as the part below, where the shells have an altitude of thirty-one feet, exceeding the height of any other recorded mass of shells in the world. The dense growth of

WHALEBACK MOUND, DAMARISCOTTA.

pine and spruce trees, which cover the whole peninsula and encroach upon the shells, makes it difficult to ascertain the exact width of the heap. The widest portion appears to extend about seventy-five feet inland; but there are traces of shells in the rear of this, consisting mostly of small circular mounds, the exploration of which is not easy on account of the tenacious roots that permeate the soil in all directions. The present appearance of the shell-bank gives an indication of the enormous losses which it has suffered by erosion from the river since the shells were deposited. This fact will at once be discovered by the most superficial observer, as he traverses the little shelly beach which lies in front of the bluff. Wherever the altitude of the shells is not too great, he will see a vertical wall of closely packed shells lying above the yellow soil. It is evident by a glance that the shells did not originally terminate in this wall, but that the land once extended many yards out in front, giving room for the natural slope of the shells as they were thrown on the ground in the original piles. In the higher parts of the bluff the shells could not well sustain a vertical position and have fallen upon the beach in steep slopes. It has been a frequent pastime for boys in their sports to wallow with glee in the shells from the top of the steep incline down to the beach.

This heap has sustained other losses than those caused by the depredations of nature. For many years the "Oyster Banks" was a favorite place for the denizens of the surrounding towns to obtain material for walks and other purposes. In consequence of this demand hundreds of tons of shells were taken away by scow and cart. A lime kiln was also erected at the southern end of the great mound and many tons were burned therein. Of late years, however, the owners of the property have shown a laudable desire to preserve the features of the mound, and have allowed no encroachments to be made upon it. All along the edge of the bank trees and shrubs are growing. Trunks of trees have fallen upon the shore, dragging soil and shells after them, and have been floated away by high water and by retreating ice in the spring. It is a pleasant occupation to draw up one's boat on the shelly beach and explore along the base of the mound. In one place successive hands have picked away the shells underneath the roots of a tree and have hollowed out a little cave large enough for one to sit in. Its side and roof are of compact shell, white as alabaster, and we may have the pleasure of plucking away a few shells to make the concavity larger.

Up to a few decades ago it was generally assumed that the banks were natural beds of oysters. But just be-

WHALEBACK MOUND.

fore the war of the rebellion Professor Chadbourne of Bowdoin College made a brief examination of the mounds and showed conclusively that they had been left there as remains of savage feasts at a period in the past whose limits he did not attempt to describe. Besides the larger heaps, he found frequent occurrence of shells in piles ten or fifteen feet in diameter, two or three feet deep. The soil beneath was made up of the diluvial deposit of sand, gravel and boulders, like all the land in the vicinity beyond the shells. He also noticed scattered among the shells numerous bones of animals broken into fragments, as if by some instrument, — bones of birds and beavers, and some sturgeon's plates. A dark line was seen near the bottom of the large mound, probably vegetable mould formed during temporary abandonment of the heap, and in places along that line the shells for a few inches underneath were decomposed, or turned to lime, as if acted upon by fire. The shells of clams, quahaugs and other bivalves, moreover, were found scattered through the heap.

A hundred yards down stream, on the same side of the river as the deposit just described, is another bank of shells, extending about eight hundred feet along the shore, and broken at the lower end into several small heaps. In some places it is seventy-five feet wide, and its greatest depth is eleven feet. This heap is at the lower edge of what is now a large field, in which, during the progress of cultivation for many years, countless numbers of arrowheads and various other aboriginal tools and weapons have been disclosed. Evidences of the local manufacture of Indian implements have here been found, and it is beyond doubt that this field and its immediate vicinity formed the site of a long-continued aboriginal encampment. The shell deposit hereto annexed is covered with grass and a few scattered trees of large size. Upon digging into the bank from the beach are found the roots of great trees whose upper parts, having been exposed to the air, long since became dust and vanished from the landscape. Like the mound on the peninsula, this mound also has been subjected to great erosion along the shore, and like the other has lost large quantities of its shells. There is no exaggeration in the statement that both these shelly banks have lost fully one-half their original contents. This mound is now exposed along its whole front. On account of the lesser height, however, it is by no means so conspicuous to the view as its neighbor above, and is therefore the object of less attention. Many who have idly explored these deposits will receive with incredulity the statement that the lower heap contains fully as many shells as the peninsula mound; but a careful examination will convince one of the correctness of this conclusion.

About twelve years ago a business man from abroad attempted to buy the deposits on the western shore of the river, for the purpose of grinding the shells, to be used as food for hens and fertilizing material for the soil. He was unable to secure these deposits, however, and turned his attention to the eastern bank, where traces of shells were seen outcropping upon the

A SECTION OF WHALEBACK MOUND.

shore three hundred feet across the river, and directly opposite the peninsula mound. By few, if any, had the extent of this new deposit hitherto been suspected. Scientific and idle investigation had on the western shore found so many shells to manipulate, where the water had made easy access to them, that the possibilities of the neighboring heaps had received only casual thought. As the process of removing the incumbent soil was continued and tentative

excavations were made on the heap, it became apparent that an immense deposit of shells had been discovered. The prospective dealer in hen food lost no time in securing the property and erecting at the river bank a large drying and grinding mill. From early spring until late in the autumn a large crew of men was at work upon the heap, and when the snows of winter began to fall and financial coolness settled upon the enterprise, only a small portion of the mound was left.

Many years ago, Professor F. W. Putnam, of the Peabody Museum at Cambridge, in company with the distinguished scientists, Jeffries Wyman and Edward S. Morse, had made explorations of the shell deposits in this vicinity, and had collected a good deal of material, especially from the peninsula mound. Since that time other contributions have been made to the Peabody Museum, so that now this famous institution contains a large and well classified assortment of pottery, implements and bones from the shell banks in the region of the Damariscotta river. Professor Putnam learned of the intended depredations upon the newly found heap, and, realizing the importance of securing complete data in regard to the structure and contents of this mound, purchased for the Museum the right of all relics found in the deposit. A competent local antiquarian was engaged to be constantly on the ground, for the purpose of obtaining relics, measurements and pertinent facts about this great deposit. As a result of this labor a large amount of material was forwarded to the Peabody Museum, together with photographs and other important data concerning the mound. This material, on account of

shells were less than a foot deep. The mound was a solid and compact mass of shells with a comparatively great depth throughout. It had the appearance of an immense whaleback, and converted what was once a slight depression of the land into a hill. The greatest height of the shells was sixteen and one half feet, and it was estimated that the average height was nearly ten feet. Yielding in some degree to sentiment, the workmen left for a long time a great turret-like

PENINSULA MOUND — REMAINS OF WHALEBACK MOUND IN THE FOREGROUND.

lack of room in that large but already crowded edifice, is still unclassified and not yet on exhibition. We are able, nevertheless, to present here most of the important facts concerning this mound and to give reproductions of the best photographs taken during its destruction.

This newly discovered collection of shells began on the river bank and extended up hill for three hundred feet at right angles with the stream. Its width was one hundred and twenty-five feet, no measurements being taken from those points where the

body of shells standing in the centre. During the process of excavating, the fame of this great monument went far and wide, and it was visited during a few weeks of summer by many sightseers from Squirrel Island, Christmas Cove, Pemaquid and other popular summer resorts near the mouth of the Damariscotta river. It is unfortunate for posterity that the financial troubles which ultimately caused the hen-food firm to pass out of existence could not have happened before this interesting part of the mound was at last removed, thereby preserving a relic that of itself

MOUND AND MILL ON THE EASTERN SHORE OF THE DAMARISCOTTA.

would be worthy of a pilgrimage from afar. When, in the autumn, the work of demolition ceased, there was left of the great heap only a few rods of its lower extremity and several large piles of sifted shells. Not long after, by a happy accident, the mill burned down, and, the landscape being no longer obscured, nature holds sway once more. Despite the loss of the bulk of the mound, that which remains, being of considerable thickness and exposed on the upper end, is still a great object of interest to visitors, — not to make mention of the large heaps that remain practically intact on the opposite side of the stream.

As a result of the investigations made by the local expert, it was ascertained that there were three distinct periods of construction in this mound, separated by intervals of abandonment, during which an accumulation of several inches of vegetable mould gathered over the deposit. The lowest stratum of shells extended over about one-eighth of the surface finally occupied by the mound, and was three feet in thickness. At the base were found the stumps of eight or ten large trees, the wood of which had decayed to powder, leaving conical hollows, around which the shells were packed. Above this stratum was a layer of vegetable mould, which measured, allowing for that which had filtered down through the neighboring shells, about four inches in thickness. The second stratum of shells extended the area of

the heap and added about six more feet to its height. Over this was another layer of mould three inches deep, and upon this layer were found the stumps of five or six large trees of unrecognizable species, which to a diameter of two or more feet had grown up entirely within and upon the shells. The wood of these trees had been somewhat preserved by the shells which had been afterwards thrown around them, so that the stumps held their form while being dug around, although the wood was easily crumbled in the fingers. The third stratum finished the heap, and at the time of destruction had over it a layer of about two inches of soil.

The evidences of aboriginal occupation scattered throughout the mound are many and various, and, were they needed, furnish conclusive proof as to the character of the people who deposited the shells. From what had been discovered in the many explorations of the other heaps, we should naturally expect to find in the whaleback mound tools and implements of Indian use. These, in truth, we do find, although in no great numbers; for it is probable that the aboriginal village, where most of these things would naturally be found, was removed at a slight distance from the immediate vicinity of the mound.

At innumerable places among the shells were small beds of ashes and charcoal, ranging in quantity from a few quarts to several bushels. These

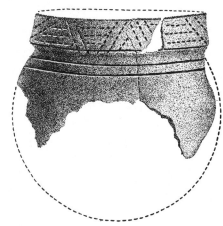

REMAINS OF AN EARTHEN VESSEL TAKEN FROM THE SHELL HEAPS.

countless beds of coal denoted places where the savages had cooked their oysters and other food. Two or three fireplaces built of stone in the form of a half circle were disclosed, each containing several .hundred pounds of stone. Upon and near these were found the remains of the banquets of savages.

In different parts of this mound appeared the bones of nearly every important animal living in this region when the first white men arrived. There were identified bones of the bear, lynx, wild-cat, raccoon, otter, mink, seal, skunk, rabbit, caribou and deer. Skeletons of a wolf and panther were also found. Parts of a turtle and numerous bones of the smelt and other fish appeared at intervals, together with the shells of the clam, quahaug, scallop and other mollusks. Many of these animal bones were in little piles of a peck or less, and in such a condition as betokened their previous servitude in a primeval soup or other similar dish. The bones were broken rather short and cracked open so as to obtain the marrow, which portion of the animal anatomy, as is known by the most unlearned, is esteemed as a charming delicacy by uncivilized peoples.

The more or less complete skeletons of six human beings were found on the heap; and of these only two showed signs of ceremonious burial, being near the top of the mound, no doubt placed there long after it was completed. Buried with them were a few beads of beaten copper and some broken pottery. The other four skeletons were lower down in the shells, and had no relics to accompany them. They appeared to lie at full length, as if fallen where they lay, and the shells had accumulated over them. The skulls were very broad, much broader than those of the ordinary Indian. To account for the presence of these skeletons in the mound is a matter of some difficulty; for it seems unnatural that the savages would bury the bodies of their dead among the refuse from their feasts. Nor on the other hand can we in these cases suspect cannibalism; for in such an event the bones would undoubtedly have been scattered far and wide. It is quite reasonable to suppose that at least the two lying near the top were placed there in formal burial at a time long subsequent to the abandonment of the heap, which period of abandonment we shall find to be a period of much uncertainty.

It is to be regretted that we cannot acquit the shell-heap makers of all complicity in masticating their fellowmen. In strict regard for truth, however, it must be disclosed that fragments of human bones were found mixed with those of other animals in such a manner as to preclude any other theory than cannibalism to account for them. Broken short and split lengthwise, they show undoubted successful attempts to procure the marrow, and, moreover, when found, they were in such location and surroundings as to prove that they once occupied a prominent position in the soup of which mention has been made.

Large quantities of pottery were taken out, mostly broken beyond repair. It is of a rude description, made of clay mixed with sand or powdered shells, and is similar in design and execution to most of the other pottery found in the East, which is never of the most expert make. The articles were commonly in the form of round-bottomed vessels from six inches to a foot in diameter. The bottom was frequently an inch or more in thickness, while the sides and top were comparatively thin. Some pieces had holes near the top, where bails or handles were inserted. Very little of the pottery was found in the lower stratum, and that was of decidedly inferior grade, plain or with scarcely any ornamentation, and having straight edges or rims. The pottery in the middle and upper strata showed a decided advance both in quality and in execution. The vessels had flaring rims and were comparatively well ornamented, — although at best the Indian ceramic art was never quite equal to that of Sèvres.

Considering the size of the mound, it was very barren of tools and implements. Two or three rude chisels of stone and a few stone flakes, together with a not very large number of bone points and deer horns with ends used as punches or spear heads, comprised about all the implements in this immense deposit. It will be remembered, however, that these heaps are merely kitchen-middens, or places of food refuse, and we should naturally expect in them little else than those relics that are directly connected with the preparation of food, such as fireplaces and pottery, together with the bones of animals and the cast off shells of the bivalves. For our spearheads, bone-points, chisels, hammers, sinkers and numerous other tools and implements, we have only to search the fields in the immediate vicinity. Indeed, the whole region for miles around, particularly the shores and islands of the river and the neighborhood of the several beautiful lakes near by, are peculiarly rich in traces of Indian life.

The two principal heaps remaining to be described are considerably smaller than the whaleback mound, and are situated on the same side of the river. One, a few rods above, is on high land and covered with soil, no part of it being visible from the river. One or two small gullies have cut into it, exposing the shells on the landward side. Many traces of shells are found in the fields near by, and doubtless if the soil were removed and extensive explorations made a large additional quantity of shells would be disclosed. The other mound is on low land near the outer angle of the river bend, and occupies a rather large area; but the depth is nowhere more than three feet, except in the case of a small barrier for a few rods along the shore. The waters of the incoming tide strike headlong against this bank, and without a doubt many feet of shells have been worn away.

It is generally noticeable that the shells in all the heaps are of great size, some of them being of immense dimensions as compared with the ordinary oyster of to-day. Those of a foot in length are repeatedly found, while a few of fourteen or fifteen inches have been secured. In the upper part of the whaleback mound a rather imperfect shell was taken out, whose cavity nevertheless was intact, measuring one foot long and eight inches wide. Its original length exceeded sixteen inches, and the animal whose habitation it had been would have filled a pint measure. The shells are found to be almost invariably single, and a long search would be necessary to find the two valves of an oyster together. They are long, narrow and somewhat curved or scimiter shaped, and are bleached white, having lost their original color. Those near the bottom of a large heap can often be crumbled in the fingers.

The total quantity of shells contained in all the mounds and smaller heaps at the headwaters of the Damariscotta river has been variously estimated. Doctor Jackson, once state geologist of Maine, by a computation the details of which are lost to history, once asserted that there were forty-five million cubic feet of shells in the

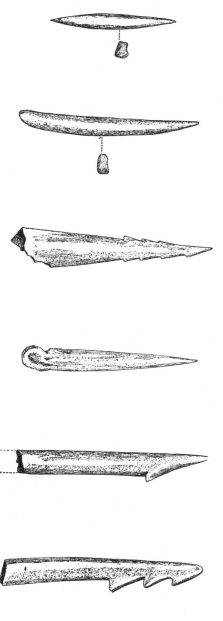

deposits at this place; but what authority he had for naming so immense a quantity passes the understanding of the present writer, — and in lack of supporting data we are obliged to pronounce his figures a great exaggeration. In fact, most of the estimates made in regard to these deposits, as well as to the other famous mounds of the world, have been greatly strengthened by a facile imagination. Making allowance for shells washed away by the river and removed by the hand of man, we may confidently assert that there were probably about five million cubic feet of shells originally deposited hereabouts. This, it will be admitted, is a sufficiently large number to make many people familiar with the virtues of these delicious bivalves. To transport so enormous a mass of shells would require one hundred freight trains, each containing forty cars. The quantity of oysters consumed by the savages in their long feeding upon these grounds would have measured nearly three million gallons. This volume of oysters would fill a structure three times the size of Bunker Hill monument, and there would be left of the succulent animals enough to fill the great tun of Heidelberg six times, with a remainder still sufficient to give every Indian in the United States a most satisfactory meal.

There are more theories than one as to the time of the origin and completion of the mounds and as to the persons who are responsible for them. To almost every imaginable people, from the Phœnicians to the Northmen, has this work been ascribed. It has appeared to some minds that the more foreign the people who could possibly be connected with this coast, the more likely were they to have left these remains at the headwaters of the Damariscotta. Because some of the bone implements here found resemble those of the Eskimos, that people forsooth held high carnival on these

BONE, SPEAR AND ARROW POINTS TAKEN FROM THE SHELL HEAPS.

grounds in primeval feasts; and because the Northmen are supposed to have once visited this coast, and there are similar kitchen-middens in Denmark, they likewise are adjudged to have fed upon the oysters of this bay and to have completed these heaps. It would seem, however, more natural, although perhaps not so ingenious, to impute these doings to the aboriginal inhabitants of the region. For every tool, implement and vessel bears unmistakable evidence of Indian occupation, no instrument having been discovered to suggest any other people. Moreover, it is highly unreasonable to suppose that these heaps had an origin entirely different from that of the hundreds of smaller mounds scattered over the continent, which were evidently laid by the Indians or other peoples who inhabited this country for uncounted centuries. To a savage the one great object of existence was to supply material for his appetite. He turned no small attention to the finny tribes. That he was not ignorant of the merits of oysters is beyond peradventure.

There are grounds for believing that the region contiguous to the Damariscotta was a favorite resort or dwelling place for the savages, being especially favored by nature in land, river and lakes. What were the characteristics of the river in the early days are shown by its name, which in the designation Damasek or Damariscotta, — the place of a multitude of little fishes, — perpetuates the Indian appreciation of its merits. The Damariscotta is in no degree unworthy of its name at the present day. In the spring millions of alewives are dipped out by nets at the falls leading from the lake, and in the winter the frozen surface of the bay is dotted with scores of small houses in which tons of smelts are caught through holes in the ice. The oysters whose shells form the great mounds were probably taken from the immediate vicinity, particularly the bay and the portion of the river leading from it down as far as the remotest heaps

extend. Solid beds of oyster shells may now be found here by one digging in the flats through several feet of accumulated mud and saw-dust; and in the clear waters of "Oyster Creek," flowing into the upper part of the bay, white oyster shells may be seen lying upon the bed of the stream. The methods used by Indians generally in securing oysters were of the rudest sort. They procured the shell fish by wading out and picking them up at low tide, and by diving. The shells were usually opened by being thrown upon beds of coal, or by being cracked on rocks.

There is no proof of the time when the mounds were abandoned, but it is generally assumed to be about three hundred years ago, or when the first white men arrived. It could in no wise have been much later, for there is on record no statement of any one who ever saw or knew of an oyster shell being thrown upon the heaps, nor has any article of European manufacture been discovered within them. But it may be a question whether the Indians in their intercourse with Popham would have reported the existence of the shell-heaps as a curiosity, were they familiar with the circumstances of construction and engaged in making periodical additions to the mounds. There is, on the other hand, good reason for believing that oysters in limited quantities have been growing in Damariscotta Bay as late as the first part of the present century; and herein lies the plausibility of ascribing a comparatively recent date to the Indian abandonment of the grounds, although it is certain that at least one hundred years ago large trees were growing upon some of the shell deposits. Oysters were once indigenous not only to the coast of Maine but also to the more northern waters of Nova Scotia, New Brunswick and Cape Breton; and artificial shell-heaps have been found in all these regions. By the gradual cooling of the water, or from some other cause, they have successively disappeared from Canadian inlets and from those of Maine and Massachusetts, until now they are found in appreciable quantities no further north than Cape Cod. One cause of the extinction of the oyster at Damariscotta may have been the large amounts of saw-dust thrown into the bay from the mills above.

In Denmark and in Japan the origin of the shell-mounds is lost in the dawn of history, while on the other hand the construction of similar mounds is known to have been going on in other places up to a recent date. The only evidence we can rely on is the condition of the mounds themselves, covered with large trees and washed away to a large degree. That so great an erosion as must have occurred on the western shore could have taken place in three hundred years is open to great doubt; but how much further back we can place the desertion of these grounds is purely a matter of speculation.

Through how long a period the savages made use of the oyster beds of this river is even beyond conjecture. In view of the small area from which the oysters were taken and the limited number of savages who could have fed here, centuries must have been required to complete these enormous heaps. If there were taken from the waters every hour enough of the bivalves to make ten gallons of the oysters ready for. eating, there would be need of seventy years, using every hour of daylight in the whole time, to make an accumulation of so vast a quantity of shells. Evidences also of long interruptions exist in the structure of the mounds themselves. It was noted previously, for example, that in the great mound on the eastern shore there were two strata of vegetable mould having a total thickness of seven inches. It is generally thought to take a hundred years for

one inch of mould to accumulate, and on this reckoning there was a period of seven centuries, during which, through causes not known, few if any oysters were obtained. In further assurance of a long period of abandonment, witness the great trees that were found to have grown up within the shells upon the second layer of mould.

From lack of historical record and the meagre internal evidence of the mounds themselves, the investigator will be pardoned if he is not dogmatic as to the beginning of this great work. Most interesting would it be if we knew what contemporary events were taking place on that day when the first few oysters were gathered by savage hands from under the waters of the river and their useless shells thrown upon ground that had hitherto known them not. But we are unable to say whether it was the time when the Athenians were marking on their own oyster shells the exile of Aristides, or whether it was at a remote period compared to which the ostracism of the famous Grecian was but as yesterday.

However wild the scenes once witnessed in this little valley, now all is calm. The countless dusky forms that we can see in panoramic vision are now only part of the dust we tread at every step. We can sit upon the shelly bank, underneath the shade of the pine trees, and muse on many things; but what we have before us is only the river with its flowing to and fro, and the pretty coves and shaded shores that are near by. We may pluck beside the shells the jewel weed, the bluebell and the primrose; and gaze at yonder rower as he glides down the stream near the setting of the sun and watches alternately the blue heron standing on the shore and the floating rafts of seaweed on which a flock of sand-pipers have settled to pick their evening meal.

5
Newport

SCRIBNER'S MAGAZINE

AUGUST 1894

NEWPORT

By W. C. Brownell

ILLUSTRATIONS BY W. S. VANDERBILT ALLEN

I

A BENEFICENT fairy of æsthetic predilections could not have arranged a composition containing more efficient contrast and balance than Newport presents in its combination of old and new, of the quaint and the elegant, picturesqueness and culture. Nowhere else does fashion rest with such feathery lightness on such a solid pedestal. The mundane extravagance gains immensely by being related, seemingly at least and as to ocular setting, to a background of natural beauty and grave decorum. The background gains a little, too. The people that inhabit it, addicted as they are to observant criticism of "summer visitors," nevertheless receive an electric fillip from their contact with what is gay and joyous and no doubt fleeting. In spite of their most conscientious efforts they are affected in a way that broadens their horizon in proportion as it sharpens their critical faculties. They "size up" the brilliant butterflies that but hover about the lovely town a few brief months in the year, and in rather remorseless fashion; but they are justifiably if secretly proud of their opportunities for doing so. What other city with any pretensions to be a watering-place has any such chance? The whole town is in consequence visibly braced up. The clerks in the shops along Thames Street betray the influence in their deportment. A higher standard of manners than would otherwise obtain is universally apparent. School-children, even, treat each other with noticeably more decorousness than elsewhere. The comedy of society is repeated, in fact, in infinite and often humorous trituration. But the result is pleasant. The hack-drivers are, socially considered, *poseurs.* They crack jokes with their fares if they divine responsiveness, but their self-respect is still more obvious than their companionability; the "old Newporter" is not above showing the place to a party of negro visitors whom he drives down the Avenue with conspicuous good-humor, but it is his good-humor that is the most striking element of the spectacle. Even in such extreme instances one perceives the effect of the social ideal due to the "summer visitor."

On the other hand, an impartial chronicle must admit that the moral effect of a foreign body of wealth, leisure, and measurable frivolity in an environment of thrifty commonplace, such as indigenous Newport for the most part is, has its weak side. Brought up in more or less close contact with and at any rate constant sight of the attractive activities of so much irresponsible wealth, the strictly Newport people—who once constituted a very honorable and peculiarly self-respecting community—have suffered a sensible demoralization. Not "hatred" nor "uncharitableness" has been the

subtle influence, with the result that "Newport" has come to mean less to them and to others. The town is still —and may be in the future still more— an interesting place to speculate about as a New England town of excellent traditions and unequalled attractions, but unquestionably it has lost something of its once very positive character through contact with ideals and examples by no means its own. Among the shop-keepers—especially among those whom recent changes in "business methods" have rather relegated to the business background—and among the householders on the streets leading from Thames Street to what used to be called "the Hill," I am sure one would find an echo of such a judgment.

At first sight and to those who take but a perfunctory view of Newport this may seem of slight importance. But to my own mind that which makes Newport what it is, is the balance hitherto

In Front of the Casino.

result of this contact with superior forces, but certainly "envy" has had a maintained between a self-respecting, organic, and permanent community and

The Casino Quadrangle—Morning.

the artificial, decorative, and more or less transitory element that makes it our chief watering-place. If the latter of these forces withdraws into exclusiveness, which to anyone who knows its composition may easily seem ridiculous, but which may nevertheless occur; or if the former declines into vulgarity and the loss of self-respect involved in the bravado of self-assertion, to which constant envy of what is quite beyond one's reach indubitably may lead, Newport as we know it now and have known it for years will certainly suffer a sea change. In other words, the future of Newport is, one must admit, considerably complicated by the peril of snobbishness, and snobbishness of both varieties exemplified by the Anglo-Saxon race. The English snob, according to an acute observer, meanly admires what is above him, the American meanly despises what is beneath him. Newport

undoubtedly has its full share of both species, but it has also, I think, the unusual advantage of sincerely attaching both to it, with the consequent prospect of circumventing each of them.

The place is supposed to owe its growth and eminence to the summer residents. It really owes these to four persons—all of them indigenous. They would nowadays be called "the Big Four." Without their foresight and realization of its potentialities, the city would still be what it was before the war, when its summer life was almost altogether a desultory and caravansary affair. It owes them, indeed, more or less indirectly, the summer residents themselves. Without their labor of preparation and seduction, opening streets and drives, modelling estates out of barren tracts, artistically cutting up the landscape into attractive lots, stimulating civic improvements, making known and visually exhibiting the immense attractiveness of the place to everyone who had taste and money, Newport would have been to-day far different in almost every trait that now makes it "Newport." They found their account in the process, of course. They were or became capitalists in the course of advancing the interests and widening the prospects of the town. And, naturally, they are now forgotten. I need mention but one of them ; but anyone who knows Newport well, or at least anyone who has known it as I have for upwards of thirty years, will appreciate what I mean to intimate in querying what the city would now be had it not been for the intelligence and enlightened enthusiasm of the late Alfred Smith, a man of ideas and imagination which, applied to anything more tangible and determinate than the gradual evolution of the first watering-place in this country, would have given him a national reputation. One needs but a passing reflection upon the imagination

upon the real Eden of America wherein to erect its "barbarian castles" and display its varied and leisurely activities.

The summer residents do not all belong to the "smart set," it is needless to say. Indeed, I doubt if any watering-place in the world of anything like equal eminence has a summer population characterized by so much elegance and refinement. There was long ago a large nucleus of elegance and refinement in Newport, and it has since grown proportionately with the increase of those whom envy and emulation have gathered around it; but certainly for these latter the way was made easy and its advantages indicated by the enterprise, energy, and enthusiasm of the men I have alluded to. Somewhat mixed the summer population now undoubtedly is. It has grown so large as to have grades and classes of its own. And to judge from the newspapers, which scrupulously record its doings, it has possession of the town from June to October. It has certainly worked a great change in the summer life of the place.

This was always artificial and exotic, and always delightfully so. But the rise and immensely increased number of great fortunes have worked changes in Newport as they have everywhere else. Less here, however, than elsewhere, I am inclined to think, and certainly less here than is generally supposed. It is a commonplace that the hotels have been supplanted by the cottages. The Ocean House survives somewhat as a landmark and a reminiscence, but in obvious isolation. You can no longer sit on its broad piazza and watch with interest the serried defile of equipages — almost all of

Exercising the Thoroughbreds.

and ideas of our American "smart set" to assure him whether or no it is likely that unassisted it would have hit

them readily to be identified. The Atlantic, the Fillmore, and the Bellevue are only memories, though to anyone

DRAWN BY W. S. VANDERBILT ALLEN.

Yacht Club and Landing-Stage.

ENGRAVED BY VAN NESS.

who knew them even in their decadence and when they no longer harbored Southern folk and Southern manners

I have even met—people who preferred a Jamestown barrack to a Newport cottage at the same price, maintaining that

An Old Revolutionary House.

with all the gayety and light-hearted *camaraderie*, characteristically Southern, they are charming memories still. Can it be that the hotel life of Narragansett Pier, for example, is a fair reproduction of its old-time Newport analogue? But this is a question of only speculative interest. As a matter of fact, hotel life has disappeared in Newport. What is curious, however, I think, is that so few people are alive to the fact that cottage life is just as feasible for persons of modest means. People go to Jamestown, on Conanicut Island, every summer and live in the hotels that have magically sprung up there at prices which would more than enable them to live in Newport cottages. Tastes differ proverbially, and I can fancy—for

the life was freer in Jamestown. I dare say it is; it is freer still at Asbury Park, N. J. Costume and manners may both be legitimately more *négligés* than would be quite seemly in a denser population and amid surroundings that suggest more decorum. But there are persons to whom a certain degree of decorum is in itself pleasant to witness and practice, and to these life in Newport during the season may be as simple as it is in a village. To such persons the only obstacle to enjoyment is the constant presence of an elaborate and expensive life which they cannot share. This has capacities for making the envious and the feeble-minded, people who have no pride of tradition or shrewdness of philosophy or instinctive

DRAWN BY W. S. VANDERBILT ALLEN.

Bellevue Avenue—Afternoon.

fastidiousness, extremely unhappy, no doubt. For others with small means the advantages of Newport are unequalled. The markets seem high-priced, especially to a New Yorker, but they are much more than counterbalanced by the low rents ; and the conveniences obtainable at low rentals, due to the way in which cottage-building has been speculatively overdone, are unexampled. Bathing, rowing, sailing, driving, walking, picnicking are to be had in perfection, under a sky of infinite delicacy, in an atmosphere of unique softness, and in an environment of natural beauty and artistic distinction that exists nowhere else.

Then there is the passing show—the social spectacle. The social spectacle as well as the summer life has greatly changed of recent years. Opening the Ocean Drive from the end of the avenue

digiously disseminated the stately procession that used to pass decorously up and done the Avenue, turning at Bailey's Beach and at Kay Street where the houses ceased. Though the procession is much augmented nowadays it no longer produces the same effect as formerly and has, indeed, ceased to be a procession ; the "establishments," as they used to be called, are strung along without cumulative effect. And owing to their greater number no one knows and can gossip about more than one in three of them. "Newport" seems less condensed in consequence. Its old lovers feel a certain lack. The procession's smartness, too (an epithet, by the way, we should not have thought of using twenty years ago), is now deeply infiltrated by plebeian elements — Stewart's, Hazard's, or other so-called "drags," with their

On the Cliffs.

to the fort made a great difference to it. Ten miles more of macadam pro-

mammoth loads of excursionists anxiously curious to see and fix in the

The Ball-room of the Casino.

memory the mansions they have read about in the Sunday papers, and also frequently recurrent vehicles of the ultra-shirt-sleeved *bourgeoisie* of the town itself, in whom the desire of parade has altogether outrun the capacity of creditably attaining it. These new elements "have a good time," in our American idiom, and certainly no place in our democratic country, not even Newport, can consistently elevate any ideal above that of providing people in general with a good time at any cost to the æsthetic or other sensibilities of "the remnant." Only, a *laudator temporis acti* in thinking of Newport may, perhaps, without feeling quite a snob, make the reflection that the present situation is the result of artificial rather than of natural selection.

This overlay of *nouvelles couches* is obvious elsewhere than in the driving procession, of course, with the result of social and political rather than æsthetic

cheer to the spectator. The accursed but convenient trolley system clangs and sizzes through erstwhile sedate Spring Street and out the wide expanse of elm-lined Broad Street, now characteristically become Broadway. The colored population has increased after its prolific racial fashion, and the anomaly of a barouche full of darky dandies and dusky belles conducted by an Irish, or even, as I have before mentioned, a native Newport driver is a frequent phenomenon. The appalling excursionist from Providence and Pawtucket, with his and her paper bags and odor of peanuts and ginger-pop, infests the squares, the cliffs, the beach, and awakens echoes with enjoyment. The Irish contingent has augmented proportionally with the African. The city government is largely in its hands, with perhaps the usual consequence of its own prosperity and a deterioration of public works in general. There are larger

Yachting.

crowds of expectorating loafers around the Post-office and the City Hall. The commercial traveller, with his samples and his manners, is more numerous. In fine, the city is no longer, to the eye as well as in fact, composed of a summer aristocracy and a resident *bourgeoisie*, its self-respecting admirers. It has moved with the rest of the world and with similar results. And with all its changes, which the dilettante or the lover of old Newport may deplore, it is perhaps more pre-eminently than ever the loveliest, the serenest, and most smiling, the most refined and decorous civic *ensemble* that the country possesses.

The quality of the summer life is its elegance, its defect is its artificiality. It is undoubtedly elegant, but its elegance is not quite a natural evolution. It is surrounded with ease, comfort, and distinction not merely material, but æsthetic. Its stage is carpeted with the loveliest of lawns and decorated with the greatest profusion of flowers anywhere to be seen. It is characterized by a great deal of high-breeding, of de-

corum triumphing over frivolity, of taste, reserve, and composure. A large element of it certainly is superior to the envious fleering or the obsequious flattery of vulgarity. Its self-respect is perfectly obvious and real. But one would like to see this carried a little farther, to the point, I mean, of unconsciousness, of absolute free play. Self-respect is admirable, but respect for one's traditions is admirable, also. The Newport summer life has traditions, and it should not abandon them in the chameleon-like way characteristic of it, and appear imitative and artificial. It is only comparatively new, and yet by its rather systematic imitation of what is positively old—by its studied modelling of itself on English country life, with which it really has but the most superficial relations in the world—it creates the effect of a reflection and not of an original. In English country life the flowers make no such display, it is true, but the lawns are deeper and richer, the houses have infinitely older associations, and the entire environment is infinitely more established and sedate. Why abandon our own heritage of vivacity and high-spirited decorousness in favor of an exotic, and to us esoteric, ideal? Anglomania is, perhaps, not conspicuous in Newport, certainly not in comparison with the rest of the East; but in Newport it is less excusable than elsewhere, and its effects more regrettable accordingly; in Newport more than anywhere else with us imitation by the new thing of the old, failure to insist on one's own idiosyncrasies, and, as Arnold says of ritualistic practices, "vehement adoption of rites till yesterday unknown," seem to imply that we do not "know a good thing when we see it."

So great, however, is the unifying their withdrawal from the beach, the summer people are certainly less in evidence than they were formerly. They make far less of a spectacle for profane contemplation and somewhat consciously and uneasily, perhaps, study exclusiveness, if not seclusion. They visit among themselves and have teas and dinners to themselves, quite as they do in their several winter social circles. It is perfectly clear that they do not have anything like the good time they or their fathers and mothers used to have; but that is their affair, and is only interesting as it affects and modifies "Newport." They still come out quite strong—as they are beginning to learn

An Afternoon Spin.

power of Newport that when its summer life appears in any concrete manifestation one feels that to inquire into it is eminently to inquire too curiously. It is true that with the extension of the drive, the decline of the hotel-life and to say—at the Casino; though the Casino has never paid for itself and is a monument to the unwisdom of its originators' efforts to domesticate an essentially foreign institution. It embodies the transplanted fancies of the staid burghers of Holland in conjunction with the predilections of the lawn-loving Englishman, and includes a restaurant more or less reminiscent of France. But it has been found to be unduly costly and adjudged to have "forced the note." Yet it has weekly concerts and dances which at all events the outer fringe of the society people do not hesitate to attend and participate in, and it witnesses one festival in the year to which they contribute their presence with the utmost cordiality—the annual lawn - tennis tournament. There are probably few prettier scenes than that of which this contest is the centre. Perfectly trimmed lawns swept by the freshest and daintiest morning dresses, young men in flannels, rosy with health and irresponsibility, fashion in its freest and least conscious manifestations, the mass of "best people" in their most attractive inadvertence, the rising seats around the courts clad in the most refreshing variety of clear-colored costumes pricked out with patches of brilliant parasols, the water-color note everywhere, as a painter would say, and the well-groomed young fellows in the centre of the composition obviously exhibiting both strength and skill—make a picture which for combined animation and refinement, both of actors and spectators, it would be difficult to match anywhere. Jean Béraud—or better still Raffaelli or Forain—would find it quite as well worth fixing as Longchamp, though the types, of course, are less various.

Newport owes, too, to the summer resident, not only a high standard of social life and a decorous employment of leisure, but also an æsthetic ideal of architecture and landscape gardening. Architecture has perhaps been as much travestied as illustrated. The feeblest whimsies abound. Reflections in frame of reverend stone *motifs* are not infrequent. The art of building is often caricatured in houses of which the only inspiration is plainly the desire to be conspicuous. And though some of the old houses, such as the Bareda mansion and Mr. Wetmore's palace, are their own excuse for being, there are not a few elaborate examples of exaggerated bad taste and worse grammar. On the other hand, such a house as the late H. H. Richardson built for Mr. Sherman, or that of Mr. Marquand by Hunt, and others easily mentioned, form a notable leaven and rectify the effect produced by perhaps the predominant inapposite sportiveness. But there is no doubt at all of the immense service to the place rendered by the summer resident's landscape gardener, who has covered broad acres of it with lawns and boscages, clumps of trees and bushes, heaps of flowery luxuriance walled in by privet and buckthorn, and has more than any other agency, except the climate and the natural lay of the land, exhibited the potentialities of elegance inherent in these latter. A good word should be said, in addition, for the way in which—often an awkward and somewhat absurd instrument in the hands of Providence — the summer resident has circumvented the purely utilitarian and ignoble activities that, left to themselves, would have done their disastrous utmost to vulgarize Newport, wholly and deplorably unconscious that the life of the goose that lays for them such golden eggs is really in peril.

II

THE old town may be called picturesque in distinction from the general pictorial effect that is noticeable. It is full of narrow streets and quaint turnings ; little squares left undisturbed by the march of municipal improvements within their old-time staid and rectilinear demarcation ; trapezoidal houses built originally, it is evident, in exemplification of the sound principle that expression of function is the one thing needful in architecture ; gently inclining gambrels in themselves a composition. But even its streets and houses, its courts, *impasses*, and docks have as detail too much character and individual sap justly to be termed the mere material of a picturesque whole. They have none of the indeterminate and huddled look of the detail of Amalfi or Assisi. They make a harmony that is sensibly organic. They are individually quaint now and then, without, however, the sharp accent that we usually

Bass-fishing Stand.

associate with quaintness, and they fit the landscape "like the paper on the wall." Some of the narrow gambrel-roofed houses have gables that gaze on the streets, on which they often look, like human faces. Cotton's Court, Wanton Avenue, and similar places, contracted as they evidently are in area, have an air of complication and variety that tempt and would reward the exploring sense. Curious juxtapositions of shop, dwelling, stable, warehouse, and what not form incomparable "nooks." The public buildings are interesting. The City Hall, admired by Allston, is a charming bit of classic, and the State House a colonial monument of much dignity and character. The jail, on Marlborough Street, is absolutely delightful and characteristically domestic; there is a legend of its one prisoner once complaining because there was no lock on her door. In all the world probably there is nothing like the Long Wharf, with its succession of boat-builders' shops, tenements, ignoble saloons, heaps of junk, sail-boat moorings and floats, terminating in the railway freight station and the steamboat wharf. It is hardly changed within my own recol-

lection. Deacon Groff's succession to James Hart, the boat-builder and letter, in whose airy shop a parliament of local sages meets now as it has for several decades, amid the shavings and spars, the oars and "tackle," to look out over the harbor and speculate on the political state of the nation and the social state of the town, is the chief variation I note, and that is not revolutionary. On the hottest day there is always a breeze here, and much to be learned besides.

Nor is there anything, I fancy, quite like Thames Street from end to end—the business street of the town—though its banks and butcher-shops, and bookstores and fish-markets, and hardware and dry-goods and haberdashery are punctuated and faintly diversified with dwellings now and then. They have been dwellings a long while, and count many generations of probably the same families. The subdued note of age, of "silence and slow time," is distinctly audible, and vibrates gently throughout the old town, with its gray and white and green blinds; but I must admit that of recent years there has been to some extent an intrusive discord of

Scene on the Beach.

DRAWN BY W. S. VANDERBILT ALLEN.

commercial modernity even here. The one-price clothing store, the bee-hives of humming retail industry, and the universal emporium are foreign bodies in the general environment and contribute a foreign color to the quaint old street—like an overflow of Fall River or Providence. But as yet they have not greatly detracted from the general character of the thoroughfare, which is still sufficient to afford one of the most piquant contrasts in the world, I think, when the drags and dog-carts, the broughams and phaetons of fashion weave their way along its narrow length at what it pleases everyone's humorous fancy to call the shopping hour. Thames Street, whatever its transformations, will indefinitely, I think, continue to perform its distinguished function of binding together summer and winter, transitory and permanent Newport with a notable welding force.

The Point, too, is a part of the old town, and is rather neglected, which it should not be. It is somewhat inaccessible, and anyone who lives there or inhabits the neighborhood for a summer has need, perhaps, of a horse and trap of some kind. But it has its advantages and qualities of its own. To begin with it is very far removed from the artificial summer life. One may live there as much in retreat as at Jamestown. Land is very cheap, and if I were tempted to "build" in Newport I am not at all sure that I should not select some site on the water's edge in this region. One could have his fill of still-water bathing, his cat-boat and row-boat, and a certain measure of seclusion wholly consonant with the most delightful out-of-doors activity and within easy reach of whatever is attractive in the town itself.

III

NEWPORT is longitudinally divided by three main streets which run north and south. Following mainly the harbor line and projecting thitherward its many slips is Thames Street, where is almost all the business of the town, extending from the cemetery, with its characteristic contrast of old and new, the old slate carvings of winged cherubs' heads hard by, the joint product of La Farge and St. Gaudens, to the lower end of the harbor. A few rods up the hill Spring Street, with its prim houses and old Trinity and other churches, parallels it, running from just above the Parade or Mall where the State House is south to the ocean. And on the crest of the ridge are the nearly straight two miles and a half of Bellevue Avenue. At its north end is the romantic and trimly kept Jews' Cemetery, celebrated by Longfellow, where sleep amid flowers and cypresses Abraham and Judah Touro and other Hebrews, who amply repaid the early toleration and respect here extended to their race long before it received them elsewhere. Next come residences, boarding-houses, a little row of lesser commerce, the Newport Reading-room—the club euphemistically so-called—the Redwood Library, now a more hushed but less hospitable bookish retreat than many old Newporters remember it, and Touro Park, where the Old Stone Mill stands and a band plays on summer evenings. Then a stretch of shops till one gets to Bath Road, the broad street leading to the beach, the Casino, and the stiff, stark caravansary of the Ocean House just beyond.

Here begins the succession of cottages and châteaux of the summer resident, set wide apart in elegant lawns bordered with hedges and blazing with flowers, that extends for a couple of miles to the sea. And the slope that shelves gently eastward from the crest of the hill that the Avenue follows has also within the past few lustra (especially in the neighborhood of Ochre Point) been covered with elaborate mansions the average of whose pretensions exceeds perhaps that of those appertaining to the Avenue itself. This is the region—the rough parallelogram formed by the Avenue, the cliffs bordering the sea a half mile or so to the east, the southern shore, and an east and west line from about the Ocean House to a point a little south of the Beach—where chiefly reside the summer people whose activities the papers chronicle so copiously, and where, better perhaps than anywhere else, an American may see his "young [and old] barbarians all at play"—to recall Arnold's application of the line to Oxford. The northwestern part of the city has grown greatly also of recent years, and is covered with cottages of modest cost and considerable architectural character. Past the Beach is another district whose houses, some of them ample and elaborate, stand in notable isolation amid rural fields, then Paradise with its farm - houses, ponds, junipers, and gray rocks, the Second Beach, and finally Sachuest Point, which brings one to the Seaconnet River and the verge of Newport. All around here and north from the town proper, delightful drives lead out into the island itself. Six miles out is the Glen, an almost artificial arrangement of romantic nature, driving whither one may stop at Mrs. Durfee's for tea and waffles, and enjoy a truly English interior. Then there are Pebbly Beach, with its unexplained geological conformations, and romantically situated, cool, and cosey St. Mary's Chapel, and Vaucluse and its deserted close, eloquent in reflections such as Mr. Swinburne has crystallized in his incomparable "A Forsaken Garden ;" and no end of quaint cross-roads and long vistas beneath overhanging elms or between trim poplars—the whole greatly vivified and highly colored by the local inhabitant, with his sturdy and salient characteristics, lounging in front of country stores and post-offices, or jogging past in his open wagon, smiling the while, with good - natured cynicism at any exuberance you and your party may exhibit.

To go back to the town itself, is there anything in the world like the two miles and more of the Cliff Walk? Setting out from the Beach the sea is on one's left, its near shallows, "with green and yellow sea-weed strewn," and beyond its stretch of varying blues and purples, the long, graceful reach of Easton's Point, at the end of which a solitary cottage stands sentinel, and shimmering in the more distant haze the shore of Seaconnet and its neighboring rocky islets around which the breakers are flashing in foam. On the right of the path, which undulates along

its edges and rises and falls with its rolling unevenness, extends that succession of lawns which, more than any other feature perhaps, sets the pitch of Newport's elegance. In these smooth expanses of soft green glowing with unexampled profusion of aristocratic flowers, the art and nature of the place meet in effective fusion. So elegant is it all that one fails to note how high and rugged are the cliffs themselves, the highest on the Atlantic coast from Cape Ann to Yucatan. On a day of storm, with the waves driving in from the ocean and beating angrily against them, they are more impressive ; but they are always picturesque and make a striking dividing line between the sea, wherein the forces of nature are always visibly at play, peaceful or turbulent, and the broad shelf of land which the hand of man has moulded and decorated with the most cultivated art. Curious, is it not, that certain proprietors of the villas to which these lawns appertain should have tried by every means to circumvent the undoubted riparian right of all the world to follow this unequalled path at its will, provided trespass be avoided ? They are newcomers, one infers, to Newport at any rate, if not to *id omne genus*, for a prolonged submission to Newport influences could hardly fail to modify the Hyrcanian hearts and Bœotian brains to which in such circumstances as these monopoly could suggest itself.

Beyond the southern extremity of the Cliff Walk, and extending westward to Castle Hill (whence one may see the fringe of hotels and cottages that compose Narragansett Pier) and Fort Adams, stretches out the charming region known of old as Price's Neck—variegated with ponds and embayments, hill and dale, rock and marsh, and skirted and reticulated with the famous Ocean Drive and its tributaries. The Ocean Drive is the finest, I think, in the world ; at least to my own taste its mingling of stimulus and suavity, its alternations of wildness and culture, its invigorating iodine-laden breezes, the sedative softness of its mists, the piquant aroma of its huckleberry bushes, the infinite variety of its "effects," combine to produce an impression to which that left by the Cornice from Nice to Genoa is a shade saccharine and monotonous. This and the Paradise country are the regions that appeal most, perhaps, to the few landscape painters who have had the sense to appreciate that in Newport they had but to reproduce, whereas elsewhere the heavy burthen of origination is laid upon them. Mr. La Farge is a notable exception, by the way ; and curiously, thus, it is the most imaginative of our painters who, almost alone, has illustrated the most pictorial landscape that we have. The Neck has been greatly changed within the last few years, and some fastidious spirits who are displeased with any intrusion of man into the realm of nature (I should greatly like to know if Mr. La Farge were among them in this instance), have esteemed it "destroyed." The change, at all events, is at the charge of the summer residents. To me, I confess, it is to be charged to their credit.

IV

ANOTHER effect of the evolution of the summer resident as an important and controlling class has been the transformation—I was about to say the destruction—of the Beach. The Beach is no longer what it used to be. The " bathing hour," with all its characteristic features, has departed. You may bathe at any hour when you can find a " house," but it is no longer fashionable to bathe at all. There are a few private houses sometimes occupied, and at Bailey's Beach others whose owners use them very constantly, but the bathing at the Beach as a feature of social summer life is over. The carriages do not come down and draw up on the sand to watch the bathers. The place is no longer a rendezvous both for bathers and spectators, as, say, the *plage* at Trouville is. " Society " has abandoned it, and in general, probably, confines itself to " tubbing." The philosophic lover of Newport must recognize the change as inevitable, no doubt, but the sentimentalist may be permitted to regret it. Perhaps it would have been asking too much of the summer people,

to preserve in this respect the simplicity and really democratic elegance which they evinced before they became consciously so much of a force as to be uneasily careful with regard to even chance companionship. And it must be confessed that of late years the Beach has been invaded by people with whom fastidiousness may excusably find it disagreeable to mingle. On Sundays it is given over to excursionists and servants, as was quite to have been expected, of course, with the increase of Newport's general popularity and its facilities of access by rail and water. But even on week-days it has " developed " immensely in a popular direction. " Pavilions " that recall Coney Island more than old Newport have arisen, and the aroma of chowder pervades them. The travelling photographer sets up his shanty. Wrapping-paper abounds, and " lunches " are surreptitiously munched. The sunshine and salt air minister to the greatest good of the greatest number. Of the " best people " in general, only those who find the bathing hygienic or positively pleasurable, enter the water, and only their immediate friends attend and observe them. Still I, for one, cannot help thinking that things might have been different but for the society fiat that bathing was to be considered unfashionable, and that the fiat itself rather unnecessarily preceded any real occasion for it. Certainly, were the natural advantages of the Beach appreciated as are those of the European watering places whose summer population is both popular and select, they would be utilized instead of neglected. They are, as a matter of fact, unequalled. There is but one natural disadvantage. The Beach fronts southward, and after a storm gets more than its due proportion of seaweed ; and seaweed is a distinct discount upon the pleasure of bathing. Otherwise it is unrivalled. It is absolutely safe. It shelves in the gentlest gradation. The water is always warm. Even at high tide there is plenty of room for carriages. The dunes are high enough to afford protection from the wind when it happens to come from the north. It is a mile in extent and affords a driving promenade at low tide of almost unique exhilaration. The "scene" is invariably animating. Indeed, it must not be supposed that in finding excuses for the "best people's" recent neglect, one really quite acquits them of stupidity in the matter—only in speaking of most of their characteristic manifestations, one is naturally more interested in explaining them than in speculating about their intelligence and tact. There are plenty of people who bathe daily in the season at the Beach, and have done so, they and their fathers and mothers, for more seasons than most of the now prominent summer residents can count, and who get along very well both without the old confraternity and with the new popular element, with whom visual association only is necessary, and that in general more interesting than disquieting. But, of course, the number of persons in any community whose breeding is sufficiently sound to give them a sense of security in such matters is comparatively limited, and however philosophic they are in this instance, I fancy they will welcome the formal social re-establishment of the Beach, even at the expense of the social differentiation by which this may be accompanied.

V

For rheumatic and respiratory maladies there are no doubt better climates than that of Newport, and there are others whose tonic properties are greater. But the Newport climate is balm to those manifold temperaments that are consciously or unconsciously threatened with any manner of nervous valetudinarianism. It is a poultice to the nerves, an anodyne to irritability, a sedative to excitement, and an assuagement of exhaustion. It not only performs the important function of keeping the skin moist, but it is balm to the tired mind. Arriving from New York in the early summer morning, the sensation of relaxed tension, of being swathed in soft salt dampness, of breathing the *primeur* of iodized air, is sybaritic. One proceeds to sleep like and long and often as a child. One may almost speak of quaffing deep draughts

of dreamless repose. And in ensuing days the blessedness of having fatigue assail only the physique and spare the faculties is unspeakable ; one is tranquilly instead of feverishly alert.

There are "dog days," of course. From July 25th to September 1st exertion is profitless and energy misplaced. The fog that drifts in from the southeast and struggles with the sun vainly in the morning and victoriously in the late afternoon complicates abnormally any unusually high temperature. It does not last long and oftenest is condensed by the wind's shifting to northeast into cooling downpours that one enjoys from piazzas, the dripping trees and damp fragrance of everything having a distinctly tonic effect. Still it is in July and August that the lotos-eating which the soft climate and insular atmosphere make an almost universal habit in Newport most prevails. The *segreto per esser felice* is not really in "a smiling mistress and a cup of Falernian"—it is, to anyone who has ever eaten of this ambrosia, in the lotos of Newport. More than anywhere else there are days here "always afternoon," days on which one may even with a sense of elation that exceeds that of virtue forget what elsewhere is duty. The most prosaic submit to the spell of the place. Everyone is physically lazy without suffering mental stagnation. A larger proportion of Newport boys return to the place of their nativity, probably, than is true of any other even New England town—drawn back, after no doubt often futile vicissitudes in the exterior world, by the loadstone of its subtle attractiveness. No one once inoculated with its serene and searching charm ever thoroughly recovers his independence, I think. His energy may be sapped by it, but his spirit is soothed and for him the battle of life is won by avoiding profitless engagements and tempering one's ambitions.

But more potent even than the caressing climate in its effect on a delicately organized sensorium is the Newport landscape—its aristocratic lines, its elegant expanse, its confident highbred air as it lies stretched out in the sunlight or yields itself to the soft en folding of sea mist. I remember a Newport lady writing from Athens itself to her little nephew at home, " Don't you think it is a piece of good fortune to live in the most beautiful place in the world? " and share her sentiment. Everything is pictorial ; every series of objects is an *ensemble ;* the vista in any direction exceeds the interest of the purely picturesque — the picturesque with its crudity, its fortuitousness, its animated and uneasy helter - skelter. Nature here is conscious—by comparison with much of our American landscape, infinitely developed. She is elegant and reserved as well as suave, and smiles at one with patrician softness and delicate sympathy, as who should say, " To enjoy me depends a good deal on yourself." At the crest of a yellow-green elevation, variegated with browns and shaded with cool grasses, the granite elbows itself gracefully out of the earth and warms itself in the moisture-tempered sunshine. A white cloud rests affectionately on it, as you look up from the hollow, truly Titianesque in its depth of fulness. The sky at the horizon is a light blue, like a child's sash. Streaks of vapor are spun across the zenith toward which the blue deepens into sapphire. The beach is white—white, however, over which every tint plays in opaline iridescence. Berkeley's rock stretches out purple, sage, and olive, toward the sea. The white sand dunes are crested with yellow sedge. Black rocks jut out on the sea horizon. The afternoon curtain of gray shadow gradually descends in front of the Purgatory ledge. Five or six dark dots of bathers (there is no " hour " for bathing at the Second Beach) move about in the ripple of the gently dissolving breakers. A wreath of children is running along the damp sand that fringes the ebb and flow, starting the sandpipers from tip-toeing into brief flight. Seaweed carts drawn by oxen and horses are hauling away their dripping loads at the other end of the two-mile crescent. The clouds are violet at the north horizon and white overhead, and long, graceful lines of shore frame the ever-changing blue-green of the ocean on two sides of the triangle of which the sky forms the third. Back from the beach is " Paradise "—but indeed paradise is all around one.

Or take a July morning down at Bailey's Beach, at the end of the Avenue and the beginning of the Ocean Drive. The sun illumines every cranny of the rocks. Above them are slopes covered with bright - green, shiny huckleberry bushes, and beyond a little grove of artistically placed pine saplings. Over the hill is an elaborately picturesque house. Seaward the sand glistens and sparkles, wet from the spray, the water folding itself over it in narrow hems. The rocks are seamed and spongified and accented with gold-brown seaweed, and their own local color runs the gamut from brown with pinkish tints to cool gray, from fawn and mauve to pearl. Above are the constant Titianesque clouds, overflowing with opaline effulgence. A bloom of gray Timothy furze rests on the deeper green of the splotches of grass. The varied blue and green of the water whose wimples are winking in the sun ranges from cobalt to malachite. Spouting Rock is booming melodiously nearby. A couple of six-year-olds in fresh light blue cambric dresses are climbing an adjoining acclivity, showing in delicate contrast of values against the green and gray hillside. Around all and unifying everything the moist Newport air tones and centralizes into a true picture the various objects that it makes contribute to a harmonious color composition.

What is especially characteristic of the Newport landscape is the co-operation it demands in the beholder's appreciation. It appeals to one's alertness, rather than to a lazy receptivity. You miss its quality entirely if your own faculties are not in a state of real activity. This does not exclude composure or imply excitement. There is nothing keyed up, nothing especially exhilarating in the soft air and suave prospect stretching out in every direction wherever one may be. Only, still less is there any enervation, any relaxing somnolency inviting to the *far niente* state of the mind. One's soul is distinctly " invited," not soothed in any narcotic sense. The appeal of the place is to an intelligent rather than a purely sensuous appreciation. You know why you like it, why it charms and wins you, why, indeed, it takes a never-to-be-disengaged hold on the very fibre of your affections, why you remember and regret it on Lake Geneva, in Venice, in Sorrento, why and how, in a word, it is beautiful.

VI

NEWPORT HARBOR is one of the best roadsteads in the world, being land-locked, easy of access, and having no bar. But its utilitarian advantages are slight in comparison with its æsthetic attractiveness. It is not merely one of the most, but, I think, from what I have heard and seen, the most beautiful of the world's harbors. Of course, such an opinion is largely a matter of taste, and a lover of Newport, so far from dissembling his partiality, is in-clined to profess it. There are doubt-less enchanting fjords in Norway, and reef-protected stretches of lovely pur-ple water in the tropics ; there are the Bay of Naples, whose beauties no amount of cockney admiration can ren-der commonplace, and the blue reaches around the Piræus and Phalerum and Salamis. There are Constantinople and the Golden Horn, and so on. So far as my own experience goes, the water view from the Athenian Acropolis gives one the nearest approach to the sensa-tion produced by Newport Harbor. Arriving at the Piræus from Naples, the Italian drop-curtain seems to have lifted and disclosed a scene of natural beauty, in whose presence one's mem-ory of the Vesuvian Bay is that of an exotic and artificial aspect. When the sensitive traveller awakes after a night on the Sound boat, now moored to Long Wharf, and notes the gradual un-folding of the placid prospect before him, as the summer sun comes up over the gray roofs and green trees of the town, and reveals the beautiful Rhode Island Harbor and its refined land-scape environment, he feels, to be sure, that his eyes, which closed the night before on the actual world, are opening on the delectable phenomena of fairy-land itself. Yet, the sense of contrast once overcome, the impression of the scene is curiously like that of the Athenian Harbor. There is the same commingled softness and freshness, the same brilliancy combined with suavity of color, the same gray-green envelope thinly overlaying the same stony geolog-ic structure, the same absence of trop-icality on the one hand and presence of exquisiteness on the other.

Newport Harbor, however, is too ac-tively characteristic for even the least fanciful comparisons. As day advances it becomes a busy as well as a beauti-ful scene. The wharves that jut out into it, covered with piles of lumber and (piquantly) heaps of junk, do not attest great commercial agitation. But the Conanicut ferry-boat issues at regular intervals from her slip, the Fort Adams and Torpedo Station and Coaster's Har-bor launches ply back and forth, the Wickford and Narragansett Pier boats, and an ever-increasing number of ex-cursion steamers from Providence, Bris-tol, Fall River, Rocky Point, and Block Island churn their way among the yachts and trading-schooners at anchor, and the fleet of cat-boats gliding breez-ily hither and thither in all directions, but plainly without specific destination and following courses laid by the fancy of absolute leisure. The sense of life and activity is omnipresent. The air is salt and full of savor. Lobster-pot buoys bump against a passing keel and bob in its wake. Fishermen with short briar pipes and sou'westers lean lazily against the tillers of their boats com-ing in from " outside " laden with the day's catch. " Naphtha boats " spin along with incredible speed, puffing stertorously. Beyond Goat Island lies one — or two or five — of the White Squadron, spick-span in the sunlight. Up at Coaster's Harbor the boys are drilling on the slope to the music of a brassy band heard faintly across the stretch of water. The " wash " of the Richmond flutters aloft. A crack cut-ter shoots by leaning over like a skater, and skimming the smooth water like a sea-gull.

Sensations are of all kinds, and the connoisseur doubtless has his prefer-ences. For myself I know no sensu-ous beatitude equal to that to be real-ized in the stern-sheets of a cat-boat in Newport Harbor of a bright August afternoon. It is so exquisitely poised between anodyne and excitant. You must know how to "sail a boat," and though no great seamanship is implied in the competent management of a cat-boat, in which it is said only a lubber or an expert navigator ever comes to grief, there is enough of the unexpected to be considered to demand constant attention. A reasonably spirited horse requires less of his rider, when you remember the number of extraneities to be looked out for in a populous harbor, to say nothing of wind and weather eccentricities. You may have a party or not, but with your hand on the tiller, even in the serenest sailing it is the boat and the environment that furnish the acutest pleasure, to anyone of philosophic years at least.

VII

In winter the town is still unique. The wealth of leafage has disappeared and the multitude of trees is even more noticeable in its bareness than in its clothed estate. It counts less as a restful and mysterious mass and emphasizes itself by its starkness. Myriads of sere and gray branches glisten in the bright sunshine and cast a network of shadow over the sidewalks and houses. Dusky spaces and rich boscages have given place to the staccato tenuity of arboreal anatomy—sharp accents everywhere instead of the soft toning of the deep green summer luxuriance. The quaint houses look in consequence insubstantial, tiny, and isolated ; the background in which they were set and into which they fitted so cosily is gone, and they stand out in somewhat insignificant silhouette. One divines, however, the interior comfort of contented hibernation. Spring, summer, and "the season" are coming, and even in frame structures and in icy weather such a prospect is sufficiently sustaining. The macadam is ridged and furrowed by the frost. An occasional stretch of brick pavement oozes trickling rills at noonday. The long plank walks, interspersed with ash and clinker substitutes at recurrent intervals, echo crisply to an incredible distance the tread of a brisk pedestrian of a Sunday returning from church. The air is absolutely still. Sounds carry miraculously. One may hear a dog bark or a wagon rumble as if by telephone from a spot beyond identification.

After Thanksgiving and toward Christmas a silver sheen succeeds the autumn bloom as this in its time had overlaid the summer warmth and soft suffusions of color. On a brisk December day which begins with ringing clearness and crispness it takes the sun an hour or two only to bring everything into a harmony, whose keynote, higher than at any other season here, is yet of a mellower brilliance than elsewhere in America at this time a similar temperature suffers. The lotos-eating season is over, plainly, yet there is the same agreeable absence of demand on any specific energies as in summer. The envelope of color—that delightful garment that Newport never puts off— is as evident to the senses as in mid-summer, though more silvery in quality, as I said. At noon there is positive warmth—a glow that one enjoys the more for feeling a little as if one had earned it, with other than the hot-house enervation born of whiffs of roses and orange trees and tempting one to forget the season instead of improve it that is characteristic of Cannes and San Raphael. The water is blue, beautifully blue, but of a hue more marked by crispness than suavity and full of character. There are no breakers, as earlier in the season, or as in and after foul weather, but the ceaseless folding over and self-hemming of the long, tranquil waves in regular recurrence is eloquent to the eye, as their faint but voluminous sound is to the ear, of the steady pulsations of the Atlantic, beside which the plashing ripple of the Mediterranean seems special and occasional.

Over the eastern hill and out at Paradise the turf is grown dry and brown with the frost, yet the sense perceives that Nature is only sleeping, and notes an absence of that mortuary aspect which she wears at this season in New England generally. The summer delicacy of color has grown, in steady autumnal gradation, diaphanous to the verge of dreariness, but has stopped there without overstepping the line. The slopes and fields and stretching marshes are not grayed into desolation, but harbor here and there, in little dells and hollows, or even more minutely under the lee of hummocks and tufts of herbage, warm hues and hints of green, color evidences of life reminiscent of summer luxuriance, and softening the austerity of the prospect with an undertone of deeper and richer hue. And in key with this background the wealth of Paradise cedars and junipers contribute their evergreen freshness and vitality, and attest the vigor of the deep-lying sap of Newport earth, the consciousness of whose presence prevents one from

> " ——petting
> About the frozen time."

The sky, which always unites every detail under it into a pictorial composition in Newport, counts in winter more than ever in the fading competition of elements terrestrial. It is cloudless and of a soft cobalt hue during the early part of the day, if the sun be shining and if the curtain of gray mist and cold colorlessness that, of course, drops in winter with more frequency and less charm than in the summer season, be lifted. But noon once past, on these bright winter days, a soft glowing light creepingly suffuses the western sky, and is faintly reflected in the eastern firmament. The most delicate of yellow-greens imaginable quietly distributes itself as background, upon which purple cirrhus clouds speedily spread themselves in long, feathery plumes. Then the zenith becomes sapphire, flushed at the fringe with salmon and pink wreaths of vapor. Filaments of mauve stretch themselves in haphazard fret-work across the heavens. The eastern half of the vault takes on a pervasive rose - leaf tint of pink.

Then, as the sun sinks and the temperature falls and twilight comes on, there is a sudden burst of deep - red, that fades out into infinitely long horizontal ribbons of orange ; the zenith grows dull and declines in lead color ; when finally the sun disappears beneath the rolling stretches of Conanicut, the clouds become more and more diaphanous and fade away into the everlasting ether, that now shows itself unfathomable and austerely blue, with two or three stars just blinking themselves into the reach of human vision.

Walk down quaint and quaintly-called " Wanton Avenue " — an alley bordered with picturesque and preposterous frame buildings, one inhabited by an old Newport " character ; " the next a storeroom ; the next a boathouse—and look out over the incomparable harbor at such an hour as this —the hour of a winter sunset with the shades of night drawing themselves slowly together over the lovely scene. The water is steel-blue—a hard and chilling light reflected from its fretful wavelets. White cat-boats and sloops anchored near by bob briskly with the desultory rise and fall of the breeze-roughened water. There are faint red lights struggling with the coming obscurity and the dying daylight on Goat Island. Fort Adams is a dark and not unromantic mass of sombre lateral extension. The cold has blended all colors into a harmony of frigid witchery. Familiar objects—the City Wharf, with an unloading coal-schooner alongside ; Alger's and Groff's rickety piers ; the vast white mass of an Old Colony steamboat lying next the end of Long Wharf ; the chimney of the torpedo station on Goat Island—take on a romantic aspect as the accidents of a purely artistic and immaterial *ensemble*. An hour or two later the boat leaves for New York. It is as hard to take it and leave this permanently enchanted spot, as if the season were midsummer.

6
Cuttyhunk

GOSNOLD'S ISLAND.

CUTTYHUNK.

By Arthur Cleveland Hall.

WENTY miles south of New Bedford, where Buzzards Bay opens into the broad Atlantic, lies Cuttyhunk. The little island is almost unknown now, but it played an important part in history nearly three hundred years ago. Here was located the first settlement by Europeans on New England shores, if we except the coming of the Northmen to Vineland. The ruins of the house the settlers built could still be seen early in the present century, and the information obtained from Cuttyhunk in 1602 was most useful in inducing the English emigration to New England which followed. While "Good Queen Bess" was yet alive, and but fourteen years after the Spanish Armada dashed itself to pieces on the British coast, Cap-

tain Bartholomew Gosnold "did set sail from Falmouth, on the five and twentieth of March, 1602, being Friday, in a small bark of Dartmouth called *The Concord,* holding a course for the north part of Virginia." There accompanied him "32 persons, whereof eight (were) mariners and sailors, twelve proposing upon the discovery to return with the ship for England, the rest to remain there for population."

Among these bold voyagers, two, "Gabriel Archer, gentleman and journalist," and M. John Brereton, wrote accounts of the expedition. In the following pages these old manuscripts, of necessity much condensed, are followed as closely as possible.

The names of the ship's company, so far as they are known to us, were Bartholomew Gosnold, commander; Bartholomew Gilbert, second officer;

Robert Saltern, who was afterwards a clergyman; Gabriel Archer, gentleman and journalist; John Angel, William Streete, John Brereton, Robert Meriton and ——Tucker.

"The wind favored us not at first, but enforced us so far to the southward, as we fell in with St. Mary, one of the islands of the Azores; but holding our course directly from thence we made our journey shorter (than hitherto accustomed) by the better part of a thousand leagues. Yet were we longer in our passage than we expected, for that our bark being weak, also our sailors few and they none of the best, we bear (except in fair weather) but low sail. Besides, our going upon an unknown coast made us not over-bold to stand in with the shore but in open weather.

"On Friday, the 14th of May, early in the morning, we made the land, being full of fair trees, the land somewhat low, certain hommocks or hills lying into the land, the shore full of white sand, but very stony or rocky. And standing fair along by the shore, about twelve of the clock the same day, we came to an anchor, where eight Indians in a Basque shallop with mast and sail, an iron grapple and a kettle of copper, came boldly aboard of us; one of them appareled with a

waistcoat and breeches of black serge, made after our sea fashion, hose and shoes on his feet. All the rest were naked, saving near their waists sealskins tied fast like Irish dimmie trowsers.

"These people are of tall stature, broad and grim visage, of a black swart complexion, their eyebrows painted white; their weapons bows and arrows. It seemed by some words and signs they made that some Basques of St. John de Luz have fished or traded in this place, being in the latitude of 43 degrees.

"Coasting along to the southwest, we came to anchor near a great cape, where in five or six hours we had pestered our ship so with codfish that we threw numbers of them overboard again; and surely I am persuaded that there is upon this coast better fishing than in Newfoundland, wherefore we named the place 'Cape Cod.'

"Sailing round about this headland almost all the points of the compass, we were come at length amongst many fair islands, all lying within a league or two one of another, and the outermost not above 5 or 7 leagues form the main. Coming to an anchor under one of these, Captain Gosnold and some others of us went ashore, and going about it, we found it

THE SOUTH SHORE OF CUTTYHUNK.

to be four English miles in compass, the place most pleasant, but without house or inhabitant. The chiefest trees of this island are beeches and cedars, the outward parts all overgrown with low, bushy trees three or four feet in height, which bear some kind of fruit, as appeared by their blossoms; strawberries, red and white, as sweet and much bigger than ours in England; raspberries, gooseberries, whortleberries and such an incredible store of vines, as well in the woody parts of the island, where they run upon every tree, as on the outward parts, that we could not go for treading upon them; also many springs of excellent, sweet water, and a great standing lake of fresh water an English mile in compass, which is maintained with the springs running exceeding pleasantly through the woody grounds, which are very rocky. This island we named 'Martha's Vineyard' [now No-man's-Land, a desolate island just west of the present Martha's Vineyard]. Here also we saw great store of deer, diverse fowls in great plenty, also great store of pease, which grow in certain plots all the island over; and on the north side we found many huge bones and ribs of whales.

"The four and twentieth of May we set sail and doubled the cape of another island next unto this, which we called Dover Cliff [now called Gay Head, at the west end of Martha's Vineyard], and then came into a fair sound, where we rode all night. The next morning we sent off one boat to discover another cape that lay northwest of this, between us and the main, from which were a ledge of rocks a mile into the sea, but all above water and without danger [now known as the "Sow and Pigs" reef]. We went about them and came to anchor in 8 fathoms, a quarter of a mile from the shore, in one of the stateliest sounds that ever I was in [Buzzards Bay]. This called we Gosnold's Hope, the north bank whereof is the main, which stretcheth east and west. This island Captain Gosnold called Elizabeth's Isle [now Cuttyhunk], where we determined our abode.

"It containeth many pieces or necks of land, which differ nothing from several islands, saving that certain banks of small breadth do like bridges join them to this island. In mid-May we did sow (for a trial) in sundry places wheat, barley, oats and pease, which in 14 days were sprung up 9 inches and more. The soil is fat and lusty, and the sowing or setting is no greater labor than if you should set or sow in one of our best prepared gardens in England. This island is full of high timbered oaks, their leaves thrice so

THE VILLAGE.

broad as ours; cedars straight and tall, beech, elm, holly, walnut trees in abundance, hazle-nut trees, cherry trees, sassafras trees, great plenty all over the island, a tree of high price and profit; also divers other fruit trees, some of them with strange barks of an orange color, in feeling soft and smooth like velvet. In the thickest part of these woods you may see a furlong or more round about.

"On the northwest side of this island is a stage or pond of fresh water, in circuit two miles, on the one side not distance from the sea 30 yards, in the centre whereof is a rocky islet containing near an acre of ground full of wood, on which we began our fort and place of abode disposing itself so fit for the same. This lake is full of small tortoises, and exceedingly frequented with all sorts of fowl, much bigger than ours in England. Also in every island and almost in every part of every island are great store of ground-nuts, 40 together on a string, some of them as big as hen's eggs; they grow not two inches underground, the which nuts we found to be as good as potatoes. Also divers sorts of shellfish, as scollops, muscles, cockles, lobsters, crabs, oysters and wilks, exceeding good and very great.

"But not to cloy you with particular rehearsals of such things as God and Nature hath bestowed on these places,

in comparison whereof the most fertile part of England is but barren,—we went in our light horseman from this island to the main, right against this island some two leagues off, where coming ashore, we stood a while like men ravished at the beauty and delicacy of this sweet soil; for besides divers clear lakes of fresh water, meadows very large and full of green grass, even the most woody places do grow so distinct from one another upon green grassy ground as if Nature would show herself above her power, artificial. Immediately there presented unto us Indians, men, women and children, who, with all courteous kindness, entertained us, giving Captain Gosnold certain skins of wild beasts, which may be rich furs, tobacco, turtles, hemp, artificial strings colored, chains and such like things as at the instant they had about them.

"These are a fair conditioned people, who being emboldened by our courteous visage and some trifles which we gave them, followed us to a neck of land which we imagined had been severed from the main; but finding it otherwise, we perceived a broad harbor or river's mouth which ran up into the main, and because the day was far spent we were forced to return to the island from whence we came, leaving the discovery of this harbor [probably

THE CLUB-HOUSE.

New Bedford harbor] for a time of better leisure.

"The next day, being the first of June, we employed ourselves in getting sassafras and the building of our fort on the little island in the lake before mentioned. On the following day we wrought hard to make ready our house for the provisions to be had ashore to sustain us till our ship's return, in building whereof we spent three weeks, covering the house with sedge, which grew about this lake in great abundance. Now, on the fifth of June, as we continued our labor, there came unto us ashore from the main 50 savages, stout and lusty men, with their bows and arrows; among them there seemed to be one of authority, because the rest made an inclining respect unto him. The ship was, at their coming, a league off, and Captain Gosnold aboard, and so likewise Captain Gilbert, who almost never went ashore, the company with me (Gabriel Archer) only 8 persons. These Indians in hasty manner came towards u , so as we thought fit to make a stand at an angle between the sea and the fresh water, being loath they should discover our fortification. I moved my-

self towards him 7 or 8 steps and clapped my hands, first on the sides of my head, then on my breast, and after presented my musket with a threatening countenance, thereby to signify unto them either a choice of peace or war; whereupon he using me with mine own signs of peace, I stepped forth and embraced him; his company then all sat down in a manner like greyhounds, upon their heels, with whom my company fell a bartering. By this time Captain Gosnold was come with 12 men more from aboard, and to show the savage seignior that he was our captain, we received him in a guard, which he passing through saluted the seignior with ceremonies of our salutations, whereat he nothing moved or altered himself. Our captain gave him a straw hat and a pair of knives; the hat a while he wore, but the knives he beheld with great marveling, being very bright and sharp; thus our courtesy made them very much in love with us.

"On the seventh the seignior came again with all his troop as before, and continued with us the most part of the day eating and drinking with us. The

THE CLUB-HOUSE GARDEN.

rest of the day we spent in trading with them for furs, which are beavers, luzernes, martins, otters, wildcat skins, very large and deep fur; black foxes, coney skins of the color of our hares, deer skins, very large; seal skins and other beasts' skins to us unknown. They have also great store of copper, some very red and some of a paler color; none of them but have chains, earrings or collars of this metal. They head some of their arrows herewith much like our broad arrow-heads, very workmanly made. Their chains are many hollow pieces cemented together, each piece of the bigness of one of our reeds, a finger in length, 10 or 12 of them together on a string, which they wear about their necks. Their collars they wear about their bodies like bandeliers a handful broad, all hollow pieces like the other, but somewhat shorter, 400 pieces in a collar, very fine and evenly set together. Besides these they have large drinking-cups made like sculls, and other thin plates of copper made much like our boar-spear blades. The necks of their pipes are made of clay hard dried; the other part is a piece of hollow copper, very firmly closed and cemented together. All of which they so little esteem, as they offered their fairest collars or chains for a knife or such like trifle; but we seemed little to regard it. Yet I was desirous to understand where they had such store of this metal, and made signs to one of them with whom I was very familiar, who, taking a piece of copper in his hand, made a hole with his fin-

ger in the ground and withal pointed to the main from whence they came. These Indians call gold *wessador*, which argueth there is thereof in the country.

"They strike fire in this manner: Every one carrieth about him in a purse of tewed leather a mineral stone (which I take to be their copper), and with a flat emery stone (wherewith glazers cut glass and cutlers glaze

THE POST-OFFICE.

blades) tied fast to the end of a little stick, gently he striketh upon the mineral stone, and within a stroke or two a spark falleth upon a piece of touchwood (much like our sponge in England, and with the least spark he maketh a fire presently. We had also of their flax, wherewith they make many strings and cords, but it is not so bright of color as ours in England. I am persuaded they have great store upon the main, as also mines and many other rich commodities which we, wanting both time and means, could not possibly discover.

"These people, as they are exceeding courteous, gentle of disposition and well conditioned, excelling all others that we have seen, so for shape of body and lovely favor I think they excel all the people of America; of stature much higher than we; of complexion or color much like a dark olive; their eyebrows and hair black, which they wear long, tied up behind in knots, whereon they prick feathers of fowls in fashion of a coronet; some of them are black, thin bearded; they make beards of the hair of beasts, and one of them offered a beard of their making to one of our sailors for his that grew on his face, which, because it was of a red color, they judged to be none of his own. They are quick-eyed and steadfast in their looks, fearless of other's harms, as intending none themselves; some of the meaner

"Many other such trials we had, which are here needless to repeat. Their women (such as we saw, which were but three in all,) were but low of stature, their eyebrows, hair, apparel and manner of wearing like to the men, fat and very well favored, and much delighted in our company; the men are very dutiful towards them.

"And truly, the wholesomeness and temperature of this climate doth not only argue this people to be answerable to this description, but also of a perfect constitution of body, active, strong, healthful and very witty, as the sundry toys of theirs cunningly wrought may easily witness. For the agreeing of this climate with us we found our health and strength all the while we remained there so to renew and increase as notwithstanding our diet and lodging were none of the best, yet not one of our company (God be thanked) felt the least grudging or inclination to any disease or sickness, but were much fattter and in better health

A FISHERMAN'S HOME.

sort given to filching, which the very name of savages (not weighing their ignorance of good or evil) may easily excuse. Their garments are of deer skins, and some of them wear furs round and close about their necks. They pronounce our language with great facility; for one of them one day sitting by me, upon occasion I spoke, smiling to him, these words: 'How, now, sirrah, are you so saucy with my tobacco?' which words (without any further repetition) he suddenly spake so plain and distinctly as if he had been a long scholar in the language.

than when we went out of England.

"But after our bark had taken in much sassafras, cedar, furs, skins and other commodities as were thought convenient, some of our company that had promised Captain Gosnold to stay, having nothing but a saving (*i. e.,* money-making,) voyage in their minds, made our company of inhabitants (which was small enough before) much smaller, so as Captain Gosnold, seeing his whole strength to consist but of twelve men, and they but meanly provided (with victuals), determined to return for England, leaving this island (which he called Elizabeth's Island) with as many true sorrowful eyes as were before desirous to see it. So the 18th of June, being Friday, we weighed, and with indifferent fair wind and weather, came to anchor the 23d day of July, being also Friday (in all bare five weeks) before Exmouth."

In an appendix to the account of John Brereton, which he addressed to Sir Walter Raleigh, is "A brief note of such commodities as we saw in the country notwithstanding our small time of stay." These are classed under trees, fowls, beasts, fruits, plants and herbs, fishes, colors, metals and stones. It is rather amusing to find under fish "whales, tortoises, seals, lobsters, crabs, muscles, wilks, cockles, scollops, oysters" and, last of all, "snakes four feet in length and six inches about, which the Indians eat for dainty meat, the skins whereof they use for girdles."

Cuttyhunk to-day is greatly changed from the fair, wooded island discovered in 1602. The stately trees have passed away. In 1858 not one was

THE LIFE-SAVING STATION.

growing there; not even a decaying stump could be seen above ground. But now there are a few silver-leaf

poplars near the houses on the east of the island; and two or three fruit trees, solitary survivors of many planted, still struggle through the cold blasts of

CHURCH AND SCHOOL

winter. Long, low sand bars, deeply strewn with sea-worn stones, connect the different parts of the island as of old, and off to the west the reef of "Sow and Pigs" spouts like a geyser in a storm. Rocky hillocks, interspersed with steep little valleys, where six or seven hundred sheep find pasture, decline gradually to a fresh water pond on the northwest, where Gosnold's Islet rises green above the blue water. The identity of the places visited by the bold voyagers of 1602 can scarcely be doubted, so minute and exact was their description of them. Early in this century the cellar of Gosnold's house and fort were distinctly to be seen; but unfortunately since then the ground of his little island has been ploughed over and cultivated; so that hardly a vestige of the ruin remains. Possibly a careful excavation would again reveal portions of the cellar which Dr. Belknap, the historian, found on his visit to the island in 1797.

In 1817 several members of the Massachusetts Historical Society visited the Elizabeth Islands (Gosnold's name for Cuttyhunk having since been transferred to the entire group), and an account of their visit may be found in the fifth volume of the North American Review, from which I make the following extract:

"In the western end of the pond is a high islet surrounded by a rocky margin and covered with a very rich soil. . . . The stump of a red cedar stood near the shore, and we brought home a piece of it as a remembrance of our expedition. On the northern bank of the islet, about ten yards from the water, we found a small excavation number and not disposed in any apparent order. On digging in other parts of the islet we found more of the same kind. We conjectured that the first excavation was all that remained of Gosnold's cellar and the latter a part of the trench dug for the purpose of forming the fort."

The desirability of some simple monument to commemorate this first European settlement in New England, and in memory of Bartholomew Gosnold, who died August 22d, 1607, and

A WRECK AT CUTTYHUNK.

overgrown with bushes and grass, on one side of which were three large stones in a row at the distance of three feet from each other, having under them other stones of the same size lying in the same direction. Between these were smaller stones, which appeared by their form and smoothness to have been taken from the beach. In another slight excavation twenty yards south of the former, near the centre and highest part of the islet, were similar stones, but very few in was buried in an unknown grave at Jamestown, Virginia, has often been suggested. Nearly three hundred years have passed, and at present Gosnold's Island is adorned with a deserted henhouse.

None of the Elizabeth Islands retain their primitive appearance, except Naushon, the largest of them. Here noble forests of beech, oak and other trees cover the land, while the wild grape and other vines grow luxuriantly among the branches. The islands have all preserved their Indian names, which have been put into rhyme:

"Naushon, Nonamesset,
Onkatonka and Wepecket,
Nashawena, Pesquinese,
Cuttyhunk and Penequese."

Cuttyhunk is contracted from the Indian name Poo-cutohhunkounoh, which may mean Place of Departure. Quawck was the Indian name for Gosnold's Islet. A lofty promontory running out from the north of Cuttyhunk was called by the Indians Copicut, or Cappiquat, meaning thick, dark woods. This name it still bears. Canapitset is the name for the passage between Nashawena and Cuttyhunk. Nashanaw was the collective aboriginal name for the whole group, and probably means Our Father's Islands.

THE LIFE-SAVING CREW

The modern visitor to Cuttyhunk will find much to reward him if he has eyes and ears to know the sea and the rocky, wreck-strewn shore; if he loves to feel the salt wind blow, full of life, from the bounding waves, and will watch the play of light and shade on the rainbow-colored cliffs of fair Gay Head.

After a storm at sea great waves roll in around Cape Cod and Martha's Vineyard and hurl their "thunderous snow" upon the rocks of Cuttyhunk; often when all is fair o'erhead. Sometimes one may see great billows driving in to the shore in the very teeth of a northeast gale, which cuts the foam from off their crests and tosses it, a wind-blown sheet of sparkling spray, far out behind each charging wave.

The island affords almost nothing to do; but the beauty of it is the visitor to Cuttyhunk does not want to do anything. First impressions are likely to be amusing. A harbor without a wharf, a village without a street, country without a tramp—such is Cuttyhunk. The coming of the mail steamer is the event of the week, in

THE LIFE-SAVING CREW AT PRACTICE.

A GLIMPSE OF THE ISLAND.

way (made largely of old ship planking) leads to the foot of the hill on which the straggling village rests. Here a short halt gives time to let down the bars from a gate and the party proceeds upwards a hundred yards or more to where a short flight of ship steps mounts securely beneath the wide, upright plank of a board fence. The upper planks have been removed, and a little agility and caution will enable the stranger to pass on his way rejoicing. Next you ascend to a partial opening in a stone wall, and higher still some strictly natural stone steps, surmounted by a swinging gate.

Once on the other side, you have attained the goal of your desire, and are in the heart of the little settlement of perhaps twenty houses. Gates still confront you on every side, gates adorned with relics of many an old wreck and swinging open by aid of weights,—a heavy ship's pulley block or the shackle to an anchor. But the ways are free to all—the island dogs are as amiable as their kind-hearted owners—and, arrived at last under some hospitable roof, one learns the good results of sea breezes and recent gymnastics in satisfying a voracious appetite with delicious lobster, fish, fresh vegetables and many imported delicacies.

Meanwhile the distribution of the mail is progressing at the postoffice,— a whitewashed shed in the rear of one of the cottages. Here, before a large assemblage of the islanders, the postmaster or his wife calls off the names of fortunate recipients, letter by letter, and then the meeting adjourns until

the summer the event of each day. Entering the harbor a number of small catboats are seen, standing on and off, ready to convey passengers and baggage, live stock and freight—whatever comes their way—through "the narrows" into "the pond," where a landing can be made. The channel runs close to a long, low sand spit, covered completely with heaps of wave-washed stones and shattered wreckage.

"Mamma, what is that horrid thing with teeth?" asked a trembling little girl, as the boat swept toward a great, black, jaw-like wreck of a schooner's bow, high and dry on the rocks.

When the tide runs out through "the narrows" and a head wind is blowing the island expressman comes into service before the baggage is put ashore. Over the stones and into the rushing water go the stout horse and wagon, a rope is heaved from the boat, and, thanks to the harmonious action of sail and horsepower, the boatload is soon safe beside the little dock in the quiet "pond." Landing, you cross a bit of sea marsh by a narrow, raised causeway of boards. If two fat men meet here at high tide a retreat or a bath must follow.

Such minor difficulties avoided, the

time for the next mail. If you do not happen to be present, and no one brings your mail, you can step into the deserted postoffice and look for yourself over the pile of letters yet uncalled for. No one thinks of locking up anything on the island. Why should they, when all are honest and almost everybody related, so that secrets are all in the family?

Fifty years ago, when New Bedford and Fairhaven had almost four hundred whale ships, the Cuttyhunkers' business was largely pilotage. Seven men earned a good living in this important work; and there are still several pilots hailing from the island. Many a deed of daring or narrow escape from death one hears from their lips.

Two of them were sailing one very foggy day in the Sound, when suddenly a schooner's bow loomed up right above them. "Catch hold for your life!" one pilot called to his fellow and leaping on to the martingale, made his way quickly to the deck, where it required about a minute to make the astonished crew understand that they had run down a pilot boat and must lend a hand to rescue the other pilot. They found him clinging to the bowsprit chains, with just his head above water, and soon hauled him aboard. Next day the pilots, left on the lightship, discovered their boat

bottom up, righted her, bailed her out, and went back to business as if nothing had happened.

One pilot has named his fishing boat the *Never Budge*. Another catboat is called the *Mikado*, which, so a fisherman said, "is the title of some big official, I don't remember just where. Hold on a bit. Yes, its Switzerland, that's where it is."

The islanders are great borrowers. If a man is building a shed or doing anything for which some materials have failed to arrive from the mainland, he goes round among "the neighbors" till he finds "suthin' that'll do," and borrows it. A favorite Cuttyhunk story relates how a man, buying salt to cure his fish, purchased two bags full, one for use himself and one to lend friends. When any salt was borrowed it was always returned and put back; yet the bag for lending was empty almost as soon as that for home consumption.

Lobstering is now the principal business of the islanders. Formerly a successful man could lay by one thousand dollars besides supporting himself during a good season, which lasts from March till late December. The years vary greatly; 1896 was the worst on record. In late September one man said he had not cleared twenty-five dollars over expenses. An old lobsterman said he had seen a steady de-

THE SURF AT CUTTYHUNK.

VINEYARD SOUND AND GAY HEAD (GOSNOLD'S DOVER CLIFF) FROM CUTTYHUNK.

From a painting by C. H. Gifford.

crease in the number of lobsters caught during the last twenty-two years. Laws have been passed to remedy this, fining anyone with lobsters under ten and a half inches long five dollars for each "short lobster" in his possession, but the laws are hard to enforce.

One grizzled Cuttyhunker lives half the year in an old warehouse just above ordinary high water. In storms or very high tides everything on the ground floor is awash; but the old salt said: "I don't mind that nothin'. The salt water has been swashin' round me all my life." All his household goods are safely stored away in the upper story underneath the eaves. A ladder with a rope hand-rail affords ready access. One long window has a canvas shutter, fastened by rope lanyards when the wind blows too strong for comfort.

"I like ter live down here," said he. "It's so handy to my work. I start off lobsterin' sometimes 'tween three and four o'clock in the mornin', and eat just a bite before startin'. Get in nigh on ter two in the arternoon, hungry as a bear. Don't want ter have to climb way up to the village and wait to have things cooked. Here everythin' is handy, right by the dock. I eat whatever's ready while I'm cookin' suthin' more, — or when my wife's here, she cooks it."

He is a strong, honest, quick-witted specimen of a Yankee fisherman grandfather, weighing a hundred and eighty pounds, working early and late, owning a farm in the centre of Martha's Vineyard and an orange grove in Florida. But he says: "There ain't nothin' in farmin' nowadays. The wife she says wool is sellin' for only twelve an' thirteen cents a pound. Think on it!" As for the orange plantation, he declares: "I won't never git my money back again"; but in winter he goes down South to "have a look at it." The dock just in front of his warehouse is taken up in the autumn, the props knocked from under it, and all tied up and anchored as securely as

possible on the bank; but the winter storms play havoc with it nevertheless.

Cuttyhunk has a neat little school-house, a church and a library of three hundred books. The school is in session three-quarters of the year, and the church the other quarter; for it is only in the summer that the islanders can have a minister, or, more properly speaking, a young man who hopes some day to become a minister. The stores are in private houses and closely connected with the kitchen department. If the good housewife gets tired of keeping certain things for sale, a neighbor will undertake to supply them next season. The candy store moves often, occupying a dark closet now in this house, now in that.

Forty or fifty people live on the island all winter, fourteen households, besides the men at the life-saving station. Most of the hard work comes in the spring, summer and fall. In winter the men make lobster pots, smoke, play cards, lie around and take things easy. Almost all the islanders come from old New England stock. They are strong, courageous and hard-headed, slow to make friendships and slow to break them; true as steel to those they love, and hospitable to all who come to them.

Until two years ago no horse had reached Cuttyhunk. The island turn-outs were two-wheeled carts, drawn each by a stout donkey. Cows, sheep, turkeys and hens roam freely almost everywhere. Old fishnets are hung on poles to protect flower-beds and choice bits of kitchen garden. With the exception of the few acres in and around the village, the whole island (of between six and seven hundred acres) is owned by the Cuttyhunk Fishing Club. "The farm" is rented out for five hundred dollars a year, but of late it has not been a success, although corn and other vegetables grow well. The reason seemed to be, as one of the natives expressed it: "The man who runs the farm won't make nothin' outin it. Cause why? He hain't got no headpiece."

The clubhouse stands on a bold bluff looking off on the broad Atlantic to the southwest and across Vineyard Sound, that highway of ships, to where Gay Head rises glorious from the waves. In 1864 some New York gentlemen discovered that striped bass could be caught from the rocks of Cuttyhunk. A club was soon organized, and the clubhouse erected. Its walls are decorated with paintings of great fish caught; but the bass have decreased very greatly in numbers since the early seventies, when nearly seven thousand pounds of the striped beauties were landed in a single year. The largest bass on record weighed sixty-four pounds. But even should the fish desert the island entirely, there is little danger of the club members following. Most of them are well on in years, and regard Cuttyhunk as one of the most delightful of places for a summer's rest. One old Texan has spent twenty-two successive seasons at the club. Another member has never failed to appear in the last thirty-two years. Behind the clubhouse a really beautiful garden glows with many-colored flowers, and long rows of healthy vegetables give evidence that the club table is not neglected. On the south a well-kept lawn reaches down to the edge of the cliff; and a fine spyglass, mounted on its tripod, invites to watch the passing ships.

But the central point of interest to Cuttyhunk visitors is apt to be the life-saving station, established by the United States government in 1889. As early as 1847 the Massachusetts Humane Society had erected stations on the Elizabeth Islands, supplied with approved life-saving appliances, for the use of the brave islanders, who would not brook the sight of fellow mariners shipwrecked and perishing before their eyes without an attempt at rescue.

Many are the crews whose lives these stout-hearted volunteers have saved at the risk of their own. In February, 1893, when the brig *Aquatic* was wrecked on the "Sow and Pigs" reef, five of the six members of the volunteer crew perished in their attempt to reach the vessel. That was a terrible day for Cuttyhunk.*

But a few nights before, a four-masted schooner, the Douglass Dearborn, was wrecked on the rocks to the southward and her half-frozen crew rescued with great difficulty, one by one, in the breeches buoy. The life savers were worn out by their exertions. Suddenly came the terrible news: "A brig wrecked on Sow and Pigs—the sea will break her up before morning!" In haste the undaunted islanders made their way to the west end of Cuttyhunk, where blazing torch-lights on the wreck flared out of the darkness, above the seething combers, raging in to the shore. "No boat can live in such a sea," said a brave old salt. "Oh! yes, she can," answered Tim Akin, Jr., and he called for volunteers. Five men stepped out and the surf-boat was quickly launched. Slowly she staggered forward, up and down amid the waves. Captain Tim was a man who never knew fear. "Come on, boys,—ain't this fun!" he shouted from his place at the steering oar. Just then, close by the brig, a gigantic comber overwhelmed them and the men upon the wreck saw four ghastly faces upturned to theirs as the gallant rescuers, clinging to their overturned boat, were borne swiftly past, helpless, into darkness and death. One man, Josiah Tilton, was carried by the waves toward the brig's stern. The bight of a rope was flung him and he was saved, yet he alone of the life savers could not swim.

Contrary to all expectation, the brig held together until the following noon, when all aboard her were rescued from the foretop where they had taken refuge. The men had wrapped the topsails about them and crouched under the lee thus made. But they were drenched by the icy seas, and

*See poem "Cuttyhunk," by Edward Payson Jackson, in the New England Magazine, June, 1893.

their clothes were frozen stiff in the biting wind gusts. A little longer exposure would have ended their lives. A fund of $30,000 was subscribed and divided among the families of the drowned heroes, and the Canadian government made a grant of $1000 for the same good purpose,—for the wrecked brig hailed from St. John, N. B. The men who perished had rescued many a shipwrecked crew. Their rewards were sometimes $3, sometimes $5, and never more than $15 per man. Cuttyhunk is a rough mother and rears strong and fearless sons. The voice of duty is strong within them and courage is as the air they breathe.

A generous emulation exists between the government station men and the other islanders to see who shall be foremost in the noble work of saving life. At the present time there are, as an old lobsterman said, "three humane buildings" on Cuttyhunk. "The Captain" who has charge of them has invented many a useful life-saving apparatus, and has medals from Paris and Havre commending his work. He has on exhibition at the Board of Trade building, Gloucester, Mass., a model of a life-saving car, to be built of aluminum bronze. Its general adoption by coasting vessels would result in the saving of many lives. The captain's interest in his invention is purely philanthropic, for he has never applied for a patent.

At the government station seven or eight men are always on duty, except during June and July. All night long and every foggy day they patrol the cliffs and stony sand reaches along the west and south shores. Each man carries two Coston signals, whose bright red glare has warned many a ship approaching too near the dangerous coast or given promise to wrecked mariners that help is not far distant.

In the handsome station, finished in hard polished wood and kept as neat as wax, two big surf-boats are ready for emergency, mounted on their long carriages and supplied with oars, life-preservers, ropes and other necessaries. The beach-cart is there loaded with hawser, shot-lines, Lyle gun and ammunition. There are the breeches-buoy, the life-car and all things needed to send a strong rope out to the wreck, along which rope when fastened to the mast the breeches-buoy or life-car makes its perilous way through dashing surf and blinding spray safe to the welcoming shore.

On the last July night, just before the men go on duty, a dance is usually given at the life-saving station. The home of life-cars and surf-boats is bare, save where upon the walls lanterns, life-belts, blocks and tackles serve half as ornaments, half as a sombre setting for the bright, girlish faces and the muscular, sunburnt men, who look so well in their uniforms of blue and white. Through the great open doorway a group of spectators can be dimly seen, leaning against a life-car, standing, or sitting upon coils of rope, while beyond the sea drags the pebbles over the singing beach and the half moon rides through a cloudless sky. Promptly at twelve o'clock the fiddle and the banjo, those instruments of Cuttyhunk gaiety, cease. Two guardsmen take clocks and signals and start on their four-hour watch, which is to continue every night and foggy day through cold and sleet and driving rain until the summer comes again. These men receive sixty dollars a month; and one may some of the islanders speak of the life-fisherman's life from the fact that some of the islanders speak of the life-savers as having "a good berth and an easy time of it."

7
Evolution of the American Fishing Schooner

EVOLUTION OF THE AMERICAN FISHING SCHOONER.

By Joseph William Collins.

H, see how she scoons! The startling tones of an excited bystander cleft the air with this exclamation, as he witnessed the "peculiar skipping motion" of a little fishing vessel that received its baptism in Gloucester harbor one hundred and eighty-five years ago. This "ketch" was rigged in a new and remarkable manner, having gaffs to her sails instead of the lateen yards previously in general use, and the luff of the sails bent to hoops on the masts. Her builder, Captain Andrew Robinson, who invented this novel arrangement of spars and sails, was apparently undetermined as to her name up to the moment of launching; for history indicates that he was quick to catch the inspiration of the curious words of the looker-on and, breaking a bottle of rum over her bow, shouted: "A scooner let her be!"

Thus the "scooner" was christened; and the word so impulsively uttered and so promptly utilized thenceforth furnished the typical designation of vessels similarly rigged and has continued in use until the present, when the white sails of schooners gleam on all waters that wash this continent and are familiar objects on many foreign seas, from the frozen north to the distant isles and capes of the southern hemisphere. Not only has the rig been found well adapted to our ocean fisheries after nearly two centuries of trial, but it is popular on yachts and pilot boats, and is fast superseding all other rigs on large American vessels engaged in the coastwise trade, and even in foreign commerce.

When, in these closing years of the nineteenth century, schooners of immense size, some of them carrying cargoes ranging from 2,000 to 3,000 tons, sail to South America and the West Indies, cruise along the coast of the United States, and easily outstrip lofty ships in crossing the Atlantic, it is not difficult to realize the importance of the rig to commerce. Previous to its adoption, ships, snows, ketches and shallops were employed in the American fisheries. The last two, being of comparatively small dimensions, were chiefly used by the colonists; and many ketches were built in Massachusetts ports for fishing and trading. The latter rarely exceeded forty tons burden, and generally were much smaller. They were full bowed, round bottomed craft, with the mainmast nearly amidship and a second and smaller mast near the stern. It is probable that most of the ketches, particularly those employed in fishing, carried lateen sails, possibly with a square topsail on the maintopmast, although old prints indicate that the typical ketch, used for war purposes, had square sails on both masts.

The ketch rig, though popular in the seventeenth century, was peculiarly unsuited to the variable winds on the New England coast, for the lateen yards had to be lowered and changed when tacking, thus involving much labor and hardship to the seamen. It is therefore evident that there was a potent incentive to invent a new rig for fishing vessels, for it was pre-eminently desirable that they should be able to change their course at the shortest intervals and to sail equally well on either tack, without the necessity for lowering and setting the sails.

Captain Robinson apparently made

no attempt at that time to improve the hull of the vessel; for it is explicitly recorded that he "built and rigged a *ketch*, as they were called, masted and rigged it in a peculiar manner."* It is probable that the "scooner" resembled vessels of the same rig built at a later date, which, as is well known, had heavy square sterns and short quarter decks. The fancied resemblance of those vessels to an inverted shoe, the quarter deck simulating the heel, gave to them in subsequent years the nickname of "heel tappers."

The new rig apparently met with favor from the outset, though there is little to base opinion upon, except that mention is made of the employ-

curing their cargo they would go to Lisbon, Bilboa or Cadiz, and bring back wines, salt, etc." Shortly after the middle of the eighteenth century, nearly all vessels employed in offshore fisheries were of this type. Before the Revolutionary War, Massachusetts alone had 542 vessels engaged in the fisheries, most of these being "scooners," as may be readily assumed when it is known that 326 of them belonged in Essex County, where the rig was very popular. They were generally without bulwarks forward of the quarter deck, or at most with a strip spiked to the top timbers, this form of construction being adopted because, at that time, it was

MARBLEHEAD COD-FISHING SCHOONER, 1750.
From a drawing by J. W. Collins.

ment of a "scooner" in 1716, in the fisheries off Cape Sable. In subsequent years the fleet increased rapidly; "about 70 of these 'scooners' were owned in Gloucester in 1741, and nearly all of them engaged in fishing on the Grand Banks, where after se-

* Babson's History of Gloucester, Mass.

believed unsafe to have anything to stop the free sweep of water across the main deck. Indeed, the same idea found expression in building seagoing vessels for commercial purposes until after the beginning of the present century, and even as late as 1815, many had no bulwarks forward of the fore rigging. The quarter deck on one of these old "heel tappers," being so much higher than the main deck, was comparatively dry in a gale, when the main deck would be all awash; therefore, when anchored on the banks in rough weather, the crew stood there to fish, which they could do very well, since at that time only half the men engaged in fishing at the same time, as their rule was to fish, watch and watch, each half of the crew taking its turn of four hours in regular rotation.

The cabin was aft, and entered through a small companionway, in the after end of which the binnacle was usually located. A rude fireplace, built of brick or stone, served for heating and cooking. The culinary operations were of the most primitive sort. Berths were arranged around the cabin, which was also equipped with a board table and locker seats. Sometimes this apartment was painted, but generally its dingy hues were attributable solely to smoke and grime. A rude log windlass worked by handspikes, heavy hemp cables and a long tiller were details of equipment that continued in use until near the middle of the present century, though in the meantime fishing vessels had undergone material changes in other respects. There was in these early schooners no attempt at ornamentation except in rare instances, when a broad white or yellow band stretched along the side, or when representations of windows were painted on the stern. Ordinarily they had only a plain gammon-knee head and were coated with tar, at least as high as their bends. They had long floors, with barrel-shaped bottoms, and excessively full ends. This form continued in vogue until early in the nineteenth century.

A long high-steeved bowsprit, two rather short, clumsily made masts — the foremast stepped well forward — a maintopmast, and rather short main boom, projecting just beyond the taffrail, constituted the more important features of the spar plan. The hemp sails had very little angle to their peaks; they were baggy and ill-formed, when considered from present standards, and one marvels how such vessels, with no light sails and with such a diminutive sail area, managed to make passages to and from the distant banks or, stranger still, to European ports. Only three sails were usually carried — jib, foresail and mainsail; but the desire for supplementary sail area in light winds led to a modification in the rig, to the extent of having in addition a single square foretopsail and sometimes a flying jib. The gafftopsail and maintopmast staysail, now so generally used by fishing vessels, had not then been adopted.

While we may cheerfully concede the improvement which resulted from Captain Robinson's innovation, it is difficult to imagine a

A CHEBACCO BOAT, 1790.
From a drawing by J. W. Collins.

stronger contrast in naval architecture than is presented by the picturesque old-time fishing schooner and one of the yacht-like fabrics that now pursues the fisheries of the North Atlantic. The difference, striking as it appears, is the result of changes which have come gradually. Some of these have been the result of conditions that

were of necessity left to rot in the harbors during the Revolutionary War, while the brave men who sailed on them, and exacted tribute from old ocean's living treasures, joined the Continental army, served with Captain Tucker,* a naval hero of the time, or swarmed on privateers that harried the commerce of Britain and made

A PINKY OUTWARD BOUND, 1836.
From " Fishing Industries."

affected the whole nation, but more generally they have been due to a desire for improvement, particularly in the matter of speed,— though modifications have often been attributable to the necessity for adaptation to local conditions or the requirements of special fisheries.

The New England fishing schooners, the sails of which had been seen from New York to the Newfoundland banks, and even in Southern Europe,

English merchants realize the cost of war.

At the conclusion of the war, the fishermen were generally unable to provide themselves with vessels large enough to visit the distant banks. At this period the chebacco boat came into extensive use. This diminutive type of craft derived its specific name from the place where it was first built,

* Captain Samuel Tucker, of Marblehead, who is credited with capturing more guns and more British tonnage than Paul Jones or any other commander of the Revolution.

the parish of Chebacco, now a part of the town of Essex, Mass., which has always been famed for its prominence in the construction of fishing vessels.

At first these boats were usually built with sharp sterns. They ranged from five to ten tons in size, and were only partially decked, having so-called standing rooms in which the crew stood to fish. There was a little cuddy or cabin beneath the forward deck which served for sleeping quarters and for cooking. A small fireplace of stone or brick, with wooden chimney above deck, was provided for the latter. At a later date the size of the boats increased until a maximum of twenty tons was reached, and some were built with square sterns. These were called "dogbodies," to distinguish them from the sharp sterned craft. Both kinds, however, were cat rigged, with two masts, the foremast standing as far forward as possible.

The stem was a most noticeable feature of the chebacco boat; it always stood high above the bow, was generally painted bright red, and, because of its fancied resemblance to an ancient battering ram, a vessel of this type was often called a "ram's head boat." The stem served the special purpose of a bitt head, over which was placed the eye of the hawser that held a boat to its mooring when in harbor.

It was an easy and natural evolutionary step from the sharp sterned chebacco boat to the schooner-rigged pinky. The requirements of ocean fishery led to a gradual increase in size of vessels, until finally the addition of a bowsprit and jib to the rig became necessary; and thus the chebacco boat, deprived of its high red stem as well as its distinctive rig and specific name, was transformed into the pinky, a type of small vessel celebrated for its seaworthiness and extensively employed in the New England fisheries for several decades. It came into general use after the war of 1812-15; was most in favor between 1820 and 1840; but pinkies were built in some of the Maine ports as late as the fifties.

The pinky's chief characteristics were a full round bow with plain gammon-knee head, long floor with more or less barrel-shaped bilge, a short, well-formed run, strongly raking sternpost, and a heavy drag. The special feature was the extension of the rail and bulwarks posteriorly until they met and fastened to a narrow, raking, V-shaped arch board (formed like the stern of a dory), hollowed out like a crescent at the top to serve as a crutch or resting place for the mainboom. This was the "pink," from which this type of vessel derived its specific name, and it usually curved rather sharply upward from the general sheer of the vessel. The cabin was forward; it was dingy and dark, being lighted only by the companionway and two or

A DOGBODY, 1790-1820.

Drawn from a model in the National Museum at Washington, D. C.

A SCHOONER OF THE "ROMP" TYPE, 1848.

three small dead lights of thick glass. At night the dull and flickering glare of a tallow dip furnished the entire illumination.

But while the pinky superseded the sharp sterned chebacco boat, the legitimate successor of the dogbody was the square sterned schooner, with low quarter deck, which appeared in the thirties, and rapidly superseded the pinky in the following decade. Vessels of this type were, as a rule, larger than the pinkies, and there was soon apparent in their construction some attempt at ornamentation. Short cutwaters with carved fiddle heads, and sometimes figure heads, came into fashion with the square stern schooner, and in the last half of the forties some attempts were made at ornamenting the stern with painting. At first the fiddle heads were painted in imitation of fruit and leaves, but later the tendency was to gild them.

The schooner of this period was a distinctive improvement over the old type of high quarter deck craft. Although the lines were still very full, they were more symmetrically proportioned. Instead of an open waist, the bulwarks were filled in from deck to rail; the long low quarter deck made such vessels better adapted to the mackerel hook and line fishery; and the introduction of jibbooms and additional light sails increased their speed and efficiency in summer weather. They were much better adapted to the needs of ocean fishery than the pinky, since the yawl-boat or dingy had to be stowed on the deck of the latter, thus limiting the deck space, while it could be hoisted to the

A FISHING CLIPPER OF THE SEVENTIES.

schooners. Practically nothing had been done in building yachts at that time. Pilot boats were regarded as examples of the most approved forms of swift vessels. Attention was also directed to the clipper schooners of Baltimore that had gained celebrity; and these were soon utilized for the mackerel fishery.

The first notable attempt to produce a clipper fishing schooner north of Cape Cod was in 1847, when the *Romp* was built at Essex. She had much easier lines and a sharper floor than her predecessors, while her stern was somewhat narrower, though the counters were low, so that, when loaded, this new clipper had a box-like form aft above the water — a feature that was continued in fishing vessels for many years. Instead of the short head theretofore prevalent, she was provided with a much longer head, which, with other innovations, served to characterize her as a new type. The *Romp* would now be called anything

stern davits of the schooner, leaving the deck clear for fishing or for temporarily stowing the catch. Then, too, the cabin was aft, and the accommodations for sleeping and cooking were more commodious, if not yet luxurious.

The adaptability of this type to the mackerel fishery led to extensive employment of it during the forties, and, since the jig was the chief implement of capture, they were often called "jiggers," though the same name was sometimes applied to pinkies. The mackerel fishery, which had suffered a long period of adversity, owing to scarcity of fish, became prosperous again in the closing years of the first half of the present century. The demand for mackerel was good, and large catches readily sold at remunerative prices. Complete success, however, often depended upon the speed of vessels, and consequently the thoughts of fishermen and designers were turned toward producing swifter

A MODERN CLIPPER, 1894.

but sharp or clipper like; but so fixed
had ideas become at that period that
men feared to sail on her because she
was so sharp, and tradition relates that
her skipper had difficulty in securing a
crew to man her.

The decade succeeding the building of the *Romp* was one of experi-
mentation in the construction of
fishing schooners. The *Romp* was a
somewhat close approximation to the
pilot boat of that period and, despite
the evil prognostications of conservative fishermen, who predicted that in
a heavy sea she would "dive and never
come up," she proved a remarkably
seaworthy vessel, as well as much
swifter than those in common use at
that time.

The rivalry between the fishermen
in the matter of speed resulted in the
production of many diverse forms of
schooners, each designer striving to
outdo others. The tendency of the
times, about 1850, was to build
schooners on the "cod's head and
mackerel tail" principle. Generally
they had fairly easy lines forward, but
with the bow strongly flaring at the
top; their greatest width was usually
about one-third to two-fifths of their
length from the stem, and there was
a gradual tapering from that point to
the stern, which was narrow and deep.
They were rather straight on top, had
a heavy drag — being shallow forward, and with a large draft aft, and
were sharp on the floor, — in these
particulars as in others, having a
strong affinity to the Baltimore clippers. A striking feature on many of
them was an exceedingly long pointed
cutwater or head, having a gilded fiddle head at its extremity, also carved
and gilded trail-boards along the sides.
It also became customary to have
gilded moldings on the sterns, and in
some cases this style of ornamentation
was carried to excess. The schooners
were usually painted black above
water, with one or two white stripes,
while the bottom was green. Often
there was a narrow white line which
separated the green on the bottom

GLOUCESTER HARBOR, SHOWING A FLEET OF FISHING SCHOONERS.

RELATIVE SIZES.

No. 1.   40 feet long.
No. 2.   45 to 60 feet.
No. 3.   50 to 65 feet.
No. 4.   75 to 120 feet.
No. 5.   80 to 130 feet.

No. 1. "The Sparrow Hawk," which sailed from England with forty passengers in the year 1626 and wrecked on Cape Cod.
No. 2. "The Pinky Tiger," built in 1820—the style of boat used at that time to bring frozen herring from Newfoundland.
No. 3. "The Rebecca," built at Marblehead in 1798 for Grand Bank cod fishing.
No. 4. Type of 1860 fishing schooner.
No. 5. Type of 1895 fishing schooner.

Photographed from models in John R. Neal's museum, T wharf, Boston.

from the black above; and this improved the appearance of the new clipper. The rig was copied largely after the Baltimore vessels; the masts generally raked very strongly, for at that time the erroneous belief prevailed that speed was enhanced materially, especially in windward sailing, by such an arrangement of spars.

The builders of fishing vessels in those days had no fine-spun theories about "lateral resistance" and "centre of effort" of sails, and were content in their experimentations to follow in the footsteps of others or work out their own ideas by rule of thumb process. Some of the early clippers, which were commonly called "sharp-shooters," were built on extreme lines, having very sharp bows, while they were shallow and poorly fitted to meet the exigencies incident to winter fishing in the Atlantic. The result was that some of these met with fatal disaster in the gales to which they were exposed, and went down at sea with all on board.

During the period referred to, a considerable number of vessels of the type ordinarily termed "bay boats" were purchased from Baltimore for employment in the New England summer mackerel fishery; a few of these also engaged in the winter oyster trade between the Chesapeake Bay region and Boston. They were loftily rigged, some carrying a foretopmast and a large square sail on the foremast; consequently they sailed well in light summer winds; but they were shallow, with deep waists, and had small under deck capacity for cargo, so that when exposed to gales, which often arise very suddenly in the Gulf of St. Lawrence, they were too frequently found unsafe and dangerous.

Builders at New London and vicinity produced a much better style of schooner for the deep-sea fisheries, which proved to be both seaworthy and swift, it having greater depth and fuller midship section than the Baltimore type, while the lines were also comparatively easy. Vessels of this type had shorter and better formed heads than many of the others, and were copied to a greater or less degree by the progressive builders of Essex and other points north of Cape Cod.

One of the most noted builders of clipper fishing schooners about the middle of the present century was Samuel Hall, a well-known naval architect at East Boston. With large experience in designing, and holding advanced ideas as to the elements needed in a vessel, he practically produced a new form, which combined many of the best features of the Baltimore and New London schooners, though being an improvement on both, so far as speed and adaptation to requirements were concerned. The vessels he designed were intended for employment in the mackerel fishery in summer and for freighting oysters from the Chesapeake Bay region to Boston in winter. Among the first schooners built in his yard were the *Telegraph* and *Express*, launched about 1849. These vessels were larger than the other first-class fishing schooners used at that period, being approximately 100 tons, old measurement. Their advent in the fishing fleet caused a sensation, for not only were they more powerful under sail, and swifter than vessels previously seen, but they were very loftily rigged and carried a large area of canvas.

The first vessels launched by Hall proved so satisfactory and popular that they were followed by others for service in the oyster and mackerel trades. Donald McKay, the famous builder of clipper ships, also constructed a number of fishing schooners in the fifties. But his designs were less popular than those made by Hall, which were extensively copied and, with some variations, continued in use for more than thirty years. The fact remains, nevertheless, that vessels of this style, although perhaps well suited to the summer mackerel fishery, as well as to the oyster trade, where moderate draft was required, were, owing to their shallowness, not able safely to encounter winter gales in the open sea.

The attempted improvements after 1855 can scarcely be considered advantageous, for the tendency was to increase the size of the vessels chiefly by making them longer and wider, while little was added to their depth. They were also made much sharper forward and hollowed out excessively in the run. The stern remained broad and heavy, with flat counters, giving almost a box-like form to this part of the vessel. Thus, from 1860 to 1885,

THE LATEST "FLYING FISHERMAN."

the clipper fishing schooner of New England, though having a sharp and well-formed bow, was so badly designed in its after section that it failed to develop a high rate of speed except when running free. Although it had large initial stability, its shallowness, and the fact that it was commonly ballasted with stone, stowed inside, made the centre of gravity so high that the righting power was reduced almost to a minimum. It was therefore an unsafe type of vessel, particularly in winter when exposed to severe storms, and it too often happened that there was an appalling loss of life and property. In many instances the loftily

rigged schooners were thrown on their beam ends by the fierce drive of a terrific wave and, unless by rare good fortune they righted, nothing more was heard of them; vessels and crew found a common grave in the stormy Atlantic.

While a single gale sometimes exacted its dreadful tribute of ten or a dozen schooners and reaped a ghastly harvest of more than an hundred drowned men, those who came straggling back to port after the hurricane's wrath was exhausted had gruesome tales to tell of hair-breadth escapes from sudden death. On such occasions the local press told of vessels that were rolled completely over like toys in the grasp of the rushing sea; others lay with masts or sails in the water, with men struggling among the waves or clinging to masthead or topmast rigging until the lucky moment of righting came, while the canvas of some had been torn to shreds by the tempest and they came limping home under jury rig or, in one case at least, with bed clothes sewed together to form sails. So frequent and so dreadful were such disasters, that the loss of life and the horrors of winter fishing became proverbial. Often whole towns were in mourning for the brave men who had gone hopefully forth to the distant banks, but failed to return, and distracted and destitute widows and helpless children waited and watched for the gleam of returning sails that never came, or peered through the darkness for approaching lights that they hoped might be borne by the barks that their loved ones had sailed on. But tidings came not, and hope faded into deep despair; the list of "missing" bore the names of their dear ones. Then came the struggle for bread, scanty aid doled out with provident hand by the relief societies, and the oblivion that gaunt poverty throws over her victims — until, perhaps, a new disaster recalled those of former years.

Mention should not be omitted of the fact that there was a material change in the size of fishing schooners from 1840 to 1885, during what may be termed the first period of the development of the clipper type. About 1840 and for several years thereafter vessels employed in the fisheries seldom exceeded 45 or 50 tons, old measurement, equal to about 25 or 30 tons of the present tonnage; a schooner of 70 tons was sufficiently uncommon to create much comment. The most marked innovation in the matter of size was the building of the oyster carrying schooners already alluded to. The first of these were soon followed by others of larger dimensions. The advantage of having vessels for the mackerel fishery with greater capacity than the average schooner was soon apparent; and since the frozen herring trade with Newfoundland reached considerable proportions in the fifties and sixties, and such schooners were better adapted to it than those of smaller size, an impulse was given to their production. While therefore some of the largest clippers found employment in winter in freighting oysters or frozen herring, others engaged in the fruit trade or in special lines of commerce for which they were suitable.

But there was a general disposition to increase the dimensions of the schooners, and they gradually developed in this particular, so that by 1880 the average size of off-shore fishing vessels of the first class was about 75 tons register, or from 100 to 110 tons old measurement. Although the change in this particular has perhaps not been so pronounced since that time, it is nevertheless true that with the advent of a new type larger vessels were built than had before been common, if we except the few isolated instances when attempts were made to introduce three-masted fishing

schooners in the cod and mackerel fisheries — ventures that did not prove popular.

Notwithstanding the losses suffered by the New England fleet, nothing was done for many years to make the schooners more seaworthy, and, with the exception that they increased materially in size, averaging almost twice as large in 1885 as they did thirty years earlier, they remained practically unchanged in hull and rig. However, the decade ending in 1890 witnessed a marked innovation, if not a revolution, in the design of American fishing schooners, both as to hull and rig.

Being impressed with the fatal fallacy of employing shallow vessels in the ocean fisheries, the writer was impelled in 1882, to publish a series of articles in the Gloucester papers earnestly advocating the introduction of a deeper and safer schooner, and changes in rig which study and experience indicated might prove beneficial. The discussion was continued in subsequent years, and the letters on the subject were supplemented, in 1885, by a practical demonstration of the ideas previously promulgated.

At that time, the late Professor Baird, desiring a schooner for the work of the United States Fish Commission, and also feeling anxious to improve the opportunity to make helpful suggestions to fishermen, placed in the writer's hands the work of designing the new vessel. The *Grampus*, as the schooner was named, was a radical departure from the prevailing form and was in reality a new type of American fishing vessel. She was about two feet deeper than the ordinary schooner of the same length; the after section was more V-shaped, with easier horizontal lines; the stern was not so wide and had a much stronger rake; while the stem was nearly perpendicular above water, though curved strongly below. Many other new features were introduced in her construction to insure greater strength or adaptability. Among these the most noticeable were in the rig. The foremast was made considerably shorter than the mainmast, and the foretopmast, instead of being of the same length as the maintopmast, as had previously been the custom, was not so long by several feet. The schooner was also rigged to carry a forestaysail — the forestay coming down to the stem head — and a comparatively small jib, this arrangement of head sails being considered preferable to the large jib until then in almost universal use. Wire rigging was used instead of hemp.

The exhibition at Gloucester of the model and plans of the *Grampus* led to prompt attempts to imitate her. Several schooners embodying many of her features were designed after her construction was begun, and as the work on them was pushed with utmost rapidity they were launched weeks or months before the *Grampus* was completed. The appearance of the *Grampus* on the fishing grounds in the summer of 1886, and the fact that she proved exceptionally swift, easily sailing away from the typical fishing clipper of the period, especially when close hauled or reaching, attracted much attention to her and prompted the ambition of fishermen to excel her if possible. This led them to avail themselves of the skill of Edward Burgess, the famous yacht designer, and D. J. Lawlor, long distinguished for designing pilot boats, yachts and fishing schooners. Others also entered the field, and the employment of competent talent resulted in producing a sweeping change in designing fishing vessels. So great has the change been that the modern craft is not only immeasurably swifter than the clipper of the early eighties, but her superiority is perhaps most noticeable in her safety and efficiency in heavy weather. For it has often happened in recent years that, when vessels of the old type had to lie to and drive to leeward in strong off-shore gales, the new boats sturdily faced wind and wave and came bravely into port, forcing their passages to windward, even

though they were sometimes coated so heavily with ice that they looked almost like moving icebergs with sails set on them.

In form and rig it seems that the modern clipper fishing schooner of New England has nearly attained perfection, so far as that can be reached in sailing vessels of moderate dimensions. It is, in fact, a sturdy sea-going yacht, with all the grace and easy sweep of lines that characterize the highly specialized pleasure vessel, but generally carrying inside ballast* and necessarily being somewhat wider in proportion or else having a smaller area of canvas than is carried by the lead-keeled yachts. Iron is largely used for ballast now. On most of the new vessels boiler punchings are placed in cement between the floor timbers, and pig iron is stowed above this. Thus the centre of gravity is much lower than it was on the shallower schooners, and the chances of righting, if knocked down, are materially increased. Indeed, the ability of the new clipper to right has been fully tested in the gales to which it has been exposed, and numerous instances are on record where it has escaped from the peril of foundering when shallow vessels would doubtless have gone to the bottom with all on board.

The double head rig is now universally in favor, a long light bowsprit without jibboom being found far more suitable than the clumsy rig of former years. The long head is also discarded, as is the big stern and flat counters, while wire rigging has been extensively adopted.

But while the fishing schooner of the region north of Cape Cod has undergone many changes, and consequently has exerted a strong influence on other sections, little alteration is observable since 1850 in the vessels of other parts of the Atlantic coast, and the builders as well as the fishermen

* Since this article was written schooners have been designed for the Atlantic fisheries with cast-iron keels; part of their ballast at least is thus carried outside, which is a decided innovation in the construction of this class of vessels.

of some sections seem quite content with the boats they have. Even as late as the decade closing in 1890, the fishing schooners of southern New England showed little improvement over those built thirty or forty years earlier.

The same is also true of the schooners employed in the oyster industry of the Chesapeake Bay region. The pungy of to-day is almost the exact counterpart of the oyster schooner built more than forty years ago, and those who use it seem to continue in the belief that perfection of form and rig has been attained. In view of the enterprise shown by the builders of the Chesapeake in the first half of the century, when the "Baltimore clipper" became famous for speed and beauty, it is somewhat remarkable that their fishing schooners of recent years evidence no marked change, and that the extravagantly raking masts, long heads, convex lines and wide thin sterns of nearly half a century ago are still universal, despite all that experience has taught to the contrary. It is true that the Chesapeake pungy, with its wide deck, which affords room for oysters, and its raking stem and sternpost, which insure quick turning, is well adapted to the work it has to do; still it is undoubtedly susceptible of much improvement in speed and other qualifications, while retaining all of the excellencies that have made it so popular.

The smacks employed in the fisheries of Key West have been copied after the Connecticut schooners that first went there to develop the fisheries, and to a less extent this is true of some other southern ports. Elsewhere, however, in the South, the typical New England schooner prevails, since most of the vessels have either been purchased or built to order north of Cape Cod. This is particularly true of Pensacola, where some of those employed in the market fisheries are of the latest and most improved forms.

Several of the Gloucester schooners have rounded the Horn to engage in the fisheries of the west coast or in trade. The *Romp* was one of the first of these, and they have mostly been of the old class of clippers, though a few of comparatively recent date have made the voyage.

Thus the influence of the humble fisherman who built and rigged the original schooner has been felt on oceans and inland seas and, though his creation was crude, in keeping with the time in which he wrought, the germ has developed until now, when no safer or more graceful craft floats than the trim fishing schooners, those gleaners of sea harvests, that boldly sail forth oceanward from the old harbor that bore on its bosom the first of the type. And, whatever may be said of the ancient "scooner," we have but to see one of these modern clippers under way in a good breeze, tearing along like a trained race horse of the sea, to feel the impulse to cry: "Oh, how she scoons!"

8
Le Beau Port

THE WHARVES OF GLOUCESTER

LE BEAU PORT

THE SEA-BROWNED FISHING TOWN OF GLOUCESTER

By JAMES R. COFFIN

Illustrated from photographs by H. W. Spooner

OF the above titles, the first is that by which Gloucester Harbor was, with singular felicity, descriptively named by the great Champlain in 1606, this being his second visit to the point which he considered one of the most important, strategically and commercially, on the coast. The sub-title is from the pen of the Rev. Cotton Mather, who in 1680 visited the colony, which at that time had already attained to considerable importance.

Time has done nothing to change the aptness of either phrase. Gloucester is still a fishing town, sea-browned, while its beautiful location attracts thousands annually, during the months of the great shoreward migration that is so engaging a feature of modern life.

From the beginning the Gloucester fisheries have been a force in the building of the nation. Passing over the earlier visits of white men to the shores of Cape Ann,—the semi-mythical landing of the Norsemen and the romantic but futile explorations of Captain John Smith, who named the harbor after the Turkish lady who had intervened for the saving of his life and the three islands from the three luckless Turks whose heads he had cut off,—we come to the settlement made by the "Dorchester Colony" in 1623.

The object of the settlement, in which wealthy English gentlemen were interested, was the pursuit of the fisheries, which had been so profitably followed on the New England coast since 1606, and for which the location of Gloucester was and is so eminently well adapted.

The site of the settlement where was erected their "stage," or wharf, is that which is now known as Stage Fort, and is appropriately held as a public reservation. It lies just to the south of the present city, a fair eminence, rock-girt, and commanding a noble view of the harbor and the sea beyond.

In 1624 Roger Conant was appointed governor and the settlement attracted marked attention. The Plymouth colony claimed jurisdiction over it, and went so far as to attempt to make good their claim by force of arms, an expedition under command of the doughty Miles Standish himself laying siege to the strongly barricaded quarters of the independent colony. Conant succeeded in pointing out the way to peace without bloodshed, and a *modus vivendi* was established. The fisheries were successful, the first cargoes of Gloucester fish going to Bilboa, Spain, and proving very profitable. The agricultural portion of the colony, however, did not find the situation so favorable. The whole region is very rocky and the amount of arable land small. The farming part of the community accordingly moved southward, leaving

THE BELL-BUOY AT NORMAN'S WOE REEF

Gloucester a strictly maritime settlement. The name Gloucester, by the way, had already been chosen in remembrance of the beautiful English cathedral city from which so many of the adventurers had come.

Thus for nearly three hundred years Gloucester has maintained its character and still ranks as the most important fishing port in America. The seafaring life has bred a hardy race of men, who have played an important part in our great national struggles; from Bunker Hill, where two companies of Gloucester men were engaged in the battle, and the disastrous campaign before New York City, where the fishermen of Massachusetts, by their firmness and intrepidity, saved Washington's army from annihilation,

to the late Spanish war, in which five hundred Gloucester fishermen responded to the nation's call for skilled mariners.

This long period of continuous development along one line is unique in American life, and confers upon Gloucester a stamp of individuality that is as interesting as it is unusual, at least on this continent.

The growth of the city has been remarkably even. In 1873, after two hundred and thirty-one years of corporate life, the town government was changed for a city charter. The present population of the city is about 33,000. It is thirty-three miles from Boston on the Gloucester Branch of the Eastern Division of the Boston & Maine Railroad, and is the metropolis of the great North Shore summer colony.

This summer life is certainly an important and growing feature of the place. Cape Ann, surrounded by water on three sides and perpetually swept by ocean breezes, is virtually free from fog, and its cool, clear atmosphere affords grateful relief to the city toiler. It is said that among the earliest summer visitors to this district were the Brook Farm Transcendentalists, who made Pigeon Cove the point for their annual summer pilgrimages, doing the distance from Boston by stage—a long, hard, day's journey—and that was only seventy-five years ago. To-day it is an easy hour's ride, and at least fifteen thousand people annually seek its salubrious summer climate and the refreshment afforded by its scenic beauty and varied recreations.

But what of the fisheries? Have they prospered? Are they followed to-day with the old-time vigor and enterprise?

I think that the contrary has been generally reported and believed. As a matter of fact, Gloucester-cured fish is a very much finer product to-day than it ever was, and the market is a growing one. The business is carried on by a number of very strong firms, and their trade is national in its scope. The method of conducting the business has unquestionably changed, and, as is always the case, the period of transition and adaptation to new conditions has been one of depression. But the past year has been one of the best that the Gloucester fisheries ever knew, and there is every reason to believe that this is but the beginning of a new era of prosperity.

There are three principal reasons for the renewed prosperity of this ancient trade. The first has already been re-

higher price for the product than they would if a portion of it had to be sold at a reduced price. In the packing of the fish, also, the scientific spirit of the age has introduced many improvements. Formerly it was not practicable to attempt to sell packed fish in the summer months. To-day Gloucester packed fish products keep in perfect condition throughout the summer months. And this lengthening of the

CAPE ANN LIGHT, SHOWING "MOTHER ANN" ON THE EXTREME POINT

ferred to. It is the improvement of the product. The packers no longer accept fish from the vessels unless they are in prime condition. Formerly fish were graded and cargoes that were in a very bad condition could still find a sale at some price. The adoption of stricter regulations has resulted in no hardship or loss to the fishermen, for they are simply compelled to take greater pains to properly salt and pack their catch on board and receive a

season is the second element that enters into the growing prosperity of the Gloucester fisheries.

The third important factor in this growth is that the great packers have entered upon a campaign of advertising that introduces their product into thousands of homes where it was formerly unknown as an article of diet, and this extension of the market seems to possess almost limitless possibilities.

But will the fisheries be able to

THE WINTER RIG OF THE GLOUCESTER SCHOONER

supply this increased demand? Unquestionably, yes. The fish are in the sea, and granted a market that will make their catching and packing remunerative, there will be no difficulty, and never has been any difficulty, in securing them.

As the question of feeding the immense human population of the globe becomes more and more acute, so tremendously important an element of diet as that of packed fish will assume larger and larger proportions in our national balance sheet. It is an interesting fact that to-day practically the entire Gloucester catch is sold to the home market. There is practically no export trade in Gloucester-packed fish, for the simple reason that the home demand absorbs the present supply at the present price; but the supply could be enormously increased at a very slightly increased price.

The prosperity of Gloucester is founded upon that bedrock foundation, a primary article of world dietary.

It has been quite widely believed by those who are only cursorily informed that the Gloucester fish business has been and is being steadily transferred to Boston. This idea is founded upon misinformation. Boston to-day, and not Gloucester, is the centre of the fresh fish trade. Gloucester still is, as it always has been, the center of the fish-packing business.

In this connection a few items of statistical information will be informing. Considerable pains have been taken to make the following figures authoritative. They are furnished in part by Mr. Arthur L. Millet, the expert statistician and commercial reporter of the fisheries; Mr. J. E. Lenhart, wholesale fish dealer and chairman of the publicity committee of the Board of Trade.

The Gloucester fishing fleet numbers about 275 sail, with a gross tonnage of about 22,000 tons. Large fishing schooners predominate, but there are many small craft; also small steamers and gasoline propelled craft. Some of the large vessels and quite a number of the smaller craft are also fitted with gasoline auxiliary power.

The fishing grounds frequented by Gloucester vessels extend from Cape Hatteras to Greenland, and the length of trips varies from a day or two for the little boats to five and six months for some of the larger vessels which go for salt cod or "flitched" halibut, the latter up among the icefields and icebergs of the Labrador coast and Davis strait.

These figures for the number of vessels at this port do not include small craft under five tons, of which there are many.

The fisheries have been prosecuted here since the place was founded, but records of earlier losses have not been accurately reported. Since 1830 the figures are as follows:

Vessels lost	779
Tonnage	41,757
Value	$3,952,996
Insurance	$3,035,058
Lives lost	5,304
Widows left behind	1,064
Children left behind	2,144

From this it will appear that in a period of eighty years the entire fleet has been practically lost three times! These are solemn facts that throw a very vivid light on the dangers that surround the fisherman's calling. In an editorial paragraph in our New England Department will be found tabulated statistics of the catches.

It will be but a small number of our readers to whom the Gloucester fishing schooner is not familiar. This swift, staunch and beautiful craft is the creation of these fisheries. Her great strength and stability tells of the dangers in the midst of which the fisherman's calling is followed. Her speed tells of the shrewdness and "smartness" essential to success. Her general rig and style tell of the ingenuity and inventiveness of those who devised this instrument for the conquest of the boisterous northern seas. No better or more beautiful craft ever sailed on any sea.

The manning of these vessels is by crews who work on a co-operative system that is both interesting and in-

A TYPICAL GLOUCESTER SCHOONER UNDER FULL SAIL

THE FLAKES. DRYING SALTED FISH.

structive. Each man on board the boat takes his risk in the result and his share of the success of the trip. These shares are known as "lays." The system is a survival of the shares which the original adventurers took in the founding of the colony, and it is a case of the survival of fitness.

It is more than doubtful if any other system of payment would result satisfactorily. The business is one in which the individual workman needs the incentive of his own profit, for everything depends upon his energy, courage and skill. The game that he plays is one that requires a kind of fortitude and daring that is only bred of such an independence and sense of being his own master as this system produces. Whether or not the cash receipts are at the end of the year equivalent to wages may be a subject of endless discussion. So much depends upon so many ifs. Certain it is that it avoids all disputes and breeds intelligence, independence and manhood. Rough men these Gloucester sailors may be, but they are manly fellows. They certainly

lift the lid a little when they come ashore from a long trip; but there are some things that they do not do, and those things are such as might be grouped under the general heads of meanness and cowardice.

The old Yankee stock has very largely prospered out of the work, if I might be permitted to coin such an expression. They have made enough money to educate their children to callings involving less hardship, and but few of them are found aboard the fleet to-day. The crews are largely recruited from the descendants of the Scotch and English settlers of Nova Scotia. They become naturalized Americans, for they cannot hope to become the masters of vessels otherwise, and they recruit our population with a shrewd, hardy and honest body of men racially the same as our older Yankee stock. There are a number of Portuguese fishermen in Gloucester, and they are very highly thought of, too, but of other nationalities there are very few.

Thus co-operatively manned, and her decks piled high with nested dories or the great seine-boats, and her hold laden with ice or salt or both, our beautiful schooner stands out for the Grand Banks or the treacherous, uncharted coasts still farther to the north, her canvas all set and drawing — a beautiful picture. More space than we have at our disposal would be required to describe the manner of taking the fish.

The cod fishery, which is the staple industry, is pursued with hook and line, with trawls, gill-nets and with jiggers. The greater part of the cod fishing is done with a trawl. The trawl is a long line from which shorter hooked and baited lines depend. At each end of the trawl is an anchor, and a buoy or marker by which to locate the trawl, which is kept very near the bottom. Trawls are baited and coiled in tubs and set from dories, usually manned by two men, the lines being skilfully tossed overboard by a little flirting fling with a short stick. The usual equipment of a large vessel carrying ten dories is six line-tubs to each dory. Each line is 300 feet long and is fitted with from 80 to 100 hooks; so that, with all trawls set, a vessel is covering over 20 miles of fishing ground with some 30,000 hooks.

This method necessitates the dories being at considerable distances from the vessel, which is often left to be handled by the cook alone; and it is this disposition of the crew that is the principal source of the loss of life.

Next in importance to trawling is seining with the purse seine, which is the usual way of catching mackerel and sometimes of other fish.

The purse seine, as the name indicates, may be drawn together by a cord that is reeved into it top and bottom. The mackerel seine is about 225 fathoms long and is set from a seine-boat, which is a kind of large whale-boat of a peculiar Gloucester design. After a school of mackerel is sighted the crew take to the oars, and the game is to row swiftly enough to surround a good proportion of them with the long net, which is paid out as the men row in a circle and quickly gathered up with the pursing cords before the fish have an opportunity to escape. Mackerel are a fish of very peculiar habits, and there is much speculation of late as to the sudden disappearance of the great schools from their usual haunts. Whither they have gone no man can tell, or at what moment they will suddenly reappear.

THE LOBSTER-MAN AND HIS MATE

The gill net, as the name signifies, is a net that is left suspended in the water for a considerable time, until many fish become enmeshed by the gills.

Under some conditions the simple hook and line are used, each man having his position along the rail of the vessel. "Jigging" is fishing with an unbaited and unbarbed hook, which is let down (two hooks being fastened to the same line and held apart and leaded) into schools of fish, which are caught by a quick, jerking motion of the hand. Sword-fishing is done with a harpoon, and is an exciting and dangerous employment. The fish sometimes weigh as much as 700 pounds and fight desperately. Good swordfish stories are part of every fisherman's equipment. They do not have to be invented.

The methods used in the curing and packing of fish are full of interest. Cleanliness and prompt handling are the great requirements. On all the longer trips now the fish are cured on board the vessel. They are split open, fresh from the water, cleaned, thoroughly washed, and packed in pure sea salt. When a sufficient catch is made the vessel promptly sails for Gloucester, where the fish are removed from the vessel, washed and packed in hogsheads holding about 1200 pounds each. Thus they are kept to await the demands of the trade. When needed they are taken out, washed again, piled up in "kench," a process which presses out a great part of the pickle. Then they are taken to the "flake yards," where they are spread out, each fish by itself, flesh side up, and dried by sun and wind—a process in which the climate of Gloucester excels. This process calls for experience and judgment, and the excellence of the product depends upon its being properly done.

The first step in the packing of the dried fish is that of removing the fins, backbone and skin. It requires expert workmen and much skill. The next step is to pull out the remaining bones. This is done with pincers by hand, the work being carried on by young women under the most cleanly conditions.

There remains but to cut the fish into the required lengths and to pack it into the neat cartons, wrapped in waxed paper, in which form, "absolutely boneless" and perfectly cured, it is marketed.

Mackerel are cured aboard the vessel and repacked in Gloucester into barrels of about 200 pounds each, in which form they are marketed. Of late there has arisen quite a considerable business of selling extra choice mackerel in the original package, for which purpose the finest fish are taken and packed in smaller packages.

Smoked herring are handled in the winter months, the business having very large proportions. They are brought from Newfoundland lightly salted in the hold of the vessel. They are then soaked out and hung in the smokehouse until cured to that rich, golden brown tint that has made the Gloucester product famous. They go all over the country under the name of "smoked bloater herring."

Another very important article in the line of cured fish is smoked halibut. These fish are caught off the dangerous Labrador coast by the trawling method. They are cured and sliced aboard the vessel. The vessels engaged in this trade usually leave Gloucester in May and return to Gloucester in September. The slices or "flitches" of fish are taken from the vessel at Gloucester and stored in pickle until needed. Then they are taken out, washed and a good part of the salt soaked out, the water pressed out and the pieces hung in the smokehouse, where they are subjected to the curing process from a smoke that is made by smouldering fires of sawdust and oak chips.

If this brief account of the Gloucester method of packing and curing fish shall have conveyed an idea of freshly-caught fish, firm-fleshed from the cold northern Atlantic, promptly cleaned and salted and carefully packed under the most cleanly conditions, it will have left a correct impression of the preparation of a very important American food product whose market is constantly increasing.

A number of very large and important firms are engaged in the business.

The Gorton-Pew Fisheries Company, which has been established by the union of several large concerns, has done a great deal for the enlargement of the market for Gloucester-packed fish. By judicious advertising and direct contact with the trade the consumption of cured fish products is greatly stimulated. The Cunningham & Thompson Company are large owners of vessels and very large packers, make a specialty of selling high-grade packed fish direct to the consumer. This is a very important and growing line of business, in which others also are profitably engaged, notably the Consumers' Fish Company, of which Mr. E. K. Burnham, secretary of the Gloucester Board of Trade, is the managing proprietor.

The Davis Brothers Company produce a number of brands and sell to the wholesale trade exclusively.

William F. Moore & Company,

AN EASTERN POINT ROADWAY

putting up a number of well-known brands. William H. Jordan & Company are the owners of some of the finest vessels in Gloucester, including the Oriole, which is the crack fishing schooner of the world. In last year's race from Belle Isle she beat everything else by many hours. The firm is an old one and its brands are well known and synonymous with excellence.

The Frank E. Davis Fish Company wholesale fish dealers, seek to develop the export trade. The Gold Bond Packing Company are successful developers of the high-grade hotel and family trade, while the Gloucester Salt Fish Company are both producers and jobbers in a broad line, including all of the usual Gloucester products, and Charles F. Warsar & Company deal in fish specialties for the high-class grocery trade. Hugh Parkhurst & Company are producers and wholesale dealers

GLOUCESTER'S ATTRACTIVE HIGH SCHOOL BUILDING

who make a specialty of Georges tongues and sounds and Georges slack-salted pollock.

Naturally, these men get together for the common good, and the Gloucester Board of Trade affords them the opportunity for so doing. A committee of the board, meeting regularly, establishes the price to be paid for fish from the vessels, a practice which tends to eliminate the old scramble from wharf to wharf, which was more entertaining to outsiders than profitable to the parties concerned.

Mr. Thomas J. Carrol, manager of the Gorton-Pew Company, is president of the Board of Trade. Mr. Fred A. Pierce of the Cunningham-Thompson Company, vice-president, and Mr. Edward K. Burnham of the Consumers' Fish Company is secretary and treasurer. The board is active in many ways useful to Gloucester. It engages in general advertising, issues a most attractive book on Gloucester, and seeks to develop the city's commercial interests along all lines. Industries seeking a location favorable for manufacturing would learn much to their advantage by communicating with them. It is doubtful if equally available sites for manufacturing or a practical port of entry with established shipping can be found anywhere else within the same distance from Boston at anything like the same cost. Indeed, Gloucester has free sites to offer to firms that mean business.

The Business Men's Association, of which Mr. Chick, a large real estate dealer, is president, also works for the advancement of Gloucester's interests, particularly of the summer business, and the city government may always be counted upon to co-operate.

There are already established in Gloucester many forms of manufacturing outside of the fish business or closely allied to it.

One of the most important of these is the Russia Cement Company, which, as the manufacturer of Le Page's liquid glue, is known the world over. The high quality of the product of this firm is evidenced by the fact that their make of glue for the use of photo-engravers, a very exacting trade, is the world's standard. The process of manufacture is exceedingly interesting. Nothing is wasted. That which cannot go into glue is sold to the manufacturers of fertilizer. The industry affords a profitable use for the by-products of the packing industry, and is a very important feature of Gloucester's industrial life. One may go through the Russia Cement Company's plant from end to end without the slightest inconvenience from those odors which are supposed to be inseparable from the manufacture, in so cleanly a manner is the work conducted. Not the least important feature of the success of the work is the neat form in which the glue is packed for the use of the small consumer and the skill with which the product is advertised.

The Robinson Glue Company is another very large producer of liquid fish-glue of high grade for all purposes. Formerly this firm sold only to large consumers and to the wholesale trade. Recently they have extended their marketing methods to include the small consumer, and have entered upon a campaign to put their goods before the public in that form.

E. L. Rowe & Son (incorporated), sail-makers and ship-chandlers, originally established for the supply of Gloucester shipping, have extended their business far beyond these limits. They are particularly widely known at present for the manufacture of Rowe's Gloucester bed hammock, a popular veranda luxury.

One of the largest plants in Gloucester is that of the Gloucester Net & Twine Company, which has successfully extended its market beyond the Gloucester demand, and is to-day doing a business in all parts of the world.

It would be obviously impossible to even mention all of the industries located in a city the size of Gloucester. The above have been particularly mentioned because of the very direct way in which they have developed from the fishing industry of the city. The same may also be said of the manufacture of oiled clothing by the Boynton's Improved Process Company and by the Gloucester Oiled Clothing Company, the C. R. Corliss & Son Company, the L. Nickerson Company and the J. H. Rowe Company.

While nothing could be more wholesome and natural than this develop-

CITY HALL AND DALE AVENUE, GLOUCESTER

ment of manufacturing out of the by-products of the fishing industry and to meet its needs, there is an opening for other lines of manufacture in the city, which is most advantageously located for any general line of manufacturing.

The early farmers of Gloucester found, as we have previously intimated, that they had indeed cast their lot on a "stern and rock-bound coast." They did not realize that some day those very rocks would be farmed more profitably than a kindlier soil. The granite industry of Cape Ann is a very important asset for Gloucester. It is a very durable and beautiful stone, and has been employed in many of the proudest structures in the country. It is also splendidly fitted for paving, as it is exceedingly durable and non-absorbent of moisture, which makes it a very sanitary form of pavement.

The fine old city of Gloucester is by no means absorbed in its industrial life. There is a broad and fine development of social activity along the lines that minister to the higher life. There is a very fine choral organization in the city; an active camera club that produces work of unsurpasesd artistic merit—for which, indeed, it has unsurpassed opportunities; two public libraries, a fishermen's institute, master mariners' association, a most excellently conducted working-girls' club, and many other institutions that are unique and possess Gloucester individuality, besides those usual to all New England communities and excellent churches and schools.

Again and again we find ourselves returning to the topic of the beauty of the district. Gloucester scenery is not to be surpassed by that of any seashore point in the world.

There is a warmth and range of color, a softness and clarity of atmosphere and an endless variety of detail that has won for it the love of a very large artist colony, including many of our leading American painters. If a more delightful place for summer residence exists, we have yet to discover its whereabouts.

THE SAWYER FREE LIBRARY AND UNITARIAN AND CONGREGATIONAL CHURCHES

9
Old Saybrook Sketches

THE INN, SAYBROOK POINT

Old Saybrook Sketches

By M. Louise Greene

is still cordially provided at the old inn at Saybrook Point, though the tavern sign has long since found indoor housing and the carpenter's hammer and mason's chisel have transformed the big halls and cavernous fireplaces into sizable chambers and hearths proportioned to the needs of a private house. On the diminished hearthstones the fires crackle and burn and roar up the wide ancient chimneys with all the old-time hospitality, while their glowing embers recall the story of the past.

This was not the first inn in Saybrook. The earliest was kept by John Wastoll. It was on Middle Lane near the northwest corner of the then Green—divided into private lots in 1742—and not far from the church and schoolhouse. This second hostelry offered, in summer, refreshing shade beneath its great tree, and, in winter, welcome warmth beside its huge fires, especially to churchgoers, loitering between the long Sunday services. The old-time taverns were hard by the place of public punishment, which, because of the supposed salutary effect upon the community, was always administered upon Weekly-Lecture day. They were handy for training-day; they were accessible for

147

WATER STREET, SAYBROOK POINT

an adjourned town or church meeting; and, in seaport towns, were readily found by captains and sailors, eager for news and to learn the opportunities for trade throughout the country side. In Wastoll's day the town wharf ran out near Mrs. John D. Ingraham's house. To reach it from the inn, one travelled down Middle Lane to Fenwick Street, rounded into Water Street and so along the river front to the Point. Water Street was the direct road to what later became known as the "Center," and branched to the outlying settlements within the original forty thousand acre triangle of the Saybrook Patent. That had included Lyme, Chester, Westbrook, Old Saybrook, Saybrook (or Deep River and Winthrop), and Essex, including Centerbrook. Lyme was set off in 1663. The ferry thence to Saybrook in 1662 made possible the coast road to New York from New

AN OLD-TIMER

"THE LADY FENWICK," THE FERRY TO LYME

London and the eastward. The wharf at Saybrook received the river trade from Hartford and the neighboring towns; also, of course, the coasting trade soon developing into West India and later into foreign commerce.

The distance from Wastoll's inn to the Point may seem short, but the line of least resistance is always followed. Taking into consideration that there was no system of roads in Connecticut before 1700, no turnpikes until after 1776 and a bleak, open country six months of the year, there were times when the inn seemed a good distance off the main road. Moreover, after 1666, the centre of population slowly shifted inland. Trade began to bunch itself on the direct thoroughfare, Water Street. The Blague Wharf, under the present wharf of Burns and Young, was built in 1702-3. Doty's bakeshop for sailors' bread was established on the southeast corner of Fenwick and Water Streets about 1708. Both father and son were largely interested in West India trade and a little later built Doty's Wharf, thirty feet wide and to the north of their warehouse.

Tully's Wharf at Heartsease and Dickinson's Wharf followed. From 1673 the Boston postboy made irregular trips to New York. To have seen him with his pack, to have heard him chaffer with his customers and bargain for the more speedy doing of errands in the towns along his route, one would have concluded that his last and least thought was for the letters in his wallet. From 1715 his trips were fortnightly in winter and more frequently in summer.

Seeing the trend of business, a house, suitable for an inn, was built on Water Street at the head of Fenwick. All trade by land or water passed the door. Its outlook commanded the river and the roads. So the house was snugly built, every nail of hand-wrought iron; ceilings in the lower rooms of plaster, still firm as when made of clam-shell lime; a great semicircular fireplace, nine feet and six inches in diameter below stairs and a second one in the hall above, flanked by two small and one very long narrow room. As taverns were then built more for day use than night, presumably the smaller bed-

149

rooms were for distinguished guests of quality, while in the other, after a good heating before the big fire, the wayfarers hustled into beds or bunks or on to mattresses of straw, laid upon the floor. The old inventories give sadly deficient lists of what we term necessities. This inn was long kept by Daniel Kirtland. The stories told about its hearth related mostly to the first century of the settlement, for by Revolutionary times a new inn had risen almost in the shadow of the new meeting-house, which for the accommodation of her people, the church, removing from her ancient site at the Point, had erected on the triangle opposite the present Congregational building. The history of the period of settlement, of the colonial period, and of the national could be pieced together from the gossip of the three old taverns.

Many years ago, before it was the fashion to treasure every scrap of colonial history or tradition, a little Saybrook girl found her greatest pleasure in listening to her grandfather's tales of the time when he, a growing lad, hearkened to the stories his great-grandfather told beside the fire or by the wayside;—stories of the earliest Saybrook days, of how he had helped to defend, to forward and to guide the young settlement in the wilderness. Because the grandsire was a man of mark and the grandfather, surveying through the countryside for the still young colony had taken to his heart those earliest tales and added thereunto his own experience, which he retold in his still virile

HUMPHREY PRATT'S TAVERN

ACTON LIBRARY

old age, this little grandchild had absorbed a truer volume of tradition than comes to most of us. Further, she carried through life an absorbing love for all the deserved greatness that in the earlier and later days had embosomed colonial Saybrook. Story, tradition, history, comment and current event she garnered and committed to her commonplace-book, and it is my good fortune to draw somewhat from the wealth thus accumulated during many, many years.

Lord Say and Seale, Lord Brooke and others, as we know, on July 7, 1635, commissioned the younger Winthrop governor for one year at the mouth of the Connecticut. He was to overlook the property included in their patent; to protect the country from a possible Dutch investment; and to see that Lion Gardiner, an able engineer from the service of the Prince of Orange, and highly recommended by John Davenport, Hugh Peters and other influential persons, should build a proper fort at Say-

brook Point with houses suitable for gentlemen of quality; should lay out a town behind the fortification and set the foundation of a military post, so anticipating the arrival of a company, well calculated to develop a commercial metropolis, which should also, from its military character, be the bulwark of the up-river towns. To start with, Gardiner brought with him £2,000 in money, iron for two drawbridges, guns, accoutrements, materials, and twelve men with which, in December, 1635, he began the building of the fort. (An advance party of twenty men under Lieutenant Gibbon and Sergeant Willard had reached the Point, had mounted two guns, and, November 24, 1635, had driven off a Dutch sloop, attempting to land.) Inside the fort, "a redoubt of heavy wooden slabs, polygonal in shape, held in the centre an open court or parade-ground, around which were built houses for men of quality, Soldiers' Quarters and the Great Hall—which latter building,

151

surmounted with an Iron Lantern, served for a lighthouse—and also for Judicial, Educational and Religious purposes. Upon the river side a rampart of earthwork, covering the Arsenal and Commissary Department, bristled with the great guns of that day. Standing out from each angle out as agent for the company, of which he was a member, with instructions to inspect the fort and the surrounding country. Lion Gardiner had proceeded to lay out the town in six large squares. Until 1639, when he removed to Monchonack Island, he was in charge as lieutenant of the

"CAPT. MORGAN'S"

of the redoubt were hollow bastions enclosing gardens; also affording range of vision outside the wall; and which pierced with portholes enabled the flint-locks of the soldiers to tell upon the destiny of the Indians attempting to break through the stockade or to swim the moat surrounding the whole."

In 1636, George Fenwick was sent fort and was actual governor of the colony during Fenwick's absence in England, and, after his return to Saybrook, in joint charge of the interests of the post. He surveyed the lands, blazed the roads, and with twenty-four men, two women, and his infant son to protect, held the fort through the strenuous winter and spring of 1635-36 with hostile Pe-

LION GARDINER'S MILL STONE (1636)

quots tormenting the small garrison and raiding the country round about. From the Saybrook fort went brain and brawn to help in the overthrow of the Pequot nation, and had Gardiner's advice been more closely followed, some of the bloody history of that time might have remained unwritten.

With Colonel Fenwick in July, 1639, came his wife, his two sisters and a Mrs. Mary Fenwick and also as pastor, Mr. John Higginson, afterwards minister at Guilford and the author of the "Attestation" or introduction to the "Magnalia." Lady Fenwick held her title by courtesy only and as the former widow of Sir John Botelier, eldest son of Sir Oliver Botelier, Knight, of Teston, Kent, England. After her marriage to a Roundhead and their removal to America, her own family and that of the Boteliers quickly lost sight of her, preferring those who espoused the royal cause. About this lady of brave courageous spirit circles the halo of a local saint. For over two centuries the winds buffeted her lonely tomb on the bleak hillside, once

within the enclosure of Gardiner's fort; for centuries still will be repeated the story of her fair face, sweet with contentment in her husband's love and in her chosen duty though far from the pleasant English fields, the comfortable English life, the dear old friends, so dearly loved and in so many cases separated from her in the estrangement of civil and religious war. Her re-interment at the entrance of Cypress Cemetery (laid out in 1635), when, in 1870, the building of the Valley Road threatened to destroy her resting place, confirmed tradition and added to it the pathetic fact that, while the material discomfort of the new world bore hard upon her, much of her physical frailty was probably due to a well-defined spinal curvature. Her hair was as golden beneath the nineteenth century sun as when flashing back from the graceful coil and soft strands encircling her face the sunlight of a by-gone day. Flowers bloomed for her and fruits struggled up in spite of "the canker-pest."

" Wild timid hares were drawn from woods to share her
    home caresses
Uplooking to her human eyes with sylvan tendernesses."

To her and Colonel Fenwick the young colonies were indebted for fruit

SITE OF LION GARDINER'S GRIST MILL, THE
FIRST OUTSIDE THE PALISADES

trees and cattle. For her people she planned her garden, not alone with precious seed of English flowers, but also with herbs of healing. She consulted with Surgeon Pell, with the minister, and with the Winthrops (both father and son), famed for their medicinal lore, and she sought to have ever ready the simples of her time. There was digitalis, for internal use or for external swellings; St. John's-wort, for vertigo, epilepsy and madness; elderberry, for wine and for wounds,—especially for gunshot wounds; rhubarb and bryonia, for cathartics; while as "against plague, small-pox, purples and all sorts of fevers, poysons and King's evil by way of Prevention or after Infection," the best London physician wrote to Governor Winthrop to have always ready "a black Powder of which the basic ingredient was pulverized burnt toads." For certain common ailments the lady was advised to mix and mould into bullets a preparation of maidenhair fern, fennel, parsley root, two or three ounces of fresh oil of almonds and one-fourth pound of new butter.

Lady Fenwick lived her husband's handmaid, her people's almoner, her church's child, for not even the long, hard journey to Hartford daunted the sweet spirit that sought in Thomas Hooker's church a home for herself and child. In the fall of 1645 she laid herself down to rest, courageously, because her work was done and because she knew that to her husband all men looked as to "a godly and able instrument to assist in the helping to uphold the civil government of the second and third colonies here planted and to a good encourager of the Church of Christ at Hartford."

It is difficult to briefly tell the story of Saybrook's influence in Church and State, since in Connecticut to 1818 they were united, and at Saybrook was formulated the most influential document in Connecticut's ecclesias-

CONGREGATIONAL CHURCH AND CHAPEL

tical history,—namely, the Saybrook Platform of 1708.

Four churches have housed the Congregational folk of Saybrook: the present edifice; the one referred to as standing from 1726 to 1840 nearly opposite it; the church of 1646 by the old Saybrook Point green; and near the same site, the famous church of 1680, whose notable convention, assembling in obedience to the command of the General Court of Connecticut, drew up the Saybrook Platform. This document embodied the faith, discipline and authority of the forty* churches of Connecticut, and was by the Court approved and made the ecclesiastical law of the land. Through it Congregationalism, with a strong Presbyterian bias, became the state religion. On its theological side it but reaffirmed in somewhat stronger language previous confessions of faith accepted by all the colonial churches. In addition to this authorized creed, by its "Associations of Elders and Ministers" it provided for the fellowship and mutual interests of churches. It provided also a recognized authority for the admission and dismissal of candidates for the ministry. Further, in its "Articles" it established "Consociations," assemblages of delegates from all the churches in each county, and gave to these Consociations the final jurisdiction over schismatic

GRACE EPISCOPAL CHURCH AND RECTORY

* There were, in addition, one Baptist and one Episcopal church.

155

churches or their refractory members. When finally Episcopalian, Quaker and Baptist had won the right to embody in church estate and to be free from taxes and fines laid by the government for the benefit of the Congregational church, a long and bitter struggle arose. About the middle of the century, influenced by the great revival, known as "The Great Awakening," the people, discontented with the formalism that had crept into the state church, desired a simpler form of Congregationalism. The power of the Consociations, the strength of the conservative political party, united to beat back the malcontents, and it was not until 1784 that the spread of more tolerant ideas among the people caused the Saybrook Platform to be quietly dropped from the Revised Statutes, and not until 1818, under the new Constitution of Connecticut, that all kindred authority and all religious penalties were swept away. Thereafter religion was purely voluntary. Congregationalism of its own accord preserved the best features of the Saybrook Platform. The principles of "mutual co-operation and friendly confederation of the churches, which were first inaugurated and made effectual by our fathers at Saybrook," wrote Dr. Bacon, "must be regarded as of the greatest value, not only in the development of Congregationalism, but in the moral and social development of the Connecticut people."

The famous Saybrook Convention of May, 1708, was preceded November 11, 1701, by a no less memorable gathering of ministers at the house of the Rev. Thomas Buckingham. There

the first trustees of the future Yale University met for a four days' discussion of the scope and prospects of the Collegiate School of Connecticut, and came to "a comfortable and unanimous opinion" that there would be no great difficulty about the place of location, since Mr. Nathaniel Lynde of Saybrook had offered a suitable house. The large frame house, eighty feet long and one story high, on what in 1701 was Back Lane, now the macadamized road to Saybrook Point, has gone. Its old cellar, visited in 1793 by President Stiles, was "contiguous to the burying yard and near the centre of the peninsula." Its tract of land was recently added to Cypress Cemetery, and a granite bowlder marks the site of Yale's first college building. For fifteen years Saybrook was Yale's first and only home. Here the majority of her students were in residence, and though her peripatetic seniors strayed to Killingworth and Milford, they brought back their

FIRST SITE OF YALE COLLEGE

HEARTSEASE,
A VACATION HOME FOR WORKING GIRLS

teacher and rector to preside at the Saybrook commencement.

The earliest Saybrook record in regard to matters educational is of the services of John Tully, schoolmaster. The great almanac maker received £30 yearly from the town and from each male child—the only sex taught —five pounds of beef, or grain, or corn of proportionate value. The smaller boys and girls were taught at home. The schoolboys were taught reading, writing and casting up of accounts, while the older ones among them went to the master's house to be instructed in navigation and astronomy. At a later period—1783-1853—the little red schoolhouse at the Point at Neck Lane was the temple of learning. Many score of little folks sat under the watchful eye of Miss Sarah Tully, 1757-1802. In the lower half of the schoolhouse a master taught the advanced pupils during the winter term. It is said that in Revolutionary times wooden muskets with tin bayonets were furnished the little ones, and that prim New England dames marched and countermarched their young patriots. History was taught by living it; by the rush to defend the shore against British raiders; by the attempt to recapture the stores secreted at Joseph Tully's, now

Heartsease; by the sacrifice of a Saybrook captain's lands to buy shoes for his men during their winter at Valley Forge; by the building of the colony sloop, *Oliver Cromwell,* and her patrol of the coast; by David Bushnell's firing of the British ships in the Delaware and his earlier attempt in the *American Turtle* to employ a submarine torpedo. This boat was constructed at Saybrook Ferry. It was seven and a half feet long and received its name because it resembled two tortoise shells in contact, with just room for the captain, and air to last him thirty minutes. Paddles, operated by the feet, moved the boat in either direction. Most of the ballast was attached to the keel and could also be used as an anchor. A compass for steering, a barometer to estimate the distance below water, and torpedoes, with torpedo lines for anchoring them, completed the equipment. The greatest trouble was lack of light to steer by, so that, while

THE GRADED SCHOOL

demonstrating that gunpowder could be exploded under water, the *American Turtle* blew up an American schooner instead of the British man-of-war *Cerberus,* exploded a torpedo among a group of English tars sent out to examine the floating thing, and went out of commission with a price set on the much dreaded Yankee inventor's head.

When the country became a nation, Dr. Morse made for the school children their first geography, and Noah Webster improved upon the Dilworth speller of 1740. Lessons in weights, measures and coins followed the rule of three and fractions. The Bible—one for a class—wore its maxims into childish brains. Its poor print gave many a child the chance to shirk and yet save the credits by calling "rubbed out." The "Columbian Orator" and similar compilations inculcated breadth of vision by offering to the young aspirant for honors on annual inspection day, when came the minister heading the school committee, speeches from the Roman Senate, from the British Parliament and from the American Congress, with a spicy admixture of the "Sinner's End" and the "Day of Judgment."

Nowadays, supplementary to the modern graded school is the Acton Library of seven thousand volumes on Parsonage Street, corner of the old Pennywise Lane. The wisdom of the library may be had by any member who pays the yearly fee of one dollar and by any trustworthy person for six pennies the volume or three pennies the magazine. The town contributes one hundred dollars a year, and friendly contributions added to the fees support the library. Fic-

tion, being much sought, especially during the influx of summer visitors, predominates, but works of a more serious nature and books of reference have their place. A pleasant feature is the smaller memorial library of art and music books, started by the young people in memory of one of their number, and continued by the earning of its own books. During three afternoons and evenings each week the librarian has her latch-string out. She has had an interest in her charge from its earliest infancy, when a certain few bought books and circulated them among themselves. When the books became too many for this oversight, Mr. Acton first rented a home for them for two years. Later he gave the land on which the library stands, and with others contributed to erect the present building, that the library might have a larger field of usefulness.

Few Connecticut towns can count among their sons and their descendants a greater number of illustrious names than Saybrook. From camp and pulpit, from the bar and from the highest office within the gift of the people, men trace their ancestry to Saybrook either directly or through those hardy emigrants whom she so early sent into the great western territory. From Geneva, New York, to Marietta, Ohio, many Saybrook men, driving their great covered wagons, settled with their families in the towns springing up along the route and even farther west. Soon after 1783 the exodus westward became the butt of the doubting public. Newspapers revelled in the "springs of brandy" and other marvels the emigrants expected to find. The cartoonists indulged in the corpulent men "Bound for Ohio" and the emaciated "Return," and in pictures of "growing flax yielding ready-made clothing." But these did not daunt the venturesome and far-sighted.

The War of 1812, with its raid on Essex; with the locking in the Thames at New London of the American frigates *Macedonian* and *Constitution* and the consequent British patrol of the coast; and with the constant terror of an attack upon Saybrook, was destructive to her commerce. After the war, when their shipping and allied industries waned, New Haven, New London and Middletown shifted their capital into other industries. Saybrook did not succeed in doing so. Her large ropewalk was destroyed. Shipbuilding and fisheries were more successful elsewhere. Her more ambitious sons sought business away from home, and her wealth gradually dwindled as her opportunities for making it decreased. The age of steam worked on the principle of "to him that hath shall be given and from him that hath not shall be taken that which he hath." The railroad posted its station a mile and a half from the Centre and dignified it by the name of Saybrook Junction,—sometimes an important epithet. It threw its tracks into towns where streams turn the mill wheels, and rushed its side and double tracks where enterprise had added steam equipment or some of the many new plants required to produce the necessities, which the mechanical, electrical or chemical discoveries of the last half century have created. Saybrook dropped out of the race. Nor was she, like Nantucket, suffered to become as a summer resort once more famous. True, she has a summer colony at Fenwick, the little borough reached from the Point by railroad, or by the half-mile carriage bridge. There is the hotel, Fenwick Hall, and a goodly number of pretty cottages, sold or rented under terms which secure a quiet, attractive and well-ordered community. In the winter the lighthouse keepers, the winds and the tides are the only inhabitants, and the latter are frequently most unruly.

Saybrook bore her full share of sacrifice in the Civil War. While grieving and rejoicing with the nation as a whole, the most eventful day to her loyal citizens at home was August 16, 1861, when the few peace-party men in town invited their friends from the surrounding country, even as far as Hartford and New Haven, to see a peace flag-raising in front of Gilbert Pratt's house on Main Street. The Unionists quietly invited a few friends also. There was a lively scrimmage; the prospect of a big fight, led by grim, determined men, and a long tussle over the raising of the Stars and Stripes on the pole intended for the peace flag. Finally they flew aloft, and the peace party, finding the air not easy to breathe, made themselves scarce. There was a call for speeches, in which General Hawley, fresh from the front, led. Some in the crowd may have remembered that the house, first known as Humphrey Pratt's house, had, in its memorable tavern days, sheltered the great soldier and friend of liberty, Lafayette. Tradition says Washington also. Its immense ballroom, with arched roof and spring floor, had echoed since 1773 the merry Virginia reel, the graver square dance, introduced in 1776, and the dignified cotillion, footed by men and women loyal to the United Colonies and to the young nation. The unfurling of a peace-flag, the triumph of a peace-at-any-price policy would have been disloyal to the traditions of liberty and the long, gallant fight for it.

One recent gala-day of the old town should be chronicled. The Yale bicentennial celebration began with the marking in Branford of the site of the old Russell parsonage, where the ten colonial ministers gathered to consider the first steps toward establishing a college, and where tradition says each offered a portion of his precious store of books to form the nucleus of the college library. The closing event of the great celebration was the commemoration at Saybrook of the earliest years, of the small beginning of the modern university that now yearly enrolls nearly three thousand students.

The simple services on November 11, 1901, when the old town was gay with bunting and good cheer, were most satisfactory. The collation in the new Episcopal parish house suggested the good cheer and bustling hospitality of that first commencement dinner at the Rev. Thomas Buckingham's, the details of which have been handed down to us. The services in the Congregational church, the old-time hymns,

"O God, beneath Thy guiding hand," "Now thank we all our God," Luther's hymn, and "O God, our help in ages past," in their appropriateness spoke of effort, struggle and victory, and reminded one of how closely connected in the minds of the founders was the thought of preparation for the ministry and preparation for public service,—the two avowed purposes for which the Collegiate School was established. The historical address by Professor Franklin B. Dexter told in detail the story of Yale's first sixteen years, and Dr. Hart recited Saybrook's claims to "early grandeur" and her deservedly "great veneration." President Hadley, in felicitous words, spoke of Saybrook's monument, "small in size compared with the monumental buildings going up in New Haven, yields to none in the impression of external strength it conveys, carrying in its ruggedness yet a grace beyond the hand of man to better. May we prove ourselves, with our sons and daughters, worthy of our trust, so that when two centuries hence the men of that day shall look back upon the day of our small things, they will see the foundations we in our prosperity have laid by God's grace no less true, no less a living sacrifice to the cause of education, of country and our God, than those of the men who sacrificed here two hundred years ago."

10
The Catching
of the
Cod

THE CENTURY MAGAZINE

AUGUST, 1906

THE CATCHING OF THE COD

BY WILLIAM J. HENDERSON

WITH PICTURES BY M. J. BURNS

HIS is the story of the catching of the cod. It is the story of the cold calculation of man laid against the innocence of fish. It is the story of the trip of the smart Gloucester schooner *Sarah B.* from Boston to the Georges Banks and back. Cap'n Hiram has left a cargo of cod in Boston, and now he has turned his thoughts from westward to eastward. With all his lower sails and a kite or two drawing their best, he is racing past Provincetown, with Minot's Ledge Light far astern. The mounds and pits on the Georges shoals beckon him from beyond the blue rim of the Atlantic. Out yonder are leagues and leagues of water, yellow, green, and blue, and under the surface are millions and millions of finned creatures. Cap'n Hiram cares for few of the many varieties. He is a Banker, and his game is cod.

Whether you are plunging on a transatlantic greyhound through the cobalt swells on the southern edge of the Grand Banks, or cutting the shallows of the Georges on a Boston packet, or slipping across the gloomy headlands of Newfoundland in a Red Cross liner, you will see continually the festooned sails of the fishing schooner and hear always of fish. Perchance as you slide by one of the wide openings in the Newfoundland coast you will note the hundred rocking craft at anchor and say to jovial Capt. Clarke of the *Rosalind:*

"What are those fellows catching over there?"

And he will answer you laconically:
"Fish."

Your laugh will bring no responsive smile to his face, and seeing his earnestness, you will ask:

"What sort?"

"Oh, sometimes they get a halibut and sometimes they get a flounder," he will reply, "but mostly they catch *fish.*"

And then you will understand that, in the language of these latitudes, "fish" means cod.

All the way from the Cholera Banks, some twenty-five miles east of Sandy Hook, to Sambro Head, thence to Cape

Race, and thence to the eastern dive of the Newfoundland Banks into the central abysses of the Atlantic, the fishermen hunt the cod in his lair, and because, like Disko Throop, they have learned to think as cod, they catch him. So Cap'n Hiram, who works the Georges for the Boston market, is driving the *Sarah B.* under all plain sail to the eastward.

Drive her out and drive her in; that is the fisherman's way, for she must be back in time for the Friday market. If she does not catch the market, there are fish to be salted down or packed on the ice. On the Banks she will loaf and invite her prey, but now she hurries, hurries, hurries, slipping through the water like a yacht, fast and staunch, a craft to woo a sailor's eye and to line a fisherman's locker.

Cap'n Hiram carries a motley crew, part Irish, part Swedish, and part plain Yankee. He never carries all of one nationality, for then, in case of trouble, they would stand together. As it is, they will split, and there will surely be some to stand by the skipper. But they are all Bankers like himself, and they know that the luck of the craft is their luck, and the bigger the fare, the bigger each man's tally.

The eight dories are stowed in a nest, that is, one within the other amidships in the waist. The trawl-tubs and the trawls are ready.

No fancy navigation is done on board the schooner *Sarah B.* The compass and the lead are the mainstays of the skipper in finding his way, and he knows every lift and fall of the bottom, every change in the texture or color of the sand. Wake him up out of a ten years' sleep adrift on the Banks and give him two casts of the "dipsey" lead, and he 'll tell you where you are as nicely as a naval officer would after an hour's work at Sumner's method. Fair weather or foul, blow high or blow low, sunshine or fog, it is all one to him: he feels his way through it all with his leaden finger on the bottom. This time he has calculated that fish are loafing about near the north edge of the Banks, and thither he makes his way.

The wind has dropped to a light, cool air from the north when Cap'n Hiram comes upon his chosen ground. As neatly as you would bring an automobile to a door, he rounds up the *Sarah B.* and lets go the mud-hook. Down comes the mainsail and it is furled. The boom is lashed amidships and the riding-sail, a triangular piece of canvas, goes up in its place. The forward sails being in, the schooner rides to the wind under the riding-sail.

The next step is to feel the ground. The eight dories are put over and manned. Each one carries her four tubs filled with trawl-lines. Now, a trawl is an ingenious contrivance of man against the repose and security of fishdom. It consists of a main line, with a lot of smaller lines dangling from it at regular intervals. Each of these smaller lines carries a baited hook. At the beginning of the trawl is an anchor, from which streams a cable, and to the top end of this cable is attached a buoy bearing the standard of the dory, a sort of mark by which it may be identified. A long pole with a disk at its top and on the disk some sort of inscription—that is the fisherman's standard. Sometimes the inscription is a masonic emblem, signifying that the doryman is a brother of the square and level, or it may be some personal design. Two men are the crew of a dory, and dorymates are they for better or for worse. They share fortunes and they must do their full share of the work. The tally is kept by boats, and the boat which does not gather in its quota does not finger much of the profits of the run.

The heaving of a trawl is simple enough, for the line goes out over the quarter and the hooks are thrown clear of the gunwale. When the trawl is hauled in it passes over a "gurdy," or trolley, on the gunwale near the bow and is coiled down in the tub. When the first tub is emptied in heaving a trawl, the end of this line is bent to the beginning of the line in the second tub, and so on till the end of the last one is reached. At the finish, another anchor and a second buoy are put overboard. The entire trawl is now resting on the bottom, and along its entire length are the smaller lines, with their baited hooks, inviting the cod to become a commodity for that Friday market in Boston.

The weather? Well, the fishermen of the Banks are a long way from home, and they have to stay out in the streets, no matter what the weather may be. Eight dories would start from the sides of the *Sarah B.* just the same, even if the seas

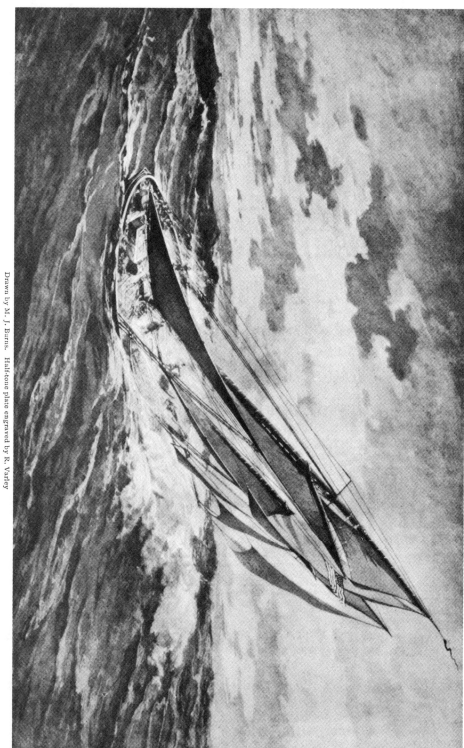

Drawn by M. J. Burns.   Half-tone plate engraved by R. Varley

"WITH ALL HIS LOWER SAILS AND A KITE OR TWO DRAWING THEIR BEST, HE IS RACING PAST PROVINCETOWN"

were ranging up against a horizon that was as close as the rims of a saucepan.

The first day they put off toward eight points of the compass—north, northeast, east, southeast, south, southwest, west, and northwest. From the schooner as a center eight long trawls radiate toward the circular horizon. It is a huge cod web, with the old spider, Cap'n Hiram, sitting in the middle, waiting for his prey. Or, if you like it better, the whole contrivance is an octopus, with its far-reaching tentacles out-spread to find out where

upon him with the deadly barbed hook in our hands and the Friday market in our minds.

Cap'n Hiram mentally blocks out a fine spacious square of old ocean. This is to be his battle-field. The top boundary of it is a line running east and west some distance south of his present anchorage. He gathers in his dories and gets his anchor. Now he sails down to one end of his north boundary,—let us say, for example, the west end,—and there he puts Dory No. 1 overboard. As he sails eastward along

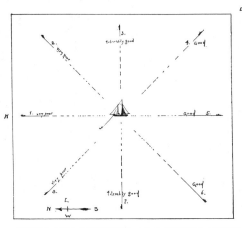

"FROM THE SCHOONER AS A CENTER EIGHT LONG TRAWLS RADIATE TOWARD THE CIRCULAR HORIZON"

THE SPIRAL PATH IN LOOKING FOR A LOST DORY

the victims are. Dory No. 1 has laid her trawl to the north, and when she hauls it she finds a very poor catch. Dory No. 2 to the northeast and Dory No. 8 to the northwest have the same sort of luck. It is evident that the cod lurks not in these quarters. Abeam of the schooner on the east is Dory No. 3, and on the west tumbles over the foaming crests Dory No. 7. They lift their trawls to report that the catch is tolerably good.

But it is from the other three dories in the southerly hemisphere of the compass that the cheering news comes. The catch is good, and as the skipper turns his gaze over the taffrail at the heaving expanse of water south of him, he knows that the fish are down there. And now it is time to call in the scouts. We have located the enemy, and the next move is to make him ours. Over the sandy, water-hidden ridges on the bottom to the south of us he is lying in fancied security. We shall descend

his line he drops the other dories at regular intervals. They are thus ranged along the line like racing crews at an intercollegiate regatta, each in its own lane of water.

When Dory No. 1 is put overboard she lets go the anchor of her trawl and pulls away directly down wind, paying out the trawl as she goes. When her four tubs are bare of line, she drops her second trawl-kedge and hangs on for a time to let the fish bite. Dory No. 2 proceeds in the same manner along her lane, and the other boats follow suit. The result is that, as all the trawls are of the same length, the eight dories bring up abreast of one another on the base-line at the south end of the skipper's blocked out field of operation.

All this sounds very simple. But stop a bit. The land is far away, many miles to the westward. There are fifty fathoms of green water between the surface and the

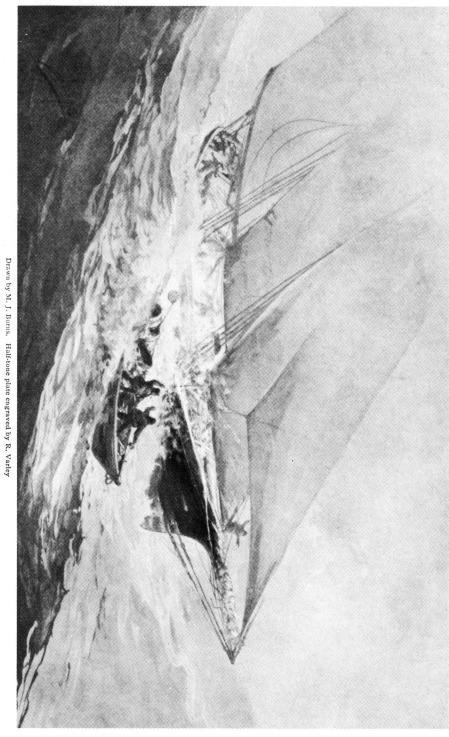

Drawn by M. J. Burns.   Half-tone plate engraved by R. Varley

"ALL THE DORIES SAVE ONE HAVE BEEN SIGHTED"

Drawn by M. J. Burns. Half-tone plate engraved by H. C. Merrill

"LEAPING, AND PLUNGING BOWS UNDER"

bottom. The Atlantic spreads two thousand miles to the eastward, and the deep-sea swell runs ceaselessly day and night. The pitiless winds torture the sea forever. Calms come sometimes in the sweet summer months, to be sure, but with them comes fog, the deadliest enemy of the liner and the fisherman alike. To be lost in a fog in an open boat more than a hundred miles from the coast is not a thing for which even a fisherman learns to have a liking, yet it is not an uncommon

boundary, trying to sight all his dories on the way and to ascertain if all is going well with them. As he navigated out to the Banks, so he bisects diagonally his square. The compass holds him to his southwest course and the lead line discloses to him the secrets of the bottom. He knows that bottom as you know the floor of your room, and when he reaches the southwest corner of his fishing lot he is at the precise spot where Dory No. 1 should drop her second trawl-anchor.

Drawn by M. J. Burns. Half-tone plate engraved by R. C. Collins

"SENDS A LONG, WAILING BLAST DOWN WIND"

experience for him. In autumn come the gales, and then to hold fast to a trawl, with the dory pitching bows under and the heavy line threatening to drag her to destruction, is not a pleasing diversion.

Now Cap'n Hiram of the *Sarah B.* finds himself on the Banks in ordinary conditions. It has grown again to a wholesail breeze, and the schooner piles up a smother of foam under her lee bow as she plunges over the roaring crests at a seven-knot gait. But Cap'n Hiram is an old hand at the game. He makes his first move according to the established rules. From the east end of his north boundary, where he dropped Dory No. 8, he sweeps with the wind over his starboard quarter right down to the west end of the south

Now Cap'n Hiram puts the helm of the *Sarah B.* hard up, and jibes, while the cook, the only member of the crew left on board, shifts the head sheets. Now the skipper stands across the base-line of his ground to the eastward. He can run that line with great accuracy, and his purpose is to ascertain whether the eight trawls have been set. The wind is "breezing up," as sailormen say, and the sea is rising. That makes little difference to the *Sarah B.;* she is snug enough for anything short of half a gale, and she threshes through the foaming windrows, a little queen of the salt surge. The dories, having dropped the anchors at the southerly ends of their trawls, start back to the north. It is now their business to reverse their first process. They lift their trawls and get the fish. Fish is what they came for, and the Friday market is beckoning down behind the western horizon.

Cap'n Hiram, having come to the easterly end of his base-line, starts to sweep up his fleet. He reaches all the way across the field on a wide starboard tack, with his sheets lifting a little, so that the schooner is not quite closehauled. His eyes peer ahead on both sides, for the skipper is looking to sight the dories as he quarters his ground like an old setter in a quail-field. All the way across to the westerly side the schooner skims, and not a dory sighted.

Helm 's alee, and about she goes. Now on the port tack, the *Sarah B.* heads to fetch the middle of the easterly side. Something ought to heave in sight soon. It 's a little thick up to windward, and the observation is limited. But wait a moment. Almost as the schooner's helm goes down for her tack on the easterly line, Dory No. 8 heaves into view. She was the last to be put overboard at the northerly end of the line, and she is not over half-way up to the start. Tubs and fish lying in her bottom show that her two men have not been idle.

The *Sarah B.* sweeps thundering into the shining hollows just to windward of her. Hoarse shouts ring across the few rods of intervening water. Cap'n Hiram knows how the catch is coming. The schooner slips away on the starboard tack again, off for the other side of the cod-lot. Two more tacks bring her up to the north end of the field. All the dories save one have been sighted. There are signs of fog, and Dory No. 3 is missing. Where is she? There is no question about one thing: wherever she is, she is holding fast to her trawl. To lose it would be to go helplessly adrift, with fog driving down upon her, the wind hardening, and the sea getting up a very nasty kick.

Cap'n Hiram must gather in his other dories, and then he must hunt for No. 3. The first thing to do is to try the spiral path. Picking up No. 1 as she lies over her anchor at the starting-point, the skipper bears down, with the wind on his port quarter, for the center of his field. He can find that center with the faithful lead-line. Once there, he begins to sail from

that point around and around in a series of constantly widening circles till he has swept over his entire field and even beyond its limits. In this sweeping he picks up his other dories, but where is No. 3?

The thickness grows, and over it begins to creep the dimness of late afternoon. The blue of the leaping sea hardens into a cold gray. The silver foam feathers into snowy smoke. Down in the gathering shadows Dory No. 3 is leaping, and plunging bows under. The spray hurls itself over her sharp nose in hissing streams. She tugs at the trawl as if she would break its bonds and free herself, to go driving whither the wind would carry her. The doryman in the bow clings to the trawl. His mate bends to the oars, to ease the strain by rowing up against the sea. To make headway is impossible. All that the two can hope for is to hold their own and wait for Cap'n Hiram, who they know is searching in the fog, to come and find them.

And now all the world is gray and only a few rods wide. The ghostly waves rush suddenly out of gray nowhere on one side to vanish into it on the other. The *Sarah B.* herself begins to wear the aspect of a staggering specter as she reels across the half-hidden billows. Cap'n Hiram's face takes on a strained look. He leans forward from the wheel as if he could peer into the fog and find the dory by straining his gleaming eyes. He is too old a seaman to be deluded by that false sense of isolation which creeps over the landsman in a fog.

He knows that out yonder behind the impenetrable gray curtain lies a heaving ocean filled with moving craft. He knows, too, that while in clear weather one may cruise for miles and miles without meeting a sail, in a fog there is always something lying in wait for the sailor. But most of all he thinks of his dory. He yearns for that boatload of fish. He worries because the boat may go astray and he may have to lose valuable time searching for it. He hardly fears its entire loss, though he knows that is not an impossibility. But the weather has not yet reached an alarming state, although it would frighten a landsman almost to death to be out there in the schooner, not to speak of the dory.

The skipper has a mechanical fog-horn,

Drawn by M. J. Burns. Half-tone plate engraved by C. W. Chadwick

"DORY NO. 3 IS SEEN UP TO WINDWARD"

one of those which you blow by pumping wind through it with a crank. He leaves the wheel ever and anon and sends a long, wailing blast down wind through the shroud of mist. Every shriek of this eery voice is followed by a silence which is only accentuated by the smashing of the seas against the schooner's bows. Dreary, dreary it all is, and night coming on to make of dreariness a deadly gloom. At last a wider circle brings Cap'n Hiram and the *Sarah B.* across the northern boundary of the field, and there the skipper stops long enough to anchor a dory with a light swinging from the top of her mast at the top of No. 3's lane, so that it may act as a guide to that boat in case her crew succeeds in pulling her up to the head of the field. This same light will later on act as a mark for Cap'n Hiram when he is threshing through the night in his search for the lost boat.

His wide circle swings him outside the eastern boundary of his field and down beyond the southern end, for down there the dory might be if she had gone adrift. This, however, the skipper regards as unlikely.

"It ain't no such weather as that yet," he says to himself.

Then he hauls sharp up on the wind and begins a beat up to the top of the field once more. This time he does not sail in circles, but in short tacks from one side of No. 3's lane to the other. If she is anywhere along the lane he must find her in this way. As the night sets in, the weather grows hot and murky.

"We 'll have somethin' doin' before dawn," mutters Cap'n Hiram, as he twists the wheel another spoke.

Now the wind falls light for a time, and then it comes in from the southwest. A low mutter of distant thunder floats down across the writhing swells. The skipper scents an approaching squall, but that gives him no concern for his schooner. She is snug enough. He does begin to be uneasy about the dory, for if the weather becomes very dirty, she may not be able to hold on. Presently there is a smart puff and a rattle of snarling thunder that tell of the near rush of the squall.

The fog whirls and staggers before the rising breeze. Suddenly there is a break, and a half-buried star drops a watery gleam through the rift. Five minutes later the fog is torn to tatters and goes writhing away to leeward like the smoke of a twelve-inch gun. At the same instant the squall breaks. Pandemonium is loose. Shrieks in the rigging, crashes against the bows, and the groaning of tortured timbers, mingle with the bellowings of the thunder. The sea gets up with incredible celerity, and the schooner is tossed like a chip. Can a dory live? Indeed it can. Dories have lived through gales. There is nothing better in the way of a small boat than a dory.

Cap'n Hiram has the *Sarah B.* on the starboard tack. The seas are pounding viciously against her weather side and sending tons of spray scurrying through her humming cordage. The crew is lined up along the rail, with eyes straining into the darkness. Suddenly a cry comes from forward. It is the voice of the cook.

"I see her!"

"Get out, cookey! Your eyes are full of gravy."

But now all are tense with anxiety. Crash! The heavens are split, and a blinding zigzag of lightning rips down the sky. For an instant its glare lights up the sea, and Dory No. 3 is seen up to windward, pitching like a cork. Instinctively some hands leap to flatten in sheets as the schooner is jammed hard on the wind. It 's like a yacht race, only tenfold more wild.

"By the great hook block!" says the skipper, "she 's hanging to her trawl yet!"

Another tack, and the *Sarah B.* is brought down just to windward of the dory. One of her hands heaves the painter as the schooner forereaches on her, and it is caught by one of the fishermen on deck. The suspense is over, for in another moment Dory No. 3 and her men are safe, and the *Sarah B.'s* crew slacks away its tense cord of anxiety.

"And now," says Cap'n Hiram, "we 'll not mind a little breeze o' wind."

And wind enough and to spare the skipper has, for it blows smartly for the next three days. Nevertheless the *Sarah B.* gets her fare, for that is what she is out there to do. "Captains Courageous" Kipling called the Banks skippers, and that is what they truly are. They fish and fish and fish, and when their holds are full of fish, they go home. Meanwhile all the

Drawn by M. J. Burns.   Half-tone plate engraved by G. M. Lewis

"THE 'SARAH B.' MAKES THE PACE A LIVELY ONE"

varieties of celestial and demoniacal weather of which the roaring forties are productive come along and make trouble for them; but they plot off their squares and fish them down in spite of it all.

So when Cap'n Hiram gets his fare, he points the schooner's nose for Cape Cod. There 's a huge sea still running, but the schooner has it astern of her, and as every roarer sweeps under her, it gives her a mighty push homeward. The riding-sail has been sent down, and a double-reefed mainsail set in its place. Driven along by this, her reefed foresail, and her jib, the *Sarah B.* makes the pace a lively one, and as she toboggans down the steep olive slopes, she shoves her bowsprit clear into the smother of foam under her bows and the water roars right up to the foremast foot.

Not alone is the *Sarah B.* Out of the depths behind the rim of the ocean have risen the *Mary Brown* of Chatham, and the *Phineas Phinney* of Gloucester, and five or six others. They have all taken the breeze over their taffrails, turned tail on the Georges and headed for Boston. It 's an easy run this time, for the catch was quick and big, and the Friday market will be there for all hands.

But, nevertheless, the man who lands his cargo first will make the best of the bargain, and so there is a race for Boston Light and the land of the codfish-buyer— a race not of gingerbread yachts, but of toilers of the sea, fishermen of the Banks, storm kings every one of them.

And when the fish are landed, it is up and away again to do it all over, till days of doing are ended and final night closes over the cod-fields.

11
The Queer Folk of the Maine Coast

A CORNER IN NO MAN'S LAND

The Queer Folk of the Maine Coast

BY HOLMAN DAY

PHOTOGRAPHS BY FREDERICK THOMPSON

OF old, muskets drove the Abnakis off the coast of Maine. To-day, money is driving away another race.

Between Kittery Point and Quoddy Head " resorters " have acquired hundreds of headlands and thousands of islands. A phalanx of cottages fronts the sea. More than half the States in the Union are represented in these summer colonies. Cove and cape, the coast is pretty well monopolized by non-residents; " no-trespass " signs are so thickly set that they form a blazed trail. The man from the city resents intrusion. For that matter, the queer squatter people who have been dispossessed find little relish in being stared at as human curiosities. Therefore they have hidden themselves in the deep gashes of the coast cliffs; their little huts are now at the head of crooked coves where pleasure craft do not venture; or they have located on little nubbins of islands that city people do not buy, for these islands may be approached only at flood-tide. And in their retreats the " queer folk "

resent intrusion as heartily as do the rich folk on their reserves.

So the " queer folk " live alone—and it is said that isolation develops eccentricity. The ocean creeps to the doors of their huts, and the winter waves thunder in their ears—and there are those who say that the din of the sea beats curious ideas into the head.

Even the Maine " native " himself, the thrifty farmer who sells his produce to the city " sojourner " or takes summer boarders, does not understand the queer folk of the lonely coves very well. The nooks that they have chosen for hiding-places have no roads leading to them. The islands that they have pre-empted have been " set off " by act of the Legislature from the nearest coast towns, in order that the towns may not have the unfortunates on their hands as paupers. These people who have been abandoned dwell in a sort of " no man's land." They do not pay taxes, they do not vote. Fashion is close to many of them, just over that ridge of coast ledge or down that stretch of water—for fashion has picked most of the choice spots on the Maine coast for its sojourn. But the queer folk are not interested in any display that fashion may make. They are not envious, they do not want to beg. Where penury and pride meet in the cities there are heartburnings. But the man tossing in the battered dory in the swash of the millionaire's yacht neither sighs nor glares, provided he be one of the queer folk. For the queer folk are queer in one respect especially: they dwell content in their own world, which is often a world of illusion—for solitariness and the sea breed strange thoughts.

Ossian Dustin, of Newcastle, would not change places with a millionaire, so he says. Yet Uncle Ossian, at eighty, lives alone in a little hut with a dirt floor, and earns about fifty dollars a year by sawing fire-wood and doing odd jobs. But fifty dollars supply his frugal needs, and he has the most of his time to devote to hunting for Cap'n Kidd's treasure, in the buried existence of which he implicitly believes.

The case of Uncle Ossian illustrates the type of that content that relieves

these hidden human tragedies of the Maine coast of some of their pitifulness. During most of his long life, as often as he has found opportunity, Uncle Ossian has hunted and dug along the ragged Lincoln coast. He has toiled nights, for the most part, believing that in the night a treasure-seeker can best circumvent the enchantments laid on buried pirate spoils. He has kept vigil oftenest in the region of Cod Lead Nubble. He searches with a treasure-rod made by his own hands. He has the tip of a cow's horn, plugged with wood and containing various metals. In the wooden plug are stuck parallel strips of whalebone, and he clutches these strips, one in each hand, and walks along, balancing the tip of horn. When he passes over the famous iron pot the tip, thus is his belief, will turn down and point at the buried treasure. There is nothing remarkable in Uncle Ossian's quest, for other men in Maine have hunted for Kidd's treasure. But his radiant courage and his unfailing optimism are striking. He believes that he " is always right on the edge " of finding the gold. He says

his spade has struck against the iron pot several times, but that enchantment has whisked away the treasure. He expects that eventually his own charms will prevail over the powers of evil. He believes that the long waiting and the disappointments have been merely a test of his courage and good faith —remarkable philosophy in a man who is eighty years old and has not succeeded. He is reanimated occasionally by the sight of a figure all of shining gold that comes rowing up the reach from the sea, and he is confident that this is a good spirit sent to guide him to the treasure, and that the spirit will sometime prevail over the imps who watch the iron pot.

Uncle Ossian affirms that he has passed as happy a life as any man he knows; he says that the money will

Bushy Island, where Hermit Tripp toiled at Treasure-digging

THE DIVIDED HOUSEHOLD OF LITTLE SPRUCE

"come in handy" in his old age, and that he shall first buy a stone for his mother's grave, and then a house with a floor in it for himself. It can scarcely be said that Uncle Ossian's unfailing cheerfulness springs from any philosophy of life that he has evolved. But after our talk I came out of his dingy hut with the feeling that probably some of the proud folk in the cottages down the bay needed pity more than he.

On Little Spruce island I found three old men, brothers—William, Daniel, and Nehemiah Shanks. They have lived there all their lives in a tumble-down little shelter. They are melancholy old men. They are contented, but the sea has brought to them a strange, brooding, wistful solemnity. William and Daniel never married. Nehemiah has had a poor little romance that broke his heart. When he was young he used to go with his father to Portland to sell their fare of fish. The only woman to whom he had ever spoken was his mother—for no one except the Shanks family has ever lived on Little Spruce. A woman of the water-side in Portland made him her prey for the sake of his little hoard of savings, married him, induced him to forge his father's name and draw the family savings from the bank—and then deserted him. He went home with his confession of wrong-doing.

"Then you must look out for the boys after I'm dead," said his father, forgiving him. Nehemiah has spent his life "looking out for the boys," who are now infirm old men. "It is my duty in return for my father's pardon of my wrong-doing," he told me, "and I have tried to do my best. I am the youngest, and I am best able to work."

For more than twenty years William has never come out of the hut into the sunshine. He told me that he feared the sun might heat his brains and interfere with his life-work, which is the composition of poetry. There is a blanket hung across one end of the hut. William sits behind this blanket and fixes his eyes on the sunlight that enters through a knot-hole, and "composes." He states that now he is the author of a thousand pieces

179

of poetry. He has committed nothing to paper. He has memorized all of them, he says.

While William idles, Nehemiah tills the little garden, catches fish, digs clams, and cooks. He is cheerfully the burden-bearer, and with some pride says that he is the head of the family; for when his father imposed the trust on him he did so with a ceremony truly patriarchal: he gave into Nehemiah's hands the staff on which he had leaned for many years, saying that it should be the badge of Nehemiah's authority. Nehemiah described the scene to me, tears trickling down his wrinkled cheeks. Memory was only a partial spur to this grief.

Daniel, after more than sixty years of obedience, had become a most amazing rebel. He had declared that another flood had been prophesied to him in a vision, and that he had been ordered to build an ark on Little Spruce. Little Spruce is owned by a lady in Boston, as part of an extensive holding of islands. The Shanks brothers have been permitted to remain as squatters on condition that they do not disturb the standing timber. Nehemiah gave this promise to the manager of the estate.

Daniel, though threescore and ten, took the family axe, hand-saw, and hammer and proceeded to his labors on his ark. Nehemiah stood in front of the lordly spruce that Daniel was about to attack with the axe, and in the name of the Shanks family forbade him to chop. Daniel had the zeal of monomania and insisted. Then Nehemiah brandished the family staff and threatened to chastise the disobedient son of their father. Daniel, in a frenzy, made at his brother with the axe, routed him, captured the

HERMIT TRIPP

staff, chopped it up, and then began on the tree. He laid waste quite a section of woodland before Nehemiah got word to the agent. Then in high dudgeon Daniel built a shack of his own. He lives in it and refuses to speak to his brothers. Nehemiah, tall, grave, dignified, with the flowing white beard of a patriarch, stood upon a knoll and pointed over to Daniel's hut and told me of the unfortunate affair, sorrowfully, without anger. Daniel, realizing that his misdeeds were exposed to a stranger, shook his fists from afar and leaped up and down in what was apparently ecstasy of rage. He waylaid me before I had left Little Spruce, and informed me that after being bossed by his brother for more than sixty years he proposed to run his own affairs for the rest of his life. Nehemiah came in his turn to the shore after Daniel had trudged away to his hut, cracking his hard little fists above his head in his temper.

"I still hope to be able to meet father at the door of heaven and tell him that I kept the Shanks family together and kept it decent, as he would have liked to have me keep it," said Nehemiah, sadly. "Daniel was always hard to manage; father found him so. But I think he will come back to his home, for I am the only one in the family who can cook things as mother used to cook them."

Bushy Island, to which I came when a poor little human drama was at its climax, is a bare handful of earth without a tree on it. Quarter of a century ago Henry Tripp, after roving along the coast, settled there. He was an old man even then, bent at his hips into almost a right angle. Fourteen years ago a woman, as old as he, came from the main and dwelt with him in his little house. In fourteen years she was off that patch of island only twice.

"Hermit Tripp," as he was called, believed that Kidd had buried his treasure on Bushy. Old and decrepit as he was, he began to dig the island. He wore out shovel after shovel at his task. When he died he had shovelled nearly half the island off into the sea, cleaning the earth down to bed-rock.

He died in August, 1908. On the night of his death a summer gale swept the coast, wrecking cottages and flattening acres of trees on the main near Bushy. When the old woman realized that Tripp was dying she took a big hand-bell and, though so weak and old that she could walk only with difficulty, she went out on the high land of the island and rang the bell with all her strength, hoping that in some lull of the gale the sound would be heard on the main.

NEHEMIAH SHANKS, THE PATRIARCH OF LITTLE SPRUCE

At midnight she went to the hut to minister to the old man, and found him dead. Then she resumed her vigil on the shore, ringing the bell, blinded by the lightning, drenched by the rains, and blown about by the gale.

People heard and came off to the island the next day. But Bushy Island is one of those "set-off" places, a no man's land so far as the law goes. Three towns at first disclaimed responsibility for the burial expenses of a pauper. The old woman stayed alone with her dead a second night. Then came men and dug his grave, a pebble-toss from his hut, and laid him there. Some one read a bit from the tattered old Bible that was found in the house. Those who had buried the old man went away and left the old woman alone. Chance and idle curiosity brought me to Bushy one day. I had supposed that charity had provided a home elsewhere for the lonely tenant. But she was still there. She was ill, she was hungry, she had not

sufficient strength to walk or to build a fire. There is no fresh water on Bushy. She had a scanty supply in a jug.

It is not necessary to go into the details of the measures promptly taken for her relief. At first she concealed her name. We discovered what it was from some old letters that were flying about the little yard. She "had been some one" once on a time. She has a brother living, a worthy and prominent man in an inland town. He came promptly when I communicated with him, and went with me to visit his sister in the hut on Bushy Island. He had not seen her, had not heard from her, for many years. He had sought for her, but she had disappeared. He and she are the only ones left of a well-known family.

One can imagine how fiction would have handled this reunion. But real life has its own grim methods. It was high tide and the launch swung close to the corner of the hut, under which the waves were lapping. The brother hesitated, misery on his countenance.

"Go in first, please!" he implored.

She gave him only a careless glance when he sat down in the unspeakable shelter.

"For God's sake, take me out!" he gasped. "I can't stand this!"

We were not in the place ten seconds. He had not heart or strength to make this forlorn creature know him for what he was. He hurried into the launch and left the island. This is how fact tersely dismissed a situation that fiction would have lingered over.

It is proper in this connection to state that later the brother appointed me his agent and almoner, and before the fall grew late the woman was re-

THE OLD WOMAN OF BUSHY ISLAND

ENTERTAINING THE MISSIONARY—SUNDAY ON MALAGA ISLAND

moved from the island to a comfortable home, where she is now cared for. Her mental faculties that had been impaired by her privations have been regained in a measure, but she has never made any inquiries regarding her family. On our visits to her we find her reading her Bible and, to use her words, " preparing my soul for the great change."

This case also brought to my attention a character who ought to be interesting from a sociological point of view. He is an addition to the varied army of vagrants—he is a water tramp. While search for some honest persons who would take the old woman as a boarder was in progress, those interested in the case carried cooked food each day and plenty of dainties. She declared that she felt perfectly safe to stay alone nights—and, in fact, the hut was too wretched a place to serve as a lodging for any person except the poor old creature who had become accustomed to it.

Now appears a human derelict in a barnacled old dory! He seemed to sniff those food delicacies from afar. He billeted himself on the poor old woman, coming in the edge of the evening, re-

maining the night, and departing before charity came again with heaped hands.

This especial water tramp has been a peregrinator in Casco waters for many years, a stolid, weather-beaten man, and even the gulls of the bay take more thought as to where they may perch for the night. There are a dozen or more of his ilk scattered alongshore. The city man who comes down to his cottage in the spring and finds a window forced, the left-overs of his larder devoured, and his summer clothes gone, has this gentry of the coast to thank. The water tramp steals only what he can eat and what he can wear. He dwells in a cottage as long as it suits his taste or convenience, or until the crackers, canned goods, and firewood are gone. Then he moves to the next. He is not a good housekeeper, and the cottager who finds his débris in the spring has a bad quarter of an hour and a lively desire for vengeance. If he will keep sharp watch, he will find his old coat on the back of a " dory vagabond." But it doesn't trouble the water tramp if he is sent to jail. He goes up-country stoically, and returns to seek his living in the same old way.

But there is one who stands forth from among these petty thieves with almost the proportions of a modern Viking. He came coasting along from Nova Scotia in a gray and seamed old Hampton boat, leisurely seeking adventures and three

JAKE, GREAT-GRANDSON OF THE PIONEER OF MALAGA

meals a day, and arrived in the Pemaquid region.

He lingered there for some weeks. His name was MacTush, he had the swagger of a border chieftain, and his hair was the hair of a Norseman, and he found favor in the eyes of a wife whose husband was away upon the Grand Banks on a "mack'rel-chancin'" trip. So the stranger stole the wife, four children, and such furniture from the house as could be stowed in the Hampton boat. He sailed back to Nova Scotia.

As time went on the wife regretted. But it was not regret for the abandoned husband. Here once more fact differs from fiction. She was sorry that she had

not been able to take more of her belongings. The Viking's hut in Nova Scotia was but scantily furnished. She kept remembering certain choice things that had been left behind in the hurry of departure and on account of lack of room in the Hampton boat. She urged her new lord to go back and get another load. The story of how she urged came out later in the Lincoln County court. The Viking went back a few months after his first foray. The wife told him that the house would be locked up and the husband away to the Banks once more. The freebooter was removing the rest of the furniture— finding the house untenanted, as the wife had prophesied; but he was apprehended by friends of the absent husband. The judge in imposing sentence stated that a thief who would steal a man's wife, four children, and half his furniture, and then come back after the rest of the household goods, was too much of a rogue to expect mercy, and MacTush is in jail for a number of years.

Louds Island, off the coast of Bristol, occupies perhaps a more anomalous position than any other land along the Atlantic seaboard. It has a considerable population of thrifty fishermen and farmers; they live in good houses and are intelligent. They and their ancestors have dwelt there for more than one hundred and fifty years. But the men of the island have never voted in any election, town or State or national. They have never paid any State, town, or county taxes. They resisted the draft at the time of the Civil War; and drove the officers off the island with clubs and rocks. They say that they do not need the protecting arm of State or national government. They raise money for schools and roads, elect municipal officers to administer affairs, and seem to get along very comfortably as an independent principality. Flattering overtures have been made by Bristol; by coming into the fold the islanders would receive State school money, have an opportunity to vote, and obtain other advantages. But Louds Island will not affiliate. There has never been a crime committed on the island, no one ever locks his door, and almost every one is a relation of some one else.

While Louds Island is genially beckoned into the family by Bristol, Malaga Island is getting the cold shoulder from Phippsburg—the town that contains the site of ancient "Augusta," pioneer of all New England settlements.

As a "no man's land" Malaga has more striking peculiarities than any other island alongshore. There are about fifty persons on it, of all grades of negro blood, and most of them descendants of a runaway slave who came and hid there more years ago than any man about there remembers. These people form a strange clan. They have married and intermarried until the trespass on consanguinity has produced its usual lamentable effects. They are as near to being children of nature as it is possible for people to be who are only a stone's throw from the mainland and civilization. They lack entirely the spirit of thrift and of providing for future emergencies. Winter after winter, through all the years, they have shivered and starved, but never does November find a wood-pile on Malaga, nor a week's supply of food in reserve. To counsel on economy and to preachment on thrift they are as inattentive as little children would be. A coast missionary took in hand one especially improvident family of six—father, mother, and four children well grown. Spurred by him, they fished, dug clams, sold bait to trawlers, and at the end of the summer had saved about seventy dollars among them. Then the missionary went away, confident that at least one Malaga family would reach "March Hill" in comparative comfort. When his back was turned they used for kindlings the shingles that he had given them for the repair of their miserable hut, bought six dogs in order that each member of the family could have his own pet, and spent the rest of the money for sweets, pickles, jellies, and fancy groceries.

Charity, after a few experiences with the "Malagaites," as they are called by their indifferent neighbors on the main, grows a bit discouraged. Donations of money bring more harm to them than otherwise. Old clothes and a doling of something to eat form charity's only resource. A State agent who looks after paupers in unorganized places goes over to Malaga occasionally, thins out the dogs, travels about to see whether medical attendance is required by any one, gives those actually hungry an order on the nearest grocery-store, and does not trouble himself to give good advice; it was discovered a great many years ago that good advice is wasted in Malaga. A while ago the agent took along a notary and had marriages performed between six couples whose naïve ideas of wedlock had not reached out to the fact that a ceremony was necessary.

In summer all the people of the colony work as best they are able, but the scope of what they can do is so limited and the returns in money so small that it is not surprising that winter finds them with hands empty.

Women put on trousers and boots and dig clams with the men. Occasionally farmers on the main hire the women to work in the fields. The men are too lazy. The woman who earns the most money is one who lives in what was once the cabin of a schooner. She takes in washings from the main. As she cannot stand upright in her house, she climbs upon the roof and there toils at her tub.

Certain amateur sociologists have been wondering and planning what to do with Malaga and the Malagaites. Popular subscription has erected a neat little schoolhouse, in which a teacher, paid by the State, began her work in November, 1908. The children will be taught how to read and write, and the women will take lessons in sewing and darning and patching. There have been few needles on Malaga in the past.

The people of the island are singularly

susceptible to religious influence, and most of them row to the main on Sundays to attend church. With the exception that their ideas of the social code of morals are primitive, they are blameless so far as their relations with the world go; they are not vicious, they show none of that sullenness that marks similar strata of society, and they extend the rude hospitality of their island with touching warmth and sincerity.

The rude gashes in the coast of Maine afford good hiding-places for those who desire to leave the world behind. One day a youth dropped off a coaster and looked about a Maine fishing-village. He stayed long enough to fall desperately in love with a girl whose father owned a Grand Banks smack and was accordingly in the upper ranks of village society. The young man, poorly clad and a stranger, was repulsed, naturally. When he undertook to explain that he was a runaway from a wealthy English family he was looked upon with still greater suspicion.

He set at work digging clams for a living and feeding his soul on occasional fleeting glimpses of the girl he loved. His story had been scoffed at with so great unanimity that he did not make any more revelations regarding his prospects. But one day he appeared at the office of a lawyer in the shire town of the county, and produced papers just received from England that required only his signature and his oath to yield him $15,000 from an estate in his native country. He got the money, put it into a bank, bought out the general store in the fishing-village, married the girl, and from the butt became the boss of the place. It would be pleasing to state that he remained the boss and lived happy ever after, but again does grim fact tip over fiction's apple-cart—as life is lived in the cracks o' the coast!

That young man was instructed by the lawyer in the use of a check-book, and it did not seem like spending real money when he wrote a check. He bought all the fishing-boats for sale along that part of the coast. Every one who had anything to sell hurried up from cove, island, and far inlet and sold it to this young man, who had become drunken with flattery and adulation after having

been despised so long. Travelling salesmen heard of him, and descended and filled his store to bursting with goods—goods that he tossed out on credit to the throng that hung around him.

When, at the end of eight months or so, he got a notice from the bank stating that he had overdrawn his account he did not understand, and went to the lawyer to have the matter explained. When it was explained he was dazed. He had not thought that fifteen thousand dollars could ever be cleaned out by writing on little slips of paper!

His affairs were so mixed that he was obliged to assign, and it is easy to understand what an assignment would do to a man who did not know that fifteen thousand dollars do not make an inexhaustible treasure. I am afraid that what I have heard is true: that he is digging clams again.

But while he lasted he was the most talked-about young man along a good bit of coast. Even old "Six-fingered Simpson" of the Crumples heard of him —and the Crumples is at the end of the world! Simpson pawed over his scanty possessions, found something to sell, and came up and sold it. He had not been to the mainland before in twenty years. The list of things that Simpson had never seen comprised all of man's inventions between locomotives and phonographs. The new Midas of the coast had a phonograph, and he was willing to amaze Simpson. But Simpson was not amazed. He listened, walked around the contrivance, and declared that some one hidden down-cellar was making the noise that came through the horn. He listened to the parlor organ without comment. But when he rejoined his son, who had been waiting for him at the shore, afraid to venture among those devil gimcracks, he said:

"The most of it didn't amount to much. But you ought to have seen the critter in the parlor. His woman set down 'side of it, and it showed its teeth to her, and she cuffed along them teeth and trod on its tail, and it growled and whined away savage enough, now, I tell ye!"

So we turned at the Crumples and came home from our exploring, for it is plain that the Crumples is at the end of the world!

12
The Measure
of Content

Drawn by Sidney M. Chase.

"THEY AIN'T NO LOBSTERS," WAS THE TERSE REPLY.

SCRIBNER'S MAGAZINE

JUNE, 1908

THE MEASURE OF CONTENT

By Sidney M. Chase

ILLUSTRATIONS BY THE AUTHOR

IN the blue summer night the stars are beginning to fade. Wakened birds are twittering in the branches. A gray mist is rising from the fields, and in the air is the fresh, damp smell of early morning. Lights appear here and there in the dusky landscape, and down the silent road comes the "chug-chug" of rubber boots, as dark, clumsy-gaited figures make for the beach. Lanterns are bobbing about the tumbled cluster of fish houses, and the creak of thole-pins and the plash of oar blades tell that other fishermen are out. In the blue haze over the ocean hang the dim shapes of dories, with sprit-sails set, running for the fishing grounds. The little noises of preparation, the grating of a keel on the wet gravel, the dip of oars, and the lapping of waves against the boats, only complete the great, cool, damp silence of the morning. And the salt tang in the air is very good to smell!

If, fresh from the roar and turmoil of a large city, you will come to any one of a hundred villages on the Maine coast, and rise at three o'clock of a summer morning, you will enjoy something like what I have just described. In countless nooks and corners of that coast line, almost as if they had been swept up by the Atlantic and left stranded by the ebb tide, are battered and storm-beaten groups of fish houses, and sea-worn old salts who use them. Not so many now as formerly, when staunch and able schooners cleared from many ports, and brought back full fares from the Banks. The youth and vigor of the coast have followed the fishing fleet to Gloucester and Boston.

Only the older men are left, with a few sons and nephews—they fish by families—to use the old gear and fish the old grounds.

There is something, then, in the hardihood, the leisure, and the contentment of

When a man works from midnight till noon fishing, and then all afternoon baiting-up, and just gets a living and a little money for new gear, there must be compensations. And when you get out with

Baiting up.

these men that appeals strongly to the modern busy man of affairs. It is in such derelict villages that we, who know them, have some of our warmest friends. It is of their ways and their sayings that we like to think in the stress and worry of dollar-getting. And in intervals of business, back we go, each to his special haven, for a breath of salt air, and the companionship of men who take pleasure in simple things.

him some morning and see the ocean turn to sapphire and gold under the long heave of your dory, and smell the salt wetness all around, you know what some of them are!

If there is a "breeze o' wind" up goes the old, patched sail, and Abner lays the course for the rosy glow in the East, that touches with crimson the wet gun'ls and thwarts of the dory. Once outside the Cove, we "open out" point after point of land. The shore

Drawn by Sidney M. Chase.

An early start.

Another baited hook goes over.

fades to an irregular blue line, lost when the dory slides into a hollow of the sea.

"Don't feel no sick, dew ye?" asks Abner.

I hasten to reassure him, and inquire where he is going to "set."

"Wall, they'd ought tew be some haddick on the Middle Graound. Leander Lewis, he ketched a good mess on em aout thet way yestiddy. What's the ranges? I cal'late ef we git Blue Hill on the new meetin' haouse, and Burnt Island Light over Joel Turner's red barn, we'll be som'rs abaout thar."

The sighting over two ranges on shore in two directions gives the fisherman two lines, the intersection of which locates his fishing grounds.

From the stern of the dory I watch him get his gear ready; trawl basket on the middle thwart, sail held by a bow-hitch in the sheet, and tiller-rope in hand. Then he scans the shore for ranges.

"So cussed thick o'haze, ye can't see nothin'," he mutters, "but I guess we're 'baout right naow."

Splash goes the "kag," or trawl-buoy, and the thirty-five fathom line follows it overboard. As it floats astern, Abner heaves the "killick" after it, a heavy stone set firmly in the forked branch of a tree. That is the trawl anchor, and onto that is bent the ground-line, or trawl. The killick over, the half mile of trawl begins to run out smoothly from the maze of line and hooks in the basket. When Abner comes to a "gangin'" (or short line, with baited hook, attached to the ground-line), he flips it over side. Then six feet more trawl, and another baited hook goes over. It might be done to music.

To the landsman the ease with which a half mile of trawl and some five hundred baited hooks, coiled in apparently hopeless confusion in a trawl basket, untangles itself and runs smoothly over side, is a never-ending source of wonder. One hand is enough for the fisherman to give to his trawl. Steering and sailing the dory are sub-conscious. His real attention he gives to conversation.

"'T ain't no joke when ye git ketched aout an' it shets daown thick o' fog, an' ye ain't got no compass. Some on 'em don't never carry no compass. Haow dew they git in? Oh, jest take notice which way the chop is a-runnin'. I gen'ally cal'late tew hev one along, though, but one time mine got busted, an' me an' Levi Emery got ketched aout beyond the Island with a bo't lo'd o' fish, an' it come on tur'ble thick, an' black, an' ye jest couldn't see nothin'. Some fellers up Rocky Bottom way thet warn't much acquainted tew the Cove, they come a-rowin' by us an' hollered they was goin' in. 'Fore we got the killick up, we heered their v'ices agin an' they come a-rowin' back. 'Where yeou fellers goin'?' hollers Levi. 'In tew the Cove,' says they.

Hauling a trawl.

'Yeou won't never git in *thet* way,' yells Levi. 'Better foller us." An', by mighty, yeou, ef we didn't go and git astray with them a-follerin' of us in! I was settin' with my legs hangin' over the baow, es fur for-'ard es I could git, an' Levi, he was rowin'. An' I couldn't see ary thing! They was people on the P'int hollerin', an' I could hear Uncle Nate's v'ice—in the Cove, he was—an' he was a-hollerin'. An' when we asked him whar he was, all he'd holler was, 'I'm here!' an' thet didn't help none! Levi, he got mad, an' he ups and yells, 'Where in hell is "here"?' Bum'by we got ashore—'twas lucky 'twas ca'm. They was an' old ice haouse on the P'int, an' when I see it, I says to Levi, I says: 'Thar's the new meetin' haouse.' I hadn't no notion whar I was, tell I see the tops o' them fish haouses. It was es marster a mix-up es I ever see."

Some time later the trawl ran out, and the other killick and buoy were hove over to mark the end. While we waited for the trawl to "set," Abner and I baited a couple of hand-lines and swung them over.

"They'd ought tew be quite some fish hereabaouts," remarked he, as he sculled the dory with one hand, and sawed his line invitingly with the other. "We ain't fur frum the "Ten-Fathom Hole, an'——"

Dropping the oar, and stooping suddenly forward, he began heaving in hand over hand, his eyes fixed on the water.

"Gol a' mighty, he's a good un!" he panted.

There was a whir of taut line with drops of molten silver flying from it, an extra tug, a quick stroke of the gaff, something strug-gling and flashing rose in air, and a fifteen-pound cod fell with a heavy "plop" into the kid at my feet.

Abner surveyed him proudly but gloom-ily.

"I don't reckon we'll git nothin' much naow. We don't gen'ally like to git a big un fust off," said Abner, the pessimist.

But we did. Even as he spoke, my line thrilled and tautened, and as the wet cord sang over the gun'l, he watched me ap-provingly. "Pollock—I kin tell the way he pulls," said he. And sure enough, a gamy pollock, flashing dark green and silver, fighting every inch, came up, and Abner gaffed him in, and stunned him with a couple of blows.

And so they came splashing into the dory—pollock, haddock, and cod, and in the short intervals Abner was minded of many things.

"Git's some cold winter fishin'," he said. "I rec'lect one day last Janooary Uncle Nate put aout o' here 'n his dory. Cold es blazes, she was, 'baout ten below, an' blowin' heavy aout o' the no'the-east. Wall, a squall struck him, an' the fust thing he knowed, the mast an' sail was blowed clean aout of her, an'——"

"Whirr," went his line. "Nothin' but one o' them damn dog fish," said Abner, as he hauled him up, and gave him a vicious slat against the gun'l and overboard.

"Wall, Nate beached his dory some-haow, an' some fellers helped him haul her up. Then he walked more'n a mile thru the snow, right plum over stun walls—never seen 'em, he said, the snow was so deep—to the nearest haouse. He was wearin' a canvas jacket, an' when he got in by the fire, they told him his back was all froze up solid ice, an' he said, 'Thet so? I didn't know it!'"

While we fished and talked we had been eating our breakfast.

"I s'pose we'd better take a look at thet trawl. She's laid abaout long enough," said Abner, at length, setting his last huge mouthful of doughnut awash with a gurgle of cold coffee.

We pulled over to where our keg was bobbing on the sun-flecked water, and hoisted it aboard; then a steady haul brought up the killick, and we both bent over to sight the first hook. A streak of green and white trailed after it, and be-yond it, in the water, came another. Cod and haddock they were, for the most part, not splashing and struggling as on the hand line, but limp, the fight gone out of them. As Abner hauled the dripping trawl over the roller, he slatted the fish off the full hooks into the already half-filled kid, and re-coiled the line in the basket.

The fascinating lottery of hauling a trawl! The new interest in what each hook may bring! Great, sluggish cod; goggle-eyed skates, looking like Japanese kites; graceful, pointed pollock; a loathsome scul-pin or two; worthless England hake; beau-tiful rose-tinted haddock; and a good sprink-ling of silver-bellied dog-fish, the curse of summer fishing, who "come with the board-

Drawn by Sidney M. Chase.

"A purty good fare o' fish."

ers an' stay es long es they dew," as one old fisherman expressed it; and one five-pound chicken halibut, the prize catch—such was our loot from the great spoil of the sea.

The dog-fish Abner viciously slatted over side, cursing them the while with lurid profanity. Of one he turned the snout back, and the fish swam off in circles, unable to steer or dive. They are really small sharks, and at their worst will follow a dory and eat the fish off the trawl, leaving only a line of heads when the fisherman hauls it in.

While Abner hauled, and I eagerly watched each hook, a hail came to us across the water.

"Haow be ye makin' of it?"

We both looked around.

Seated in a dingy old dory just abeam of us and a little way off was a grizzled old fisherman. Sunlight glinted from his poised oar blades, and a lobster trap rested on the dory's after thwart.

"Fish is scurce," called Abner. "Gettin' any lobsters?"

"They ain't no lobsters," was the terse reply; and the old man, glancing over his shoulder toward the Cove, leisurely resumed his short stroke, rowing apparently with wrist and forearm only, while his old dory slipped easily along toward shore, and the "dip, dip" of his oars came more and more faintly to us over the sparkling water.

fishermen.

With the trawl all in and some three hundredweight of fish aboard, Abner stood up in the dory, and wiped his brown hand across his sweating forehead. Then he scanned the sky and the water.

"Looks like a leetle breeze o' wind," he observed. "I hope we *dew* git a leetle air. I hate most almightily tew row."

While he clambered forward to step the mast and set the patched canvas, a cool breeze came ruffling the surface of the ocean that set the water slapping the sides of the dory, and filled out the sail. With Abner steering by the tiller-ropes in the middle of the dory, I lay back in the stern, and watched the distant coast-line rise and fall. Much too soon familiar marks appeared. Then the Cove opened out, and soon we were swinging at moorings.

Others had come in, and heaps of wet, slippery fish lay on the beach. Three strokes of the knife, one sweep of the hand, and a fish was cleaned, the men splashing at work with oil pants and rubber boots knee-deep in water. The fish were flung into four-handled barrows and Ab and Lem carried them heavily up to the scales, iron steelyards swung from a timber scaffolding. Lem slipped the rusty weight along the bar till the scales swung, balanced at three hundred and twenty-five pounds. The others grunted admiration.

"A purty good fare o' fish," said old Peter Dyer. "Nothin' like them that used tew be ketched tew this Cove, though. I mind the time when——"

"Yeou kin rec'lect a dum sight more'n yeou ever ketched, Peter," put in Ab. "Yeou kin lie slicker'n old man Green. Day afore yestiddy Charley asked him haow many fish he hed tew peddle aout, an' the old man told him three hunderdweight. Then Tom Hawley come along, an' he asked him, an' Green said four hunderd and twenty-five. A little piece later somebody put Hank up tew findin' aout, an' the old cuss swore he'd got more'n five hunderd! I cal'late ef he'd a stayed any longer he'd a stuck his hoss right thar!"

Tied to the scales or standing near by were two or three dejected-looking horses, hitched to shaky carts, gray and weather-worn, with "Fresh Fish and Lobsters" painted in straggling red letters on their sides. Their owners took speedy possession of the catch and tossed the fish into their box-like carts, along with big chunks of ice. Abner's peddler picked up a piece of shingle, and made a labored calculation with a stub of a pencil. Then from a dirty roll of greenbacks he slowly extracted four, counting them with moistened thumb and forefinger. Ab stuffed them into his pocket silently. Humming a little tune, the peddler mounted his cart and with a terse "Git ap, yeou," rattled away noisily over the pebble-beach.

With his fish disposed of, Abner's morning work is done. His wage in his pocket, his blackened clay in his teeth, he strolls over to the nearest shade. No one may disturb his leisure. By and by he will go to dinner. Then he may dig a few clams, and after his trawl is baited, or his mackerel net mended, in the cool of the afternoon he will join a group of men in the shade of some fish-house, who fill the silent intervals of story telling with blue clouds of tobacco smoke.

Very far away, then, seem the hard days of winter fishing—when, in the stinging cold of a bleak December morning, the dories must be broken out of the ice by lantern light before the fishermen can make a start, and numbed hands haul endless trawls over icy gunwales. There is something inspiring in pitting a fourteen-foot dory against a fog-bound, storm-swept win-ter ocean for a few dollars' worth of cod. And the fisherman does it every day, and if he thinks much about it—he doesn't say so. Deep down in him he loves the great symphony of the sea, which for him is never twice the same. There is no discord in the whole suite, from the murmur of the tide about his wharf, to the deep-toned thunder of a north-easter on the headlands at his doorsteps. In the sparkling summer sea there is comradeship. There is challenge in the storm. Every mood of the ocean finds a responsive mood in these men who love it.

But the fisherman doesn't talk of these things. If, some afternoon, late, when the trawls are all baited, and the pipes are alight, you should stop to leeward of some old fish-house, you would be welcomed by a scant nod or so from the group of men—not in discourtesy, but from a feeling of perfect good fellowship that needs no surface greeting. You might take any vacant space, light your pipe, and feel at home.

"As many artists as usual around this year, Captain Zeb?"

The Captain, his huge brier pipe crammed with the strongest of tobacco, scratched a sulphur match on a trawl-tub and guarded it carefully from the breeze. Then he applied it to his pipe, took a hurried puff or two, removed the pipe from his mouth, and spat thoughtfully. His leathery old face broke into a thousand kindly wrinkles, as he turned toward me.

"Wall," he said, at length, "There's enough on em 'raound. Abaout twenty t' the acre." He chuckled, then paused impressively. "Abaout the humliest lot o' wimmen folks I ever see!"

There was a little stir of appreciation.

"They was some o' them artistses here tew the Cove last year," went on the Captain, "as wanted I an' old Nate should pose fer em. Wall, I hed the settin' daown job—mendin' nets, I was—an' Nate he hed tew stan' up, with his foot up on a trawl-tub, so," the Captain illustrated with a gesture of his huge hand, "an' Nate, he was tew pint with his thumb over tew a lot o' boarders in the pictur. We hed tew stan' in the blazin' sun, an', by mighty, 'twas some hot! Nate was all oiled up, from boots tew sou'wester, an' the feller'd

Drawn by Sidney M. Chase.

Toilers of the sea.

A Maine coast fisherman.

no sooner git him fixed than Nate'd hev tew turn 'raound tew spit, an' then he'd hev it tew dew all over agin. Nate, he stud it quite a spall, an' the sweat run right thru the knees o' his pants, an' he hed tew gin it up. An' then *I* hed tew set for both on em."

He paused reflectively. "I s'pose," he went on, "I was drawed aout by thet artist feller much es 'leven dollars wuth, all summer."

The Captain stopped, and Nate observed:

"Paintin' 's a good deal like fishin'. Ye go one day 'n ef ye don't git nothin', ye think mebbe ye will the next."

I mentally agreed.

"Yeou all baited, Jed?" said the Captain to a newcomer who strolled over to the group.

"Wall, I baited tew trawls, but dog fish is solid everywhar."

"Wish yeou could a seed the school o' pollock I see yestiddy," said Abner, "they was jumpin' thick an' must a' reached clean frum here ter Joe Lewis's fish haouse. They was so tame I could hit 'em on the back with an oar, an'——"

"I see a shark off tew th' east'ard o' the Island t'other day," put in Lem. "Must a been all o' thirty foot, tew."

"'T ain't nothin' tew the time me an' Jim Easton was halibutin'," said 'Liph. Harding. "Jim was haulin' trawl an' I was rowin'. Bum'by Jim, he giv a holler, an' started cuttin' the gangins off his graound line. 'Got a Hell-h'ister!' he yells. 'Halibut?' I says. 'Guess so,' says Jim. Wall, thet fish, he jest cut loose an' done things complete! Arter awhile we begun tew haul him an' Jim says he didn't feel him. 'Sure you don't feel nothin'?' says I. 'No,' says Jim, 'I don't feel nothin'

"Some o' them wimmen rusticators is turrible ignorant," at length observed the Captain. "They was a woman daown t' the Cove t'other day, an' Ike was weighin' his fish. She p'ints for Ike, an' brings up all stannin', 'baout ten foot off. She giv

Hauling his mackerel net.

much, only, mebbe, a big skate. When he come 'longside, I see he was a big un, an' I reached fer the gaft, an' layed over, an' Jim, he was so excited he flung thet halibut clean over my head an' inter the bo't! An' thet fish weighed all o' sixty-five paound, tew!"

"Sho, naow, yeou don't say!" exclaimed old Nate Parsons.

"Wall, yeou," remarked the Captain, "I ketched seven halibut once on a fifty-hook trawl, an' the smallest on 'em weighed more 'n eighty paounds!"

"I bin on George's," said Ike Martin, "when the water was so thick o' mackerel thet ye jes' couldn't see no water 'thout fish showin,' an' we hed tew look sharp tew find a small enough school tew set araound!"

"Thet's so," said Ab.

They puffed their pipes in silence for a space.

one look at the barrer o' fish an' she p'ints tew it with her parasol. 'What is them—fish?' she says. 'Damsure, them's fish,'" says Ike.

There was a general chuckle.

"They *are* cur'us critters," said Ike. "Some on 'em sails putty nigh the wind all the year so's t' hev tew weeks tew the sea shore. I knowed one feller thet stayed tew the Hotel till he didn't hev no more'n enough tew git hum on, an' they was a big storm or suthin' so's he hed t' stay 'nother day or tew, an' he hed tew walk six mile plum tew the depot."

There was a lull in the conversation, and 'Liph reached for his pipe, and plug-tobacco. I forestalled him with the offer of a cigar.

"Wall naow, yeou," he said, with satisfaction, as he chewed the end and blew out fragrant clouds of smoke, "thet *is* ter-baccer! I most gen'ally smoke 'Peace

Drawn by Sidney M. Chase.

When lines are slacked.

an' Good Will.' I s'pose," he went on, "thet I've smoked more fer my years than any man t' this Cove. I'm goin' on sixty-five, an' when dew yeou think I begun tew smoke? Wall, I begun when I were four year old!"

"Wall, yeou!" from Nate, leading a chorus of surprise from the others.

"Yes, I did fer a fact," said 'Liph. "I hed what the Doctor called catarrh o' the thro't, an' old Doc. Harvey, he allaowed es haow ef I should turn tew an' smoke, mebbe 't would dew my thro't good, an', by mighty, it cured me right up!"

"Speakin' o' smokin' an' eatin'," remarked the Captain, "I eat suthin' yestiddy I never eat afore. 'Twas a puddin' like made aout o' this dum sea-weed."

"Haow'd yeou like it?" asked Ab.

"Wall," answered the Captain, slowly, "'Twas putty fair, takin' it all araound, but 'twant what yeou might call fillin'."

The shadow of the fish houses was lengthening along the beach before us. Over the sand dunes a thin film of blue smoke rose lazily from a chimney. Their "women" were getting supper ready. One or two of the fishermen rose stiffly to their feet, stretched their arms, and yawned.

"Sun's settin' up his back stays," said one. "Good day tomorrer."

"Yes," agreed the Captain, addressing me, "yeou'll never git no faoul weather, when ye see the sun a-drawin' water."

"I see a caow stannin' on Blue Hill es I come daown," remarked Abner. "They dew say es haow ef ye see a caow stannin' on the highest p'int o' land she kin find, it's a sure sign o' rain. But mebbe t'ain't nothin' intew it."

"I never heered thet," said 'Liph, "but ef ye ever noticed a bar'l o' cod's livers in ile, ye find thet ef they rise t' the top, ye'll git a spall o' faoul weather; an' ef they sinks t' the bottom, 't will be fine."

The Captain rose slowly to his feet, and turning, snapped the huge padlock in the door of his fish house.

"I guess my supper 's abaout ready," he said.

"Wait a minit, an' I'll go 'long with ye," said 'Liph, and presently the two old friends with pipes alight clambered stiffly over the

Cleaning his catch.

pebble-beach toward their little white cottages up the road.

One by one the group diminished, with no word of farewell, as there had been none of greeting; and each with pipe going, and some with a codfish for to-morrow's breakfast in hand, followed the Captain and 'Liph up the narrow road.

The last rays of the setting sun touched the hauled-up dories and the gray fish houses with gold, and the long shadows creeping over the stones found a beach deserted save by a stray cat or two smelling about for cod heads. The only sound was the soft plash of the waves on the pebble-beach.

13
Cape Cod Folks

A CAPE COD ROADWAY

Cape Cod Folks

By Clifton Johnson

With Illustrations by the Author

IT was densely dark when I arrived at Yarmouth one October evening. Viewed from the platform of the railway station the world about was a void of inky gloom.

"If you're looking for the town," said a man at my elbow, "you'll find it over in that direction;" and he pointed with his finger. "You follow the road, and turn to the right when you've gone half a mile or so, and that'll take you straight into the village."

"But I don't see any road," said I.

"Well, it goes around the corner of that little shed over thar that the light from the depot shines on."

"And how far is it to a hotel?"

"We ain't got no hotel in this place; but Mr. Sutton, two houses beyond the post office, he keeps people and I guess he'll take you in all right."

I trudged off along the vague highway, and at length reached the town street, a narrow thoroughfare solidly overarched by trees. Dwellings were numerous on either side, and lights glowed through curtained windows. How snug those silent houses looked; and how cheerless seemed the outer darkness and the empty street to the homeless stranger! I lost no time in hunting up Mr. Sutton's, and the shel-

MOWING ON THE SALT MEADOWS

ter he granted brought a very welcome sense of relief.

When I explored Yarmouth the next day, I found it the most attenuated town I had ever seen. The houses nearly all elbowed each other for a distance of two or three miles close along a single slender roadway. Very few dwellings ventured aside from this double column. Apparently no other situation was orthodox, and I suppose the families which lived off from this one street must have sacrificed their social standing in so doing.

Yarmouth was settled in 1639 and is the oldest town on the Cape. Its inhabitants in the past have been famous sea-faring folk, and fifty years ago almost every other house was the domicile of a retired sea-captain, and in the days of the sailing vessels the Yarmouth men voyaged the world over. A certain class of them went before the mast, but the majority were ship's officers. A goodly number of the latter amassed wealth in the India and China trade. This wealth has descended in many instances still intact to the generation of today, and accounts for the town's air of easy-going comfort. But fortunes are no more drawn from the old source, and at present the ambitious youth who aspires to riches turns his eyes cityward. The sea has ceased to promise a bonanza. Even the local fishing industry is wholly dead, though it is only a few decades since the town had quite a mackerel fleet; but the little craft are all gone now, and nothing remains of the old wharves save some straggling lines of black and broken piles reaching out across the broad marshes that lie between the long street and the salt water.

These marshes are of rather more economic importance to modern Yarmouth than the sea itself; for grass and rank sedges cover them and furnish a considerable proportion of the hay that is harvested. I liked to loiter on these wet levels and watch the men swing their scythes. I noticed that they left untouched the coarse grass that grew on the strips of sand. "That's beach grass," said one of the mowers with whom I talked. "The stock won't eat that, nor any other creatures won't eat it that I know of except skunks. Thar's plenty of them chaps along the shore on these ma'shes Me 'n' my dog kitch a lot of 'em here every winter."

The route back to the town from the marsh on which this skunk hunter was at work led across a low ridge of stony pasture-land where the blackberry vines displayed their ruddy autumn foliage and brightened the earth like flashes of flame. A most beautiful little lane threaded along the crest of the ridge. It was only about a dozen feet broad, and was hemmed in by stone walls overgrown with bushes among which rose an occasional tree. The paths trodden by the cows' hoofs wandered irregularly along, avoiding obstructions, and, as a rule, followed the line of the least resistance. There was, however, now and then, a deflection which the cattle had made purposely toward the thickest of the bordering brush, intent on crowding up against the twigs to rid themselves of flies. How shadowy and protected and pastoral the lane was! I envied the boys who drove the cows and thus had the chance to make a daily renewed acquaintance with its arboreal seclusion.

Not far from where the lane emerged on the village street stood a dwelling that I looked at with interest every time I passed. It was a low and primitive structure, and behind it was a little barn surmounted by a sword-fish weather-vane. Sword-fish, or ships, I observed, were the favorite vanes

everywhere for Cape Cod outbuildings. The attraction of this home with its serious air of repose under the shadowing trees, grew, until one day I ventured into the yard. Near the barn a gray-bearded ancient had just hitched a venerable horse into a wagon, and

was preparing to grease the vehicle's wheels. I spoke with him, and after some preliminaries said, "It appears to me that you have about the oldest house in town."

He gave me a sudden look of surprise out of the corner of his eyes, the purport of which I did not at the moment understand, and then went on with his work. "Ye-ye-yes," he replied in his hasty, stammering way; for his thoughts seemed to start ahead of his tongue, and the latter gained control with difficulty. "Ye-ye-yes, he is old, but he's a good hoss yet!"

"Oh, I didn't say horse," I remarked quickly, "I was speaking of your house."

"My h-h-h-h-house, hm-m-m! That —that's one of the old settlers. Must be two hundred year old; and do you see that pear tree thar with the piece of zinc nailed over the bad place in the trunk, and the iron bands around up where the branches begin, so't they wont split off? I s'pose that pear tree's as old as the house."

"What kind is it?"

"It-it-it it's wha-what we call the old-fashioned button pear. Uncle Peter Thacher that had this place years ago used to pick up the pears and sell 'em to the boys for a cent apiece. They ain't much larger'n wa'nuts. They're kind of a mealy kind of pear, you know—very good when they first drop off, but they rot pretty quick."

The man had finished applying the wheel-grease now, and he clambered into the wagon and drove off, while I walked on. I passed entirely through the village into a half-wild region beyond, where much of the land was covered by a dense pine wood. There were occasional farm clearings; but I noticed that the houses of this outlying district were generally vacant. Opposite one of the deserted homes was a corn-field that attracted my attention because the tops of the cornstalks had been cut off and carted away, and the ears left on the stubs to ripen. This was a common way of treating corn

years ago, but is seldom seen now. Here and there in the field were scarecrows,—sometimes an old coat and hat hoisted on a stake; sometimes a pole with a fluttering rag at the top and, suspended a little lower down on the same pole, a couple of rusty tin cans that rattled together dubiously in the breeze. As I was leaning over the roadside wall contemplating this cornfield, a man came along and accosted me, and I improved the opportunity to ask him why so many of the houses of the neigborhood were unoccupied.

"Wal," said he, "people don't like to live outside o' the villages nowadays. Sence the fishin' give out, the young folks all go off to get work, and they settle somewhar else, and the old folks move into the towns. In this house across the road, though, an old woman lived, and she died thar two years ago. She was kind o' queer, and some

THE CRANBERRY PICKERS

say she wa'n't a woman at all. She wore women's clothes, but she had a beard and shaved every mornin', and her hair was cut short, and she carried on the farm and did the work just like a man."

My acquaintance spit meditatively and then inquired, "Have you seen Hog Island?"

"No," I responded.

"You'd ought to. It ain't fur from to'ther end of Yarmouth village. You go down the lane along the creek thar and ask the way of Jimmy Holton that lives by the bridge. He'll tell you. It aint really an island, but a bunch o' trees in a little ma'sh, and they grow so't if you see 'em from the right place they look just like a hog—snout, tail, and all."

The man had in his hand a large scoop with a row of long wooden teeth projecting from its base. This is the kind of implement used in gathering most of the Cape Cod cranberries, and the man was on his way to a berry patch he cultivated in a boggy hollow not far distant. I accompanied him and found his wife and children on their knees each armed with a scoop with which they were industriously scratching through the low mat of vines. Where they had not yet picked, the little vines were twinkled all over with ripe berries—genuine autumn fruit, waxen-skinned, ruddy hued, and acid to the tongue—as if the atmospheric tartness and coolness had helped the sun to dye and flavor them.

The bog was not at all wild. In preparing it for cranberry culture it had been thoroughly tamed. Brush and stumps had been cleared off and the turf removed. Then it had been leveled and coated with a layer of sand. It was encompassed and more

213

ON THE BORDERS OF A CRANBERRY BOG

or less cut across by ditches; and, in the process of clearing, steep banks had been heaved up around the borders.

"Cranberries are a great thing for the Cape," said my friend. "They're the best crop we have, but it's only late years we've gone into 'em. When I was a boy, the only cranberries we used to have was a little sort that growed in the bogs wild; and we never thought nothin' o' dreanin' the marshes and goin' into the business the way we do now.

"My bog aint first class. A man's got to put a lot o' work into raisin' cranberries to do the thing just right; and when you only got a small bog you kind o' neglect it. There's one bog about a mile from here that's got sixteen acres in it, and they're always tendin' to it in one way and another the year around. They keep it clean of weeds, and if there's any sign of fire-bug they steep tobacco and spray the vines. If there's a dry spell they rise the water, though that don't do as much good as it might. You c'n water a plant all you want to, but waterin' won't take the place o' rain.

"Pretty soon after we finish pickin' we flood the bogs, and they stay flooded all winter, if the mushrats don't dig through the banks. The water keeps the plants from freezin', and seems to kind o' fertilize them at the same time. The ponds make grand skatin'-places. They freeze over solid—no weak spots —and they aint deep enough to be dangerous, even if you was to break through."

This man's statement as to the importance of cranberry culture to the dwellers on the Cape was in no wise exaggerated. When I continued my journeyings later to the far end of the

ANCHORING THE HAYSTACKS

peninsula I saw reclaimed berry bogs innumerable. There was scarcely a swampy depression anywhere but that had been ditched and dyked and the body of it layed off as smooth as a floor and planted to cranberries. The pickers were hard at work—only two or three of them on some bogs, and on others a motley score or more. It seemed as if the task engaged the entire population irrespective of age and sex; and the picking scenes were greatly brightened by the presence of the women in their calico gowns and sunbonnets or broad-brimmed straw hats. Often the bogs were far enough from home so that the workers carried their dinners and made the labor an all-day picnic, though I thought the crouching position must grow rather wearisome after a time.

Aside from the fertile and productive bogs the aspect of the Cape was apt to be monotonous and sombre. The cultivated fields appeared meagre and unthrifty, the pastures were thin-grassed and growing up to brush, and, more predominant than anything else in the landscape, were the great tracts of scrubby woodland covered with dwarfed pines and oaks, often fire-ravaged, and never a tree in them of respectable size. Ponds and lakes were frequent. So were the inlets from the sea with their borderings of salt marsh; indeed, the raggedness of the shore line was suggestive of a constant struggle between the ocean and the continent for the possession of this slender ou'reach of the New England coast. The buffeting of the fierce sea winds was evident in the upheave of the sand dunes and the landward tilt of the exposed trees, which had a very human look of

PROVINCETOWN WHARF

small sailing-craft in and about the harbor, and always a number of schooners, and occasionally a larger vessel.

The inhabitants love the sea, or else are involuntarily fascinated by it. They delight to loiter on the wharves and beach, and to sit and look out on old ocean's wrinkled surface and contemplate its hazy mystery. One would fancy they thought it replete with beneficent possibilities and that they were willing lingerers dreamily expecting something fortunate or fateful would heave into view from beyond the dim horizon. The children seek the beach as assiduously as their elders. It is their playground, their newspaper. They poke about the wharves strewn with barrels and boxes, spars, chains, ropes, anchors, etc.; they find treasures in the litter that gathers on the sands; they dig clams on the mud flats; they race and tumble, and they learn all that is going on in the shipping.

The most exciting event while I was in town was an unexpected catch of squids in the harbor. Squids are the favorite bait of the cod fishermen, but at Provincetown there is rarely a chance to get this bait so late in the year. The squids sought the deepest portion of the bay, and a little fleet of small boats collected above and captured them by the barrel. One mid-day I stood watching the boats from a wharf. Two men who had come on to the wharf soon after I did were regarding the scene from near by. "It's queer how them squids hang in that hole thar," said one of the men.

"They bring a good price for cod bait, I believe," said I.

"Yes. Willie Scott that lives next door to me, he made seven dollars this

fear and seemed to be trying to flee from the persecuting gales, but to be retarded by laggard feet.

At the tip of the Cape is Provincetown snugged along the shore, with steep protecting hills at its back. It is a town that has an ancient, old-world look due to its narrow streets with houses and stores and little shops crowded close along the walks. It is a fishy place, odorous of the sea, and the waterside is lined with gray fish-shanties and store-houses. Many spindle-legged wharves reach out across the beach, and there are dories and

OVERHAULING THE FISHING TACKLE

mornin' and he has gone out again. I'll bet his eyes are full of squid juice this minute. The squids don't trouble much that way, but they'll flip up a smeller (that's what we call their arms) and give you a dose once in a while spite of all you can do. It makes your eyes sting, but it don't last long."

"How large are the squids?" I asked.

"Oh, they're small—not much, more'n a foot and a half, smellers and all."

The other man now spoke. He was short and dark, had rings in his ears, and his accent was decidedly foreign. "Cap'n Benson," said he to his companion, "I seen the butt end of a squid smeller big as this barrel what I'm settin' on."

Cap'n Benson puffed a few times judiciously at his pipe. "Yes," he acknowledged presently, "there's a good many kinds of squids, and they do kitch 'em large enough so one'll last a cod schooner for bait a whole v'yage. We only git a little kind here."

The wharf we were on was nearly covered with racks on which a great quantity of salted codfish had been spread to dry, and "Cap'n" Benson informed me there was plenty more fish awaiting curing in the hold of a slender-masted vessel that lay alongside the wharf.

"She's a Grand-Banker," he continued, indicating the vessel. "We aint got but six Grand-Bankers now, and only fifteen fresh fishermen. The fresh fishermen you know don't go farther'n the Georges and the West Banks. Forty years ago we had two hundred fishing schooners in the town and we had sixty-seven whale ships where now we got only three. Provincetown is played out. This mornin' me and this man with me didn't have

217

but one hour's work, and we won't have over two hours this afternoon. How you goin' to make a livin' at twenty cents an hour with things goin' on that way? Forty years ago you couldn't get enough men at three dollars and a half a day."

The man with the earrings had picked up a piece of shell and was attempting to drop it from the height of his shoulder through a crack in the wharf. He failed to accomplish his purpose though he tried again and again.

"Mr. Klunn, if you want to drop that shell through thar, just mention the minister," advised "Cap'n" Benson.

He had hardly spoken when Mr. Klunn let the shell fall, and it slipped straight through the crack. "By Godfrey!" exclaimed the Cap'n, "I did it for you. I never known that to fail. When I been whaling, and we was cuttin' up a whale, you couldn't sometimes strike a j'int. You'd try and try and you couldn't strike it, and then you'd stop and say, 'Minister!' and it was done already—you'd hit it right off."

"I seen a whale heave up a shark the half as big as a dory," remarked Mr. Klunn after a pause.

"To be sure," the "Cap'n" commented. "Howsomever there's people say a whale can't take nothin' bigger'n a man's hand; but I guess that's after he's been eatin' and had all he wanted."

"By gosh! a whale got a swallow so big enough, if he hungry, he swallow a man easy," Mr. Klunn declared. "Some people ain't believe about Jonah, but they believe if they seen as much whales that I have."

"I'm thinkin' about them squids,"

Cap'n Benson said as he shook his pipe free from ashes and slipped it into the pocket of his jacket. "I guess when the tide comes in to-night I'll haul out my boat and see if I can't get some of 'em."

"I aint had no boat sence the big storm," observed the man with earrings.

"What storm was that?" I inquired.

"It was when the Portland went down in November, 1899," explained "Cap'n Benson. We had a awful time, —wharves smashed, boat houses carried off, and vessels wrecked. It begun to blow in the night. Fust thing I knowed of it was my chimley comin' down."

"I was sick that time," said the ear-

ring man. "The doctor had to give
me murphine pills. I was in bed two
three days, and I lose 187 dollars by
the storm. You remember that schooner, Cap'n Benson, what the two old
mens were drownded on?"

"Oh, I remember—washed overboard out here in the harbor, and the
wind took the schooner bang up agin a
wharf, and the Cap'n, he made a jump
and landed all right; and he never
stopped to look behind to see what become of the vessel nor nobody. He
run up into the town and he took the
next train for California."

"Yas, that's true," Mr. Klunn affirmed.

Later, while stopping over night at
a Truro farmhouse a few miles back on
the Cape, I heard more of the great
storm. "Thar was three days of it,"
said my landlady, "startin' on Saturday. It thundered and lightened on
Sunday and it snowed Monday. Everythin' that wa'n't good'n strong was
blowed down. It blowed the shed off
the end of our house, and it blowed a
window in upstairs, and it blowed the
saddle board off the roof and some o'
the shingles. We had the highest tide
we've ever had and there was places
where the sea-water come across the
roads. Monday the bodies begun to
be washed ashore from the Portland,
and they kept comin' in for two
weeks."

Truro is a scattered little country
place. Its homes dot every protected hollow. The only buildings that
seemed independent of the smiting of
the winter blasts were the town hall
and the Baptist, Methodist, and Catholic churches. These stood in a group
on a bare, bleak hilltop. The church-
yards were thickly set with graves, and

VILLAGE WATCHMAKER'S SIGN

among the stones grew little tangles
of sumachs and other bushes, but the
sandy height had not a single tree.

On this hill, years ago, stood still
another public institution—a windmill.
"It sot high up thar so't it was in sight
all over town," said my landlady.
"You could see the miller puttin' the
sails on the arms, and then when they
got to turnin' we'd know which way
the wind blowed. But some days there
wouldn't be no wind, and the sails
might hang there and not turn the
whole day long. We used to raise this
yaller Injun corn then a good deal

more'n we do now on the Cape, and we raised rye, and we'd take the grain to the mill to grind. You can't buy no such corn meal or rye meal now as we used to get from that old mill. We e't hasty pudding them days, and it used to be so nice! and we had Johnny-cake and hasty-pudding bread."

"Hasty-pudding bread — what's that?" I asked.

"It was made by putting some of the hasty-pudding into flour and mixing 'em up into dough together. We didn't have yeast then like we use now. Instead o' that we had what we called 'emptyin's' that I s'pose come from dregs of beer or other liquor got sometime at a distillery; but they kep' emptyin's fermentin' to use makin' bread at every farmhouse, and if yourn run out you could always get some at the neighbor's to start again. We'd stir up the dough and set it behind the stove to rise, and our emptyin's bread would be light as could be."

Of the churches on the hill the Catholic was the newest. It was a little shed of a building with a gilt cross surmounting the front gable. The attendants were chiefly Portuguese, the nationality which at present constitutes the great majority of the coast fisher-folk. Most of the fishing is done in rowboats, and the fish are caught in nets fastened to lines of stakes off shore. These fish-traps, as they are called, are visited daily. The crew of a rowboat usually consists of a "Cap'n" who is pretty sure to be a Yankee, and seven men who are likely to be all Portuguese. Truro had four rowboats thus manned. They started out at three in the morning and returned anywhere from noon to eight in the evening.

"It's hard work," explained my landlady, "and the Yankee men don't take up fishin' late years the way they did. I reckon they c'n make more money farmin'."

I wondered at this. The sandy soil did not look productive, and yet the houses, as a rule, were painted and in good repair and conveyed a pleasing impression of prosperity. The people with whom I talked seemed to be satisfied. "We git good crops," said a farmer I questioned about agricultural affairs. "We c'n raise most all kinds o' vegetables in the hollers, and good grass, too, though our heaviest crops o' grass we git off'n the marshes. The cows like salt hay fully as well as they do fresh hay, and they like sedge best of all, because its sweet; but you have to be careful about feedin' 'em too much of it, or the milk'll taste. Of course we got plenty o' pasture on the higher ground and plenty o' timber sich as 'tis. The trees don't flourish, though, and you won't find many that are much bigger'n your leg. This is a great country for wild berries,—blue-berries, blackberries, and huckleberries. Our Portuguese here—land! they git half their livin' in the woods. Besides berries there's beach plums and wild cherries. But the cherries we don't use for common eatin'. We put 'em up in molasses and they kind o' work and are good to take for the stomach and the like o' that."

I climbed over the hills round about Truro and tramped the sandy, deeply-rutted roads faithfully. It was weary work to one used to solid earth. Such lagging progress! I could never get a good grip with my feet and slipped a little backward every time I took a step forward. Except along the watercourses nature's growths never attained the least exuberance. The grass on the slopes and uplands was very thin, and with the waning of the season much of it had become wispy and withered. It was mingled with goldenrod and asters that hugged the earth on such short, stunted stems as to be hardly recognizable.

The landscape, as viewed from a height, had a curiously unstable look. Its form had not been moulded by attrition, but the soil had been blown into vast billows that had the appearance of a troubled sea whose waves were on the point of advancing and overwhelming the habitations and all the green growing things in the vales. Some of the dunes really do advance, and the state has been obliged to make appropriations and devise means for checking their depredations. The work has chiefly been accomplished with the aid of beach grass. This has an affiliation for sand, and you can stick one of its coarse wiry tufts in anywhere and it will grow. It only needs to be methodically planted, and the shifting dunes are fast bound and the winds asail them in vain.

Some of the characteristics of this beach grass seem also to be characteristics of the people of the Cape. They have the same hardinesss and endurance, and, like the beach grass, have adapted themselves to their environment and thrive where most would fail. With its omnipresent sand and dwarf woods, the Cape, as I saw it at the fag end of the year, appeared rather

A LONE PICKER

dreary, but the prosperous look of the homes was very cheering. These are nearly all owned free from debt, and that nightmare of the agriculturists in so many parts of New England—a mortgage—is, happily, almost unknown among the Cape Cod folks.

14
Bar Harbor

By *F. Marion Crawford*

ILLUSTRATIONS BY C. S. REINHART

THE first impression made by Bar Harbor at the height of its season upon the mind of one fresh from a more staid and crystallized civilization is that it is passing through a period of transition, in which there is some of the awkwardness which we associate with rapid growth, and something also of the youthful freshness which gives that very awkwardness a charm. The name of Mount Desert suggests, perhaps, a grim and forbidding cliff, frowning upon the pale waves of a melancholy ocean. Instead, the traveller who crosses the bay in the level light of an August afternoon looks upon the soft, rolling outline of wooded hills, on the highest of which a little hotel breaks the sky-line, upon a shore along which villas and cottages stretch on either side of a toy wooden village, which looks as though it were to be put away in a box at night, and upon the surrounding sea, an almost land-locked inlet, in which other islands, like satellites of Mount Desert, are scattered here and there. As the little steamer draws up to her moorings the groups of people waiting on the pier stand out distinctly, and the usual types detach themselves one by one. The clusters of hotel-runners and express-men are lounging listlessly until they shall be roused to clamorous activity by the landing of the first passenger ; in knots and pairs, those serenely idle people of all ages, who, in all places and seasons, seem to find an ever-new amusement in watching the arrival of trains or boats, are as deeply interested as usual ; the inevitable big and solemn dog, of nondescript breed and eclectic affections, is stalking about with an air of responsibility. And yet the little crowd is not quite like other gatherings on other piers. Girls in smart cotton frocks are sitting in shining little village carts, with grooms at their horses' sleek heads, wedged in between empty buckboards that look like paralyzed centipedes, the drivers of which wear clothes ranging from the livery of the large stables to the weather-bleached coat of the "native" from Cherryfield or Ellsworth, who has brought over his horse to take his share of the "rusticator's" ready money during the short season. There are no hotel omnibuses, no covered traps of any kind, as becomes a holiday place where winter and rough weather are enemies not meant to be reckoned with ; everybody seems either to know everyone else, or not to care if he does not, and there is an air of cheerful informality about the whole scene which immediately makes one feel welcome and at home. In order not to be behind every self-respecting town throughout the Western world Bar Harbor has a Main Street, which plunges violently down a steep place toward the pier, and which is beautified for a short distance by a mushroom growth of tents and shanties, the summer home of the almond-eyed laundryman, the itinerant photographer with a specialty of tintypes, and the seller of weary-looking fruit, of sandwiches that have seen better days, and temperance drinks of gorgeous hues. Plymouth Rock also vaunts its "pants," and young ladies are recommended to grow up with Castoria. Then come the more necessary shops—the tinsmith's, at whose door a large bull-terrier benevolently grins all day ; the tailor's, where one may study the fashions of New York filtered through Bangor ; the china shop, where bright-colored lamp-shades spread themselves like great butterflies in the window, and the establishment of Mr.

Bee, the locally famous and indispensable provider of summer literature, and of appropriate alleviations for the same, in the shape of caramels, cigarettes, and chewing-gum. Directly opposite stands a huge hotel, apparently closed or almost deserted, but evidently built in the years when the gnawing tooth of the national jig-saw grievously tormented all manner of wood-work, a melancholy relic of an earlier time when, as "Rodick's," it was almost another name for Bar Harbor itself. No lover of Bar Harbor has been found bold enough to say that Main Street is pretty ; and yet, between ten and twelve o'clock on a summer's morning, it has a character, if not a beauty, of its own. Alongside of the "board walk," which takes the place of a pavement, the buckboards are drawn up, waiting to be hired ; in some of them, often drawn by four horses, are parties of people, consisting usually of more women than men, as is becoming in New England, already starting upon one of the longer expeditions, and only stopping to collect a stray member or to lay in a stock of fruit and sugar-plums. Farmers' carts, with closed hoods like Shaker sunbonnets, are on their rounds from one cottage to another, meandering through the crowd, and driven with exasperating calmness by people who sit far back in their little tunnels, and cannot possibly see on either side of them to get out of anyone else's way. Then there are all sorts of light private traps, usually driven by women or girls bound on household errands or visits, and psychologically unbalanced between their desire to speak to the friends who meet them on foot, and their anxiety lest they should be forced to recognize the particular acquaintance on whom they are just going to call. Along the board walk there is a row of little shops, some of them scarcely larger than booths, the proprietors of which perch like birds of passage, pluming themselves in the sunshine of the brief season, and taking flight again before the autumn gales. In one window a lot of Turkish finery looks curiously exotic, especially the little slippers, gay with tassels and embroidery, turning up their pointed toes as if scorning the

On the Corniche Road.

stouter footgear which tramps along outside. Another shop is bright with the crude colors of Spanish scarfs and pottery ; in another, Japanese wares manage to keep their faint smell of the East in spite of the salt northern air, and farther on you may wonder at the misplaced ingenuity of Florida shell jewelry, and be fascinated by the rakish leer of the varnished alligator.

By one of the contrasts which make Bar Harbor peculiarly attractive, next door to these cosmopolitan shops there still thrives one of the indigenous general stores, where salt fish are sold, and household furniture and crockery, and the candy peculiar to New England stores and New York peanut stands, which keeps through all vicissitudes a vague odor of sawdust, and where you

may also buy, as was once advertised by the ingenuous dealer, " baby carriages, butter, and paint."

Should you wish to give a message to a friend without the trouble of writing a note, the chances are more than even that you will find him or her any morning on the board-walk, or in the neighborhood of the post-office, for as there is no delivery at Bar Harbor, and as the mails are often delayed, there is ample opportunity to search for an acquaintance in the waiting crowd. Here also congregate the grooms in undress livery, with leather mail-bags slung under one arm, who have ridden in from the outlying cottages, and who walk their horses up and down, or exchange stable notes with their acquaintances ; sailors from private yachts, usually big, fair Scandinavians ; mail orderlies from any men-of-war which may happen to be in port ; boys and girls who do not find the waiting long, and all that mysterious tribe of people who look as if they could not possibly receive a dozen letters a year, and yet who are always assiduously looking out for them. As usual, the post-office is a loadstone for all the dogs in the village, and as there are many strangers among them, of all breeds and ages and tempers, walking round and round one another with stiff legs and bristling backs, unregenerate man is kept in tremulous expectation of a dog-fight as free as any in Stamboul. But somehow the fight rarely comes off, though the resident canine population has become fearfully and wonderfully mixed, through the outsiders who have loved and ridden away. One nondescript, especially, is not soon forgotten, a nightmare cross of a creature in which the curly locks and feathery tail of the spaniel are violently modified by the characteristic pointed breastbone and bandy legs of a dachs-hund.

Wandering through the streets of the little village one is struck again and again by the sharp contrast between what may be called the natural life of the place and the artificial conditions which fashion has imposed upon it. In some of the streets almost every house is evidently meant to be rented, the owners usually retiring to restricted quarters at the back, where they stow themselves away and hang themselves up on pegs until they may come into their own again. Here and there a native cottage has been bought and altered by a summer resident, and over the whole there is the peculiarly smug expression of a quarter which is accustomed to put its best foot foremost for a few months of the year. But in the back lanes and side-streets there are

still the conditions of the small New England community, in which land is poor and work is slack during the long winter, so that although there is no abject poverty in the sense in which it is known to cities, there is also little time or inclination for the mere prettinesses of life. An element of the picturesque is supplied by an Indian camp, which used for years to be pitched in a marshy field known as Squaw Hollow ; but with the advent of a Village Improvement Society certain new-fangled and disturbing ideas as to sanitary conditions obtained a hearing, and the Indians were banished to a back road out of the way of

Canoeing.

sensitive eyes and noses. They claim to be of the Passamaquoddy tribe, speak their own language, and follow the peaceful trades of basket-weaving, moccasin-making, and the building of ured balls of fat in all shades of yellow and brown—roll about in close friendship with queer little dogs, in which the absence of breed produces a family likeness. It is curious to see in the

The Landing-Stage.

birch-bark canoes. Their little dwellings—some of them tents, some of them shanties covered with tar - paper and strips of bark—are scattered about, and in the shadow of one of them sits a lady of enormous girth, who calls herself their queen, and who wears, perhaps as a badge of sovereignty, a huge fur cap even in the hottest weather. She is not less industrious than other " regular royal " queens, for she sells baskets, and tells fortunes even more flattering than the fabled tale of Hope. Some of the young men are fine, swarthy, taciturn creatures, who look as though they knew how to put a knife to other uses than whittling the frame of a canoe ; but one does not feel tempted to rush upon Fate for the sake of any of the dumpy and greasy-looking damsels who will soon become like their even dumpier and greasier mothers. The whole encampment is pungent with the acrid smoke of green wood, and many children—round, good-nat-

characteristic work of these people the survival of the instinctive taste of semi-savage races, and the total lack of it in everything else. The designs cut on the bark of their canoes, the cunningly blended colors in their basket - work, are thoroughly good in their way ; but contact with a higher civilization seems to have affected them as it has the Japanese, turning their attention chiefly to making napkin-rings and collar-boxes, and to a hideous delight in tawdry finery, which is fondly, though distantly, modelled on current American fashions.

Bar Harbor drinks the cup of summer standing. In mid-April the snow may lie six feet deep, and before the end of October long icicles are often hanging on the north side of the rocks, while even in August the northern lights shoot up their quivering, spectral spears from the horizon to the zenith. Some fierce days of heat there are in July, but on the whole the tem-

DRAWN BY C. S. REINHART.

Climbing Newport Mountain.

perature is decidedly arctic, especially to one accustomed to a less rigorous climate. In New York we are used to having the kindly fruits of the earth brought to us long before their natural season, and it sounds strangely to be told at Bar Harbor that the first garden strawberries may be looked for about the fourth of July, and that June lilies will bloom early in August; but such trifles only give one a feeling of chasing the summer, as climate-fanciers follow the spring, and are certainly not to be reckoned as grievances. The people who have a certain very slight right to complain are the artists, who, having heard of the beauties of Mount Desert, come prepared to carry away at least a remi ıder of them on canvas or paper. They find that they have fallen upon a spot almost entirely deficient in what painters term "atmosphere," and of which the characteristic effects almost defy reproduction. In what is known as a "real Bar Harbor day" the air is so thin and clear that there seem to be no distant effects, and objects lose their relative values. The sea is of a darker blue than the sky, and the rocks are very red or very gray, and the birches are of a brighter green than the firs, which stand out against the sky with edges as sharp as those of the tightly curled trees on wooden stands in the toy Swiss farm - yards dear to our youth. But that is all. Even the clouds seem to abjure mystery and take definite outlines; the water is spangled with shining points where the light breeze ruffles it, and one can see every patch on the sail of the old fishing-schooner making her leisurely way to her anchorage. Any attempt at a faithful rendering of such dry brilliancy is apt to have a fatal likeness to a chromo-lithograph, and the artist usually ends by leaving his paint-box at home, and giving himself up to enjoyment of the keen air that tingles through his veins like wine.

The truthful chronicler is forced to admit that the climate of Bar Harbor has two drawbacks—high wind and fog, one usually following the other. Out of a clear sky, without a cloud, while the sun grins away derisively overhead, a southwest gale will often blow a whole day, filling the village streets with stinging dust and the whirling disks of vagrant hats, and making the little fleet of catboats and launches in the harbor duck and strain at their moorings; turning venturesome girls who try to walk into struggling pillars of strangely twisted drapery, and even in the heart of the warm woods tearing at the crowded trees so that they sigh and creak as they rub their weary old limbs against one another. The second day is gray and cloudy, on the third it rains, but still the wind blows, a nervous wind that makes one long to pick a quarrel with one's best friend. And then the wind drops as suddenly as it rose, and

"Landed."

A Yachting Party.

the next day all discomfort, past and to come, is forgotten for awhile in sheer delight of beauty. For the air is still, and the sun shines gently on a dull green sea over which little shivers run now and then, and far in the offing there is the gray line of a fog-bank. Slowly it comes in with the southeast wind, stealing along the surface of the water, now closing softly round an island, then rising from it like a wreath of smoke, here piled into a fleecy mass, there turned to silver and scattered by a sunbeam, but coming on and on, and creeping up and up, until the trees on the Porcupines have their feet in the clouds like Wagnerian heroes; and presently they also are hidden, and the whole harbor is swathed in a soft cloud, from the depths of which come now and then the muffled, anxious whistles of the little steamers which ply about the bay—the Silver Star, from Winter Harbor; the Cimbria, from Bangor; and louder and deeper, the hoarse note of the Sappho as she feels her way across with passengers from the ferry. When the oldest inhabitant is asked how long a fog may last he will shake his head, shift his quid, and decline to commit himself. There is a legend of a young man who came in on a yacht some years ago, duly prepared to enjoy himself and admire the scenery. His skipper groped his way to an anchorage in a mist so dense that he could not see fifty feet ahead or astern ; the luckless young man went about for nine mortal days, swathed in a soft, smothering blanket ; on the tenth day he sailed away, still in a thick fog, and swearing mighty oaths. Even when the fog lies over the bay the air may be quite clear inland, and after a drive among the hills it is a curious sensation to come back to the shore. In the wooded uplands all is sunny and cheerful, but when the village is reached a cold breath is stealing through it as though the door of an ice-house had been left open, and on turning down a side-street a gray wall of mist blots out trees and shore alike.

To anyone not familiar with it, catboat sailing in a thick fog does not suggest itself as an amusement. It has a strong attraction of its own, however, for the breeze is usually steady, and the entire obliteration of the familiar landmarks gives an element of uncertainty and adventure. The course must be steered by the compass, and it is necessary to have accurate notes of the local bearings. If the harbor is at all crowded the little boat feels her way out slowly, close-hauled, as carefully as though she were alive ; but once in the freer water the sheet is started, and she slips forward into infinite mystery. Every sense is strained to take the place of sight, which is baffled and almost useless in the thickly pressing veil that now and then grows thinner for a moment, only to close in again more densely. The sharp lapping of the water against the sides of the boat, the wash of the rising tide upon some island, the shrill scream of a gull overhead, the whistle of a launch astern in the harbor — all these make to themselves echoes, and by and by the far-off beat of a side-wheel steamer throbs with a great palpitation in the stillness. Boats which ply for profit or sail for pleasure are apt to make noise enough in a fog ; but the fishermen give themselves less trouble, and slipping along, ghost-like, one may be suddenly aware of a larger and darker phantom ahead,

to which it is wise to give a respectfully wide berth, without insisting too much upon the privileges of the starboard tack and the possible right of way, when the water is over-cold for much swimming. There does not seem to be any particular reason for ever turning back, when one is not bound for any visible point, and you may dream your dream out before you come about and run free for the harbor again. The fog is, if anything, thicker than when you started, and it is no easy matter to find your berth ; but the boat seems to "kinder smell her way," as an old sailor once remarked in a like case, and at last she bumps gently against her mooring-buoy.

The most beautiful effects of fog at Bar Harbor are to be seen from Newport Hill, which is about a thousand feet high, and is a mile or two out of the village. At first the path leads upward among thick woods, through which the sunlight falls in yellow patches, and where the squirrels chatter angrily from the spruce boughs. This part of the way is very pretty, though it is apt to be warm, and in early summer the black flies make succulent meals on the nape of the pilgrim's neck. A little farther on, the path leads out over broad open stretches of granite rock, scratched and furrowed by a primeval glacier, with scrubby tufts of mountain laurel growing in the stony hollows, and blueberry bushes holding on for dear life everywhere. Oddly enough, it is the easiest thing in the world to lose the path, although it has been considerably marked with a line of small cairns, which, however, are set at varying distances apart, often as far as a couple of hundred feet each from the next, and are built up of fragments of the rock itself, so that they are hard to distinguish in a failing light. To miss the path means wandering aimlessly over the slippery rock-slopes, or striking down the hill-side through the almost impenetrable underbrush, with the further penalty, especially if one happen to have a companion of the other sex, of being unmercifully jeered at ; for to have lost one's way on Newport Mountain is as well-worn an excuse at Bar Harbor as

Anemone Cave.

it is, in town, to say that one's cab did not come. Once fairly at the top, and having conscientiously looked at the view all round, there is no lack of sheltered corners for smoke and contemplation. On the one hand the open sea stretches out, a sheet of gray steel, with great patches of speckled froth and foam here and there, near the shore, like white leopard skins, flung off by the grim puritan rocks that will have none of such heathenish adorning. On the other hand the mainland stretches its cruel, jagged line beyond Schoodic, and the lighthouse on Egg Rock stands up straight as a sentinel to guard the bay. Two or three big men-of-war lying in the harbor might be taken for neat models of themselves, and the little craft moving about them are like water-beetles or flitting white moths. But the sea has changed suddenly, and it shivers all over as though the cold water could feel yet colder, and all at once the fog-bank that has been lying so innocently outside begins to unfold itself and steal forward over the surface. There does not seem to be much air above, and the trees on the Porcupines are still free. But on the right all is very different. Through the deep gorge or cleft between Newport and Dry Mountain, into which the sun has been beating all day, the chilly fog-wind now draws hard, and the fleecy cloud pours after it. Nothing, perhaps, could be less like the stern side of Dry Mountain than the gracious sweep of Mount Ida, and yet, as one looks, the lines of Tennyson's "Œnone" rise to the memory:

" The swimming vapor slopes athwart the glen,
  Puts forth an arm, and creeps from pine to pine,
  And loiters, slowly drawn."

But you will do well not to loiter too long yourself, for gray cairns are ill to find in a gray mist, and you had better gain the woods by the time the top of Newport is swathed in cloud as though it were a real grown-up mountain.

Mount Desert is lucky in its proper names of places, having been discovered as a summer resort late enough to escape the semi-classical namings of "Baths" and "Mirrors" and "Bowers," which have sentimentalized the rocks and pools of the White Mountains. A few French words still linger as a reminder of the time when Louis XIV. gave the original grant to the Sieur de la Motte Cadillac; but most of them, like Hull's Cove and Town Hill, have an honest colonial American ring, while about Pretty Marsh Harbor there is a certain echo of romance, and "Junk o' Pork" and "Rum Key," two little islands, or rather rocks, in the bay, have a very nautical, and even piratical, suggestiveness. At the first glance the island, on a map, reminds one somewhat of the dejected lamb which hangs by his middle in the order of the Golden Fleece. The deep indentation is Somes's Sound, running far inland, with Somesville at its head, a quiet New England village, with a white meeting-house, and many other houses, most of them also white, and standing among gnarled apple-trees, in a gentle, dozing tranquillity from which the place is roused when parties drive over from Bar Harbor to eat broiled

Cottage Life — a Luncheon Party.

Eagle Lake.

chickens and "pop-overs" at the local hotel, and to drive back by moonlight —expeditions which are considered to have sufficient local color to entitle them to notice, without omission of the pop-overs, in Baedeker's recent "Guide to the United States." In the neighborhood of Somesville the characteristics of the native population are much more noticeable than at Bar Harbor, only eight miles away, where a watering-place has been grafted on a fishing village. At some time or other in his life almost every islander seems to have followed the sea; the man who drives your buckboard may have been more than once to China, and it is extremely likely that the farmer who brings you your green peas has been tossed for many a week of hours in a crazy dory off the

DRAWN BY C. S. REINHART.

A Buckboard Party.

ENGRAVED BY WITTE.

deadly Banks, which cost us every year so many lives. In nearly every home there is some keepsake from far away lands, some tribute from arctic or tropic seas, and when at last an old captain makes up his mind to stay ashore it is certain that there will be something about his house to show his former calling — a pair of huge whale-ribs on either side of the front door, flowers growing in shells that have held the murmur of the Indian Ocean, and, instead of a cock or banner, a model of some sort of boat perched on the barn for a weather-vane. That a sailor-man is a handy man is true the world over, but the Maine man seems to have an especial knack with wood, from the lumber - camp to the cabinetmaker's bench, and many a carpenter working by the day will turn out a well-finished sideboard or an odd piece of artistic furniture from the roughest sort of pencil sketch. They are good smiths, too, and the best of their wrought-iron recalls the breadth and freedom of the early German and Italian work.

Society at Bar Harbor does not now differ in any particularly salient manner from good society anywhere else, except that it is rather more cosmopolitan. When the guests at a small dinner or luncheon may have come from New York, Philadelphia, Boston, Washington, and Chicago, it is impossible that the conversation should fall into that jargon of a clique which often makes the talk of the most centralized society, like that of Paris or London, seem narrow and provincial to the unfortunate outsider. One amusing survival of the simpler early days is the habit of going out in the evening in uncovered traps. There are a few private broughams, but if you are dining out, and happen to reach the house as a lady drives up, the chances are that you will help her to alight from an open buckboard, her smart French frock shrouded in a long cloak, and her head more or less muffled and protected. One or two of the livery-stables have hacks which must have been very old when they were brought from Bangor, and which now hold together almost by a miracle. A year or two ago one of them could never be sent out without two men on the box, not indeed for the

sake of lending the turn-out any fictitious splendor, but because one of them had to "mind the door," which was broken, and could neither be shut nor opened by any one inside. If two or three entertainments take place on the same night there is telephoning loud and long for these antediluvian vehicles, as the only other alternative is to take a sort of carry-all with leather side-curtains which have a treacherous way of blowing open and dropping small water-spouts down the back of one's neck.

It would be out of place for a mere visitor to launch into predictions regarding the social future of Bar Harbor. But one thing at least seems certain—it can never be in any sense a rival to Newport. The conditions which make the summer life of the latter more brilliant than that of any other watering-place in the world, mark it also as the playground of a great commercial metropolis, and a large proportion of its pleasure-seekers would not dare to be eighteen hours distant from New York, as they must be at Bar Harbor, until our means of getting about shall be singularly improved.

Then there are not the opportunities for display of riches and for social competition which already exist at Newport. The villas and cottages are scattered and isolated ; there is no convenient central point of general meeting, and the roads are too hilly for any but light American carriages. Some victorias manage to trundle about, but the horses which draw them, or hold back their weight, look far from comfortable, and although occasional coaches have made a brief appearance they have not been a success, as on most of the thickly wooded roads their passengers are in danger of the fate of Absalom. There is an Ocean Drive which is fine in parts, and another road runs above the upper bay, seeming in some places to overhang the water, and affording a charming view of the Gouldsboro' hills on the mainland ; but on the whole there are few roads. There is no turf on which to ride, and the pleasure of keeping horses, except as a convenient means of getting from one place to another, is limited. But there is always the sea, and to that one comes back with a love that is ever new. Men who know what they are talking about say that Frenchman's Bay is apt to be dangerous for small craft, on account of the sudden squalls which come over the hills and drop on the water like the slap of a tiger's paw, and it would certainly be hard to find a place in which there can be at the same time such an amiable diversity of winds. It is not at all uncommon to see two schooners within a couple of miles of each other, both running close-hauled or both before the wind, but on the same tack and in opposite directions. Another experience, familiar but always trying, consists in starting with a light but steady southeast breeze which feels as if it would hold through the morning, but which drops out suddenly and completely within half an hour, leaving one bobbing and broiling in a flat calm, until, without warning, it begins to blow hard from some point of the west. Sometimes there is a good sailing breeze at night when the moon is near the full, and to be on the water then is an enchantment. The glistening wake has here and there a shining point of phosphorescence; the familiar lines of the islands are softened with a silver haze; and the whole scene has a certain poetic quality which the positive beauty of daylight cannot lend to it. One is reminded of a woman of the world whom one has known as always sure of herself and almost hard, until in a moment of weariness, of weakness, or of sadness, of fatigue or despondency, the gentler nature glimmers under the mask.

Entirely apart from the question of exercise nothing perhaps affords such lasting amusement at Bar Harbor as rowing, for it rarely blows so hard that one cannot get out, and one is independent of calms and master of one's own time. All along the shore the granite rocks come down to the edge of the water, which in many places lies deep under sheer cliffs. The tide rises and falls about a dozen feet, and one may do duller things on a hot morning than pull slowly, very slowly, along in the shade at half-tide, watching the starfish that hold on to the face of the rock with their red hands, and the brown weed rising and falling as the water swings slowly back and forth. If the tide is not too high one may explore the moderately thrilling recesses of the caves which abound on some of the islands, and if the hour is not too late one may have agreeable converse with some old gentleman who has been visiting his lobster-pots, and who has probably sailed every known sea in his time. Of late years several of our ships of war have been at Bar Harbor every summer, and more than once a whole squadron; and the yachts of the New York and Eastern Clubs put in either separately or in little parties. While they are in port the harbor is gay with bunting and laughter and music, and as one sits on the deck of a yacht in the evening the lights of the village, as they go straggling up the hill and along the shore, have a very foreign look, and the cardboard masses of its wooden hotels loom up as if they were really substantial habitations.

After being a few days at Bar Harbor one begins to feel some curiosity about the phases through which it must have passed. There are now a number of cottages, most of them simple, with here and there a few that are more elaborate, and about a dozen hotels, three or four of which seem to be always full and prosperous, while some others find it at least worth their while to keep open; but there are still others which have frankly given up the game, and are permanently closed and for sale, though no one seems anxious to buy them. Yet they must have been needed when they were built in the bygone days, which were not long ago, and after exhausting a friend or two with questions one learns that Bar Harbor already has a past which does not seem likely to repeat itself. It was discovered nearly thirty years ago by a few artists and students roaming, like Dr. Syntax, in search of the picturesque, and most of them, if they survive, can be moved to rage like the heathen, even at the present day, by reminding them that they could then have bought land for a song by the acre where it now sells by the foot. A few comfort themselves with the reflection that they were only rich in youth and strength in those days, and had no money wherewith to buy land anywhere. Year by year the fame of Bar Harbor spreads far and wide, and as one hotel became too crowded another sprang up beside it, until about twelve years ago the place was in the full height of popularity. The few private houses were extremely simple, and nearly everybody lived either in the hotels or in little wooden cottages with no kitchens. The cottagers had to go to one of the hotels for their food, and were known as "mealers" if they were near enough to walk, and "hauled mealers" if they had to be collected with a cart. The little houses were very uncomfortable, and the things to eat at the hotels very bad. Biscuits and preserves formed an appreciable part of the visitor's luggage, and the member of a table who could and would make good salad-dressing.became a person of importance, for fresh lobsters and stringy chickens could be bought cheap, and a judicious regular subsidy to the hotel cook was an excellent investment. If one was asked to dine at a private house it was thought better taste not to boast of it beforehand, nor to talk of it overmuch afterward, and the host on his part always expected to provide enough food to satisfy a crew of famished sailors. For several seasons men rarely wore evening dress, and such unusual occasions required previous consultation and discussion, lest one man should seem to be more formal or ostentatious than the rest. This was among the quieter "cottage colony," but at the large hotels, of which Rodick's was the most popular, there was little question of sumptuary laws, and at the occasional "hops" young fellows in flannels and knickerbockers were the partners of pretty girls gay in the fresh finery which a woman seems able always to carry in the most restricted luggage.

The principal characteristic of the place was an air of youth—it did not seem as if any one could ever be more than twenty-five years old. Parties of half a dozen girls were often under the nominal care of one chaperon, generally chosen because she was good-natured and not too strict, but as a matter of fact the young people protected themselves and one another. Large picnic parties frequently went off for the day in buckboards, and there is a lonely sheet of water among the hills, called Eagle Lake, which used to be a favorite goal for afternoon expeditions. There were canoes and row-boats to be had, and in the evening supper was obtainable, and better than in the Bar Harbor hotels, at a little tavern where the prohibition laws of the State were defied. The usual result followed, and very bad things to drink were sold at very high prices, after paying which the party came home, making the wood-roads ring with laughter and singing. That is all changed now. The tavern is burnt down, a great wooden box in the lake marks the sluice which takes the village water-supply, people only cross it on the way to Jordan's Pond, and on moonlight nights it hears but the occasional splash of a fish, or now and then the wild laughter of the loon. Although parties were popular enough, the pairs who happened to have a temporary affinity were generally in each other's company all day long, wandering over the hills, rowing or paddling on the bay, or sitting on the rocks and islands, each pair out of ear-shot of the next. On any one of the "Porcupines" there were always sure to be two or three row-boats or canoes drawn up on the little beach; and, as many of their navigators were not used to so high a tide-rise, the skiffs frequently floated off, and it was part of the boatmen's regular business to pick them up and rescue the helpless couples to whom they belonged. In the evenings when there was moonlight the sight on the bay was really charming. The meal called tea at the hotels tempted no one to linger over it, and as soon as it was over the board-walk was alive with boys and girls hurrying down to the landing-stages, the young man in light flannels, sunburnt and strong, with his companion's bright shawl flung over one shoulder, while the maiden pattered along beside him, her white frock drawn up over a gay striped petticoat, after the fashion of those days, and often her own special paddle in her hand, perhaps with her initials carved carefully thereon and filled in with sealing-wax, rubbed smooth. Then there was a scramble at the floats, and a few minutes later the harbor was covered with boats and canoes, while those who were crowded out consoled themselves by sitting on the rocks along the shore. Slowly each little craft drew away from its neighbor on the quiet water, the young man pulling lazily or wielding the paddle silently with sweeping strokes of his bare brown arm—the girl sitting luxuriously in the stern-sheets, or on a deer-skin in the bottom of the canoe. The sun went down toward Hull's Cove; and as the red glow faded on the upper bay and the moon rose behind Schoodic, twilight merging into moonlight, the rippling note of a girl's laughter or the twang of a banjo ran softly over the water, a white speck showed where a boat was beached on the shingle of an island, while another floated like a black bar into the silver wake of the moon. Late in the evening the boats came in, one by one, and for those who could afford it there were little supper-parties at Sproul's restaurant, while others contented themselves with mild orgies of biscuits, jam, and the sticky but sustaining caramel. The famous "fish-pond" at Rodick's was a large hall in which the young people used to assemble after breakfast and the early dinner, and in which the girls were supposed to angle for their escorts. It must have been a curious sight. Some of the prettiest girls in all the country were gathered together there, and the soft vowels of the South mingled with the decided consonants of the Westerner. As a school of manners the fish-pond had its drawbacks for young men. They were always rather in the minority, and a good-looking college boy was as much run after as a marriageable British peer, with no ulterior designs, however, on the part of his pursuers, but only the frank determination to

"have a good time." People who belonged to the elders even then, and bore the mark of the frump, still tell how startling it was to see a youth sitting on the broad counter of the office and swinging his legs, with his polo cap on the back of his head, while two of the prettiest girls in the world stood and talked to him, in smiling unconsciousness of his rudeness. Of course such conditions were only possible in a society which still had traditions of a time not very remote, when boys and girls had tramped to and from the village meeting-house and singing-school together, and on the whole it does not seem that any particular harm came of it at all. A few imprudent early marriages, a large number of short-lived betrothals, kisses many, and here and there a heartache would sum up the record of a summer at Bar Harbor in the old days. The young men got over their heartaches and married girls whom they would have thought slow at Mount Desert; the beauty of the board walk married a quiet man who had not been there, and advised her mother not to let her younger sister go, and after a while the newspaper correspondent began to accumulate the stock of stories about summer girls and engagement rings, on which he has been drawing ever since. The quiet people who liked the climate got tired of living on fried fish and lemon pie, and built themselves houses in chosen spots, with kitchens, and each of them is convinced, and ready to maintain, that he occupies the most thoroughly desirable spot on the island. Fortunately, so far as that is concerned, the wanderer is not called upon to decide where owners disagree, and with happy impartiality he may put away his visit, with all its associations, in the safe cupboard of his pleasant memories.

15

The North Shore
of Massachusetts

SCRIBNER'S MAGAZINE

JULY 1894

THE NORTH SHORE OF MASSACHUSETTS

By Robert Grant

ILLUSTRATIONS BY W. T. SMEDLEY

O those who live in Boston and its vicinity the North Shore of Massachusetts, or The North Shore, as it is always called, has come to have an identity as a summer-resort quite as distinct as that of Bar Harbor, Newport, or Lenox. Even New Yorkers, enlightened as to its advantages by those who go down to the sea in yachts, have learned to think of it respectfully as a very pretty place to which Bostonians who wish to keep cool, and yet be able to see the gilded dome of the State-house through a telescope, hie themselves from June to October. One would suppose that its accessibility, its coolness, its freedom from either democratic or plutocratic crowds, and the unique combination of the seaside and the country which it affords would have attracted before this the people from large cities who wish to be comfortable without being devoured by mosquitoes, to be cheerful without having to be riotous, to get enough to eat without being obliged to fight for it, and to sit on their piazzas without exposure to kodaks, picnickers, or surf flirtation. And yet the comfort-seeking public still passes it by in favor of abandoned farms, sylvan camps, islands on the coast of Maine, and the various other refuges from the life of the average summer watering-place. Perhaps the reason is to be found in the argument that it is too near Boston, which is a polite way of expressing reluctance to invade the sacred precincts of the most critical society in America for fear of not pleasing. If such be the case, this attitude of caution acts as a two-edged sword, for if there is any plea to be urged against the attractiveness of the North Shore it is that the society is so exclusively Bostonese. The families from a distance are almost to be numbered on the fingers of one hand, and you meet in your walks and drives and social intercourse the self-same people with whom you have dined and slummed, or whom you have seen at the Symphony Concerts all winter. If it is meet that man should not live alone, it is almost equally desirable that he should for a month or two in every year lose sight of all his family, except-

The Beverly Shore.

ing his very nearest and dearest, and his entire customary social acquaintance. But this is a privilege which only those who are not tied by business exigencies to the apron-strings of their native city are able to enjoy with any degree of regularity.

By the North Shore is meant the northern coast of Massachusetts Bay, from Nahant and Swampscott on the southwest to Gloucester and Cape Ann on the northeast. Cape Ann is the end of everything except the Atlantic Ocean, and civilization properly ceases before you come to Gloucester, the famous fishing-town of this portion of the world, which lies thirty-one miles from Boston in a tolerably direct line by rail. Along the borders of this rocky coast, which abounds in marvellous curves and indentations, including several fine harbors, stands a succession of villas, of various types of architecture, and for the most part at sufficient intervals from one another to insure privacy, for a distance of fifteen miles. Swampscott, Phillips Beach, Marblehead Neck, Beverly, Pride's Crossing, Beverly Farms, West Manchester, and Manchester, are among the names by which, for the sake of municipal or railway convenience, one strip of shore is distinguished from the next ; but except for the purposes of taxation the aggregation of villas may be said to be part and parcel of no town, and to be a community unto themselves. In the same category should also be included Nahant, a watering-place far older than any of these, a

rocky promontory stretching out into the sea, nearly at right angles with the coast from Lynn, to which it is joined by a narrow line of sand beach, three miles long, traversed by a single road. The late Thomas Gold Appleton fastened upon Nahant the epithet of " Cold Roast Boston." It has for several generations been a favorite summer-resort for old Boston families, and its popularity has never waned among those who by descent or purchase have acquired an interest in its limited territory. For invigorating coolness of atmosphere, boldness and picturesqueness of rock effects, and the complete illusion of being at sea, which one experiences on many a piazza, Nahant has attractions at least equal to those of the rest of The North Shore. There is indeed a mild rivalry between its cottagers and those of the Beverly coast, whose favorite taunt, that Nahant possesses only one drive, can never be refuted, and only counterbalanced by the claim that those who sleep at Nahant can enjoy a delicious sail to the city by steamboat, instead of being obliged to undergo a heated, dusty, railway journey. The rapid and luxurious evolution of summer life along the North Shore has had a marked effect upon the appearance of Nahant, and to some extent upon the manner of life there. Twenty-five years ago Nahant was the aristocratic watering-place of Boston ; but there were few if any trim lawns to be found upon its territory, and there were no trees except an occasional clump of weather-beaten balm of Gileads. White weed, dandelions, and butter-cups, the red honeysuckle, and common prickly roses ran delightful riot in front of every piazza, and the not infrequent cry of "Cows on the place," was a pleasant slogan to the rising generation. To-day all these primitive beauties have disappeared beneath the harrow of the landscape gardener, and given place to cultivated verdure, æsthetic-looking bushes, and a very respectable number of trees, so that it is no longer possible for the Beverlyites to declare, as formerly, that there is not a reputable piece of foliage on the peninsula. Moreover, a very successful club or casino, organized within the last five years, acts as a central magnet to draw the cottagers from their piazzas and to promote social circulation. And still along the water's edge, especially on the eastern side, stands a splendid array of cliffs which no one has ever attempted to improve, and which are more impressive in their ruggedness and bold beauty than any on the North Shore. There are, indeed, none on the coast, excepting perhaps at Bar Harbor, which surpass them in grandeur. Here is the well-known Pulpit Rock, so named from its shape, to the top of which, in the days of the old hotel—burned more than thirty years ago, and never rebuilt—an adventurous damsel climbed, only to discover that she had to be lowered by ropes. Tradition tells us that Nahant was originally traded by an Indian for a suit of clothes; and it is probable that the simple savage felt that he got quite as good a bargain as William Blackstone did when he parted with Boston. Where in the world is there such a delightful dormitory as Nahant, distant by either sea or land only an hour from the city, where the tired business man may refresh his brow and lungs and eyes, and his children may breathe ozone day in day out, and learn to swim like ducks in the coldest of cold waters?

The North Shore proper, which begins at Swampscott and extends beyond West Manchester, represents, unlike Nahant, the growth of the last twenty years. It is a fringe of aristocracy skirting the coast of the noble County of Essex, whose towns of Salem, Beverly, Marblehead, and Gloucester have, in the past, been such intelligent and honest factors in the welfare of the State and nation. But the once well-known Ocean Street, Lynn, should not be passed over in any itinerary of this shore. This short, straight avenue, on the ocean confines of the shoe town of Lynn, was, twenty-five years ago, divided into perhaps a dozen and a half beautiful estates, of from one to three acres in extent, ranged side by side in precise stateliness. The villas were elaborate for that time, and the places were tended far more carefully than those of Nahant, and made in most instances to display beautiful lawns and fine trees and flowers. They fronted on the avenue, and backed directly on the full expanse of the portion of Massachu-

Looking Toward Swampscott from the Cliffs at Nahant.

Cape Ann.
"The end of everything except the Atlantic Ocean."

setts Bay which lies under the lee of Nahant, and they were owned by Boston people of wealth and social prominence. Under the combined influence of the tide of fashion, which was moving farther along the coast, and the increased demand for summer residences, which suggested to real-estate speculators the possibilities of subdivision, these fine estates began to drop into the market about twenty years ago, and have since been cut up into smaller building lots and traversed by connecting streets. The old villas have been pulled down, and in one or two cases have been superseded by much more elaborate structures, the homes chiefly of the wealthy manufacturers of Lynn. But the greater portion of the new cottages are of the every-day Queen Anne pattern, and, though they command the same beautiful ocean outlook as formerly, they are too much commanded by the windows of their next-door neighbors. In short, Ocean Street has become more like its next-door neighbor, Swampscott, a community of small estates on the edge of the sea, grouped closely together with an eye only to keeping cool and to looking seaward in summer. Ocean Street, however, as has been stated, has been appropriated chiefly by the rich shoemakers of Lynn, who live there the year round, whereas Swampscott's single shore road, which runs out of Ocean Street, has for years and years been the camping-ground of

people from Boston and its vicinity who have been content to allow its fishing-village aspect to remain unaltered except in a very few instances. Here are two large hotels, and a host of boarding-houses, and a sand beach, and a railroad station within easy driving distance to accommodate the business men who wish to live at the sea-side with as little trouble and expense as possible, and at the same time to be close to town. This simplicity of architectural and social effects is true, particularly of the village proper. Beyond it the shore, which stretches to Marblehead, has become occupied by more elaborate cottages, some conspicuously ugly and others of very tasteful design. Many fine water-views are obtained from these, notably from the beautiful Galloupe's Point, which is shut out from the dust of the high road and other suggestions of urban proximity. In brief, it may be stated that the last twenty years have seen the erection, along the hitherto unoccupied shore from Swampscott to Marblehead, of colonies of cottages inviting the proprietorship of the increasing class of well-to-do people who desire to live comfortably in summer, interspersed with an occasional hotel of ample dimensions, the prices of which terrify the democratic beachcomber whose ambition is bounded by a fishing-pole, clams, and pink lemonade.

In an indenture of the coast formed

DRAWN BY W. T. SMEDLEY.

On the Piazza of the Eastern Yacht Club at Marblehead

by the harbors of Marblehead and Salem, and on a smaller harbor of its own, is situated the ancient village, but modern shoe town, of Beverly, from which the picturesque strip of shore which stretches thence to Cape Ann takes its name. For almost a generation there has been a nucleus of beautiful estates on the shore, beyond the street limits of the town, where the same class of people who went summer after summer to Nahant lived in peaceful enjoyment of broad acres of woods, marsh, and beach, undisturbed by thrifty cogitations as to their market price. The houses, like the original houses at Nahant, were square, comfortable-looking, dull-colored edifices, surrounded by broad piazzas, protected by sloping roofs unenlivened by the modern shingle stain, and the landscape wore a rougher appearance than at present. To the northeast, as far as the eye could see, lay a marvellous coast,

with here a curving beach and there a wooded point, and here again a superb reach of cliffs, each and all provided with a background of undulating fields and rich dark foliage. All this edge of ocean, with its wealth of country behind, was practically unoccupied, and large tracts of it could be purchased at what now seem pitiful figures from the fishermen farmers who held it in fee. To the south-southwest, across the water, the Beverly cottagers looked at the queer old town of Marblehead without a suspicion that there was a handsome fortune staring them in the face in the shape of the spit of land which forms the outer bulwark of the harbor, where to-day the white-winged yachts almost outnumber the white-winged gulls. Twenty years ago and less, Marblehead Neck, as it is called, was in the general estimation a bleak headland which no one cared to build upon. Now it fairly bristles with small habitations, which have sprung up in such close proximity to one another, and on such primitive lines, architecturally speaking, as almost to suggest a camp-meeting settlement. A little apart from these stands the club-house of the Eastern Yacht Club, the meeting-place on shore of the yachting brotherhood, whither, at the time of the sojourn of the New York or Eastern squadrons, comes all the fashionable Shore to dine and dance and visit the racing machines and the graceful floating boudoirs which fairly crowd the tranquil waters of the snug harbor below. Outside this same harbor, where the pleasure yachts of two friendly countries contend for silver cups in eager emulation, the Chesapeake and the Shannon fired broadsides at each other in the same summer weather not far from a hundred years ago.

It is at and beyond Beverly, however, that the true

Looking Toward Boston from Nahant.

The Cliffs at Nahant.

grandeur of the North Shore begins. Marblehead Neck is bold and reaches out to sea, and the old town of Marblehead, which lies directly across the narrow harbor, provides, by its quaint streets and its legend of Skipper Ireson with the hard heart, abundant material for the edification of those who take an afternoon drive in that direction. But the true glory of the North Shore, that uniquely picturesque and ever-varying combination of sea-side and country which distinguishes it from the rest of this shore and from other shores, begins at Beverly. It sounds like a paradox to state that you may there look out from rugged cliffs over a summer sea and inhale its salt fragrance, and yet by a turn of your heel find yourself face to face with a landscape of rustic meadows and stately woods. Yet such is exactly the case. The dweller in this paradise scents on his piazza the mingled aroma of brine and pine, of storm-tossed seaweed and new-mown hay; and, moreover, in this instance man has joined hands with nature to preserve the beauties of the scene, in that he has refused to subdivide his lands. A succession of magnificent estates follows the shore, but almost invariably the houses stand in the midst of several acres, and are frequently sheltered by woods or surrounded by a more or less cultivated park. This gives an elegance to the landscape which serves to heighten the effect of the splendid scenery, and these conditions have been maintained in the rapid development of the shore which has taken place during the last ten or fifteen years.

The sudden increased demand for sea-side residences, and the. rapid and extraordinary trebling and quadrupling of values consequent thereon, which has been a part of the recent history of the entire New England coast, has been more remarkable in the case of the Beverly shore than in that of any other resort except Bar Harbor. Large tracts of wooded lands along the sea's edge, and strikingly beautiful points which had been suffered to remain unoccupied for generations save by local

At Manchester-by-the-Sea.

farmers, have changed ownership at fancy prices and been made the sites for villas of the most improved modern architecture. From Beverly you come to Pride's Crossing and Beverly Farms, beyond which lies West Manchester, Manchester and the Masconomo House —the one hotel of that immediate shore —and Magnolia; and everywhere the same class of habitation is to be seen, more elaborate and luxurious, perhaps, the farther you proceed. The eager purchaser has occupied every available piece of shore, and in many cases has bought it from poetic but far-sighted individuals who anticipated the demand. It sometimes happens in this wicked world, though perhaps too infrequently, that the practised acumen of the real-estate speculator is put to the blush by the more discerning wisdom of the seer.

Unlike Newport, Lenox, and Bar Harbor, the North Shore is first of all a dormitory. The busy men of affairs, who spend the summer at Beverly Farms or Manchester, go to Boston every day and return home in the early afternoon, content to sit on their piazzas enjoying the breezes from the ocean, or to drive or ride. Until within the last few years the evening meal was a high tea, at which the rising generation could entertain their contemporaries without compelling *paterfamilias* to do more than brush his hair, or depriving him of his evening paper. Many people on the Beverly shore now have late dinner; consequently there is more formality and circumstance, and he who would fain lie in a hammock and listen to the trembling of the sea may have to choose between green mint, curaçoa, and benedictine, and try to forget that he is to take the early train in the morning. But, after all, the entertaining of this kind is not extensive. *Paterfamilias* is a long-suffering biped, but his good nature is apt to give way after missing once or twice the A.M. train, which he had hoped would be later than he; and even the most energetic spirits in the family —naturally the unmarried daughters who need do nothing all day but breathe ozone—prefer to spend the evenings in their hammocks. A ball or evening reception such as we know at Lenox or Bar Harbor, or even the hotel hop, which is common enough at the hotels along the Swampscott-Marble-

A Yacht Race at Marblehead.

Pavilion at " The Masconomo."

in order to give them women luncheons—sometimes rather elaborate luncheons—where the conversation may be about art and literature, or may be about yachts and hunting, according to the aspirations of the hostess. Three afternoons a week, during July, August, and September, there is the opportunity, of which many avail themselves, to see the members of the Myopia Hunt Club play polo on the club grounds at Wenham, four or five miles inland to the north from Beverly. This is a favorite meeting-ground. To reach it you enjoy a delightful drive, and while there you are afforded a panorama of the toilettes and equipages of the Shore while watching the an-

head coast and at the Masconomo, is unheard of on the Beverly shore. Occasionally small parties drive through the woods to Chebacco Lake to sup on broiled chickens, thin fried potatoes and champagne, to dance a gay waltz or polka or two, and drive home by moonlight; but apart from occasional dinner-parties, this is the limit of the social gayety. A few of the younger matrons complain, as a consequence, that the Shore is dull and needs awakening; but the sentiment of the busy men, that rest after a warm summer's day in town is the best form of recreation, appeals to most wives and daughters, who indeed on their own account are delighted to make the most of the out-of-door life, to look after their lawns and shrubbery, to drive and walk, to go yachting if there is a yacht in the family, and in general to break away from the social diversions of life in town. There is some calling, and women invite other women from Nahant and elsewhere to stay with them

tics of the players. During the summer of 1893 the Essex County Club, a casino situated a little inland from Manchester, has been completed. This will doubtless prove a convenient uniting point for those who crave greater social activity, though, owing to the fact that its patrons are scattered along ten miles of shore, it is likely to be occasionally empty. A cynic might be disposed to suggest that the success of the Club at Nahant was the controlling reason why it was built.

The New England gentleman of fifty years ago, if he could see the way we live now, would open his eyes at the importance which the horse and his accoutrements have acquired in the eye of the present generation, and undoubtedly would come to the conclusion, on the whole, that our ancestors were bigoted in their association of a semblance of sin with a free use of the quadruped in question. Certainly the gay vehicles, bright harnesses, and sleek, stylish animals which are to be

DRAWN BY W. T. SMEDLEY.

Magnolia, from Norman's Woe Point.

Entrance to the Grounds of the Essex County Club.

this hunting element, many of whom do not hesitate to risk life and limb in their almost hysterical enjoyment of the transplanted ancient sport. The Hunt Club has a modest club-house at Hamilton, where a pack of hounds are kept, and in the course of the last five years a colony of horse-loving spirits has absorbed and settled upon the most attractive of the surrounding farms, some of which possess an old-fashioned picturesqueness which suggests brass andirons and gilly-flowers. These hunting men and women have succeeded in maintaining friendly relations with the Essex County yeomanry, over whose corn-fields they dash in pursuit of a real or imaginary reynard, and who were inclined at first to resent this new invasion of red-coats as undemocratic impertinence and a legal trespass. But well-mannered tact, especially if it go hand-and-glove with liberal indemnity, will mollify the wounded pride even of a New England farmer. By degrees the hard-headed countrymen, who sniffed at fox-hunting as mere Anglomania, have become genuinely, though grimly, enthralled by the pomp and excitement of the show, and take almost as much interest in following the fortunes of the riders as though they themselves were booted and spurred and swathed in pink. To cement mutual good feeling a ball is given every autumn, at which the wives and daughters of the country-side dance with the master of the hounds and his splendid company, who valiantly, if vainly, endeavor to cut pigeon-wings in emulation of the country swains.

If the temper of the Beverly-Manchester shore is equine, no less is it nautical. The telescopes on every piazza command the entrance to Marblehead Harbor, and the womenkind unable to distinguish a cutter from a

encountered nowadays along the country roads of the strict old county of Essex, are a vast improvement, from an æsthetic point of view, over the sombre chaises and inelegant nags by means of which our forefathers endangered their chances of salvation. The charms of out-door life on the North Shore have fostered a taste for riding and driving which has proved, alike in a hygienic and a liberalizing sense, of great benefit to both the sexes. Riding, at which most young ladies and many men in the North used to shy, has become, in several sections of the country, and conspicuously on the Beverly shore, a favorite form of exercise and recreation. Under the conduct of the Myopia Hunt Club, fox-hunts after the English pattern engage the enthusiastic attention of a considerable number of young and middle-aged people during the early autumn months. The beautiful inland country about Wenham, Hamilton, and Topsfield has become a race-course for

stone sloop or fishing schooner are in the minority. On fine sailing days a bevy of yachts, of every cut and length, is to be seen on the broad sweep of the horizon, and often so close to land that you would seem to be able to toss the traditional biscuit aboard until you made the attempt. And yet the number of vessels owned by the actual owners of the Shore is not so large as might be expected. Not everybody by any means keeps a yacht, and only an intermittent chain of moorings follows the coast. Now and again some cottager of means buys a steam-yacht for a season or two, in which he runs to town when he is not pressed for time, and invites his friends to make the return trip with him at the close of the business day. Others keep a comfortable full-fledged schooner, with a trusty sailing-master, at their doors as a family convenience, to be enjoyed whenever the spirit moves and the elements invite conjointly—which sometimes is not for days at a time, such are the caprices of women and children, the contrariety of weather, and the business obligations of man. There is, too, a moderate number of small craft—catboats and sloops—in which yachtsmen of sixteen and some of maturer years, who deem the pleasure of handling the tiller superior to that of following the dictates of a sailing-master, tempt the deep. But whether it is that the coast is an exposed one, so that yachts cannot lie there safely in a southeaster, or that the responsibilities of maintaining a white-winged racer seem to the average business man analogous to those of maintaining a white elephant, there is rather a dearth of yachts actually owned along the Beverly shore, in spite of the fact that in the racing season the coast is fairly gay with them. There are few more beautiful spectacles than the series of races annually conducted under the auspices of the Eastern Yacht Club, when the grand flotilla of visiting New York yachts, in all their high-priced majesty and gracefulness, join the united craft of the New England coast, and spread their wings under a deep blue sky before a rattling breeze. Only second to this display is the captivating spectacle of Marblehead Harbor viewed from the piazza of the Eastern Yacht Club, when the yachts, great and little, lie packed together at night, their wings folded and their sides and rigging aglow with electric lights and lanterns which make them seem like huge fireflies afloat on the dark waters of the basin. Hither to Marblehead Neck come crowds from Boston and the surrounding towns to see the Mayflower, the Volunteer, and the huge steam-yachts in which some of the conspicuously rich men of Gotham take their summer outings.

A casual observer might suppose that the only live issues on the North Shore were horses and yachts. The wave of the discovery that there are many ways of amusing one's self profitably and harmlessly in our vale of tears, the very idea of which was an abomination to those who laid the foundations of the Republic, has not spared this delightful region in its sweep across the country. But surface indications are apt to be deceitful, and it may truthfully be said that, even in the way of surface indications, the life along the North Shore has but few of the purely volatile features which distinguish many of the doings at Newport, for instance. And just as at New-

The Hounds—Myopia Hunt Club.

Avenue of Pines, near Manchester-by-the-Sea.

port and Bar Harbor there are hundreds of delightful people who live apart from the fashionable rout, because it bores them to jump and change feet all the year round, so this class along the North Shore is even larger, partly because of the more conservative spirit of the population, and partly for the reason already referred to, that the cottagers are chiefly active business or professional men who go to Boston every day. The North Shore is essentially a Paradise for men of comfortable means, who do not wish to be separated from their wives and children in summer, and who wish at the same time to give their families a thorough change of scene and atmosphere. Neither his interest in horses nor yachts, nor the desire to be socially rampant, induces the well-to-do Bostonian to settle along the North Shore. He thinks rather of the comparative ease with which he can exchange the parboiled pavements and the scent of tepid watermelon for the delicious breeze from the sea which greets him on his own piazza, where he can sit through the afternoon on a long cushioned chair and watch the yachts sail by, waxing proud in his belief that he is able to distinguish one from another. He thinks of the delightful and numerous drives in every direction, and of the safe beaches and shaded groves in the enjoyment of which the hue of health will be deepened in the faces of his children and of his wife and grown-up daughters, provided they do not wear veils. He thinks, in short, that he will be delightfully comfortable; that his household can be kept amiable by out-of-door amusements, while he enjoys the rest which middle-aged human nature ought to enjoy in the sweltering season, and that if he chances to feel frisky, he can drive over to dine at the Marblehead Club-House, or feast his eyes on the pink-coated pageantry of an aniseed hunt. And, not to leave the finer sensibilities out in the cold — you may be sure he

DRAWN BY W. T. SMEDLEY.

The Pleasure of Handling the Tiller.

Residences on the Point at Manchester-by-the-Sea.

bears them quietly in mind, this Bostonian cottager—there are unsurpassed and rarely paralleled effects of sky and water, and winds and woods, and sunset and moon-glory, continuously appealing to his love of nature with endless variety. The ocean on the north shore of Massachusetts Bay possesses a wider range of expression than on the other side, where it begins to woo the sands of Cape Cod and to yield to the milder moods of the Gulf Stream. It is a veritable lion here, and the rugged, rock-bound coast seems to be a necessary bulwark to stay the fury of the elements. The very temperature of the water, and the fresh, bracing vigor of the winds, suggest a strength and majesty which is sometimes trying to human constitutions which lack vitality. But though a lion when roused, this northern sea has a nobleness of disposition which makes you forget its cruelty on the very morrow after it has strewn the beach with salvage, and dashed in gorgeous spray well-nigh up to your chamber window. Then there

is a depth of blue in the sky and water, and a life-giving, life-stirring warmth in the sun which fills the soul with gladness; and when at nightfall the breeze dies away, and the pink and saffron clouds paint themselves upon the peaceful deep and the silent landscape, what a joy it is to sit and watch the twilight fade into night, the stars appear, and the light-house beacons come out like other stars along the horizon. How still, refreshing, and soothing is the night! You only just catch the refrain of the automatic buoy-whistle guarding the Graves, appropriately known as the Melancholy Bull, telling, from across the Bay, that the storm has been; and once and again a cool, salty puff announces the advent of the night-breeze. Now rides the moon, and far away across her glittering wake glides some coaster like a phantom ship. Can this be the ocean which yesterday seemed so cold and cruel and revengeful, as you listened to the roar of the wind upon the roof? Even the "Reef of Norman's Woe," that poetic sorrow of

The Reef of Norman's Woe.

the coast, the Mecca of the tourist who visits Gloucester, has lost its treacherous leer, and suggests for a moment to the ever-hopeful soul that nature has become the slave of man. Such days, such nights are the frequent recurring boon of the dweller by the North Shore.

Those who regard the continued individual ownership of large tracts of land, or even of an acreage sufficient to keep one's neighbor at a respectful distance, as inconsistent with true democratic development, will be likely to look askance at the beautiful estates along the North Shore. It may be that in a few generations we shall all live cheek by jowl with one another in houses built and painted after a stereotyped model, with exactly the same number of square feet of land in our front-yards, and under limitations as to the number of flowers we may grow in our pitiful little gardens, for fear of seeming to outstrip the luxury of those who are too indolent to grow any. Such a period may become necessary in the process of giving all men an opportunity to enjoy equally the fruits of the earth and the fulness thereof. But whatever the dim future may bring to pass in this regard by dint of positive law or ethical argument, there is no doubt that, at present, the beautiful sea-side estates which have been cut out of the coast-line from farthest Maine to the limits of the shore of Buzzard's Bay, during the last twenty years, are among the most precious of human possessions, and that the class of people seeking for them is increasing in direct ratio to the growth of refined civilization over the country. More and more do we realize that a residence at a summer watering-place hotel is apt to leave soul, mind, and body jaded, and that to bang about in the hot weather at fashionable beaches and promiscuous springs may amuse for a fortnight, but suggests by the close of a season the atmosphere of the *corps de ballet* or a circus. We are learning as a nation to rest in summer, instead of to gad, and those who have been the fortunate pioneers in the movement are indeed to be envied, for though the sands of the sea are said to be unnumbered, the coast of New England has its limitations. *Beati possidentes!*

16
Block Island

BLOCK ISLAND.

By Samuel W. Mendum.

"Lonely and wind-shorn, wood-forsaken,
With never a tree for spring to waken,
For tryst of lovers or farewells taken,

"Circled by waters that never freeze,
Beaten by billow and swept by breeze,
Lieth the island of Manisees."
Whittier—"The Palatine."

TWENTY-FIVE miles southwest of Newport and ten miles from Point Judith, the nearest land, lies Block Island, which has of late years grown so rapidly in favor as a summer resort with those who love the ocean and like to feel that they are so far removed from things continental that not even a land breeze can be mixed with the pure sea air they breathe.

The island has been in years gone by the scene of so many wrecks that it might naturally enough be thought that its name is the logical result of its position as a block to navigation; but in truth the name represents the sum total of immortality which the world has conferred upon one Adrian Block, a Dutch explorer, who seems to have thought it worth his while to land and formally "discover" the island, though ninety years before, in 1524, the French navigator Verrazano sailed around it and recorded its shape as triangular and the island as "full of hills and covered with trees." The last observation is of peculiar interest, as the island is now and has been for a hundred and fifty years utterly barren of timber, save for a few fruit and shade trees here and there, which by the most persistent nursing are helped to a precarious existence, so fiercely do the winds of winter blow upon them. The island has not yet been beaten out of the triangular shape by the terrible blows of the Atlantic; a map of it looks like a huge mutton-chop, the small end toward the north. It is also still so full of hills that its surface seems to have become solidified while fiercely boiling. The northern end, called Sandy Point, is low, but the bubbling surface gradually rises toward the centre, the highest point, Beacon Hill, being rather more than two hundred feet above the sea. Toward the southern end this high level is generally maintained, and abruptly terminates in perpendicular bluffs one hundred and fifty feet high, which the waves of the Atlantic, driven by "sou'easters" dash against, often with damaging effect.

The geology of Block Island has always been interesting, and of late certain questions have arisen as to the age of the underlying strata which make the island one of special interest to the geologist. According to Prof. O. C. Marsh, the eminent Yale geologist, who has given recent study to the island, the foundation clays, which still constitute the bulk of the island, were evidently much eroded before the glacial drift was spread over them. The depressions in these clays form the impervious stratum for the

bottom of the numerous ponds
for which the island is noted. The
opinions of Professor Marsh,
given in an article written last
September, and published in the
American Journal of Arts and Sciences (vol. 152, p. 295), are very
interesting. Professor Marsh says:

"The clays all appear to be
fresh water deposits, and should
certainly contain vertebrate fossils. I found none in the limited
time at my command, but more
careful exploration would undoubtedly bring them to light and
thus determine the geological age
of these interesting beds. . . .
The massive clay beds of Block
Island were derived from the decomposition of the granite rocks
to the north, and were deposited
in quiet waters. The iron ore now
in them came also from the northern crystalline rocks, mainly a
magnetite which may still be seen
in the sands of all the beaches of
the island, and on one of them
this mineral sand was for a while
used in making metallic iron.
. . . The glacial drift covers
most of the surfaces, and the hills
and shores are strewn with boulders of crystalline rocks, granite,
gneiss, quartz, etc., that came
over the ice from the mainland on
the north. Large masses of both
the porphyritic and the garnet-bearing gneiss, waifs from the
Rhode Island shore, may be
easily recognized; and in the
beach sand resulting from the
attrition of the latter, the separate
garnets may be found. On some
of the glacial hills, near the shore
or around the Great Pond, shell
heaps of considerable antiquity
may be observed, but so far as I
could learn none of them have
been explored. . . . The presence of such great masses of
stratified clay, evidently of high
antiquity, on this diminutive island facing the Atlantic, opens up

BLOCK ISLAND HARBOR,

many questions of interest beyond the mere geological age of the deposits. These beds of clay must be the remnants of a great formation which extended out far beyond the present coast line, and being of fresh water origin and laid down in quiet waters, they prove the former existence of an extensive barrier along the continental border between them and the Atlantic depths beyond."

Professor Marsh thinks there is reason to believe that the Block Island beds are as old as the Potomac beds, and may be assigned to the late jurassic, the middle period of the reptilian age. He is confident that future investigations will reveal fossils to confirm this belief.

It is a pity that old Block's title to the island's name has not been set aside for the older and more beautiful Isle of Manisees, which is Indian for Little God's Island, and gave the name to the first known inhabitants, the Manisees Indians, a branch of the famous Narragansetts. Before the actual settlement of the island, Captain John Oldham visited it for trading purposes, but lost his life at the hands of the savages, who butchered him mercilessly. It is often claimed that investigation generally proves a white man to be the original offender in cases of trouble with the Indians, and there is a tradition, not very widely known, that Oldham had sold the Maniseeans onion seeds, which he told them would yield a crop of gunpowder if planted. Soon after Oldham's death, the island was subjugated by Colonel Endicott, under authority from Massachusetts, as a punishment for that ruthless murder; and in 1637 the ownership of Massachusetts was acknowledged by Miantonomoh, the great Narragansett sachem. He made good his acknowledgment by paying a yearly tribute of one hundred fathoms of beads or wampum into the colonial treasury.

In 1658 the island was transferred to John Endicott, Richard Bellingham, Daniel Dennison and William Hawthorne, who sold it two years later for four hundred dollars to sixteen individuals, who "bought to improve." The purchasers built their vessels at Braintree and sent them around Cape Cod to Taunton, where the party embarked for Block Island, to become its pioneer settlers and the ancestors of its hardy people. A few years later the island was annexed to Rhode Island. It must have presented a far more beautiful sight in those

SOUTH LIGHT AND BLUFFS.

CLAY HEAD.

days than now, for dense forests covered it, while to-day its bare and remarkably uneven surface is unrelieved by foliage. For hardly more than sixty years was there timber enough for the settlers; one of the rarest and most proudly exhibited relics on the island is an old stave dug up from the original canal connecting the Great Pond with the sea, and confidently asserted to have been hewn from native timber.

The disappearance of the timber was looked upon with alarm by the inhabitants. More than a hundred and fifty years ago a town meeting was called to consider the matter, and it was stated in the preamble to the call that there was "great scarcity of timber and fencing stuff, and many people hath not enough for firing and fencing, and the mainland being so far off from this place, so that if we do not endeavor to preserve our timber and fencing stuff, the inhabitants must be forced to depart the island."

In spite of these formal proceedings the timber disappeared; but the population did not go with it, for kind Nature had provided in abundance substitutes for "firing and fencing stuff." In some places the pioneer settler could hardly have taken a step without treading on a stone, though singularly enough there is not a ledge on the island. These stones are now found in cellars and in the finely built walls which bound the fields and roads. It is estimated that there are more than three hundred miles of stone wall on the island.

For firing, there was a treasure which bountifully supplied the inhabitants until the use of coal became general. That treasure was peat, which for over one hundred years was the fuel of the island. Almost every farm has its peat bed, thanks to the innumerable pockets between the hills where vegetable matter has been deposited. Owing to the hard work in getting the peat from its beds, it is generally known upon the island as "tug." As soon as it is taken out it is moulded into balls by the hands, and when partially dried is stacked up in pyramids like piles of cannon balls, until it is thoroughly dry, when it is stored in the "tug-house." So late as 1875, 544 cords were dug; and it is still used to a limited extent.

The island had the vicissitudes of Indian, Colonial and Revolutionary war, common to all New England settlements, though it appears to have been singularly free from the persecution of the Indians. After their complete subjugation in 1637, there was constant fear of outbreak, but none actually occurred. During the progress of King Philip's war the islanders felt considerable alarm, and it is recorded that the total strength of the island, seventeen men and a boy, challenged the Indians, twenty times that number, to a pitched battle. The challenge was not accepted, and the victory thus won was so complete that ever afterwards an unbroken friendship continued between the Maniseeans and the whites.

Probably no body of Americans exhibited more admirable courage than the inhabitants of Block Island at the outbreak of the Revolution. When they unhesitatingly cast in their lot with the Colonies, it must have seemed even to themselves that they were to be subjected to incessant danger from their exposed and defenceless position.

A town meeting was held, March 2, 1774, with John Sands, Esq., as moderator. Among the resolves passed at that meeting were the following:

"We, the inhabitants of this town, being legally convened in town meeting, do firmly resolve, as the opinion of said town, that the Americans have as good a right to be as free a people as any upon the earth, and to enjoy at all times an uninterrupted possession of their rights and properties. That a tax on the inhabitants of America, without their consent, is a measure absolutely destructive of their freedom, tending to enslave and impoverish all who tamely submit to it. That we will heartily unite with

our American brethren in supporting the inhabitants of this Continent in all their just rights and privileges."

Here was as good a declaration of independence as the famous document signed at Philadelphia two years later. And the courage of those brave men at Block Island was given even a severer test than they could have anticipated. In addition to the dangers of their exposed position, with scant protection provided by the American government, they were deprived not only of their live-stock, but of their trade, by Rhode Island herself. In order to prevent the resources of the island from inuring to the benefit of the enemy, a vote was passed by the Rhode Island Assembly in 1775, ordering all neat cattle and sheep upon the island, "excepting a sufficiency for the inhabitants," to be brought to the continent; and this order was carried out. But this was not all. It was feared that unrestricted intercourse between Block Island and the mainland might enable the enemy to secure information; and in 1776 the Rhode Island Assembly voted that the inhabitants of Block Island be "prohibited from coming from said island into any other part of this state, upon pain of being considered as enemies to the state"; and imprisonment was the penalty for violating this law. An exception was made in favor of those who left the island for good, and such action was urged upon the Block

PEBBLY BEACH.

THE BREAKWATER.

Islanders. It is recorded that one Mr. Hazard was instructed to "earnestly exhort the inhabitants of New Shoreham to remove off from the island."

The condition of the islanders was indeed pathetic. It would seem that they were poorly rewarded for their brave declaration of independence. The island must have been depopulated, had not the Assembly modified its action and empowered certain persons to permit trustworthy islanders to come to certain parts of the mainland for purposes of trade. Surely it was a time of thanksgiving for Block Island when in May, 1783, the glad message from the Assembly, "That all the rights, liberties and privileges of the other citizens of this state be restored," was read to them.

During the war of 1812 Block Island was proclaimed neutral; and her character seems to have been so well known and respected by the English commanders that, according to Rev. S. T. Livermore, the historian of Block Island, "not a murmur of complaint against English plunder lingers upon the island."

Farming, fishing and the saving of wrecks, these have been the industries which have supported the islanders until the entertainment of summer visitors began to attract attention and capital. There are good farms upon the island, though it is only by the most persistent attention that the soil can be made productive. For the Block Island farmer Nature has furnished a valuable fertilizer in the vast quantities of sea-weed thrown upon the island by the waves. The shore is divided into claims, from which the respective owners hasten to gather the sea-weed during or immediately after the storms. The summer hotel business has given a decided stimulus to agriculture on the island, and a very creditable amount of garden truck is raised to supply the hotel tables. Many flocks of sheep graze upon the innumerable knolls, where the pasturage is always good, owing to the bountiful supply of water with which the island is blessed. It is doubtful whether there is so small an area in the world possessing so many ponds as Block Island. The island at its greatest length is hardly six miles long, and nowhere is it more than four miles wide; yet there are at least one hundred ponds which do not become dry once in ten years. They are of all sizes, from a little duck pool to the Great Pond, which covers nearly a thousand acres. On the highest parts of the island there are quite sizable ponds, which have no apparent inlets or outlets, and never become dry. These ponds are well stocked with fish; so that one can enjoy both salt and fresh water fishing at Block Island. The writer has seen taken out of

Sand's Pond a string of pickerel and bass that would do credit to northern Maine; the largest of the pickerel weighed over four pounds.

It need hardly be said that up to the time that Block Island became a popular summer resort, salt water fishing —fishing for business—was by far the most important industry. At the present time it is probable that the income from summer visitors is considerably in excess of the receipts from fishing. In the spring and fall deep sea codfishing is carried on to a large extent. In the summer more attention is paid to the bluefish and swordfish. Bluefishing is the leading attraction in the way of pleasure fishing. About the first thing a man does who is not a hopeless landlubber is to make arrangements with

to say: "I want you to understand that I caught that fish—and he pulled like fate; if you don't believe it, look at my fingers." The marks of the rough fishline, sixty or seventy feet of which he has had to pull in while a powerful seven or eight-pound bluefish has been trying to go the other way, are probably visible in cruel lines across his fingers. The next time he goes bluefishing he will provide himself with heavy felt finger-tips.

The bluefishing is done in large catboats, which are so peculiarly broad that one is tempted to call them "tubs," but they are so strongly built and so skilfully handled that one

OCEAN VIEW HOTEL AND BEACH.

grows to admire their liberal lines and general air of safety. One could hardly find more

one of the many skippers whom he meets at the landing for a try at the bluefish. Of course the luck varies with bluefishing as with other fishing; but it rarely happens that a week of perseverance fails to bring ample reward to the fisherman. Then, too, even bad luck in bluefishing is not time wholly lost; for there must be a good wind for the trolling, and one is sure to have a fine sail even if the fish refuse to "catch on."

Proud indeed is the man who has caught his first bluefish and sits before it at table in the presence of his friends, looking upon it as if he wished

courteous and careful men than the skippers. They sniff a storm with wonderful accuracy, and always give themselves the benefit of any doubt. I have yet to hear of any loss of life at the hands of these prudent sailors.

There is excellent swordfishing, too, in the waters about Block Island, and a small steamer, "The Ocean View," leaves the harbor almost every day to look for swordfish. Her luck is announced by the steam whistle, one whistle for every fish caught, as she enters the harbor on the return trip. One day last summer eleven beauties was her catch.

I have used the word "harbor." The harbor question has been a most vital one for Block Island ever since its settlement by the men of Massachusetts. Block Island is without a natural harbor. This discouraging fact was duly noted by the early settlers, for in the agreement to purchase and settle the island, in 1660, we find the words, "There was no harbor." One would think that such a statement would have discouraged the pioneer, who knew that fishing was to be his principal means of livelihood; but we of this generation are often forced to believe that our forefathers courted natural disadvantages. If it be true that necessity is the mother of invention, we may not be surprised that Yankee inventive genius is famous.

In the northern half of Block Island is the large body of water called Great Pond, which covers, as mentioned above, nearly a thousand acres, and is of very good depth, in some places twelve fathoms. On the west side this pond is separated from the sea by a very narrow and low strip of land. There have been many attempts to connect this point with the ocean; and it is recorded that as far back as 1680 a Harbor Company was organized to make and maintain the connection. But the men of those times were without the machinery for dredging which we now have, and the difficulties encountered in the attempt to keep open the breach were so great that the enterprise was abandoned in 1705, when, "by the providence of God a prodigious storm hath broken down the above said harbor." Various other attempts at creating a harbor were made, but none succeeded. Finally, in 1816, a unique harbor was begun. It was known as the "Pole Harbor,"—and was really no harbor at all. It consisted simply of rows of oak poles sunk five or six feet and projecting from ten to fifteen feet above the surface of the water. Between these rows of poles stones were sunk; and thus primitive piers were obtained. To the poles the hardy fishermen tied their boats; but in stormy weather

IN THE BASIN.

they were obliged to haul them up on shore, all the fishermen becoming, for the time, a co-operative association for the preservation of their craft.

This harbor was better than none, and served until 1870, when the present government breakwater was begun, a little north of the "Pole Harbor," on the east side of the island. This breakwater runs out into the sea some 1500 feet, and faces the southeast, from which come the heaviest storms. There was finished in 1894 another breakwater, facing the northeast; so that now Block Island has a well protected harbor on the east side, though it is not very large and has facilities for only two large excursion steamers at the same time. Inside the harbor formed by the breakwaters, like a wheel within a wheel, is a square dock called the "basin." This is the mooring place of the home fishing craft and the steamer "Danielson," which is the regular packet and mail boat sailing to and from Newport the year round, weather permitting. This steamer is owned and manned by Block Islanders.

A few years ago some radical spirits determined again to test the possibilities of a Great Pond harbor. After much opposition from the conservative element, particularly from the farmers, who saw in the project increased taxation without the assurance of success, appropriations were voted by the town of New Shoreham, which is Block Island's corporate name, aggregating $40,000, to which was added the sum of $60,000 appropriated by the state of Rhode Island. The work has been pushed to a successful issue, and now a canal 400 feet wide and 18 feet deep connects this land-locked harbor with the open sea.

The steamer "Block Island," which makes daily trips from New London during the season, and has hitherto made its landing in the government harbor, now uses the Great Pond harbor, and for the first time in the history of Block Island there is direct steamer connection with New York. The breach is protected by two jetties of "rip-rap" stone, which run out into the sea from either side of the canal. If the sand can be kept out, Block Island will have a permanent and safe harbor, surpassed by none on the coast. As a mooring place for pleasure yachts it is without parallel, and no doubt its surface will be brilliant throughout the summer season with pleasure craft of every character.

For bathing Block Island is peculiarly well situated. It is probable that the temperature of the water is affected by the Gulf Stream, for to one who has tried bathing at points in the vicinity of Boston or upon the North Shore, the water at Block Island always seems warm enough to tempt even the most sensitive to take a plunge in the surf. The distance of the island from the mainland, too, is a decided advantage, for the water is remarkably pure. The islanders take the greatest care to prevent any contamination of the water. There are stringent rules as to the dumping of waste matter, and the foul-smelling fishhouse, so common at seaside resorts, is not found at Block Island where it can annoy.

The bathing beach is a portion of a beautiful crescent-shaped shore two miles and a half long on the eastern side and in fair weather, the clean

NORTH LIGHT.

BEACON HILL.

surf rolls in so gently and with so little undertow that bathing is indeed a pleasure and not a danger. When there is a storm, however, there is surf enough and to spare. In the summer of 1893 there were two storms during the month of August so violent that no steamer left or came to the island while the storms lasted. During those storms the surf was grand. It broke over the great breakwater in a continuous mass of white foam from twenty to thirty feet high.

An interesting point to visit during a storm is the Mohegan Bluffs. These bluffs rise in a solid mass of clay from the ocean a hundred and fifty feet below, and if one visits them during a "sou'easter" the view of the ocean lashing against them is magnificent. A

good idea of what the wind can do in the way of rapid transit can be obtained here, and one feels while trying to face it that a very little more would take one off one's feet. These bluffs are classic ground. History tells us that here the Mohegan Indians, who invaded the island nobody knows how many centuries ago, were cornered and starved by the Maniseeans. A splendid lighthouse was built on the bluffs in 1874, and its light, furnished by a lantern which consumes one thousand gallons of oil annually, can be plainly seen at a distance of nineteen miles, and has been made out at a distance of thirty-five miles. There is another lighthouse at the northern end of the island, called Sandy Point Light.

Block Island is indeed a stumbling-block in the pathway of navigation, and its wrecking history is thrilling enough to satisfy even a dime-novel boy. In days gone by wrecks were far more frequent than now; for, thanks to efficient lighthouses, fog signals, a signal station and two life-saving stations, the loss of life and property has been greatly diminished. There has been much misapprehension as to the wreckers of Block Island. It is probable that the character of the pirates who were wont to infest the island two hundred years ago was unjustly transferred to the islanders themselves. There are records of captures of pirates about the island; and so late as 1740 the Rhode Island General Assembly voted an appropriation of 13£ 13s. "for victuals and drink to the pirates at Block Island and their guards." Though the pirates confined here were foreigners, yet the island suffered from the fact in the estimation of people at a distance, much as towns suffer which have state prisons and insane asylums within their limits. The traditional belief entertained by people of the mainland, that the wreckers of Block Island were merciless despoilers of the unfortunate craft driven on its shores, has been recognized by Whittier in the beautiful poem entitled "The Palatine," where there is, perhaps, enough that is complimentary to the island to atone for what appears to be an unfounded reflection upon the character of the islanders of the time referred to. The prose story of the wreck of the "Palatine," divested of the traditional, according to the investigations of Mr. C. E. Perry, is as follows:

The "Palatine" was probably an emigrant ship hailing from some German or Dutch port and bound for Philadelphia. It is believed that the captain died or was killed on the passage, that the officers and crew plundered the helpless emigrants, and finally abandoned the vessel, which drifted ashore, in the week between Christmas and New Year's, 1752. The passengers were all landed except one woman, who refused to leave the ship. Many of the passengers, weakened by the exposure, soon died, and the place where they were buried is well known. Whittier's lines thus tell the story:

"Old wives spinning their webs of tow,
Or rocking weirdly to and fro
In and out of the peat's dull glow,

"And old men mending their nets of twine,
Talk together of dream and sign,
Talk of the lost ship Palatine,—

"The ship that, a hundred years before,
Freighted deep with its goodly store,
In the gales of the equinox went ashore.

"The eager islanders one by one
Counted the shots of her signal gun,
And heard the crash when she drove right on!

"Into the teeth of death she sped:
(May God forgive the hands that fed
The false lights over the rocky Head!)

NATIONAL HOUSE.

LOOKING TOWARD BEACON HILL.

"O men and brothers! what sights were there!
White upturned faces, hands stretched in prayer!
Where waves had pity, could ye not spare?

GATHERING SEA-WEED.

"Down swooped the wreckers like birds of
prey,
Tearing the heart of the ship away,
And the dead had never a word to say.

"And then, with ghastly shimmer and shine
Over the rocks and the seething brine,
They burned the wreck of the Palatine.

"In their cruel hearts, as they homeward
sped,
'The sea and the rocks are dumb,' they said:
'There'll be no reckoning with the dead.' "

It is natural that there should be
some feeling on the part of the islanders in regard to these reflections. In
explanation of his lines, Mr. Whittier
wrote the following to a friend:
"In regard to the poem 'Palatine,' I
can only say that I did not intend to
misrepresent the facts of history. I
wrote it after receiving a letter from
Mr. Hazard of Block Island, from
which I certainly inferred that the ship
was pillaged by the islanders. He
mentioned that one of the crew, to
save himself, clung to the boat of the
wreckers, who cut his hand off with
a sword. It is very possible that my
correspondent followed the current
tradition on the mainland. Mr. Hazard is a gentleman of character and
veracity, and I have no doubt he gave
the version of the story as he had
heard it."

It is not only very possible, but extremely probable, that Whittier's informant followed nothing more than a
tradition, for there appears not to be
a particle of historical foundation
for the cruel incidents recited in

Whittier's poem. In the same poem,
Whittier refers to the famous "Palatine Light":

"Behold! again, with shimmer and shine,
Over the rocks and the seething brine,
The flaming wreck of the Palatine!

*   *   *   *   *   *   *   *

"For still, on many a moonless night,
From Kingston Head and from Montauk
light
The spectre kindles and burns in sight.

"Now low and dim, now clear and higher,
Leaps up the terrible Ghost of Fire,
Then, slowly sinking, the flames expire.

"And the wise Sound skippers, though skies
be fine,
Reef their sails when they see the sign
Of the blazing wreck of the Palatine!"

This light has given rise to no little
speculation. There are those who
stoutly maintain that they have seen
this particular light, while others
scout the idea altogether. Mr. Livermore has this to say in regard to it:
"That a phenomenal light, at different
times and places in the Sound, in sight
of the island, has appeared during the
last century is quite certain, and superstition has associated it with the
"Palatine." That an inflammable gas
should rise through the water and
burn upon its surface is not impossible, as in the case of burning springs
and brooks."

If one may judge the inhabitants of
the island one hundred years ago by
the present generation, it is very cer-

tain that no such cruelty as tradition has handed down in regard to the "'Palatine" can be charged to them. The Block Islanders are a square people. They possess the trading qualities of the Yankees, and are industrious and thrifty, but in their dealings with one another and with strangers they are upright and generous.

There are probably few places in America which have seen so little change in the character of the population as Block Island. The present inhabitants are for the most part natives and descendants of the original settlers. In 1877 the population was

the next step in Block Island's progress will be an electric railway to connect the Great Pond with other parts of the island. The company has been chartered and officered, and it is expected that the road will be in operation by the season of 1898.

The situation of Block Island is such that it is conveniently reached from Providence, Newport or New London. The sail from Providence is particularly delightful, as one enjoys both a river and a sea trip. The distance is fifty miles, which is covered by the swift steamer "Mount Hope" in about three hours. From

THE SEARLES MANSION.

1,147, of whom 1,138 were American born and 1,032 born upon the island. According to the official state census of 1895, the population was 1,300, all natives with the exception of about 20.

It is noteworthy, too, that the development of the island has been accomplished by the inhabitants themselves. The hotels, representing a capital of $400,000, are, with few exceptions, owned and managed by Block Islanders. The government breakwater and the signal station were the result of the tireless efforts of the late Hon. Nicholas Ball, a native of the island, and his energetic fellow-islanders, and the prime mover in the Great Pond harbor project is State Senator Champlin, also a native of Block Island. The new harbor having become a success,

Boston the most convenient way to reach Block Island is by the way of Newport and the steamer "Danielson." The United States signal station supplies telegraphic facilities for the public.

After all, it is difficult to describe with pen and ink a delightful spot far out in the blue ocean so that it shall give the reader an idea of the pleasure which actual presence affords. If the Alps or the Italian Lakes could be satisfactorily described, fewer would visit them. And even the poet, who brings imagination nearest to reality, hardly satisfies us when he says of Block Island:

"No greener valleys the sun invite,
On smoother beaches no sea-birds light,
No blue waves shatter to foam more white."

17
The Lobsterman's Island

Drawn by Sidney M. Chase.

Oil-clad figures, . . . knee-deep in a quicksilver sea of herring.

The Harbor.

THE LOBSTERMAN'S ISLAND

By Sidney M. Chase

ILLUSTRATIONS BY THE AUTHOR

SEARCH a large map of the Maine coast, and you will find opposite one of its busy seaports a little group of islands—the largest a mile wide by two miles long, with a population of some two hundred people. If you miss them, I shall not blame myself, for I will say frankly that I do not mean to tell you their real name. They are quite unknown to the thousands of summer visitors who throng the coast of Maine. Many down-easters, even, have never heard of them. An old sea captain, who had once put in there, told me of *the* Island and its lobster fishermen; and I resolved to see for myself this isolated settlement, untouched by the annual blight of the summer invasion, though in the very track of it.

Somewhere among the shipping of a certain seaport town I found a diminutive steamboat, which, summer and winter, three times a week, carried the mail to my Island of lobster fishermen.

After some inquiry I located the Captain. He was comfortably smoking on the wharf with two old sea dogs. "Yes, he cal'lated to go next mornin'." "Could I get lodging on the Island?" "Well," he said, doubtfully, "they don't gen'ally have many strangers come there, but you might find somebody to take you in."

Next morning, not long after sunrise, I boarded the little steamer. As I dropped from the wharf upon her upper deck, I found I was the only passenger! After a time two women and a little girl came aboard. At length, the Captain, after a final look shoreward, joined us. The whistle blew, our big hawser splashed, the white water churned astern, and we were off.

Past the harbor light, the steamer turned her nose straight out to sea, but even with my glass, I could make out no hint of land. Only when the Captain directed my gaze, could I imagine a tiny bit of blue on the

281

horizon denser than the surrounding haze. "That's Lobster Island," said he.

We passed fishermen hauling trawls—one luxuriously at work under a big advertising umbrella. We had gotten under way about seven and it was after ten when the blue shape of the Island took clear outline. It seemed cleared land, little wooded, and I made out only a handful of houses. Presently we passed close under Smoky Head, to the south of Barren Rock, with its thousands of scolding gulls. Then the harbor opened out with its busy tangle of masts and jumble of fish houses and wharves, rambling in disarray over the gray rocks. Once more our whistle sounded—a needless form, for all the world of Lobster Island was on the wharf.

The next morning when I emerged from my feather bed in my snug lodgings to see the sun rise over the harbor, I began to feel that I belonged. After breakfast I made for the water, and climbed over wharves piled high with lobster pots. A half-dozen fishermen in wet oil clothes were dipping

little silver herring out of their dories, and others were lugging them up to the fish houses. Occasionally one stopped to light his pipe, or dash the sweat out of his eyes. Then the work went on. All around rose the evil smell of herring rotting in the sun. I sat down on a broken lobster car beside a grizzled old fisherman. His pipe lighted, he turned and regarded me with kindly curiosity.

"Stranger t' th' Island, ain't ye?" he said. "Come in on the bo't yestiddy?"

I admitted it.

"Them's herrin'," he said. "Pooty leetle fellers, ain't they? What do we do with 'em? Salt 'em daown fer lobster bait, 'n' use 'em all winter. 'Lije and Dave Eaton was over t' the no'the o' Mosquito last night, seinin'. Sartin—seine all night an' salt 'em daown 'n the mornin'. Wall, 'tis tol'able hard work while 't lasts. Takes clost to a week, ef herrin's plenty. Yeou want t' go? Wall, naow! They was a feller from Freedom Caounty went one night, 'n' he said 'twas the pootiest sight he ever see! I dunno but what Eben 'd take ye. Eben, here's a young man wants to go seinin'."

A tall, blonde man, all muscle and whipcord under his gray flannel shirt, straightened up slowly, and nodded to me.

"Wall, we was goin' t'night ef the wind don't haul into the no'the-east. Guess you could go along. Ain't never been seinin'? 'Tis some excitin'. We cal'late t' be out all night, 'n' ye won't ketch much sleep."

Promptly on time, with borrowed oil clothes and sea-boots, I tumbled aboard the "pea-pod" (which the fishermen call a small double-ended rowboat, much in vogue at Lobster Island) and was set aboard the sloop. With much creaking of tackle we hoisted the big mains'l, and, under sail and motor, left our moorings. Aboard our sloop were "Eben" and his cousin, a husky young fellow of twenty. Towing astern was the seine boat with the big seine. In a moment three other

"I s'pose 't would be tew some folks," he said.

The winter lobstermen.

mains'ls had run up, and three sloops, each towing a dory, filled away in our wake.

"Yes," admitted Eben, "it's nice t' th' Island in summer, but it gets some cold and lonesome in winter time. 'Taint no harbor to speak of, opens t' the no'the-east, an' when we git a gale o' wind I've seed seven lines of breakers t' once reach-in' clean acrosst the harbor. See thet shed on the steambo't wharf? Wall, we got a no'ther last winter thet carried half of it plum away. When a sloop breaks her moorin's in a blow like thet, 'taint nothin' left of her but kindlin'."

Once past the low rocky points that form the only protection agairst the north-east storms, the wind freshened and the low seas began to slap our bows. To leeward of Barren Rock we caught the clamor of thousands of gulls—some nesting in the tops of the scrubby spruces, and others wheeling about against the sky. And then we were fairly outside with the other sloops flashing abeam in the warm afternoon sunlight.

"Quite a little chop outside," remarked Eben's cousin," but 'twon't be blowin' none 't sundown."

"Herrin' is cur'ous," observed Eben. "They're marster thick 't Mosquito. Nary one 't home this year." He yawned. "Guess I'll git a mite o' sleep," he said.

"Didn't git none last night, an' dum little night before." He dropped into the roomy cabin and in a moment he was snoring.

After a time Eben's cousin pointed to an island ahead. "Lobsterin' here," he said, as some buoys bobbed past us. "We don't do none 't home this time o' year—git our bait an' gear ready."

Presently we rounded a spruce clad is-land, and ran into the calm water of a little cove, its quiet waters reflecting the dark, wooded hills above. The sun was getting low as our four sloops let go their anchors.

"'Most supper time," said Eben, sud-denly sticking his tousled head out of the companionway, and rubbing his eyes.

I heard him busy below, and before long savory smells came to us from the little cabin cook-stove, telling us that the fried eggs and bacon, piping hot and still sizzling, were ready, with biscuit, fresh doughnuts, and coffee. We needed no second invitation.

After a time Eben tossed his coffee-cup into the cabin, seized his pipe, and dropped over side into the seine boat. In the grow-ing dusk dories slipped across from the other sloops, and the men began overhaul-ing the great seine. Evening quiet settled down on the loneliness of the cove. Only the rattle of gear and an occasional remark came to me across the silence; and there was no light but the glow of the pipes against the darkening sky.

The seine ready, tense silence followed. Over beyond the eastern hills it grew a little light. Jared, Eben's brother, who

Drying fresh-painted lobster buoys.

had come aboard our sloop, puffed his pipe and swore softly.

"Gosh, Eb, look at 'em playin'!—thick enough to git down an' walk on 'em everywhar ye look!" Tiny, almost undiscernible, ripples were all about us. The men had hurried into oil clothes. Now four tumbled into the seine boat. Two took oars. Jared and Eben stood aft by the big seine. The latter surveyed the water on all sides. The rowers awaited his signal.

"There they be t' starb'd—Holy Mackerel, what a school! Lay to it, boys, 'n' give her hell!" And things began to happen.

The seine boat leaped from the water under the powerful strokes of the oars; the keg buoy on one end of the net splashed overboard, followed by great armfuls of seine as Jared hove it out; a long curve of floats followed the foaming wake; then, the boat, after describing a broad, circular sweep, shot past the keg again. Eben pulled it aboard. Spreading out from the seine boat lay a wide circle of dipping floats. Then, peering curiously over the dark sky line at the unusual sight, came the rim of the harvest moon.

The school surrounded, the seiners jumped to "purse up" the net. It was quick work. Men hauled desperately and the bottom of the seine came together, catching the fish in a huge bag. Not until the gap was closed did the seiners draw breath.

"Guess we ketched all the herrin' in Black Cove," grunted Jared, wiping his

sands of herring beat their lives out on the deck planks. Scoop after scoop of molten silver followed, lifted by tugging, wet, oil-clad figures, plastered white with fish scales, and knee-deep in a quicksilver sea of herring.

Four sets were made that night. In the

"Cool weather makes 'em lively," he said.—Page 8.

wet face with a wetter hand. "Look out for them floats!"

Foiled at the bottom, the herring struck upward to the surface and drove at the floats in silver streaks of light. Here and there floats went under, and men in dories were busy holding them above water. Baffled above and below the fish made the water boil. Quickly a sloop was brought up, and the seine made fast. Then the seiners "shortened in" until the fish were thrashing in a deep bag between seine boat and sloop.

Eben thrust a long-handled scoop-net from the deck of the sloop down into the seething fish, and with two men helping, landed the load of flashing silver fair on deck. Then came a muffled drumming, as thou-

second the net fouled on bottom, and through the rent the herring got away. The deep, fervent, full-souled cursing that followed was wonderful to hear! Repairs were quickly made, however, and by half-past two in the morning the last corner of the last sloop was dripping herring. Then came the two hours sail home over tossing gray seas between the waning moonlight and the growing dawn.

The following afternoon I felt like a discoverer as I took the grass-grown lane that led into the interior of the Island. Not toward the main settlement—because there isn't any. The little snug, painted houses seem to have been shaken out of some big

"Thar's Uncle Dan'l haulin' his string."—Page 8.

toy box, and then set upright exactly where they happened to fall. The haphazard character of the settlement is increased by the several grassy cart tracks, which meander over the Island, and end doubtfully in rocky pastures. Stone walls with great swinging gates cross these roadways separating one farm from the next. On every hand were rich vegetable gardens, and the front yards were gay with sweet peas. Seated on a stone wall, looking out to sea, I found my old friend of the herring beach. He was watching a bark under full sail just passing the Island.

"What does 'Kenahgook' mean?" I asked him, presently, referring to the Indian name of the Island.

"I ain't jest sartain," he answered, "but I've heered my father say that som'rs in an old guv'ment report he see that it come from two Injun words meanin' 'Fishtaown.' That wouldn't be fur wrong, naow, would it?" he chuckled.

"What sort of a government do you have out here?" I said.

"Wall," he replied, meditatively, "its cur'ous 'baout that. We didn't use to hev no reg'lar guv'ment. Some say we got along jest as well, tew. But others warn't satisfied, an' 'long, back 'most a hunderd

years, they made us what they call a 'Plantation.' Means, near 's I can see, that we pay taxes t' the State an' git 'em back agin to run our own Island."

"Isn't it pretty lonely here in winter?" I asked him.

He had risen to his feet, and stood looking thoughtfully after the bark.

"I s'pose 't would be tew some folks," he said, after a moment, "but most of us was born an' brought up here. We git the mails pooty reg'lar, an' we c'n go t' the Main when we *hev* tew. Wust is 'f any one takes sick. Two year ago last Febooary little Myry Phelps took pneumony o' the lungs, an' 'Bije hed t' go to Deep Harbor fer a doctor. 'Twas blowin' a livin' gale, with snow 'n' a nasty sea runnin'. Twicet goin' over 'Bije thought he was hove daown fer good. The doctor, he didn't say nothin'—jes' come aboard, quiet. Comin' back 'twas wuss. Didn't seem 's though nothin' could live in them seas. 'Bije never knowed haow he made the harbor, an' got the doctor thar 'n time. Cal'lated he jest *hed* tew."

His faded blue eyes softened and he passed his great brown hand over his grizzled beard.

"'Tis bad sometimes," he said, slowly,

"but this is our home, an' we've kind o' got to like it."

In the following days that I spent about the wharves the fishermen were busy. The bait salted down, there were the lobster-pots to mend, the buoys to repaint, each man in his own colors, new gear to make, and a hundred things to do.

"You goin' to stay into next month, ain't ye?" asked True Barker, lob-sterman, one day. "Fust of the month law's off on lobsters, an' its a sight t' see when all them sloops load solid o' lobster-pots, and start out to set 'em. 'F ye do," he went on, "I'll take ye out some mornin' an' let ye haul a few lobsters t' see how it's done."

It was not many days later, when, one morning, the crimson flush of sun-rise found us out in True's double-ender, True stand-ing at the oars, and me in the stern. It was a wonderful In-dian Summer morn-

The lobster smack.

ing, with a long lazy ground swell that hardly splashed on the wet rocks along shore. Outside lay a sloop, her sails slack, while the "put-put" of her motor came faintly across to us.

"Them's my buoys," said True, as he deftly slid the boat alongside a red and white float and dropped it aboard. Catch-ing the line attached to it, he hauled stead-ily until a dripping lobster-pot rose sudden-ly beside the boat. True swung it aboard, and two lobsters snapped for his hand as he flung the lath door open. He tossed them carelessly into the tub forward. "Cool weather makes 'em lively," he said. From the bait tub he took a net bag stuffed with

herring, stuck it on the iron spear in the lobster-pot, and closed the door. Splash, it went overboard, line and buoy following.

"Lobsters climb int' the pot through that hole in the nettin' 't the end," explained True. "Eat the bait, 'n' then, bein' more'n common stupid, can't find the hole t' git out agin." The method was simple, after all.

True said the lob-ster fishermen at the Island averaged to have one hundred and sixty traps each, and of these they hauled half every day. Double-enders and sloops are gener-ally used, for the flat-bottomed dory slides out of position too easily. The traps are often hauled over trawl rollers set in the boat's gunwale.

"Thar's Uncle Dan'l haulin' his string," said True, suddenly, pointing to an old-timer work-ing away steadily in the morning mist. "He's the luckiest man thet ever ketched a fish. I mind the fust time he went marster of a vessel—his father fitted him out complete when he was eigh-teen year old with a bran' new vessel. Shipped a crew o' boys 'n' started in a sou'-easter—smart lot they was!—bound fer Cape Sable. Then come a ca'm easterly, thick o' fog, an' he beat an' beat, he said, tell it seemed 's if he'd beat fur enough to go clean acrosst the hull Atlantic. Last he sounded an' got right water, with fine cod an' haddick jest solid. When he was lo'ded, he didn't have no room on deck fer a cord o' wood all sawed, an' hed to heave it overboard! Then the fog riz, an' whar do you think he was? Right off Thunder Island! Right to hum, with as fine a fare o' fish as you ever see! When the others

Drawn by Sidney M. Chase.

Stooping over, he tossed them, two at a time, upon the "culling-board."

come back frum Cape Sable they didn't hev no fish 't all, scurcely. Thet's what comes to some fer not knowin' nothin'—'tarnal fool luck!"

I laughed at the story of Uncle Daniel and his luck, and meantime True had finished his string with a good average of lobsters in the tub. He debated a moment. "Might haul t'other string off Goose-berry Island," he said. "No," he decided, "le's go home. Done enough fer to-day. Can't do everything tew once."

The summer had lengthened into fall, and my days at Lobster Island were num-bered. Regretfully I bade good-bye to "Uncle Asy," the gull warden of the Is-land. We sat on the front step of the old house where he lives alone, and he showed me the tansy that his "ancient grand-mother" brought from Marshfield.

"Sho, now, thet's too bad!" he said. "Comin' daown next year, ain't ye? When ye goin'? Wall, naow, my nephew's skip-per of a lobster smack, 'n' he's due here day after termorrer. He'll git his lobsters 'n' then he kin take ye right straight t' the Main. Do it jest 's well 's not."

Two days later, just as Eben knocked the ashes from his after-dinner pipe, a trim little schooner rounded Smoky Head and made for the harbor entrance. She came in prettily, sails drawing, and the "bone in her teeth" emphasizing her speedy lines. Then in one breath she swung into the wind with shaking sails, and her anchor rattled down. Jibs and fores'l followed.

She anchored among lobster cars—ob-long wooden pens, seven by twelve feet, moored in position, their tops floating level with the water. The planks of the cars are separated, and the water circulating between, and frequent feeding, keeps the several hundred lobsters inside alive. Im-mediately the harbor became a busy scene.

On all sides lobstermen dropped into boats and paddled out to the smack, Eben and I with the others. As we came along-side Eben nodded to the skipper.

"What ye payin' fer lobsters now, Lon?"

"Twenty-three," returned Lon. "Mar-ket's fell off some lately."

"Twenty-three cents for a lobster?" I said to Eben. "Why we pay more than that a pound at home!"

"Wall," he answered slowly, "us fisher-men does the hard, cold work, 'n' the fellers ashore gits the profits. Don't seem right to me, some way."

While we talked, Jared's car, which lay alongside, was hoisted out of water by the schooner's tackle level with her rail. Jared unlocked the heavy cover, and jumped into the car, kicking the snapping lobsters away with his leather boots. Stooping over, he tossed them, two at a time, upon the "cul-ling-board," a short board slanting from the gunwale to the deck. Lon, measuring-gauge in hand, pitched them through the hatchway into the "well." Now and then he measured a doubtful one, and threw the little lobster back to Jared, who accepted it with good grace.

Lon explained that the lobster smack was divided into three parts: two watertight bulkheads fore and aft, and the centre one filled with water (which circulates through holes in the planking) and is called the "well." This holds hundreds of live lobsters till they are transferred to the large cars of the mainland shippers, whence they are packed in ice and re-shipped to market alive.

"I see Cap'n Obed over t' Deep Harbor t'other day," said Lon to the group of lobstermen on deck. "'Hello, Obed,' says I. 'Ain't seed the old Mary 'n' Lucy over t' the Port fer quite a spell.' 'No, Lon,' says he, kind o' solemn, 'I've giv up fishin'. I'm plannin' to take a few summer board-ers,' he says."

"Yeou don't say!" said Uncle Daniel. "Obed Dwyer runnin' a dum 'sylum fer rusticators! He allus was a leetle tetched. 'Taint so long since him an' me was traw-lin' t' the Banks. I rec'lect the fust time he come aboard. Didn't weigh no more 'n a thole pin, green es grass, an' ker-ried a carpet-bag! I've knowed a carpet-bag to spile the luck on the best vessel afloat. When Obed was below our Skip-per lashed the bag ont' the main hal'yards, and yeou'd oughter seed Obed's face when he come on deck an' see his new carpet-bag swingin' aloft from the main truck!"

"How 'bout that time you an' Obed was dory mates t' 'Quero'?" said Eben, with a wink at Lon.

Uncle Daniel scratched his nose reminis-cently.

"Thet time me an' Obed was 'high line,'

d'ye mean?" he asked. "Thet *was* fishin'! I never see nothin' like it afore nor sence! Our dory was solid full an' settlin'. Obed kep' a-sayin' 'She'll hold 'em, Dan'l, she'll hold 'em!' He was haulin' trawl 'n the boaw, an' I was coilin' of it in. He was plum crazy, an' when a big cod—must a been all o' forty paound—tore aout the hook, Obed jumps overboard an' grabs him, an' yells, 'Dan'l, git the gaft!' Thet cod was 'poke-blown,' an' couldn't sink easy, so we got him. When he was aboard, aour gun'ls was awash. I see a little comber comin', an' I hove aout the trawl tubs, an' a almighty big halibut we hed in th' starn, but it was tew late! 'She's goin', Obed!' I yells. 'N' daown she went, an' turned over complete. The vessel warn't fur to wind'ard, but a little wisp o' fog hed blowed in, an' we lost sight of her. There was quite a sea heavin' up, an', bein' fall o' the year, 'twas some cold. Me an' Obed was hangin' ont' the dory's plug straps. 'Thar, ye dum fool,' I says, consid'able riled, 'ye done it now!' 'I know it,' says Obed, 'I hate like all git aout tew lose them fine fish.' We hung on, an' bum'by the fog riz, an' thar was our vessel half a mile t' looward. They sighted us an' bore daown, all hands t' the rail. 'N' thar was us, lookin' like two turtles, our dory bottom up, with gear an' big fish gone complete."

So the stories went while boat after boat with lobsters from the different cars came up and discharged their cargoes. Presently the last car was emptied, and one after another, dories made off from the smack. Only Eben and True were left.

"Wall, good luck to ye," they said to me. "Come daown next year, 'f ye can," and casting off their line they dropped into their double-ender, and with Eben standing at the oars and True stolidly smoking, the boat slipped away toward shore.

While I stood looking after them, our anchor chain rattled in. Jibs were hauled to windward. Then the creaking fores'l rose jerkily upward, wooden hoops scraping the mast. Slowly the afternoon breeze swelled the canvas, and little ripples widened out in our wake. The shores of the Island began to slip past us. Then the deep blue ocean opened out beyond the rocky points that made the harbor entrance. Almost before I knew it we were outside, past Silver Island and Barren Rock, with the fresh wind fair on our quarter heeling the smack down to meet the swash of water along her leeward rail.

Sitting on the cabin roof, with Lon at the wheel, I took a long look back. There, far astern lay the Island, a purple outline in the blue afternoon haze. And while I watched, it faded, and then disappeared into the mystery of the horizon, whence it had come, leaving me only a memory of content.

Setting lobster pots

18

Great Fights in Early New England History

GREAT FIGHTS IN EARLY NEW ENGLAND HISTORY

By H. ADDINGTON BRUCE

I. THE STORMING OF FORT MYSTIC

ON May Day, 1637, the General Court of Connecticut—which had been founded by the immortal Thomas Hooker only the year before, and boasted but three tiny settlements, at Hartford, Windsor, and Wethersfield—held one of the most memorable meetings in all its history. It was a meeting called to consider the situation created by the persistent attacks of the Pequot Indians, a fierce and warlike tribe that had been harassing the settlers almost from the time of their first arrival in the fertile Connecticut Valley. Aid had been begged from the parent colonies of Plymouth and Massachusetts, but no aid had been received; and now the men of Connecticut were confronted with the alternative of giving battle on their own account or abandoning their log-cabin homes and fleeing to the older and more populous settlements to the north.

All told, they did not have among them more than two hundred and fifty men fit to bear arms, while the Pequots could easily put into the field nine hundred or a thousand warriors. But not a voice was raised in favor of retreat. Embittered by the memory of loved ones treacherously shot down or carried into a terrible captivity, the cry was all for war. And knowing this, the General Court soon reached a decision. It would send against the Pequots all the men who could be spared from garrison duty, and it would trust to them to deal a blow that should ensure a lasting peace. Hartford it called on to provide forty-two soldiers; Windsor, thirty; and Wethersfield, eighteen—in all, a force of ninety.

Ninety against nine hundred! But the ninety were men of no common mold, and they were given for leader the best commander the General Court could possibly have chosen for the work in hand. This was Captain John Mason, a rugged, sturdy, cool-headed, and lion-hearted citizen of Windsor. He was still a young man, little more than half-way through his thirties, but he had already proved his worth. He had been trained to a soldier's life, and in the early stages of the Thirty Years War had seen service in the Netherlands. Coming to America, and settling at Dorchester, he found occupation to his fancy in hunting down pirates and planning fortifications for Boston. Later, such was the esteem he enjoyed, he was chosen to represent Dorchester in the General Court of Massachusetts Bay. But, tiring perhaps of the theocratic atmosphere of Massachusetts, he joined in the Hooker migration to the country about the Connecticut, and there he took root and flourished.

What was most advantageous for the undertaking in which he now engaged, he had a thorough knowledge of the Indian and his ways, and he was in a position to secure Indian allies for the campaign against the Pequots. When he first came to Windsor he had fallen in with a native chieftain named Uncas, who, though a full-blooded Pequot, had seceded from his tribe with a small following and settled on the banks of the Connecticut. It was Uncas's ambition to overthrow Sassacus, the grand sachem of the Pequots, and win for himself supreme control of the Connecticut Indians; and in the coming of the English he saw his opportunity. He was careful to refrain from hostilities against them, he denounced the outrages committed by his kinsfolk, and he cultivated the acquaintance of the colony's leading men. He became particularly intimate with Mason, and Mason for his part worked hard to persuade Uncas and his Mohegans, as the seceders styled themselves, that their wisest course would

295

be to enter into an active alliance with the whites. So successful was he that Uncas readily consented to serve under him in the projected expedition. This meant only a small numerical addition to the pathetically diminutive Connecticut army, but it gave it something that was greatly needed — experienced guides who knew every inch of the Pequot country. And in the end it meant far more than that to the Connecticut English, for it was the beginning of a league for mutual defence that lasted many years and more than once saved the settlers from fearful disaster.

However, not being able to lift the veil of the future, there were few light hearts in the colony the day that Mason and his men started on their campaign. It was felt that theirs was indeed a forlorn hope, and that if they failed utter annihilation would be the fate of the settlements. Some feared, too, that Mason was making a mistake in enlisting the services of the Mohegans— that they would betray the brave ninety into the hands of their enemies. But Mason, who knew how bitterly Uncas hated Sassacus, was confident that he had no thought of treachery. Grimly he assured the men and the weeping women who crowded about the departing soldiers that they might make their minds easy on that score; and then, having listened to a farewell and solemn exhortation by Hooker, embarked his troops and set sail in three vessels down the Connecticut.

At the mouth of that river the settlers had built a fort, Fort Saybrook, and had placed in it a small garrison, commanded by a Lieutenant Gardiner. According to the plan of campaign laid down by the General Court, Mason was to hasten to Saybrook, and thence sail up the Sound to the Pequot River, better known to us of to-day as the Thames. It was in the country between the Pequot and the Mystic that the enemy's strongholds were located, and Mason carried peremptory orders to lose no time in landing and attacking them. Circumstances soon convinced him, however, that if the expedition were to be a success this programme would have to be considerably modified.

Although it was early May, the water in the Connecticut was very low, and the heavily laden vessels — described in the quaint language of the times as a pink, a pinnace, and a shallop — repeatedly grounded. Such were the delays from this cause that it took a full week to make the short journey from Hartford to Saybrook. Meantime the Mohegans, grumbling at the slowness of the voyage, insisted on being put ashore, and marched overland to the fort. There they met with a cold reception from Gardiner, who refused to admit them unless they could produce satisfactory evidence that they meant to act in good faith with the English. Rightly interpreting this as a request for some Pequot scalps, Uncas and his braves surprised a small party of Pequots, killed half a dozen, and brought one as a prisoner to Saybrook, where he was tortured to death. As Mason realized when he arrived at the fort, no surer means could have been found for putting the Pequots on guard against a surprise.

On the other hand, he learned with delight that, thanks to the diplomacy of Roger Williams, the Pequots had been unsuccessful in an intrigue to induce the Narragansett Indians of Rhode Island to unite with them against the English. And he also rejoiced at finding at Saybrook twenty Massachusetts men, the advance guard of reinforcements that were now being raised in the Bay Colony. Their leader, Captain John Underhill, was, like Mason, a veteran of the Thirty Years' War, and a gallant and dashing soldier. But it was his opinion, as he frankly told the Connecticut commander, that it would be madness to attack the Pequots with the troops in hand, and he strongly advised delay until more soldiers should arrive from Massachusetts. This was Gardiner's opinion too, but it met with a blunt veto from Mason. He had come to fight the Pequots, and fight them he would, with or without Underhill's aid. And more than that, he purposed sending back twenty of his own men, who were not in condition for a hard campaign.

Both points he carried after a stormy controversy; and in another and more important matter he demonstrated his masterfulness. Underhill and Gardiner, once the decision to fight had been reached, were for following out the instructions of the General Court and making a direct attack on the Pequots. Mason argued, on the contrary, that this would indeed be suicidal, as the enemy were undoubtedly prepared for them and would overwhelm them by sheer numbers. He proposed, instead, to sail up the Sound to the Narragansett country, land there, and make a rapid march back to the Pequot forts. The Pequots would see the ships sailing past their coast, would imagine the campaign had been abandoned, and would be lulled into a false feeling of security. After-events proved how well he had calculated. Underhill and Gardiner, however, objected that he had no right to depart from the orders of the General Court. For hours they wrangled in angry debate. Then, and nothing could throw into more striking relief the profound religious convictions of the pioneers of early New England, they decided to leave the matter with God. "Good Master Stone," said Mason, to the chaplain he had brought with him from Hartford, "commend our condition to the Lord this night, to direct how and in what manner we shall demean ourselves." Next morning Chaplain Stone reported that it was God's will they should sail for the Narragansett country, and off they put without further ado.

It was Friday, the seventeenth of May, when the journey was resumed, Gardiner and his men being left at Saybrook Fort, and Underhill's twenty taking the place of the twenty Mason had sent home. Head winds so delayed the vessels that it was not until Saturday night that they entered Narragansett Bay. It was then too late to make a landing, and the next day, precious as every hour was, Mason would not let his men go ashore, because it was the Sabbath. Monday morning a tremendous northwest storm set in, continuing until Tuesday sunset, when a landing was finally made at a point not far from where Narragansett Pier now welcomes summer visitors. Leaving thirteen men aboard, with instructions to keep the ships at anchor until late in the week and then drop down to meet the expedition at the mouth of the Pequot River, Mason hurriedly marched his troops to a near-by Indian village, the home of Canonicus, the grand sachem of the Narragansetts.

"I do not come to make war against you," he told Canonicus, "but to punish the Pequots, who have cruelly slain and captured the English. I ask you, therefore, for permission to pass through your country, that I may punish the Pequots, your own enemies, as they deserve."

It was a masterly move, and if all the Indian fighters of New England had been gifted with Mason's genius for statecraft and warcraft some of the tales that will find a place in this series would never have had to be told. Canonicus greeted Mason kindly, entertained him overnight, gave a hearty approval to his intentions, but warned him that, with so small an army, he was courting almost certain disaster. Unshaken in his resolution, the stout-hearted man from Windsor roused his followers at dawn, and, after a hasty breakfast, started them on their overland journey for the Pequot country. All day they travelled with scarcely a halt, and by nightfall reached a Narragansett fort on the Niantic River, the boundary-line between the dominions of Canonicus and those of Sassacus. Here they found fully two hundred Narragansetts, who flatly refused them admission and acted generally in so suspicious a way that Mason set a strong guard around the fort, fearing that some of its inmates might try to carry a warning to the Pequots.

In the morning he was awakened by a loud shouting, and springing to his feet saw that it was occasioned by the approach of a large body of Indians. His first thought, doubtless, was that they were Pequots intent on surprising him; but to his great relief he soon learned that they were Narragansetts who had been sent by their sachem to aid the English. Seeing how the case stood, the Indians in the fort now came out with smiling faces, and begged that they too might be taken along, vehemently proclaiming their hatred for the Pequots and boasting of the valiant deeds they would perform. It must have been a striking scene,— the palisaded fort in the background, the English and Mohegans in the foreground, and between them and the fort some four hundred Narragansetts, swinging around in a great circle and chanting their war-songs.

Gladly Mason accepted the assistance thus unexpectedly tendered, and without more delay began the second day's march. Just before starting, a runner came in with news that a body of troops from Massachusetts had arrived at Providence, and that their commander wanted Mason and Underhill to await his coming. It was felt, though, that after so many delays there was greater need for haste than ever, if the Pequots were to be caught at a disadvantage. So the order was given to advance. It was then about eight o'clock in the morning of a day that gave promise of being unseasonably warm. As the hours passed, and the sun rose higher, the soldiers in their heavy buff coats suffered intensely from the heat. To add to their troubles, the country which they now entered was exceptionally wild and rough, stretches of miry swamp alternating with barrens of bristly rock. Several of the men fainted outright, overcome with the heat and lack of food, the provisions having given out; but, on being revived, they pluckily struggled forward again. Not so with the Narragansetts. The nearer they approached the Pequot strongholds the more rapidly did their valor ooze away. Some, in fact, complaining that the heat was too great, refused to proceed farther. In great anxiety, Mason called Uncas to him.

"What does this mean?" he demanded. "Do they intend to leave us? You heard them boast, brother, that we durst not look a Pequot in the face, whereas they themselves would do great things."

"That," said the Mohegan sachem, "was but their talk. They are great cowards. They fear the Pequots and will never fight them. I warn you, brother."

"And will you, too, desert us, Uncas?"

"Not though all others should. Nor I nor my braves will leave you. Brother, you may trust me."

Satisfied, Mason and Underhill exhorted the soldiers to quicken their weary steps. "We must sleep to-night," they told them, "within striking-distance of the foe." The immediate objective was a large, stockaded village, just across the Mystic River, and situated within the limits of the modern Connecticut town of Groton. This "fort," as it was called, was one of the two principal Pequot strongholds. Here, according to reports brought in by Mohegan scouts, some hundreds of warriors were gathered, celebrating the fancied retreat of the English up the Sound. Mason smiled grimly at the news, but relaxed not a jot the caution that had characterized his movements ever since the departure from Canonicus's village. Marching stealthily until one hour after sunfall, he encamped in a little valley "between two hills"— supposed to be at Porter's Rocks — and threw out sentinels to guard against a possible surprise. Then,

anxious though they must have been about the events of the morrow, he and his soldiers pillowed their heads on the stones and, completely worn out, fell into a dreamless sleep.

It was scarcely dawn when they were astir again, their carbines and muskets ready for action, and their one desire an intense longing to get at and be through with the ugly business that lay before them. The previous night the Mohegans had pointed out a narrow path which they said led directly to Mystic Fort. Along this the troops now made their way in single file. For two miles the path ran through a swampy thicket; then it came to a sudden end at a corn-field. Peering forward in the dim light of the early morning, Mason saw a long, circular structure just ahead, on the top of a difficult hill. "That is the fort," whispered Uncas.

The Indians had built about their village a stout stockade of logs, ten and twelve feet high, loopholed at a fighting-height, and enclosing an area of some two acres. There were only two entrances, on opposite sides, and each of these had been barricaded by tree-tops, with the boughs turned outward. The taking of the village, even if the assailants gained the top of the hill without alarming the Pequots, would undoubtedly be no easy matter. Still, Mason did not hesitate to arrange a plan of attack. Then, for the first time, he noticed that no Narragansetts were in sight. He motioned Uncas to him.

"Where are the Narragansetts?" he asked.

"Many have fled," was the answer; "others are back in the forest, making ready to flee."

"Go, then, and bid them not to flee, but to remain until they see whether Englishmen can fight or not."

To Underhill he gave other orders, in quick, incisive language. He was to lead his Massachusetts men against the south entrance. Mason himself, with a party of fifteen or sixteen, would try to force his way in through the entrance on the north side of the stockade. The rest of the English, together with the Mohegans, were to surround the fort as reserves. It was a daring, reckless scheme, but it appealed to the spirit of the men who had followed him those weary miles of sea and land. Silently but rapidly, the little storming-parties started up the hill.

Suddenly, the barking of a dog was heard, followed instantly by the cry, "The English! The English!" With ready wit, Mason turned and signalled to the soldiers who were still standing in the corn-field. "Come up," he shouted, "come up, all of you, and fire at them through the palisade." At the first volley there rose a chorus of shrieks and groans, mingled with the dread Pequot warwhoop. Racing madly forward, Mason and his stormers flung themselves at the north entrance and, before the Indians fully realized their purpose, were through it. Underhill's party were less fortunate. When they reached the top of the hill they were thrown into some confusion by the stoutness of the leafy barrier opposed to them, and this gave the Pequots time to rally to the defense. One, at close range, drove an arrow through the arm of the first Massachusetts man to show himself, a young soldier named Hedge. Wounded as he was, Hedge cut the Indian down, and in quick succession dispatched three others. By his side, Underhill slashed and thrust; and, the barrier now giving way completely, the stormers and the reserves poured in with a fury that would not be denied. Breaking, the Pequots fled to their wigwams, which stretched along both sides of a wide lane through the centre of the village.

Forming anew at Mason's command, the soldiers now charged against the wigwams, to be repelled by the shower of arrows which met them from every side. Right and left the winged missiles flew, one finding its billet in Captain Underhill's thigh. Two men fell dead; others dropped with ugly wounds. Outside they could hear the Narragansetts shouting like madmen, but keeping well beyond the danger-line. Clearly, they were fighting a losing fight, yet one which admitted of no retreat. Mason, resourceful as ever, took a sudden resolution. "Look, you," he cried to Underhill, "we must burn them out."

And, before Underhill could make reply, he had plunged into the nearest wigwam, sword in hand. When he emerged, a moment later, his sword was dripping with blood, and he carried a blazing brand plucked from the wigwam fire. Next instant, as he touched it to the dry matting with which the wigwam was roofed, a pillar of flame shot towards the sky.

No pen can adequately describe the scene that followed, as the fire, with lightning-like rapidity, spread through the fort. The English and the Mohegans, carrying their wounded with them, retreated outside the stockade, and massed themselves at the two entrances to prevent the escape of the tortured Pequots. At a little further distance the Narragansetts, now brave enough, threw themselves about the fort in a vast circle, to cut off any fugitives who might evade the bullets and swords of the inner guards. Many — men, women, and wailing children — perished miserably in the flames. Others, who burst from their blazing homes and rushed blindly to the stockade openings, were slain without regard to sex or age. Those who hoped to find safety by leaping the stockade and disappearing in the forest were mercilessly hunted down by the Narragansetts. There were some, the braver warriors, who mocked at foe and flame alike, discharging their arrows through the stockade loopholes until, if the old records are to be believed, the very strings were burned from their bows by the all-consuming fire.

In a word, the slaughter was thorough and complete. In its upshot, it was nothing less than a massacre, and some historians have been unsparing in their condemnation of Mason and Underhill and their mates. Yet their terrible course was not without its justification. It was either the Pequot's lives or theirs, and with their fate was bound up the fate of the Connecticut settlements. The firing of the wigwams was the only thing that could possibly have saved the little army from annihilation, and in the slaughter that followed they were guided by the certain knowledge that every Pequot who survived would be the tireless and vengeful foe of the white man. In fact, the march from the ruins of the smoking fort to the mouth of the Pequot River was a succession of fights with the remnants of the tribe; and not until a year afterwards, when a series of reverses had completely broken the power of the Pequots, was the safety of the colony fully assured. In this later and less dramatic fighting, Captain John Mason was again prominent, and Connecticut is well warranted in accounting him, as she does, among the really notable figures in her history.

19
The U.S. Naval Torpedo Station

The U. S. Naval Torpedo Station*

By Grace Herreshoff

A S our late war with Spain has quickened the interest and increased the activity in our new Navy, so the greater Civil War set on foot more ambitious projects and offered wider opportunities for inventions, "changing the old order and giving place to the new." A wonderfully able navy was that of the sixties; but one of the most essential elements the present day organization possesses, it lacked: the torpedo, which, previous to the Civil War, was in the most embryonic state, needing the activity of actual warfare to bring it into prominent notice. In the general revitalization of all governmental departments, a spirit engendered by the final demonstration of the Nation's power, attention was turned to the powerful explosives then recently brought into use by the Navy, and the subject seeming to open up unknown possibilities, it was thought wise to pursue a special course of study and experiment upon torpedoes. To this end, Admiral Porter selected, as the home of the "Torpedo Station," Goat Island, forming one of the protections of the harbor of Newport, Rhode Island, convenient to and yet removed a safe distance from the city. The little island—it is hardly a mile and a half long—was the property of the Army, however, and had hitherto been known only for its disused Fort Wolcott, where the Naval Academy boys had been drilled during war-time; but Admiral Porter's scheme was too excellent to pass unnoticed, and the value of Goat Island was finally fixed at $50,-000, a yearly rental of $5,000 being decided upon.

Accordingly, on July 29, 1869, the island was transferred from the War to the Navy Department, only by lease, however, for the possession of anything so stable as dry land is denied those whose domain covers all the seas of the earth; a torpedo corps was organized, and under the direction of Commander E. O. Matthews, as Inspector in Charge, took possession of Goat Island in September. Until

---

* It was by the courtesy of Commander Mason that the writer was enabled to visit the Station.

THE COMMANDANT'S HEADQUARTERS

the routine should be regularly established and adequate working-space provided, the old army barracks were transformed into lecture-rooms and laboratories, while a machine shop and store house were evolved from the few shelters the naval cadets had left behind.

During the first five years of the station's growth, were erected its most important buildings, which are those in present use; they were the machine shop, store house, electric and chemical laboratories, several cottages for the officers, and the inspector's house, which latter was built over the old barracks and includes also various offices. In 1881 a comparatively large gun-cotton factory was built on the west shore, and for a period of years that explosive was manufactured exclusively at Goat Island, though of late only a small quantity for experimental use is yearly turned out. It being found impracticable to mass in one building so great a quantity of sensitive explosives—the factory was

destroyed by fire, with some loss of life, in 1893—a number of small buildings were erected along the west shore, and built into the embankment which was cut out to receive them. This scheme was rendered the more necessary by the introduction of smokeless powder into general use; for, in each little building, only one step in the transformation of the raw cotton can be effected, thus reducing to a minimum the danger of explosion.

Goat Island, or the Torpedo Station, as it is invariably called, is entirely surrounded by a heavy sea-wall of stone and masonry, begun under the direction of Captain, then Commander, Converse; and it was only by the timely construction of this barrier that the island was saved from the uselessness to which the constant wear of the waves threatened to reduce it. From its northernmost point—Goat Island, long and narrow, extends almost due north and south—a heavy stone breakwater stretches some one thousand six hundred feet up the bay,

304

ending in a light-house of the usual neat, white-plastered variety. Both the breakwater and "Goat Island Light" were built long before the creation of the Torpedo Station,—about 1840, in fact; while even previous to that date a small light had been maintained on the point, its keeper inhabiting a house near by.

the station. Even a few tenderly cared for trees flourish before the commandant's quarters directly opposite the landing-pier, though elsewhere the neatly marked paths and roads gleam white in the sunlight. And let it here be noted that the extreme neatness prevalent at the Torpedo Station is such as to remind one forcibly of the

THE ELECTRIC LABORATORY

The aspect which the station presents, as one approaches it on a summer's day, is not without its beauty; with the winter days it is best not to concern one's self, for then the bleak winds, sweeping up and down the bay, seem to render even one's foothold insecure. In the summer, the ground is grass-covered, and vines embellish the six severely plain cottages, marshalled in a row along the south part of the island, which are occupied by the officers constituting the personnel of

"holystoned" and orderly appearance of a great battle-ship. Over in front of the machine shop a number of ponderous torpedoes and tubes of obsolete make, with other objects of that nature, are regularly disposed on the lawn, and clumsy old submarine mines (one "ancient" example is dated 1880, such is the haste of modern invention!) mark the corners of the paths.

And here, north of the inspector's quarters and scattered over the widest part of the island, within and about the embankments of the old fort, stands the little group of buildings which shelter the forces that go to make up the Torpedo Station,—that little speck on the great map of the United States which exercises on the Navy an influence out of all proportion to its size. For the purpose of the Torpedo Station is to manufacture, instruct, and primarily, to experiment. Every invention of use to the Navy,

and the power which these insignificant objects possess is symbolical of the importance of the Torpedo Station. They are, generally speaking, small round receptacles of brass, one or two inches in length, filled in the case of primers and fuzes, which ignite gun powder, with a very fine meal powder; but the contents of exploders and detonators, which explode the gun-cotton in a torpedo and are of necessity

OFFICERS' COTTAGES

except in the line of propelling machinery and heavy armament or "ordnance proper," passes through or has its birth at the station. Here also a large number of officers and men receives instruction on matters of vital importance.

Though gun-cotton and smokeless powder are no longer manufactured exclusively at the station, there are produced here the primers and fuzes, exploders and detonators, which fire the charges of guns and torpedoes;

more powerful, are composed mainly of fulminate of mercury. A recent invention at the Station was the combination primer, which, as the name indicates, unites in one primer the forces of two different classes; so that if, say the electricity, should fail to act, the charge would still be fired by virtue of the power of friction which the primer also possesses—and vice versa.

On the floor above the machine shop is the torpedo lecture room, a large hall in which officers and men are instruct-

ed, fairly lined with torpedoes, most of which are the modern automobiles; but in one corner hang three obsolete forms, one of which possesses an historic interest in having been taken from the Spanish war-ship "Maria Teresa." The Whitehead automobiles, however, predominate in interest, for they are the torpedoes in common use at the present time. The Howell—also an automobile—is occasionally used, to be sure, and is most successful in actual warfare; but its delicate and complex mechanism (it is propelled by a revolving disc instead of by compressed air, as is the Whitehead) renders it impracticable for instruction or "exercise" use.

The modern torpedo is a cylindrical case of steel, 11 feet 8 inches, or 15 feet, long (the Whitehead is used in two sizes) and nearly 18 inches at its greatest diameter, tapering to the bluntly rounded "head" at one end and to the slender pointed "tail," carrying the rudder and propellers, at the

other. Into three sections is the wonderful torpedo divided: the head, holding the explosive; the air flask—which is the middle section—containing the driving power of air at a high pressure; and the after-body, in which are the engine, shaft and steering-gear, together with various appliances controlling the idiosyncrasies of this miniature submarine vessel. For such the torpedo really seems to be, guiding itself, and entirely independent of any outside agency from the time it leaves the tube, until the little war-nose projecting from the head touches a solid substance, when the gun-cotton with which the war-head is packed explodes and the torpedo, with its target, is blown to atoms.

But in carrying out its purpose of destruction upon the opposing force what an exquisite piece of workmanship is sacrificed in the torpedo! Its interior is filled with numerous delicate and complicated mechanisms which automatically regulate its course, every possible contingency being provided for.

That it may the more resemble an actual boat, one small compartment is called the engine-room; within this the little engine, occupying a space hardly a foot in diameter and driven by the force of compressed air, accomplishes thirteen hundred revolutions every minute. Though racing at this tremendous rate, it can and does stop on the instant without injuring in the slightest, without even jarring the delicate machinery surrounding it. The speed made by the miniature ship in passing through the water, which, it must be remembered, offers resistance to its entire surface, is twenty-six knots an hour for a run of eight hundred yards, and amounts to about thirty knots when half that distance is to be covered. As a matter of comparison, let it be noted that the engines of the torpedo boat "Dupont," gigantic in contrast to the dainty mechanism under consideration, cannot make more than four hundred revolutions to the minute; yet with this power the boat, encountering to be sure, less resistance, can make over twenty-eight knots an hour—nearly the greatest speed of which the torpedo is capable. What, then, would be the speed of the "Dupont," could her powerful engines, without destroying themselves, even approach the high rate reached by a torpedo's machinery!

As torpedoes are in constant use for both instruction and experiment, it would of course be dangerous and even impossible for them always to carry their charge of gun-cotton; each one is accordingly provided, besides the war-head, with an exercise-head, which is filled with water, in order

that its weight may equal that of the former.

A torpedo is fired from a tube, the upper half of which projects, roof-like, over the mouth, as a shell from a gun, that is, by a charge of powder ignited by a primer; but with this difference, that the torpedo travels under its own propelling power, whereas the shell gains its momentum from the force of the ejecting charge. It requires, however, great care and skill to set correctly the different regulators in a torpedo, preparatory to the run; and it is both interesting and ludicrous to watch the proceeding of the novices at "target-practice," for they are prone to forget the most important adjustments. A "surface-run" is most remarkable to witness: then the huge cigar-shaped object goes skimming across the water, occasionally leaping several feet into the air, looking and behaving exactly like a porpoise, it is said, while making a great rushing and whirring noise, like the sound of a train speeding through a tunnel, a fact not at all strange when one remembers that the fifteen-foot torpedo is running at a rate of twenty-six to thirty knots an hour. Perhaps the steering gear is left to its own devices: immediately the torpedo proceeds upon a course most bewildering and even terrifying to the beholder, turning in circles, running up against some object, only to be headed off in another direction, and, when the compressed air is finally exhausted, describing an arc in the air before ending its gyrations at the most unexpected spot. Occasionally a torpedo will be lost, burying itself in the mud or following so eccentric a course beneath the water as to evade the vigilance of the searchers; but it is usual-

ly recovered eventually, as was the case with a torpedo found recently by the divers under instruction at the station. Though having lain a year and five days beneath the water, it was found to be intact, and will perhaps be used eighty or a hundred times for exercise purpose during its future existence.

It is hardly possible to realize that this remarkable mechanism is the result of so humble a beginning as the primitive spar torpedo. This explosive, it can hardly be called a missile, came into existence about the time of the Civil War, and was nothing more or less than a cast-iron box filled with coarse gun powder, and fastened to the end of a long spar, or "boom," which was carried alongside a launch, though projecting some distance in front of the bow. As this torpedo could not be exploded until the launch was beside the object of attack, and as this act was accomplished by means of a primitive friction primer, manipulated by a cord, the danger to the operators was nearly as great as to the enemy. Though spar torpedoes have been superseded by automobiles they have been constantly improved: the shell is now of steel, the charge has become gun-cotton, ignited by an electric detonator. At a recent experiment in the waters near Goat Island, four of these modern spar torpedoes were exploded, sending great beams of wood two hundred feet into the air, while the solid column of smoke and debris seemed to extend up into the clouds themselves.

The next step from the spar was the towing torpedo, dragged by careful manipulation of two lines at some dis-

tance off the quarter of a vessel, and made to dive beneath her adversary. An approach to the automobiles were the Lay, Lay-Haite, Ericsson and Edison-Simms torpedoes; but these, although propelled by their own power, were hampered by the cables controlling them from the boat or shore. In 1870, before the adoption of the Whitehead by our Navy, the so-called Station torpedo, resembling the English one, was constructed and experimented with at the island; it gave way, however, to the Howell, which, though a later invention, was introduced here at about the same time as the Whitehead, the most recent and by all odds, the best.

It is a remarkable, and perhaps not fully realized coincidence, that during the Spanish War not a single torpedo was fired by our vessels, the torpedo boats having been mainly useful as despatch boats, defending themselves, when necessary, with the small guns with which they were provided. Consequently the first explosion of a Whitehead under actual conditions of war took place only year before last in Narragansett Bay, when the United States Torpedo Boat "Porter," running at full speed, fired the torpedo at a distance of eight hundred yards from the target, the beach of Prudence Island; then immediately turned about and fled to a safe distance. Several other torpedo boats were assembled, with a number of officers on board to witness the experiment, which resulted most satisfactorily, effectually proving that with the discharge of a single torpedo the "Porter" could destroy the enemy's ship and herself escape with practically no damage.

Mines were originally intended to receive as much attention at the station as torpedoes; but shortly after its beginning the mine department was removed to Willett's Point, not however before Captain Converse had made an important invention in that line. The Naval Defense mines are invariably loaded at the station, and at the time of the Spanish War the employees were kept very busy filling the countermines.

FIRING A WHITEHEAD TORPEDO

Not only are mines and torpedoes loaded there, but it is at the Torpedo Station that the torpedo outfit of every vessel in the Navy is assembled; and on going out of commission it is there a ship returns her outfit, to be repaired or, if necessary, replaced. The regulations, moreover, provide that an overhauling of the outfit shall take place every three years. With the "rush in business"entailed by the tremendous growth of the Navy during recent years, it is not surprising to find the pay-roll of the employees at the Torpedo Station increased from about $100 per month in 1872 to about $400 per day in the present year.

The experiment manœuvres at the island are by no means confined to torpedoes. Back of the machine shop stands the electrical laboratory, a neat little building crowned by the search light tower, in which is given practical instruction on this weapon of the new Navy. In the lecture rooms are to be found examples of every kind of electric light used on board a vessel, from the huge search light, down to the

minute one-half candle power incandescent, with which the inside of a torpedo is illuminated for examination. The dynamo room is also the place of particular investigation and practical instruction to both officers and men.

Leaving the electric laboratory, one approaches an archway cut through the high embankment which formerly surrounded the fort; one approaches, but may not pass through, for within the enclosure stand two buildings closed to the outside world. The larger is the chemical laboratory, in which are conducted experiments in the line of explosives; in the small building to the right of the entrance the blocks of wet gun-cotton are shaped, by means of a circular saw, to fit snugly into the oval war-heads. Sawing gun-cotton sounds as if it were a decidedly hazardous proceeding; but as the material is saturated with water and every possible precaution taken, the workmen are nearly as safe as are those in the machine shop,—more so than the workers on detonators, perhaps, for a careless blow, be it ever so light, on the sensitive fulminator may result in the serious, if not fatal, wounding of the workman.

In one wall of the white plastered archway is cut the name of the French engineer, very modestly, thus:— "Rochefontain Enginr." He it was who threaded the embankments with passages, partly underground; leading into these are little doors at intervals in the walls, one of which, in a corner of the enclosure, opens into an old prison in the tunnel.

Again, back of the enclosure is another, but solid embankment, which extends thence along the west shore nearly to the breakwater; it is this embankment that shelters the six gun-cotton and smokeless powder houses, entrance into which, it is hardly necessary to state, is strictly forbidden.

Buildings 1, 2 and 3 comprise the guncotton factory. In the first of these the raw cotton is picked apart and dried, a certain brand of English cotton being always used, as it is the most successfully treated in the manufacture of the powder. The second step is the nitrate bath, out of which the cotton, now nitrocellulose, is wrung and washed, then carried to building 3 to be reduced to a soft pulp; after a final wringing the gun-cotton is ready to be taken to building 4, which, with 5 and 6, is the smokeless powder factory. From building 4 the cotton emerges transformed into smokeless powder, and having the appearance of sticks of glue; but a process of drying and seasoning, accomplished in the next building, is now necessary, and after that the powder undergoes a final test, lying stored in the last building,

under different degrees of temperature, before it is issued for use.

The preparation to which the guncotton is subjected, the ingredients of which are known to very few, is of course constantly experimented upon and, as the results show, greatly improved, for the smokeless powder of the present day has obtained a considerable advance in velocity over that of a few years ago. Many of the experiments in the action of gun-cotton and smokeless powder are conducted on Rose Island, which lies to the northwest of the station, and where a guncotton magazine is also situated. The subject of nearly as much study as the powder itself is the elimination of danger from explosion during its manufacture, and of disease to the workmen; and to that end the buildings have been so constructed that they may be frequently and thoroughly cleansed, while some progress has been made in protecting the men from the "noxious vapors" arising from the chemicals.

As a place of instruction, the Torpedo Station holds a position of importance in the Navy. Not only are classes of officers engaged there every summer in practical study on torpedo work, electricity, the chemistry of explosives, etc., but each year two classes of seamen, the pick of the enlisted men, are thoroughly trained in electricity and torpedo work, and, if they so desire and are physically fit, in diving. The course in torpedoes renders the men capable not only to fire the missiles, but to give them proper care and to repair them, to some extent, when disabled. A lasting proof of the excellence of the Station's diving course was furnished by the work and condition of the men diving on the wreck

THE EFFECT OF THE EXPLOSION OF A TORPEDO

of the "Maine" in Havana harbor. So thorough had been their physical training, that after 50 days of continuous work in the filth and stench of the harbor, in a hot and oppressive climate, not one of the naval divers suffered any ill effects or was in any way injured—a most unusual occurrence in any wrecking company. As to their ability, though the New York press was at first inclined to criticise, comparing the "sailors" unfavorably with the professional divers, at the last it was eager to admit their undoubted skill and bravery.

With their previous six months' training in the gun-shops at the Washington Navy Yard the men qualify as seamen gunners after this seventeen weeks' course, and are usually ordered at once to sea; later, those who possess sufficient ability rise to the rank of warrant officers.

A small portion of their time of study at the station is spent on board torpedo boats, the men thus becoming somewhat accustomed to sea-duty, though of course the majority are sent on board battle-ships and cruisers, gun-boats and other smaller vessels, whose numbers predominate over those of torpedo boats. Life on the latter, it must be understood, is quite a different matter from that on any other ship in the Navy. In the first place, torpedo boats are not built for men to live on, far less with a view to comfort; in fact, the question of ex-

THE MACHINE SHOP

In the foreground may be seen many torpedo tubes taken from the Spanish vessels at Santiago.

istence on board was so far
forgotten in the cases of
the "Craven" and "Dahl-
gren," that no spaces
were allowed for the
galleys, and on their completion it was necessary to
construct them between
the stacks on deck! It is
however, well known that
these boats were not the
result of American talent.

Beyond the primary
purpose of discharging
her missiles, the objects
of a torpedo boat are facil-

"THE ARCHWAY"

ity of control and speed, speed that will
enable her to outstrip any other class of
vessels whatsoever; save only the torpedo boat destroyers, which are merely
torpedo boats raised to a higher power,
size, armament and speed increased,
but not altered.   But to attain this
speed a torpedo boat must be of a slender shape and lie low on the water, in
order to escape observation as well as
to offer the least possible resistance;
further she must not be uselessly en-
cumbered with elaborate fittings, but
every portion of her make-up must be
reduced to the least weight, while her
machinery must embody in a compact
form a tremendous amount of power.
Fully as high as her speed qualifications must be her ability to respond to
the lightest touch on the wheel, to reverse, stop, or start her engines at a
second's notice; for she depends in
battle not upon the material protection
of heavy armor-plate, which would
weigh her down and detract from her
swiftness, but upon her own insignifi-
cance and cunning in escape.

A torpedo boat is, in proportion to
her size, without an exception the fast-

est vessel afloat.   Though the "Dupont" is but 175 feet in length, with a
displacement of 165 tons, the 3,800
horse power of her engines is equal to
that of the Sound liners, such as the
"Plymouth," for instance, a boat of
vastly greater tonnage and perhaps
150 feet longer.   Yet the "Plymouth's"
speed is hardly two-thirds that of the
torpedo boat.   A comparison with a
modern ocean liner, whose proportions
more nearly approach those of a torpedo boat, is also interesting.   Rough-
ly speaking, the "Deutschland"—fast-
est of the ocean greyhounds—measures about four times the "Dupont's"
length and breadth; but against a hun-
dredfold increase of tonnage, the
"Deutschland" can develop only a nine
times greater horse power, with the
result that her speed lacks about five
knots of the "Dupont's."   The latter
craft, be it noted, was built to attain a
speed of only twenty-six knots; but on
her official trial she exceeded this contract rate by about two and one-half
knots.

The power of endurance against the
ceaseless battery of waves and ice in

our northern waters is not considered one of the requisites of a torpedo boat; but the "Dupont," with the smaller "Morris," refuted the idea that these vessels must be hauled up or sent south during cold weather. Both of these boats successfully weathered the hard winter of 1898-99, moored to a dock in a sheltered cove of Bristol, R. I., harbor; the "Dupont" going there directly after the terrible November storm of that season, while the "Morris" joined her later—in good time, however, to pass through the novel experience of being frozen in the ice for many weeks. But though the boats stood the test well, the crews endured untold discomforts.

Two members of the latter, nevertheless, seemed to enjoy life in the cold weather to which they were so unaccustomed. Both of southern birth, they were "Chic," the lively little fox terrier mascot of the "Morris," captured from some Spanish merchant-ship; and "Dupont Bill," basely kid-napped in infancy from his Cuban home, a goat which gladly devoured the candy, with its paper bag, so frequently offered him by the sailors, as well as, on one occasion, the feathers decorating a visitor's hat! For a short time last winter, the "McKee" was rejoiced with "Bill's" presence as a guest, and it was on one of her trips that he narrowly escaped a watery grave. The trip was memorable in the boat's career as well as in "Billy's."

The "McKee," which is the smallest of her class,—hardly one hundred feet in length and of only sixty-five tons displacement—left New York one stormy day for Newport, expecting to arrive in about eight hours. A short distance along the Sound, however, her blowers gave out and she was forced to proceed under natural draft, crawling along at about three knots an hour, while the seas literally swept over her, nearly sweeping poor "Billy" overboard. At last he was lashed to the smokestack, and though

316

half smothered by the water, weathered the twenty-four hour nightmare of a trip; meanwhile the executive officer, "Bill's" only companion on deck, was forced to grasp the supporting stack in a close embrace.

Innumerable are these unofficial records of runs bravely accomplished under conditions with which no torpedo boat was designed to cope; but so enjoyable can warm, fair weather render a short trip, that one would forever scorn the most luxurious steam yacht after a single rapid, exhilarating run on a torpedo boat.

The "McKee" has been mentioned as the smallest vessel of her class. Still smaller is the "Stiletto," the only wood torpedo boat in the navy; be the other slips crowded or deserted, she is always to be found at her dock at the Torpedo Station. Moored near her, last summer, was that representative of a new type, the submarine torpedo boat "Holland;" and very strange and weird, like some deep-sea monster newly dragged into the light of day, appeared that part of her fifty feet of length which is visible when she rises to the surface. As far as the question of life on board (or is it within?) is concerned, the "Holland" is a little more comfortable than a diving-suit, and can be stored with sufficient air and food to support her crew of five for forty-eight hours; as to the question of destruction upon an outside force, this submarine vessel is an undoubted success, as was proved in the fleet and harbor defense manœuvres held at Newport last summer. It was reported on this occasion, that the "Holland" could have "torpedoed" (synonymous with "destroyed") probably three ships of the blockading fleet. In strange juxtaposition to this modern invention, an old submarine boat, designed by Admiral Porter, lies near the docks at the Station. It is a box-like structure of iron, divided within into compartments, one of which contains an ancient smoothbore gun, and intended to be sunk to a stationary position.

It has been almost entirely through the ceaseless activity of its many excellent commandants and assisting officers that the Torpedo Station has attained its prestige. The present Inspector is Commander N. E. Mason, the well-known executive officer of the U. S. S. "Brooklyn" during the Spanish War, who distinguished himself at Santiago; Lieutenant - Commander Rees, formerly executive officer of the island, but ordered to sea duty August, 1901, most ably performed the duties of executive officer on no less a ship than the "Olympia," at Manila, under Admiral Dewey. It is hardly necessary to add that the Department strenuously endeavors to appoint the personnel of the Station from among the most active and efficient officers of the navy.

Many years ago Rear Admiral Sampson was Inspector at the Station, and little known to the general public. With the increase of the new navy he has come into prominence, and by his ability has shown to the world her power in war,—a power the growth of which is typified by the progress made at our Navy's Torpedo Station.

20
Historic
Salem

NEW ENGLAND MAGAZINE

January, 1905

Historic Salem

By Mary H. Northend

THOMAS Wentworth Higginson, during a recent visit to Salem, Massachusetts, remarked that there was about the city a more distinct colonial flavor than about any other in New England. The annals of the past show that this remark is well founded. The complete history of our country perhaps can furnish no more interesting chapters than those relating to the settlement and growth of this famous, old town.

Salem is the chief city in Essex County, and it was here that the first permanent settlement of the old Massachusetts Bay Company was instituted. Roger Conant with a few followers came first to Cape Ann in the autumn of 1625, to establish a settlement for farming, fishing and trading purposes, and was made "governor." But his little colony proved a failure, and there was so much dissatisfaction among the settlers that, in the autumn of 1626, he led those of his little band who would follow him, further up the coast, and came to Salem, then called "Naumkeag," which name in the Indian tongue, like the word

Salem, signifies "peace." About twenty-five followed Conant to Salem, and after looking over the land, they decided to locate upon a sandy strip near Beverly, which is now known as Bridge street, the early settlement following the course of the North River. This was the first permanent colony in New England distinct from Plymouth.

One cannot but admire the determination of men like these, who to win a foothold for civilization on these shores, and unswerved by the desertion of their followers, and by the entreaties of their comrades, remained firm at their post for two long years, "the sentinels of Puritanism on the Bay of Massachusetts."

But their long lane had a turning at last. On September 6, 1628, the good ship "Abigail" cast anchor in the land-locked harbor of Naumkeag, having on board John Endicott, the first Governor of the plantation, his wife and others. Roger Conant and his companions were waiting on the shore to welcome them. In their excitement and joy they even carried Endicott ashore

JOHN ENDICOTT

in their arms, so that he should not wet his feet. The two sets of colonists at once united to form the town of Salem. The spirits of the first settlers revived, and from this time on, in spite of adverse circumstances and lack of harmony between them and those who came over with Endicott, the little colony throve under the jurisdiction of a man of sound judgment and of stern principles. Governor Endicott was well fitted to advance the interests of the infant colony over which he kept a firm hand. He was sent to Salem by the "Company of the Massachusetts Bay in New England" to govern the district lying "between three miles to the north-

ward of Merrimac River, and in length within the described breadth from the Atlantic Ocean to the South Sea."

Interest in the plantation was awakened in England, and more colonists were sent over, among them the Rev. Francis Higginson, and the Rev. Samuel Skelton. They found "that Naimkeeke contained at that time about half a score of houses built, and a faire house newly built, for the Governor, also an abundance of corne planted." The little settlement then numbered about three hundred souls. On their arrival Governor Endicott set apart the twentieth of June, 1629, as "a solemn day of humiliation for the choyce of a pastor and teacher at Salem." The vote was taken in writing, and resulted in Mr. Skelton's being chosen pastor, and Mr. Higginson teacher. A few weeks later "the confession of faith and covenant" was adopted.

In this year the first child was born in Salem, John Massey by name. His father, Jeffrey Massey, was a companion of Conant. At a church meeting, many years afterward, the old church Bible was presented to Massey as the "first town-born child."

The government of the company remained in London, till 1630, when it was transferred to New England, and John Winthrop was sent over to supersede Endicott. Winthrop first landed at Salem, but he was not well pleased with the town as a place of settlement. He founded a colony at Charlestown, and withdrew the seat of government from Salem to that place. This withdrawal, of course, was a cause of great regret to the people at Salem. They had hoped that the town would become the metropolis of the new country, and be the centre of trade. But they bowed in submission to the decree, feeling that the movement was for the welfare of the public. Endicott was made one of Winthrop's assistants. Later he became Governor, and removed to Boston.

For a time Salem increased very slowly, but fourteen or fifteen years after the coming of Endicott, the fisheries began, and all other towns were left behind in commercial enterprise. Roads were laid out, and houses built, one of which, still remaining as a landmark in the city, deserves more than passing notice. This is the Pickering House on Broad street, built in 1651, on land

COL. TIMOTHY PICKERING.

that originally belonged to Emanuel Downing, who sold it to John Pickering, so tradition says, to pay for the commencement dinner of his son, Sir George Downing. Sir George was a member of the first class that was graduated at Harvard.

This house was the birthplace of Colonel Timothy Pickering, who was one of the most remarkable men that Salem has ever had. During his life he held scores of offices both civil and military. He was admitted to the Essex Bar, and became the leader of the patriots in Essex County. He also wrote and delivered the famous address from the citizens of Salem to General Gage about the Boston Port Bill, and he was the colonel in command of the troops at the North Bridge, when Leslie was repulsed. He served in the Revolution under Washington, and was made Adjutant General Later he served in three different positions in the Cabinet, and was made United States Senator. His local offices were innumerable. He was a warm, personal friend of

Washington who called upon him in Salem, when he was making his tour through the states. The locust tree to which Washington tied his horse is still standing.

When Timothy Pickering entered the Continental Army, his brother John took his place temporarily as Registrar of Deeds, with the intention of restoring the office to him on his return. But John became so accustomed to the work, that it was

The Rev. Hugh Peters and Mr. George Corwin, a merchant of Salem, were foremost in encouraging the fishery interests, and for years it was the staple business of the town. The rivers and harbor abounded with fish, which were indeed so plentiful that they were used even as an enrichment for the soil. Winter Island, lying just off from Salem Neck, was for years the headquarters of the fishing industry,

INTERIOR OF SITTING ROOM AT PICKERING HOUSE.

decided that he should remain permanently in the office. At one time he became, as it was thought, fatally ill, and his opponents began to canvass for a candidate for the office. On hearing this, and that his brother Timothy's name was not mentioned, John became so enraged that he announced that he needed no successor, and recovered straightway from his illness.

and it was also the centre of the ship-building business, which sprang up in the wake of the former trade.

A little later began the commerce of Salem, which sent her ships into all parts of the globe, and brought prosperity and wealth to her sons. As early as 1664 there were some very rich merchants in the town. The first ship to circumnavigate the globe, a deed which was then considered something to marvel at, was the "Minerva," owned by Clifford Crowninshield and Nathaniel West.

The story of Salem's commerce reads like a bit of fiction. Her ships led the way from Cape Cod around the Cape of Good Hope, to the Isle of France, and to India, and China, and were the first to open trade with St. Petersburg. Her hand-made charts of unexplored coasts were employed for years afterward by those who followed the sea, and were used even in our navy on Commodore Perry's expedition to Japan. The sturdy seamen everywhere glorified the name of Salem by their daring deeds of heroism, whether attacked by pirates on the high seas or thrust into prisons in foreign lands.

ELIAS HASKET DERBY.   FROM THE PAINTING
BY JAMES FROTHINGHAM.

Philip English was a good type of the early merchant. He came to Salem before 1670 and in less than fifteen years afterward he had prospered so that he had built a grand house on the lower part of Essex street. It was such a fine house that it was known for long after his death as "English's Great House." Besides this house, he owned twenty-one vessels, a wharf and ware-house on the Neck, and fourteen buildings in the town. So rich was he, and so elated were he and his wife over their good fortune that their spiteful neighbors accused them of being sorcerers, during the witchcraft craze. However, they were both acquitted of the charge.

Then there was Richard Derby, who came a few years later. He exported fish and lumber to the West Indies, and brought back the products of those islands. He then proceeded to Spain, Portugal and Madeira with assorted cargoes of these same products, and came back with wine, fruit, iron, lead and handkerchiefs, to America. When one learns that these vessels rarely exceeded sixty tons burden, one begins to realize the dangers that beset such small craft, laden down with their rich cargoes, and a prey not only to the wind and wave, but to the buccaneer and to English and French cruisers.

But the commerce of Salem received its greatest impetus during the Revolutionary War, and from that time until the embargo preceding the War of 1812, the prosperity of Salem was at its height. The three most noted names in commerce were Elias Hasket Derby, William Gray, and Joseph Peabody. These three merchants owned nearly all the vessels of Salem, which sailed to every port, and brought back cargoes from nearly every country in the world. The Salem merchant was honored and respected the world over. In 1807, Salem had sixty ships, seven barques, forty-five brigs, forty schooners, and three sloops in the merchant service, and one hundred fishermen, and coasters.

With the Revolution, privateer-

JOSEPH PEABODY.

ing became the leading business of Salem. Mr. Joseph White, a merchant, was the pioneer in this. He with Mr. Cabot's assistance, bought a sloop, the "Come Along Polly," rechristened her "Revenge," fitted her out with ten guns and fifty men, and set sail in her himself as commander, to revenge the wrongs he had suffered at the hands of the British.

Every vessel that was strong enough, was made into a privateer, and people came flocking to Salem to engage in that exciting and profitable business. Rich cargoes were unloaded from the prize ships which would often extend from Naugus Head to Throgmorton's Cove, so large a fleet would be anchored at once in the harbor. But this golden era came to an end with the conclusion of the war, and gradually the commerce of Salem declined, for the "merchant princes" could not stand up against the competition that came in the train of great railroads. Their "mountain pile of wealth began to dwindle," and Derby street which once resounded to their footsteps, is now one of the poorer districts of the city, and the large colonial dwellings with their stately columns, have fallen from their high estate, and have become tenement houses.

These old merchants knew well how to build for both comfort and beauty. Their houses were square and stately edifices befitting their stately life and manners. The present Custom House stands where the elegant mansion of George Crowninshield once stood. This was a two-story, wooden building with heavy pilasters on its water front, and it was placed about sixty feet back from Derby street. It was surmounted by a cupola, on the top of which was a wooden image of a merchant in the dress of the pre-revolutionary period, holding a spy glass through which he was scanning the horizon for his returning argosies. Back of the house were the stables and a luxurious garden.

Another of the same name, Mr. Benjamin W. Crowinshield, Secretary of the Navy in Madison's administration, also built a house on Derby street. This is the fine mansion now occupied by the Old Ladies' Home. When President Madison made his four days' visit in Salem in 1817, he occupied this house, and at a grand dinner given to him here, there were present Commodores Perry and Bainbridge, Generals Miller and Dearborn, Senator Silsbee, Lieutenant governor Gray, Judge Story, and other men of note.

Nothing brings back to one the palmy days of Salem's commercial prosperity more than the Museum with its store of curious treasures gathered from all parts of the world. The East India Marine Museum was organized in 1799, its membership having been confined to "persons who had actually navigated the seas beyond the Cape of Good Hope or Cape Horn, as masters or supercargoes of vessels belonging to Salem." It was the delight of the old sea-captains, when commerce was at its height, to add to the interesting collection, and they vied with one another to bring home strange and unheard-of treasures from foreign lands. Time was when the rooms in which the collections were formerly sheltered, were the daily haunts of these master mariners, who there exchanged stories of their adventures on land and sea, and spun sea-yarn after sea-yarn. But when Salem's commerce declined, this sturdy race of men disappeared from the old town, and they are now, "as scarce as hens' teeth," as one of the last survivors facetiously remarked.

In 1824 the present East India Marine Museum building was erected, and the accessions were numerous during the "following years." Then the membership fell off, and money was lacking with which to support the Museum. In 1867 Mr. George Peabody of London placed one hundred and forty thousand dollars in the hands of certain gentlemen, who purchased the hall, refitted it, and were incorporated as the Trustees of the Peabody Academy of Science. Since then the Museum has been systematically arranged, and is one of the most interesting institutions of its kind in the country.

Commerce naturally brought in its wake the Custom House. Previous to the erection of the present building in 1818, the customs were collected in various localities in Salem, and for a long period the customs officials transacted their business in their own houses, thus giving rise to the complaint of the old sea-captains that they never knew where to find the Custom House on their return from their voyages. It was in the present building that Nathaniel Hawthorne served for many years as Surveyor of the port. His time of service was when the commerce of Salem was at its lowest ebb, and his duties were evidently not arduous; for after he had relinquished the office, he wrote to his friend, Horace Ingersoll, "If I had stayed four years longer in the Custom House, I should have utterly rusted away, and never been heard of more!"

While Hawthorne was the Surveyor of the port, General James Miller was the Collector of Customs. There was no love lost between the two men, however, for it was General Miller whom Hawthorne caricatured in his prologue to the "Scarlet Letter," which ro-

HON. WILLIAM GRAY.   AFTER STUART.

mance he tells us he found in manuscript in one of the rooms of the Custom House. The present edifice was built to accomodate the hoped-for increase in trade which even at that time was declining. It was much too large for the business of the city, even in its most prosperous days. However, the commerce of Salem, since the days of Hawthorne, has become a much more important item in the trade of the city. In fact, the amount of tonnage at the present time is larger than even in the days of foreign trade, and the beautiful harbor is often crowded with sail waiting for a fair wind. But the lumbering schooner has taken the place of the majestic ship, and instead of rich cargoes from the Indies, come lumber from Maine, and coal from Pennsylvania. Never again will Salem excite the wonder of the people living along the Mediterranean by the "beauty, luxury, and magnificence" of her floating palace, "Cleopatra's Barge." The good ship "Mindoro" the last in her line, lay rotting at Derby wharf—a fitting symbol of the past that is gone forever.

" 'Square riggers' here came by the score,
Well laden with wealth in days of yore.
Mindoro! hail! good words to thee—
Type of the ships we used to see!"

Returning to our colonists, we find that Salem slowly and gradually took on the semblance of a town. "Townsmen" were elected in 1633 who transacted the municipal affairs, and the first records of Salem, the "Book of Grants" and the "Town Records," a portion of which is in the handwriting of Governor Endicott, bear the dates, 1634 and 1636. Then a Town House and a Court House were built, and a Prison and an Almshouse. The pillory, the whipping post, and stocks were used as a means of punishment, and scolding wives were ducked. Also certain malefactors were hanged. Persons in those days were expected to walk circumspectly and in the fear of the Lord.

Recalling to mind the reason of their coming to this country, it would seem as if the persecution suffered in their native country would have taught the colonists a tolerance for the religious belief of others. But their stern and uncompromising natures could brook no difference of opinion in these matters. They banished Roger Williams and Anne Hutchinson, and they fined, whipped and hanged the Quakers. These Friends began to arrive in the Colony as early as 1657. In the following year severe laws were passed against them, and people were punished even for attending their meetings. In 1661 eighteen Quakers were publicly punished. The colonists' idea of ridding the town of this "spiritual plague" seemed to be to whip and mutilate, while the Friends, in turn, glorying in persecution, returned repeatedly to suffer for righteousness' sake. The Society of Friends, though small, still lives, several of the members being direct descendants of those who suffered in 1658.

About thirty years after the persecution of the Quakers, there broke out in Salem, that strange delusion which made the year 1692 a most melancholy date in the annals of the town. During this period no less than nineteen persons were tried and executed on the charge of sorcery, while many others were thrown into jail on the same accusation. During the excitement which prevailed, men cast all common sense to the winds, and listened to every slight tale with credulity.

The witchcraft delusion began in the home of Rev. Samuel Parris, pastor of the Church of Salem Village. Here a party of girls, friends of his daughter, met, and practised the arts of fortune telling and magic, till they became very proficient in that direction. Then they began to act very strangely in public places, and often broke up the church services with their spasms, crying out

and the new court acquitted all the accused. During this sad time, however, so many people moved away from Salem, that it lost fully one-fourth of its population.

During the troublous times preceding the Revolution, Salem was at the front, firmly maintaining that "taxation without representation" was illegal. When the duty on tea was imposed, Salem voted that none

OLD WITCH HOUSE, AS IT WAS IN 1854.

that they were bewitched. And they accused certain persons of sorcery. These persons were arrested on this charge, tried, and found guilty, and many were hanged at Gallows Hill. The excitement began in February, and lasted until September of the same year; then the tide turned, and the delusion died down as suddenly as it appeared. The stern judges, John Hathorne and Jonathan Corwin, were divested of their power,

of that article brought from foreign lands should be used. But there was one woman who refused to obey that ordinance. This was Mistress Page who lived in that part of Salem which is now called Danvers. She was a Tory at heart, and saw no harm in drinking what her Mother Country had provided. But her husband, a strong patriot, had ordered that no tea should be drunk in his house. So in his absence she

SALEM CADET ARMORY, FORMERLY COL. FRAN-
CIS PEABODY'S RESIDENCE.

invited her Tory friends to go up to
the roof of the house with her, and
there she entertained them with the
forbidden nectar. The bulk of the
inhabitants, however, were good
patriots.

The first armed resistance to the
British was at Salem, and the first
blood of the Revolution, though
flowing only from a bayonet wound,
was spilled here. On a Sabbath
morning, February 26, 1775, Colonel
Leslie at the head of about three
hundred British soldiers sailed from
Boston, landed at Marblehead, and
marched to Salem, to seize some
hidden cannon which had been
loaned to the Provincial Congress.
Met by the militia under Colonel
Timothy Pickering, he was stopped
at the North Bridge, where he
found the draw raised to prevent his
going on.

For the first time in the history of
the colony, the British troops received a check; for the first time
blood was drawn in strife between
the colony and the mother counry.

In a slight scuffle, Joseph Whicher,
one of the defendants of the bridge,
received a wound from a British
bayonet, from which the blood
flowed. He was afterward very
proud of the wound. Others were
slightly scratched, and Colonel Leslie seeing that these men were determined in their resistance, gave
up his purpose, and returned to
Marblehead without the guns.

Among the prominent men who
guarded the bridge, was Joseph
Sprague, Captain of the first uni-
formed company of Salem. His residence still stands on Essex street,
and is occupied by his great grandson, William Saint Agnan Stearns.
This old colonial home is filled with
many beautiful pieces of the old
furniture of which Salem is so proud,
much of it having been brought over
from England, and remaining in the
family ever since. There is one
relic here of more than ordinary interest, a tortoise shell comb, topped
with gold, which was given by the
Empress Josephine to Mr. Stearns'
grandmother, Agnes Saint Agnan,
when the two were schoolmates together in Trinidad.

In 1789 Salem was honored by a
visit from "The Father of his Country," who was entertained for the
night by Joshua Ward on Washington street. From the fact that
Washington spent the night at this
house, the name of the street was
changed from Town-house Lane, to
the name it bears now. General
Washington was also received at
the home of Colonel Timothy Pickering and of General Stephen Abbot.
General Abbot's house is still standing on Federal street, and still contains many of his possessions. He
was the first commander of the
Salem Cadets.

The second corps of Cadets were

formed in 1785 at a tavern called "The Bunch of Grapes," located at the head of Central street. It came into existence just after the close of a bloody war, and during the Civil War it furnished one hundred and sixty commissioned officers to the Federal Army besides many non-

is taken from one of the ancient chapels in Windsor Castle, and it is wainscoted with richly carved oak in the Gothic style of the Elizabethan period. On one side is a huge fireplace, into which one may walk without bending one's head, and look directly up to the blue sky overhead.

Its Dutch jambs support a heavy chimney-piece, elaborately carved, and containing niches filled with statuettes. The central figure is Queen Victoria, with a mailed figure at either side. The whole is surmounted by a lion, guarded by a guardsman and a

WILLIAM SAINT AGNAN STEARNS' HOUSE IN SALEM.

commissioned ones. Its headquarters are in one of Salem's historic old buildings, on land that was formerly occupied by the residence of Governor Simon Bradstreet, who was superseded in office by Governor Phipps, when the witchcraft excitement was at its height.

LINDALL-ANDREWS HOUSE. RESIDENCE OF THOMAS BARNARD. BUILT IN 1775.

fashionable part of the city. With Downing, who sold it to John Pick-the prosperous days of Salem's commerce. The "Banqueting Hall" in mentioned. The design for the room

priest. Opposite the fireplace is a beautiful stained-glass window. Prince Arthur of England was entertained at dinner in this room in 1870.

With the decline of commerce the court end of the town was changed, and for a time it was thought to make Bridge street the fashionable part of the city. With this object in view several fine houses were built there. But land disputes arising, Bridge street was deserted for Chestnut street, and this is now one of the finest residential parts of the city. It is a beautiful street, with graceful elms arching overhead, and stately dwellings lining either side, in which descendants of the sturdy, first settlers still reside; while hidden behind the houses, not flaunting their wealth to the outside world, but conservative like the old town itself, are the lovely, old-fashioned gardens, so much in evidence in our grandmothers' days.

In 1714, it was voted that the spot "where trainings were held in front of Nathaniel Higginson's house shall be forever kept as a training field for the use of Salem." This Common was laid out from swampy land in 1802, through the efforts of Elias Hasket Derby, Colonel of the militia, and in the years immediately following, several fine houses were built facing Washington square as the Common is now called. One was erected by John Andrews, and is now the home of Mr. William O. Safford, one of Salem's prominent citizens. Tradition relates that the tall and stately Corinthian columns at the side were filled with rock salt, in order to give them strength. In this house Governor Johin A. Andrews often visited his uncle, and frequently remarked that it was his ambition to make his home in it at some future time—a wish never fulfilled, however.

Another house was built by the Hon. Nathaniel Silsbee, United States Senator from 1826 to 1835. This much altered, is now the property of Mr. Frank R. Kimball, a son of one of Salem's most prominent merchants. Here President Munroe was entertained when he visited Salem in 1817 ,and Henry Clay and Daniel Webster were guests there, too.

In the same year in which the Silsbee house was built, John Forrester also built a house on the Square. This was afterward the home of Mr. George Peabody, grandfather of Mrs. Joseph Chamberlain, who was a frequent visitor at her grandfather's house, and it is now owned by the Salem Club. At the entrance one is struck with the beauty of the doorway, with its beautiful fan lights and side lights, the porch being supported by dignified, Ionic columns. The interior is divided into large, airy rooms with elaborately carved woodwork, the work over the doors being especially beautiful. Back of the house, the grounds are laid out in formal flower beds.

The First Congregational Society of Salem was organized in 1629, with Samuel Skelton, pastor, and Francis Higginson, teacher. But it was not till 1634, while Roger Williams was pastor, that a building for religious purposes was erected on the southeast corner of Essex and Washington streets. It was a small, single-story structure. In 1639, it was enlarged and was used for thirty-seven years as a church. Then a larger one was built, and the former building was used as "a skoole and watch house." In 1865, the supposed timbers of this first church were discovered at the foot of Gallows Hill, and were removed to the ground of the Essex Institute where they are now to be seen set up as near like the old place of worship as possible.

The first meeting-house was only twenty feet long, seventeen feet wide and its posts were twelve feet high. It had but one room and had a gallery over the door. "No structure was built earlier for congregational worship in America." On the spot where the First Church was built, the First Unitarian Church of Salem still worships.

Not far from the spot on which the first church was built stood the Town and Court House from 1718 until 1785. This was the theatre of many stirring events. "Here Governor Burnet convened the General Court in 1728

HAWTHORNE'S BIRTHPLACE.

House of Assembly was thereupon dissolved, and the election of a new House, to meet at Salem, was ordered by the Governor, but this by later proclamation, he refused to recognize. In contempt of his authority the members met in the Town House, October 5, and after organizing resolved themselves into a Provincial Congress, and adjourned to Concord, there to act with other delegates as the First Provincial Congress of Massachusetts." Town House Square was the spot where the

THE HOUSE OF SEVEN GABLES.

and 1729. A town meeting held here in 1765 protested against the stamp act, and another in 1769 denounced the tax on tea. Here met in 1774 the last General Assembly of the Province of the Massachusetts Bay, which June 17, in defiance of Governor Gage, chose delegates to the First Continental Congress. The

CUSTOM HOUSE WHERE HAWTHORNE SERVED.

bold Endicott cut the red cross, "the sign of Popery," from the banner of New England, for which act he was admonished and suspended from the office for a year. But the deed was

RESIDENCE OF GEORGE PEABODY. NOW THE
HOME OF THE SALEM CLUB.

who slaughtered cattle without saving their hides for tanning, and butchers were fined a sixpence for every cut made in removing skins.

Philemon Dickerson was the first man to engage in the tanning business systematically. In 1639, he was granted land to "make tan pits and dress goat skins and hides." Dickerson and all the early tanners sank their pits and plied their trade in the wet and marshy land at the east of Washington Square. Remains of ancient vats and sides of leather have been unearthed in this locality, although every other trace of the business has been effaced.

The tanner of those days was hedged in by numerous restrictions, and the town kept a close watch over the quality of the wares and the honesty of his workmanship. As early as 1635 John Marsh and John Kitchen were chosen sealers and searchers of leather, and "ould Thomas Eaborne was presented by them for wronging the country by insufficient tanning."

A century later, in 1750, an old Quaker preacher in Danvers, Joseph Southwick by name, improved the method of tanning, by grinding bark by a circular stone revolved by horse power. This was a great advance; then a still further stride was made in the business when in the early part of the eighteenth century steam and water-power were used in the most laborious parts of the process. The trade increased rapid-

secretly approved by the principal men of the Colony.

Almost at the very beginning of the colony, the leather industry was started. John Endicott was above everything else a practical man, and in choosing his followers he picked out only those men who could work. Most of the men had already learned some useful trade. Shoes were essential to the life of the community, so shoe-makers, leather dressers, and tanners were among the ship's company.

Of course, at first the little colony had to depend upon their mother country for supplies, for domestic animals were too scarce and precious to be slaughtered for their skins. However, some leather was made from the skins of the wild animals with which the woods abounded.

In 1630, the cattle were increasing rapidly. Still skins were very expensive, and in 1646 the General Court passed a law punishing those

ly then, and the number of tanneries grew from four in 1768 to twenty-four in 1836, and in that year 68,677 hides were tanned.

The old-time tanners were a sociable lot of men, fond of gathering together to discuss the topics of the day. There is still standing in the heart of the present leather district, on Boston street, a small one-story building where the tanners in "the hollow" were wont to assemble. This informal club was called "The Senate," and the sign over the door of the little building read:

JOSHUA B. GRANT,
Dealer in Curriers' Tables and Tools.

There was no formality about these meetings—the different members just dropped in, and if the proprietor of the little shop were absent, and a customer appeared, the required sale would be made and charged up by some member of the "Senate."

The next industry in order in importance is the cotton cloth manufacture, which is carried on by the Naumkeag Steam Cotton Company, incorporated April 5, 1839.

Salem claims the honor of having the first glass works in New England, for as early as 1639 a "Glasse House" was erected in a field lying between Boston and Aborn streets. Glass slag has been dug up lately on this spot.

The first mill built in New England was also located at Salem. Captain William Trask, a planter erected a mortar for pounding corn on a small brook running into North River near the Lowell Station in Peabody. In 1692, the building was made over into a fulling mill, and it was afterward known as Frye's Mills.

In a community where the fisheries were the main industry, natu-rally much attention was given to ship-building. In 1629, six ship-builders came to Salem, and began to build boats at the Neck, which was for a long time the centre of the business. Salem became noted as one of the principal places in the Colony for building vessels, and many ship-wrights in Salem were famous for their skill. The majority of the merchantmen sailing from Salem were built there, and as many as two hundred vessels were turned into privateers and fitted out at Salem during the Revolution and the War of 1812. But as her commercial prosperity is at an end, so is her ship-building, and except for the building of an occasional yacht, her ship-yards are empty, and the rope-walks, the sail-lofts, and the ship chandlers' shops have disappeared.

Marine insurance in the olden times was conducted in a very different manner from the methods of to-day. To be sure there were insurance offices, but there were no organized stock companies. These offices were visited by the merchants and skippers and other individuals also. A printed policy of insurance was placed upon a desk in the office, giving the name of the vessel and the cargo, and other particulars, and any person who desired to take a risk in the venture wrote his name at the end of the policy, giving the amount he would risk. This person was called an underwriter. The proprietor of the office kept books, and had to satisfy the owner of the vessel that the underwriter was reliable. Later, in 1800, a joint stock company was incorporated as the Salem Marine Insurance Company.

Fire Societies or Fire Clubs, as they were called, were one of Salem's institutions, and were formed as early as 1744. They did great service in their day. They associated on the mutual principle of aiding one another in case of fire, and every member was provided with a bucket and a bag. Many of these old buckets are still to be seen in the Salem houses, hanging in the hallways. They were in olden days kept under the staircase, or on some projecting cornice. In addition to the bag which was given to him as a receptable in which to take property from burning buildings, each member was given a bed key with which to take down the old-fashioned bed-steads. Most of the clubs had ladders at convenient places about the town. These were active and useful organizations in their day, but, of course, are now wholly superseded by the introduction of improved fire apparatus.

The old burying ground of the Colony is on Charter street. It was originally known as "Burying Point," as it was once on a bluff which projected into the South River. It was occupied before 1637. Here were buried Governor Bradstreet, Rev. John Higginson, Judge Lynde, and Judge Hathorne of witchcraft fame. Nathaniel Mather, a precocious, younger brother of Cotton Mather, has a curious epitaph here. It reads:

"An aged person that has seen but nineteen winters in the world."

The grave of one who came over in the Mayower, Captain Richard Moore, has recently been discovered here.

Another early burying ground is the Broad Street Cemetery, where was buried Captain George Corwin, a sheriff in the time of the witchcraft delusion. Colonel Timothy Pickering was buried here, too.

In the field of literature, of science and of art, Salem has held first rank. Since the early settlement it has been the home of men of note. Nathaniel Hawthorne and Jones Very stand preëminent in the world of letters, while William H. Prescott, as an historian, has made a national reputation. In science, Salem's brightest star was Nathaniel Bowditch who became known the world over as a mathematician and a maker of charts.

In art she has many names of which to be proud. William Wetmore Story made his fame as a sculptor by his statues of "Cleopatra" and "Semiramis." Of Charles Osgood, the portrait painter, Joseph Felt in his "Annals of Salem," says, "He is deservedly ranked among the first painters of our republic."

We have seen that Salem has had a career of unusual interest and importance, making it unique among the cities of America. Settled in 1626, four years earlier than Boston, for two centuries it has occupied the second place in prominence among the towns of New England. Twice was it the seat of government, first under Governor Endicott in 1628, and again under Governor Gage in 1774. It has always been a shire town.

And the Salem of to-day? She is filled with reminders of her past, replete with dear and old associations that hover about her quaint houses, her old-time gardens, and historic landmarks—reminders and associations that draw to her strangers from all parts of the Union with irresistible power. Her beautiful, Colonial architecture which groups itself especially around the Common and on Chestnut street, her fine libraries, and the accumulated treasures in the East India Marine Museum and the Essex Institute—these too are features that give her claims to unique distinction among American cities.

But though her commerce, her fisheries and her ship-building have declined, Salem is by no means a nonentity in the busy, industrial life of modern times. Her business interests of to-day are many and important, her people thriving and prosperous, and though she looks back upon her past with pride, she is not subsisting on the husks of former glory. The present is for her an earnest reality, and the future full of promise.

21
The Development of Steam Navigation

THE DEVELOPMENT OF STEAM NAVIGATION

STORY OF THE FIRST STEAMBOATS TO SAIL INLAND WATERS—
INVENTION OF MACHINE CAPABLE OF CARRYING PASSENGERS
AGAINST STREAM BY POWER OF "ELASTIC VAPOR" WAS CONSID-
ERED VISIONARY—INTERESTING NARRATIVE AND ANECDOTES

BY

C. SEYMOUR BULLOCK

Mr. Bullock, in continuing his life-long researches into the development of steam navigation, narrates in this third article of the series the story of the first application of steam to vessels for inland waters. From apparently ill-omened beginnings and against public ridicule and incredulity, John Fitch, of Connecticut, laid the foundation of the principle upon which the great world of commerce exists to-day. This was indisputably proven by Mr. Bullock in his first article in Volume IX, Number 3, of THE CONNECTICUT MAGAZINE. That Connecticut holds six prior claims to distinction in the mastery of steam for the propulsion of vessels against wind and tide is shown by Mr. Bullock in Volume IX, Number 4, of THE CONNECTICUT MAGAZINE. When Captain Moses Rogers, of New London, Connecticut, crossed the Atlantic ocean with the first steam vessel, it was considered foolhardy. To-day the United States steamboat inspection department alone issues more than 40,000 licenses annually. Mr. Bullock's investigations have created much interest, and as a result, several prominent families are entering claims as pioneers in steam navigation. Robert D. Roosevelt, of New York, writes: "I cannot allow the discussion of this subject to pass without putting in the claim of the Roosevelt family. I trusted that some other member of the family who had the actual proofs in his possession would come forward, but we are rather careless in claiming credit—especially when the public has made up its mind in another direction. It has always been a tradition with us that my grand-uncle, Nicholas J. Roosevelt, first ran a model steamboat as finally adopted by Fulton and made a success by him. He was connected with Fitch by marriage and business, and together they afterward exploited the Western waters, leaving Fulton the Hudson. You will find models of boats with oars propelled with steam. These were failures, and the little steamboat of my relative led the way for the wonderful invention which Fulton made successful. I do not like to seem to ignore or abandon our claim, which has been quietly maintained for nearly a century and is upheld by a quantity of evidence." Mr. Bullock in the following article mentions Captain Benjamin Beecher. A detailed story of Captain Beecher, written by Hon. Frederick J. Kingsbury, appeared in THE CONNECTICUT MAGAZINE, Volume VII, Number 3, in which the author maintained that Captain Beecher invented a propeller that antedates Ericsson by several years.—EDITOR

IN the story of steam navigation from its earliest developments of the idea to which John Fitch of Windsor, Connecticut, had given practicability, we take up the chapter of the application of steam to vessels for inland waters. The demonstrations that Fitch had made on the little stream that runs through Bardstown, Kentucky, had been taken up and heralded everywhere throughout the South and Middle West. As early as March, 1801, a project was on foot to put steamboats on the Ohio river at Cincinnati. In the *Western Spy* and *Hamilton Gazette,* published at Cincinnati, there was printed at that time the following notice:

PUBLIC UTILITY. A company of persons having, at considerable expense of time and trouble, recently invented a machine capable of propelling a boat against stream with considerable velocity, by the power of steam or *elastic vapor*, and entertaining the opinion, that if reduced to practice, great advantages must flow from it to the country, as it will afford a regular and easy conveyance for property down the various navigable rivers, and a safe and speedy return, either in specie, or in the produce of the country below; take the liberty of soliciting the aid of the public, the better to enable them to carry into effect an invention which promises to be of so general utility,

The first appeal did not bring a very hearty response. The public feared the pear was not yet ripe enough for the picking. In a few weeks more they were appealed to a second time as follows:

To The Public. We, the subscribers, Samuel Heighway and John Pool, at the request of a number of gentlemen, who have expressed a wish for the bringing into effect a mechanical project, constructed for the propelling of boats against the stream of rivers, tides and currents, by the power of *steam* or *elastic vapor*, of which we are the proprietors, propose bringing it into immediate use, by the aid of voluntary subscriptions, from those public spirited persons who may feel disposed to patronize so important a discovery.

But Cincinnati was not the only centre of effort along the lines marked out by Fitch. A letter was sent to the *Spy* from Lexington, Kentucky, which bore the date of August 11, 1801, in which the writer says:

On Thursday last, Mr. Edward West exhibited to the citizens of this place a specimen of a boat worked by steam, *applied to oars*; the application is simple, and, from the opinion of good judges, will be of great benefit in navigating the Mississippi and Ohio rivers."

The letter from Lexington recalls the description of Fitch's original boat as given in the first article in the CONNECTICUT MAGAZINE on the part this state has had in the application and development of steam for navigation.

The times were ready for a change. Robert Fulton, fortunately, stood at the very threshold of the new era with his plans for the utilization of all the good points in the inventions of others and the making of such necessary changes as would bring ultimate suc-

cess where heretofore there had been faiure. Herein lay his genius and for this the world rightly gives him honor.

After the advent of the "Clermont" there appeared on the Hudson, in quick succession, a number of larger boats that were in every way improved over the original boat—the "Car of Neptune" was built the same year that saw the improved "Clermont" come onto the Hudson. The "Paragon" appeared in 1811, the "Fire Fly" in 1812, the "Richmond" in 1814 and the "Chancellor Livingston" in 1817. All these boats, with the exception of the last, which was built by Henry Eckford from plans drawn by Fulton, were built in New York City, by Charles Brown, for the North River Steamboat Company, which at this time had a monopoly of the waters of New York State for the use of steam propelled vessels. The "Chancellor Livingston" was enrolled in the New York custon house in the name of Dominick Lynch, Jr., March 29, 1817.

Several opposition boats had appeared soon after Fulton had successfully navigated the Hudson, but they were not allowed to run for any great length of time and with them we shall now have nothing to do, as they do not enter the story we have to tell of Connecticut's part in the development of the steamboat.

In 1814 the "Fulton," which was the last and greatest boat designed by and built under the supervision of the builder of the "Clermont," was ready for her commission as the forerunner of the magnificent steamers that have ever since maintained communication between the ports on Long Island Sound. In the plans for this boat radical departures were made from the type that had been followed in all the other boats of his designing. The hull was made "ship-shape," with a "dead-rise" to the floors, a keel was introduced to stiffen the hull against "working," and the ribs were bent as in the later wooden steamboats that

FIRST SCHEDULED STEAMBOAT ON LONG ISLAND SOUND

The "Fulton," 1814, the forerunner of comfort in travel by water—At her bow she carried a bust
of Fulton—With flags a-flying she steamed into New Haven March 21, 1815

ran upon the Sound. She was sloop rigged, one mast, and depended upon her sails to accelerate her speed. Her bow was like that of a sloop, very full above but receded to an angle of about forty-five degrees. She was 134 feet long and 26 feet wide, but the rails that ran along her sides gave her an additional four feet of beam. She had a "square" engine, with a stroke of about six feet, that extended but little above the sides of the paddle boxes. There was no heavy framing visible. At the bow she carried a bust of Fulton for a figurehead. An interesting feature was the queer manner in which she, in common with the boats of that period, was painted and which has been likened to the painting of a barber's pole. Her hull was painted black with white upper works, but the majority of later boats were painted white with two contrasting stripes of paint around the hull above the water line; some boats, for instance, having a green and yellow stripe, some a green and red, or

a red and yellow. The guard fender was usually painted black. The bulwark rails and other rails were generally painted yellow on the lower half with green or brown above. With their flags a-flying and the sun shining on their striped sides they presented a very picturesque appearance.

Because of the impertinent activity of a fleet of British naval vessels at the extreme eastern end of the Sound, it was not thought advisable to put the "Fulton" at once onto the route for which she had been built, between New York and New Haven. She was therefore, temporarily placed on the Hudson. Before taking up a regular schedule here, however, she first made an excursion trip to Sandy Hook, carrying about fifty passengers who had paid $3.00 for the privilege of sailing down the bay on a steamboat and looking upon the ocean.

The first announcement of the regular schedule of the new boat appeared in the *New York Evening Post* of June 4, 1814, as follows:

> The public are respectfully in-
> formed that the subscriber has com-
> menced running the steamboat "Ful-
> ton" between the cities of New York
> and Albany for the accommodation of
> passengers.
>
> This boat was built for the purpose
> of plying between New York and
> New Haven, but will be employed on
> the Hudson River until a cessation of
> hostilities (i. e. the war of 1812) en-
> ables the proprietor to put her on her
> destined route.
>
> The "Fulton" is handsomely fitted
> and furnished, and her speed exceeds
> the most sanguine expectations of
> the proprietors or patentee. The com-
> plement of passengers is limited to 60,
> and the price of passage therefore
> raised to ten dollars.
>
> The "Fulton" will start from the
> foot of Cortland street every Satur-
> day morning at 9 o,clock, and from
> Albany every Tuesday morning pre-
> cisely at 11, and will arrive in Albany
> every Sunday morning, and in New
> York every Wednesday morning.
>
> One of the days between Wednes-
> day morning and Saturday morning,
> the "Fulton" will go out on parties of
> pleasure. Notice will be given on the
> day previous to the time of starting.
>
> Elihu S. Bunker.

The "Fulton" continued to run on
the Hudson all that summer and in the
following spring made her first trip
up Long Island Sound—the first
steamboat to navigate those waters
since the days that the little craft
built by Captain Samuel Morey had
sailed from Hartford to New York
City and back again. This was as early
as 1793 and much of the correspon-
dence that passed between Captain
Morey and Professor Silliman of Yale,
relative to steamboats on the Connecticut River and Long Island Sound, is
said to be still in existence. Morey
had first built a small boat in which
he sailed from Orford, New Hampshire, to Fairlee—a Lilliputian edition of the boats that were yet to be,
in which there was scarce room
enough for the crude engine and boiler and the handful of wood to run it,
to say nothing of the venturesome
engineer. The experimental trips of
Morey's first boats were witnessed
by the Reverend Cyrus Mann who,
in 1858, published in the *Boston Recorder* a plea for the recognition of
his friend as the builder of the first
steamboat that actually sailed upon
any river in the world.

We know that John Fitch had previously won the honors in that achieve-
ment, but that is neither here nor there
in this present article. Captain Morey
maintained up to the very day of his
death that he had been wronged by
Fulton, who secretly deprived him of
his sacred rights. His story was told
to many of his friends and his neighbors all claimed to know that the story
was true. The story tells of a boat
that Morey built and sailed to New
York where he met Fulton and Livingston to whom he explained all the
parts. On his return trip these two men
who afterward enter so largely into
the history of steamboats, sailed with
him in his little craft as far as Green-
wich and suggested that the engine
be taken from the bow of the boat and
placed in the middle. This, with several other minor changes that they
suggested, required some little time
and during this time of readjusting,
Fulton visited Morey to study the progress of the boat. When all the alterations had been completed, Captain Morey once more sailed down the
Connecticut and through the Sound to
New York City, but found upon his
arrival there that Fulton and Livingston had decided to build a boat for
themselves.

But to get back to the 'Fulton" and
the opening of the New Haven line
of steamboats. The spring of 1815
found everything in readiness for the
new undertaking. On the 21st of
March, she left New York early in
the morning with thirty passengers,
and reached her destination in about
eleven hours.

STEAMSHIP "FULTON" SAILS FROM NEW YORK TO NEW HAVEN

AN ACCOUNT OF THE NOTABLE MAIDEN VOYAGE ON LONG ISLAND SOUND AS PUBLISHED IN THE "NEW YORK EVENING POST" UNDER DATE OF MARCH 25, 1815, FOUR DAYS LATER

The steamboat "Fulton" commenced her trip from New York to New Haven on Tuesday last, a little after five in the morning, and arrived at New Haven at half-past four in the afternoon, having completed her passage in a little more than eleven hours. From the performance of the boat at this time it may be concluded that she will not often, if ever again, be so long on the route. The machinery had not been tried since last season, and it was not in perfect order; some alterations had been made in the boiler which rendered it also in some measure imperfect, she having been obliged to supply herself with such wood as the New York market offered at the opening of the spring; it was the worst kind, and the least calculated to afford the necessary supply of steam. The force of steam which she ordinarily carries is from four to six inches on an average, but on this passage she seldom had more than one inch, often less and never more than two, except when the steam was increased by her having been obliged to stop several times on her return in consequence of the fog. Yet under all these disadvantages the boat had completed her voyage in the time which has been mentioned without any aid from sails. She remained in New Haven agreeably to her intentions on Wednesday. On Thursday the weather was so thick that no vessel could venture on the Sound. On Friday evening she left full of passengers, but had scarcely got out of the harbor before a fog came on which entirely obscured the land on either side, and indeed for the greater part of the time was so thick that it was impossible to see the distance of twice the length of the vessel. And from the time she left the port at New Haven till she made Sand's Light, they did not see any land so as to distinguish what it was. The wind blew a gale from the South, which was directly ahead and raised a very rough sea, but the boat, notwithstanding the disadvantages which have been enumerated and under which she continued to labor, encountered it without the least difficulty. The facility with which she passed Hell-Gate in both instances surprised everybody who was on board,

and satisfied them that no vessel can be so well calculated to navigate this dangerous channel as a steamboat. On the return passage she passed the Gate about half an hour before high water, of course against a tide running at the rate of between three and four knots, yet she worked with as much ease, certainty and quickness as any light or small vessel could have done. The "Fulton" arrived at this city about ten o'clock the next evening, having been fifteen hours from New Haven. The length of passage was owing to her having been obliged to stop and let out her steam several times, to wait the clearing up of the fog so far that the land might be seen. On her return she passed a great number of vessels at anchor.

It has been supposed that the Sound could not safely be navigated by a steamboat on account of the difficulty of passing Hell-Gate, the roughness of the sea and the impossibility of making the compass traverse when attracted by so much iron as must necessarily surround it on board the boat. But these objections the passage of the "Fulton" has proved are without foundation. She will probably never again have to encounter so many disadvantages. It does not happen but seldom that the weather is so thick and boisterous, and as to the capacity of the compass, that is tested by the fact that having no landmarks to steer by, she made Sand's Light according to the course which the needle indicated.

We have been assured that this establishment has cost $90,000 and we believe it may with truth be affirmed that there is not in the whole world such accommodations afloat as the "Fulton" affords. Indeed, it is hardly possible to conceive that anything of the kind can exceed her in elegance and convenience. Her passages will probably be made in eight or nine hours.

The beauty of the scenery through which she passed cannot be surpassed. The enterprise has not only been attained with great expense, but great risk; but we think the owners as well as the public may be congratulated on the success of the experiment.

Mention of the passing of this wonderful boat was made by all the coast city and towns of the day. In the Bridgeport papers the announcement was simple: "The Steamboat Fulton passed up the Sound yesterday bound for New Haven." Yet in that simple announcement there were tidings of but little less importance than those that told when the war had ceased.

The "Fulton" was kept on the New Haven run for some time and afterward ran to New London for a few months. Later she formed part of the first line to be established between New York and Providence. During the first few months of her running to New Haven she was frequently used for excursions, trips on the Sound and in the *Hartford Connecticut Mirror* there appeared an account of a trip made to the Capitol City which was reprinted in the *New York Herald* of May 17, 1815, as follows:

> On Thursday morning, the inhabitants of this town, and the people collected on account of the election, were gratified by the arrival in the river opposite the city of the elegant steamboat " Fulton," which regularly plies between New York and New Haven, with a load of passengers from those places. The novelty and elegance of this vessel, attracted universal attention, and it is supposed, that on that day, and the next morning, not less than seven or eight thousand persons were on board of her, who were treated with great attention and respect by Captain Bunker. On Friday, she went down the river, with a great number of passengers, for the purpose of making her accustomed trip from New Haven to New York on Saturday.

There thus came to New Haven the honor of being the first city on Long Island Sound to have regular steam communication with other cities and later of establishing the oldest steamboat company for continuous service in the whole world. The boats that now run between the Elm City and the great metropolis are owned by a company that traces its unbroken history back to the original owners of the "United States," a successor, or rather, a competitor of the "Fulton."

The "Fulton" started in to make two round trips to New York and return each week, leaving New York every Wednesday and Saturday, the rate of fare was six dollars one way. Commencing June 19, of the same year, the trips were increased to three each week, the boat leaving New York early in the morning on Monday, Wednesday and Friday. This three-trip schedule was continued till March, 1818, when another boat, the "Connecticut," was added to the line.

It is said that this new boat was built to go to St. Petersburg, under some inducements held out by the Emperor of Russia, but that a lack of funds made it necessary to make some other disposition of it and it was, therefore, sent onto the Sound under the name of "Connecticut" instead of across the ocean under the name of "Emperor Alexander."

When the "Connecticut" came to New Haven, the "Fulton" was placed under Captain Law—Captain E. S. Bunker, who had superintended the construction of the "Fulton" having been transferred to the new boat, which began running to Norwich where stage connections were made for Boston and all points east. It was not thought prudent at that time, if indeed, it were deemed possible, to send a steamboat on so long a run as from New York to New London or Norwich and the two-part line was offered as a way out of the difficulty. The establishing of this new line was hailed with great delight by travelers between New York and Boston, as it lessened the wearisome staging to a very considerable extent. Both of these vessels had engines that were fitted with the gearing peculiar to Robert Fulton's engines, and made noise enough when in motion to keep any but the sleepiest traveler awake. A strange feature in both was the arrangement made for the uncoupling of the shafts so that the wheels might remain stationary when working the engine at the dock.

The arrangement of a two-part journey was continued until May 27, 1822, when it was interrupted by legislative enactment. In that year, as a remedy for the injustice of the decrees of New York State in protecting the monopoly of the heirs of Fulton and Livingston, by which they had the exclusive right to maintain steam navigation on the waters of that state, our legislature, by a vote of 174 yeas to 11 nays, had passed a law prohibiting the Fulton Steamboat Company to land anywhere in Connecticut until they agreed to not molest the steamboat "United States." At this time it was declared that Fulton and Livingston had not made any such discovery as would entitle them to a patent and could get exclusive rights in no other way, and that the state of New York could control only its own waters.

Naturally the owners of the two boats that had begun to bring in good returns financially from the business that had been established, would not at once relinquish all claims upon the patronage of the people and a line of sailing packets was established between New Haven and Oyster Bay, Long Island, where their passengers were transferred to the steamboat "Enterprise" and carried to New York. The "Fulton" and the "Connecticut" were then placed on the New York and Providence run. Seven years had elapsed from the time the "Clermont" first sailed up the Hudson before any steamboat had come into New Haven and seven more years pass by before a steamboat enters any harbor farther to the east.

The first steamboat to round "Pint-Judy-Pint" was a little midget that Fulton had built to run to Newburg, on the Hudson. This little thing was called the "Fire Fly" and was sent down east to run between Providence and Newport. She arrived at Newport from New York, on Monday, May 26, 1817, having made the trip in twenty-eight hours. The sea was full of mad sprites as she rounded the "Pint" but she rode the waters of their turmoil so safely that she was hailed as a very beautiful boat. Under the command of Captain Smith, she made her first trip on the new route on the 28th of May, leaving Newport at nine o'clock in the morning and reaching Providence about noon. A sloop had carried tidings the night before of the approaching steamboat, and long before noon the wharves were full of people waiting for the arrival of the strange craft.

On the morning of June 28, the "Fire Fly," with Governor Knight, United States Marshall Dexter, and others on board, sailed at seven o'clock for New York to meet President Monroe and escort him to Providence. He, however, went in a marine cutter to Bristol, and embarked there on the "Fire Fly," reaching Providence about nine o'clock in the morning.

The packet masters were exceedingly jealous of this "interloper," and resorted to every lawful means to break down the new enterprise. In a fair wind, even when she hoisted her huge square sail, the "Fire Fly" was no match for a fast sloop and the masters of the sailing vessels, who were offering to carry passengers from Providence to Newport for twenty-five cents, agreed to forfeit their passage money if they failed to arrive there ahead of the steamboat. By their continued opposition these sailing masters finally succeeded in running the little innovator from the bay and she returned to the Hudson for further service.

This trip of the "Fire Fly" from New York to Providence and back again is not included in the statement that fourteen years in all passed before the introduction of steam-propelled vessels on the extreme eastern end of the Sound.

BUILT FOR EMPEROR OF RUSSIA IN 1818

Intended to go to St. Petersburg under name of "Emperor Alexander," but entered service on Long Island Sound as the steamship "Connecticut"

To come back to the text, as the preacher says, the story of the part Connecticut had to do with the development of steam navigation has a slight connection only with this carrying of the idea further to the east and we must get back to the "Retaliation Act" of 1822, and pick up the thread of our discourse where we left off.

In 1821, Thomas Gibbons began building a steamboat in New Jersey that was one hundred and forty feet long and which he fitted with a "square" engine, built by James P. Allaire, of New York City.

After the death of Fulton in February, 1815, as a result of a cold, contracted while attending court at Trenton, New Jersey, in the case of Livingston vs. Ogden, when the question of the priority of invention by Fitch as against Fulton was first raised for the consideration of the courts and decided in Fitch's favor, Allaire, who had furnished most of the brass work for the first Hudson river steamboats, leased the machine shops which Fulton had moved from their original location in Jersey City, not far from where Secor & Co. built the monitors for the Government in 1863, and which now stood at the foot of Beach street, New York City. The next year he moved the shops to the foot of Cherry street and here the engine that went into Thomas Gibbons' boat was built. This boat was named "United States"

and was intended for service on the Hudson. An adverse decision of the court left her on the hands of the parties who had bought her while yet on the ways and Captain Benjamin Beecher, Jekiel Forbes and Stephen Huggins, of New Haven, who were at that time proprietors of a line of sailing packets, hearing of this new boat, signed papers of agreement to purchase her for the New Haven-New York line.

In the Spring of 1822, preparations were made for bringing the new boat to New Haven. The prohibitory laws of New York prevented the sailing of the boat under her own steam and it was finally decided that one of the largest sloops runing on the regular packet line should be used to tow her out of the waters of the belligerent state. Captain Benjamin Beecher was accordingly sent down with the "Huntress" for that purpose. After making fast to her charge, the sloop began beating up the East River, much to the amusement of the people along the water front who put out in boats to join the procession as it made its way toward Hell Gate. The steamboats that lay at the wharves as the strange arrangement passed along, were cut out from their moorings and followed up the stream to the treacherous swirl of waters through which it must go. Every obstacle possible was put in the way of the sailboat and her steam consort in an effort to drive either one or both ashore or onto the rocks, but Captain Beecher was equal to the occasion. With a fresh breeze blowing from the "south'ard" he steered his boats through swift currents in the crowded channels and into the open waters of the Sound. The owners of the boats that followed her, who were sailing under the privileges of the Fulton-Livingston charter, had been outwitted by the Yankee from New Haven.

During the passage up the river, the crew on the "United States" had not been idle. Steam had been got-

STEAM PACKET "CHANCELLOR LIVINGSTON"— 1817

Built from plans drawn by Fulton for a corporation that held a monopoly of the waters of
New York state for the use of steam propelled vessels—Photographed from a rare old print

ten up in the boiler and everything put in "ship-shape" so that she might sail under her own power as soon as she was clear of the waters of New York. As soon as the line was crossed, the position of the two boats was reversed. The "United States" took the "Huntress" in tow and steamed off for New Haven, reaching there the same night. Captain Beecher was then transferred to the steam vessel as master, and ran upon her for years. Including the furniture, tackling and equipment, the "United States" had cost $22,-399.44. Some of the items included were: backgammon boards and lamps, $31,66; blankets, $22.25; two chessboards, $2.00; carpeting, $51.68; kitchen furniture, $109.86; bed lace, $2.50; set chess-men, $6.75; sheeting, $144.77.

Captain Beecher was noted for the forcefulness of his speech. No one had to think twice to get the meaning of what he said, even though more of his words came from the prayer book than the almanac—perhaps not always with the same meaning. On the boat with him was an "all-round man," familiarly known as "Portugese Joe." A question had come up about a consignment of freight that had gone astray and "Portugese Joe" was called as a witness. The lawyer for the plaintiff requested the court to ask the "foreigner" if he understood the nature of an oath to which "Portugese Joe" answered:

ONE OF THE EARLY SOUND STEAMERS

The "United States," the original steamboat of the New Haven Steamboat Company—Reproduction from "The Children's Magazine" of 1831

"What! do you think I ban all dese year with Captain Ben Beecher and not know an oath?"

On another occasion the Portugese had stirred Captain Ben. up quite a little and he ordered the mate to put him ashore in a small boat. As "Joe" went over the side of the steamer, Captain Beecher stood looking on and the Portugese called out: "Goodbye, Captain Ben. I have a vish for you. I hopt you die to-night and go to eafen." The whole thing so appealed to "Captain Ben," that he ordered the man and his things put back on board and they were the best of friends ever afterward.

The advent of the "United States" was a great event in the history of New England. Up to this time the mode of transportation throughout all the eastern section of the country was, at best, but a slight modification of the caravan of the ancients and the later orientals. There were swift stage coaches running over roads, perfectly kept, that carried passengers, freight and the mails. The packets were beautifully modeled sloop-rigged vessels of from seventy-five to a hundred tons burden, built with a view to speed, carrying capacity and comfort. The sides of some of them were decorated with bead work; others had polished strips of hard pine let into the sides and all were painted in bright, gay colors. The cabins were frequently finished and furnished with mahogany, and adorned in every conceivable way. These cabins were generally from twelve to fifteen feet square and from them opened the little staterooms. Over the stairs going down into the cabin, there was usually placed a mahogany letter-box to which there would be a rush of people, as soon as the boat was made fast, for letters that had come far in advance of the slow-plodding mails over the post roads. The sailing of a mail packet was full of excitement. Friends came to bid friends good-bye, and to enjoy the hospitality of the captain of the craft,

PASSENGER WAY-BILL USED ON STEAMBOAT "UNITED STATES"

Photograph from the original way-bill used on trip from New York to New Haven, Tuesday, October 8, 1822, and now in possession of the New York and New Haven Steamboat Company

who was expected to set a filled decanter and a row of glasses on the polished mahogany table, around which all gathered and drank a solemn "health" to the prosperity of the trip.

The coming of the steamboat changed all this, but the change came slow. The first cutting off of wines at the expense of the steamboat company, was attempted on the "Chancellor Livingston," of which more anon. The merchant who had dreaded his annual trip to New York for a stock of goods, found that travel had become a pleasure. With better transportation facilities he could spread before his customers a larger assortment of everything and offer late styles and patterns in all dress material. Trade, freed from the bonds that had set its limits, went forward with a mighty stride. The world was made anew.

The "United States" herself was not very much to boast about, at least, she would not be tolerated to-day, but to our forefathers she was a thing of beauty—fleet of wing and of magnificent proportions and any countryman who had not feasted his eyes

upon her was "away behind the times." She had no staterooms and the entrance to her cabin was not much larger than the companion way of a small sloop. The pilot stood in the stern and steered with a tiller— a pilot house was unknown till four years later, but as a means of protection in stormy weather, the pilot of the "United States" had rigged up a structure over the deck that at first glance might have been taken for a floating chicken coop.

Of course the "United States" could not run in New York waters and her passengers could reach the city only by stage from some intermediate point. On June 1, 1822, she started in to make three regular trips each week between New Haven and Byram Cove, with side trips to New London and Norwich. Byram Cove is on the boundary line between New York and Connecticut and from here passengers were taken to New York City, twenty-five miles, by stage. The fare was then $4.00 from city to city. This arrangement continued till 1824, when the Supreme Court of the United States decided in the case of Gibbons and Ogden that the acts of New York in giving Fulton and Livingston exclusive privileges in steam navigation were unconstitutional, and any steam vessels were free to run through to New York or upon any of its waters. Accordingly, on March 15, 1824, the "United States" began regular trips between New York City and New Haven, landing at the foot of Maiden Lane, East river, in the former city and at the end of Long Dock in the latter.

The system of tickets as now used on steamboats everywhere in this country, was first introduced on the "United States"—prior to this, passengers were way-billed, the same as freight. It was customary then to fire a cannon from the bow of the steamer when coming into New Haven, as a signal for the stages for Meriden, Hartford, Providence and Boston, to be in readiness to receive their lists. From this custom came the later one of ringing a bell and the present one of announcing the approach by blowing a whistle. The eagle that was perched on the pilot house of the "United States," when these innovations were first tolerated, saw the various improvements that were made during the next ten years and was still in its place when the boat was sold in the early thirties, after the company had bought the "Superior," built in New York in 1830, and was carried during all its vissitudes while used for passengers and as a towboat on the Hudson till she was broken up in 1840, when she was rescued and brought back to New Haven. For a long time it stood with its extended wings over the old mill down near the wharf from which it had been so proudly carried by the first real New Haven steamer. It has since then been in the family of those who first put it in place and is now to be given a position of honor in the magnificent building of the New Haven Historical Society.

It seems a far look back to the day when the "United States" first poked her nose into New Haven bay, towing the "Huntress" that had first towed her, but the years are measured by the lives of men who remember the craft as she first appeared, and recall the prophecies then made of what her advent would yet mean to the whole world.

In my following article I intend to record the interesting story of steam navigation on the Connecticut river, and to relate incidents of river traffic and river craft.

22
Mariner's Three

MARINERS THREE

By GILBERT P. COLEMAN

'TWAS in the bleak fall of 1755 that mariners three and a cask of rum were blown ashore at Sankoty, off the east coast of Nantucket, whiles the good ship *Sister Anne* was churned to splinters against the treacherous sands. A fair cask, indeed, full from head to head, stout, and nobly hooped, and sound so that not a drop of brine penetrated and mingled with its contents, precious beyond gold and gems. No wonder, therefore, that the lusty mariner with the massive beard, standing wet and shaking on the meagre cliff that o'er-looked the sea, felt his soul grow warm within him and that he gave frank utterance in gratitude for the tender mercies of a mysterious Providence.

"Ahoy, ahoy, and well-away, me mates!" says he, merrily, as he broached the cask with a touch gentle as that of a wench. "Here's to the cooper, the brave, bonny cooper, that hath fashioned this cask as a man should do!" And they drank.

And he of the quaint pigtail quoth blithely:

"Belay and stand by, me hearties! Here's to the ship that hath borne the cask in safety o'er the sea!" And they drank.

"Heave ho and avast!" quoth he of the beaked nose, and yet of the piercing eye. "Here's to the sea that hath borne the ship that hath brought the cask in safety to these shores!" And they drank.

A tempestuous night grew on apace, and the mariners three sealed up their cask and rolled it o'er the sward before them, they seeking shelter in the quaint and tranquil town of Nantucket, lying to the westward two leagues and a half.

Now, 't was in Nantucket that Ananias Tobey, a stout friend with a humble heart, walked in the paths of righteousness and virtue, setting good examples with great clearness, having put off all human infirmities; — and also where he moved about diligently with a brassy bell, he being town-crier, and sonorously shattered the silence of that tranquil town by vociferating to the peaceful inhabitants thereof the latest intelligence. True, indeed, that friend Tobey's pronouncements usually took the form and effect following, to wit:

"'T is Tuesday night, with a fair breeze from the windward, and God prospering the morrow will be Wednesday." For sure it was no fault of his that the news was scant, since the isle of Nantucket was in fact a quiet isle, lying peaceful and undisturbed at the edge of Ocean Stream.

But this very eve, as friend Tobey ascended the seven-foot hill whereon rested the ancient mill that ground the grain for winter fodder, and scanned the circular horizon, perchance to view some incoming whaler, he observed, faintly limned against the sad gray moors, a shadowy three, toiling like Sisyphus with some unknown cylindrical substance, and ever and anon disporting themselves in an unseemly and unchurchly fashion; for they seized hands and danced round said substance in a manner that was of evil consequence, well calculated to draw away the mind from heavenly things. For which reason, as friend Tobey well knew, all persons godly disposed should shun such practices as engines of Satan.

Therefore, having offended his eyes for a space sufficient to satisfy his soul's abhorrence and curiosity, friend Tobey laid heavy grip on his bell, and made haste back to the town, fraught and important with these tidings of moment.

"'T is Tuesday!" he sang loud to the tune of the bell — "the third day — and three sinful strangers approach in the offing, bearing east, northeast, one point south. Strangers are come, possessed of the Evil One. Let all beware!"

'T was at Moor's End, at the edge of the town, that the mariners three made pause, and further broached their cask before seeking the solace of strange entertainment.

"Heave plucky, me hearties," says he of the massive beard. "Here's to the cooper that fashioned the cask!" And they drank.

And he of the quaint pigtail quoth blithely:

"Steady, oh, steady, me messmates! And here's to the ship that bore the cask in safety o'er the sea!" And they drank.

"Luff, luff to the loo'ard, me laddies!" quoth he of the beaked nose, and yet of the piercing eye. "Here's to the sea that bore the ship that hath brought the cask to this island on the lee!" And they drank.

"Whoopee!" cried they all, in fraternal accord, with rising inflections and accents boisterous.

The wind howled and the snow had begun to sweep athwart the horizon when the mariners three and their cask of rum attained the centre of the village square. Knotty souls were they, and thirsty, as they sat by their cask. And they were encircled by friends of the tranquil isle, who had been shorn of their early repose by these rude sounds of riotous glee.

'T was he of the massive beard who stood on the cask of rum and would make sweet speech with these upright men of the quaint little isle; but friend Jepthro Swayne, Selectman and worker in the paths of righteousness, with heavy spectacles bridging his nose, read by the light of a lanthorn as follows from the archives of the town to those evil men of the sea:

"Be it known that Drink is the Soul of the Devil, that it leadeth to an evil Life and Conversation, and that as a Benefit and Warning to all great Lovers of Wine and strong Liquors —"

"Whoopee!" cried the mariners three.

"As a Benefit and Warning to all great Lovers of Wine and strong Liquors it hath been declared that all Wines, Liquors, heavy Draughts, Hollands, Grog, Rum and evil Waters of whatever sort be eschewed —"

"Whoopee!" cried the mariners three.

"Be eschewed, banished, forbidden, exorcised, and forever exiled from the Island of Nantucket, and that any Persons who shall introduce any of said strong Waters to said Island shall be deemed Miscreants and evil Persons, moved by the Voice of the Devil, and shall forthwith be incarcerated in the Town Gaol by the strong Arm of the Law, and said strong Waters shall be confiscated. Blessed be the Virtuous, and they that strive for Rectitude."

Whereupon, in the exercise of the strong arm of the law, there followed a blithe and soul-easing contest between those mariners three and the cask of rum as parties of the first part, and those sober friends of the isle as parties of the second part. There was much bickering and scuffling, aye, and even sundry crackings of craniums; but the mariners three, though valiant, were weak as to numbers and had perforce to contend also against the enfeebling effects of divers devoted libations of rum, which, as the kind friend had truly said, is the soul of the Devil and does grievous hurt to all that imbibe thereof to excess.

Thus it was that the mariners three were haled to the county gaol — a modest structure, forsooth, that had fallen into some disrepair through lack of employment; — it being recorded that it had last been used to accommodate a minister of a different faith, as having no visible means of support, and therefore a godless miscreant and vagrant. And the gaol stood on the bleak edge of the moor. And Ananias Tobey, town-crier, county gaoler, auctioneer, ringer of curfew, and custodian of confiscated goods, brought up the rear with the cask of rum.

Now, 't is no rare hardship for buffeted seamen who have rolled a full cask of rum two leagues against the wind and made zestful brawl with sturdy burgesses to sleep on a hard bed in tempestuous weather. Nor did these mariners three make moan when they were shown to couches of uncovered boards. Nay, soon they were buried deep in restful slumber, which comes at times alike to the ungodly and eke to those who walk in the strait path of the righteous. Yet they had not recked of the sheep.

'T was indeed a turbulent night, and the sheep that nibbled the scant pastures by day, fleeing before the restless blasts that ever swept o'er the sandy moors, sought shelter in that spot which appeared to them most convenient, most hospitable, and most humane. What wonder, then, that, spying this friendly gaol from afar, they filed gently through its open door, and disposed themselves in crowded comfort, free from the piercing blasts that blew tireless in from the sea?

But 't was long since he of the massive beard had slept on a windy moor in an open gaol, overwhelmed with curious sheep, and in good season he awoke and peered about in the grateful gleam of the lanthorn that had been placed on the cask of rum by Ananias Tobey, town-crier. And when he perceived the nature of this billowy, fleecy sea by which he was sore hard pressed, he rose from his bed of board in stalwart rage.

"Avast and belay, me messmates!" he shouted with raucous vigor. "Avast and belay yet once again!" And there awoke also he of the quaint pigtail, and he of the beaked nose, and yet of the piercing eye, and looked about them, and were amazed.

'T was he of the massive beard who advanced to the corner where Ananias Tobey, town-crier, county gaoler, and custodian of confiscated goods, was seated on the floor, his head reclining at a fond angle against the cask of rum.

He of the massive beard thrust his boot generously into the sides of the gaoler and caused him thereby to sway pendulously for a moment, and then to sink gently to the floor, his arms falling tenderly in a posture of affection about the base of the cask of rum.

"Well, shiver me toplights!" quoth he of the massive beard.

"Heave ho and avast!" cried he of the quaint pigtail.

"Blow me and blast me!" said he of the beaked nose, and yet of the piercing eye.

Whereupon these mariners three rushed out to the tempestuous moors and back into the placid town; and they roared right lustily — yea, they did shatter that holy calm as it had ne'er been shattered before, by town-crier, auctioneer, or clangorous bell that rang curfew in tower of Old South Church.

"Ahoy!" they shouted with vast good will, and abundantly well together.

"Ahoy, ahoy, and yet again, ahoy!"

Nor was it long ere lights shone in the sundry windows of these domiciles of tranquillity, for truly the evocations were dreadful to hear; and presently there appeared in the square, equipped with lanthorns and armed with muskets, against these horrid bodements, Jepthro Swayne, Selectman and worker in the paths of righteousness, together with divers and sundry of the God-fearing natives of the tranquil isle.

There was no utterance from the mariners three and them of the isle until they had reached the county gaol, whither all were led by him of the massive beard. Thereupon he spake, whiles they of the isle

glanced down at the sheep, and also at him who yet embraced the cask of rum.

"A gaol!" quoth he, with a weight of scorn in his voice; "a gaol, a pretty gaol, forsooth! And a gaoler — a pretty gaoler, forsooth! Behold now, thy gaoler,— he of the lanthorn and the brassy bell, who snores athwart our cask of rum!"

They looked, and they saw, and they marvelled much to see.

And then he of the massive beard made speech in thunderous tones, so that they of the isle who stood there in the shadowy lights of their lanthorns quaked fearfully to hear.

"Blast me, blow me, shiver me, and avast! And do ye imagine this a gaol? We be mariners three, and we have roamed and buffeted the main, and travelled wide in distant climes. Aye, and we have lodged in many a gaol, but never in such an one as this. Shiver me! Blow me! We will not bide in thy gaol, an ye do not fasten the door and keep out the sheep!"

'T was in faltering tones that Jepthro Swayne spoke when he of the massive beard had done.

"We have had peace and satisfaction in our gaol," he said, "for it hath afforded a comfort and refuge for the sheep in the night season. But thou sayest truly 't is right that we should fasten the door;" and here he looked with puzzled mien at him who grasped the cask of rum, and presently continued, in sorrow and amaze: "It appeareth that our worthy town-crier hath fallen from grace and hath sold himself to the Prince of Darkness. 'T is proper, then, that he also should be confined in the gaol."

There was a nodding of heads by the friends of the isle, and a hum of approval, for they plainly saw that the sin of the town-crier was great, and merited due penalty.

"Yet," pursued Jepthro Swayne, as he again glanced in much perplexity at him who lay caressing the cask of rum, "yet it surpasseth my wit how we may safely incarcerate him, for, be it known, our county gaoler, whom we would with justice deprive of his liberty, hath the key of the gaol in his sagathy breeches!"

And here it was that a buzzing of sympathy passed around among those bearded friends of the isle, but he of the massive beard smote the gaoler athwart the thick of the thigh so that the sound cracked forth very like unto the harsh snapping of a faggot in the flame.

"What ho, thou shameless dullard!" quoth the mariner, "what ho, and yet again, what ho! Wouldst deprive us of a hard-earned repose, aye, and thyself also, by slumbering on the key? Come, come," he said, "what of the key, man; what of the key?"

And he who cherished the cask even as a woman cherishes her child opened a slit in his eyes and, smiling with the content of the ever-blessed, made languid utterance:

"Whoopee!"

A mighty oath tore from the lips of him of the massive beard, and he pounced upon that gaoler and seized the key from the dark depths of his sagathy breeches.

"There, in God's sooth," he said, tendering the key to Jepthro Swayne, "there is the key. Now, out with the sheep, and lock us up that we may have repose."

Saying the which, he reclined again upon his board of pine, as did likewise he of the quaint pigtail, and he of the beaked nose, and yet of the piercing eye. And ere the last sheep had been ousted from the county gaol those mariners three slept, and snored — aye, and eke snortled in rich union and harmony.

But they of the tranquil isle tarried yet a while and stood about in a circle and looked with the eye of pity tinctured with scorn upon the figure of him who fondled close that cask of rum. 'T was Jepthro Swayne who spake at length in words of sapience:

"Thou hast erred grievously, Ananias, in that thou hast seen fit to tamper with the Engine of the Devil. Behold, thou art overtaken and arrested in the grim Territories of Drunkenness, which is a sin beyond all. And thou hast brought Shame upon us, Ananias, in that thou hast openly embraced a cask of Rum."

Here, however, friend Jepthro paused, and a new light of doubt and hope shone through his heavy spectacles:

"And yet, brethren," he added, "I misgive me much that friend Ananias should trifle with this horrid enemy of the soul; — 't were not his custom; mayhap this is not, indeed, rum, of which he hath partaken. Mayhap 't is some innocent liquor, and he be overcome with excess of zeal to duty.

"Friends and brothers," he continued, turning to those who surrounded him eagerly in the murky light of the lanthorns, "I have a great concern and exercise on my mind to taste of the cask and see verily whether this be rum, and whether or no we have vainly and arrogantly maligned our dear brother Ananias."

And from all that circle of hearers there was not one word of dissent.

Gently disengaging a pannikin from the feeble grasp of the gaoler, friend Jepthro tipped over the cask and drew for himself a modicum of the contents thereof. This modicum he held to his lips and swallowed with a gurgle of righteousness, while the circle of bearded friends of the tranquil isle gazed on with a painful anxiety. And they saw a heavenly light steal into the eyes of Jepthro Swayne behind the heavy spectacles that bridged his nose.

"It hath," he said, "somewhat of the taste of rum, yet as I have but imperfect knowledge of this matter I shall ask Brother Hoffin to try if it be really rum or no."

So Brother Hoffin tasted, and in an agony of doubt passed on the burden to Brother Bolger. And Brother Bolger tasted; and Brother Cardner tasted; and they all tasted; but such was the innocence and unwisdom of those men of the isle that though they tried and they tried, in humble endeavor, never were they quite able to quiet their souls whether or no 't was a cask of rum.

'T was he of the massive beard who first awoke when the sad gray dawn made its way through the generous chinks in the easterly wall of the county gaol. And as he cast his wary eye about he rubbed it in keen amaze and stared yet once again, the whiles he gave soft utterance to words that appertain to a life on the sea. And then he prodded him of the quaint pigtail, and likewise him of the beaked nose, and yet of the piercing eye. And they also did look, and stare, and swear with sweet accord.

Peradventure 't were meet they did, for there, still in a circle surrounding that cask of rum, were they of the tranquil isle; but no longer erect and scornful, and full of righteous wrath against the vessels of iniquity, but low and humble, reclining in divers and sundry poses on the barren floor of that gaol. And all of those virtuous friends were wrapped in the slumber of the innocent,— some soundless, some snoring, some wheezing, some gasping catchily, some groaning, some sighing even as the wind soughed and sighed through the generous chinks in the easterly wall.

"Shiver me!" softly crooned he of the massive beard.

"Blast me!" whispered he of the quaint pigtail.

"Alas and ahoy," murmured he of the beaked nose, and yet of the piercing eye.

And again 't was he of the massive beard that crept with cunning stealth to where Jepthro Swayne lay nigh the cask of rum — aye, even nigher than he of the brassy bell — and, removing the key from his hand, made progress back to his mates of the sea, pushing the cask before him with tender solicitude.

"'T is a Christian act we do," he quoth, as he gently oped the door and again laid the cask on the freedom of the moor. "I wot not of the habits of sheep,— their incomings and outgoings,— but 't is only a deed of charity to lock the door of the gaol against them, that these worthy brethren of the isle be not disturbed in their slumber."

Whereupon, having carefully locked the door, he and his mariner mates made off through the dawning day toward the harbor, ever rolling before them the faithful companion of their adventures, that well-hooped cask of rum.

In a staunch whaleboat it was that they embarked, setting a fair good sail, and with a favoring breeze and a restful sea 't was soon that they could gaze o'er the stern and observe the spires of the quaint old town rise nobly above the roofs, while o'er the lea, on the bleak edge of the moor, could still be discerned the modest lines of the county gaol, wherein slumbered and snored, and gurgled and groaned, the humble, the chaste, the upright sons of the tranquil isle.

And still again 't was he of the massive beard who broached the cask and cried:

"Ahoy, ahoy, and well away, me mates! We'll drink to the cooper, the brave, bonny cooper, that hath fashioned this cask as a man should do!"

And he of the quaint pigtail quoth blithely:

"Belay and stand by, me hearties! We'll drink to the ship that hath borne the cask safely o'er the sea!"

"Heave ho and avast!" quoth he of the beaked nose, and yet of the piercing eye. "We'll drink to the sea that hath borne the ship that hath brought this cask in safety to yon hospitable shore!"

Thereupon it was that they up-ended that cask, and tilted it, and moved it from side to side, and shook it, and pressed it, and squeezed it, and spoke to it in terms of hearty rage. But not a drop issued therefrom.

"Shiver me toplights!" quoth he of the massive beard.

"Blast me forehatches!" quoth he of the quaint pigtail.

"Alas, alas, and yet again alas!" quoth he of the beaked nose, and yet of the piercing eye.

And they drank not.

So these mariners three sailed o'er the sea, with an empty cask of rum.

23
New England Fisher-folk

New England Fisher-Folk

BY GUY WETMORE CARRYL

OF all those relationships between man and elemental nature which alternate so singularly in character between strife and alliance, there is none which in its various phases is more humanly appealing than the bond, or battle, as momentary circumstances may have it, between the fisher and the sea. Between aeronaut and atmosphere, chemist and his elements, miner and his ore, the relationship, if intimate, is still strictly severe, often hostile, never imbued with anything akin to this other singular sympathy.

The fisher's life, overhung as it is with the shadow of potential unexplainable death, and invested with a myriad, as if reflected, moods of the great element with which he must be in daily, almost in hourly, touch, has provided much of the poetry, and perhaps more of the pathos, in the stories of many lands, but in none more than in that of coastwise New England.

There is a singular lack of poetry, and almost of picturesqueness, in the history of the original States, founded and fostered by sectarians of a bigotry so extreme as to seem nearly akin to fanaticism, and the mark of his stern forebears is writ large in the character of the New-Englander of to-day.

Even where, as a fisher, he is brought into close contact with the element which in all time has been the most potent spur to human imagination, the trammels of ascetic ancestry are so strong upon him that we find in his conception barely a trace of the intensely vivid imagery, half superstition, half religion, with which association with the sea has imbued the fisher of other lands—notably the Breton and the Sicilian. He is eminently shrewd, keenly observant, almost clairvoyant in his estimate of character, and surpassingly deft in every detail of his craft, but, beyond and above all, a Yankee—that quintessence of practicality which may reasonably be regarded as the antithesis of romance in its any and every form.

From your fisher of Gloucester or

Cape Cod the realistic poetry which impregnates the Breton stories of Pierre Loti is as much a thing apart as the plaints of a Romeo or the imaginings of a Shahrazad. And yet that selfsame atmosphere of romance is as truly a part of the fisher of Finistère as his technical knowledge of sails and tides.

Yet—so pervasive is that subtle sea-charm which permeates all that is brought within its influence—a romance as unmistakable as that which surrounds Plougastel or Capri, though of a different quality, lies about these little fishing-towns of New England, which contrasts them strangely with the bustling commercialism of the great mercantile and manufacturing centres, so near in actual measurement of miles, so infinitely distant in every other sense.

Stranger though he be in thought and speech to aught that smacks of ideality, an influence beyond his control, as beyond his perception, has clothed every detail of the fisher's life, every most trifling accessory of his occupation, with a poetical significance unspeakably appealing to the imagination.

"They that go down to the sea in ships"—what an inheritance is theirs, what a birthright of marvel and mystery! The association, as new to-day as it was old in David's time, is inevitable. No mere insensibility to romanticism is sufficient to lessen the permanency of its influence. The sea will infallibly mark its own, and is not to be eluded or denied.

In such a village as those of which we have been speaking the sea is, in a material sense, the source of all good, and of all evil as well. It enriches or impoverishes, saves or destroys, robs or restores. Its will is the pivot on which existence revolves. So it is but natural, and far from being a fanciful supposition, that the life of the people should reflect faithfully certain broad, general qualities which may be said to be strictly characteristic of the element whereupon they are so intimately dependent. Pre-eminent among these we distinguish a vast and highly admirable simplicity, a freedom from conventionality, wherein much that is unworthily petty, suspicious, and unjust in human thought has given

place to a kindly and tolerant, while in no sense a credulous, view of men and things.

It is a supremely sane attitude of mind —sane with the clean, wholesome sanity of the sea—when contrasted with the veritable labyrinth of prejudice wherein we, whose lives are necessarily more complicated, move and have our being. One rarely hears a New England fisherman indulging in petty disparagement of a neighbor. This is not to say that his tolerance is fatuously invariable, but only that his judgment, whether favorable or the reverse, is expressed simply and broadly, without a suggestion of either favor or fear, above all, without a hint of malice. "Them Harrises be'n't no good!" said one such philosopher, and that was the expression of a simple conviction.

Disapproval is as generous and as elemental as commendation. One is inevitably tempted to a reflection upon the pains which a less simple society would be at to adduce a multitude of trivial slurs in support of this amply self-sufficient statement.

In the well-ordered regularity of life in a fishing-town the sea once more supplies the cue. Monotony, that chiefest bugbear of more elaborate conditions of existence, is less accepted as inevitable than totally disregarded in the sense of an objection.

In dependence on the sun and the wind and the tide events move forward day by day, and men rise and retire, labor and take their ease, with machinelike orderliness. And this, their submission to the requirements of routine, is parent, no doubt, to the serene repose which is so noticeable in the older men. Long before it is possible for individual preference to point out an independent line of activity, the daily round of duty has been, almost imperceptibly, laid out, and the boy finds himself pledged to the performance of certain well-defined labors, the which he accepts without argument, if not without reflection.

There are exceptions, as in all conditions of society—lads who rebel and strike out for themselves. Every battle-ship in our navy has its tale of these. But for the most part, to an

Half-tone plate engraved by A. Lockhardt

THE SON TAKES UP THE WORK WHERE THE FATHER DROPS IT

WHARVES WHEREUNDER THE TIDE MURMURS MYSTERY

extent undreampt of in our larger cities, where the ebb and flow of life is so ceaseless and so erratic, it is a case in the fishing-town of "like father, like son." The latter takes up the work where the former drops it, sails the same boat, cleans fish with the same knife, mends and remends the same nets, and spins the same yarns in his hours of leisure.

But where the fisher's life is most appealingly in sympathy with the sea is in a respect which he of all men is probably the furthest from perceiving — its profound melancholy. In this regard, if in no other, coastwise New England is nearly akin to that coastwise Finistère of which we have spoken, and which inspired *Mon Frère Yves* and *Pêcheur d'Islande.* There is lacking the fanciful imagination of the Breton, which has peopled every mood of the ocean with the personalities of saints and demons, and thereby achieved so great a degree of picturesqueness; there is lacking, too, the extremity of devoutness which associates the woe or weal of the fishing-fleet with the direct intent of the Virgin. There are no pageants, no *pardons,* no

invocations to the sea, no little porcelain *Notre Dame de la Recouvrance,* before which, when the fleet is out, the women of the village watch and pray, and tapers continually burn.

But all these, indescribably pathetic though they be, are not, it must be remembered, intrinsically so, but only in such sense as they are the manifestations, the outward signs, of a great elemental undercurrent of tragedy—the ominous, indescribably alluring relation between the fisher and the sea.

Apart from the peculiar phenomena wherein this emotion finds expression under varying conditions lies the emotion itself, vast, majestic, large with infinity of suggestion, and identical, we may imagine, the sea-coasts of the world around. Here in New England the very severity of earlier conditions seems to have bequeathed an added force to the tragedy.

It is, perhaps, not too much to say that these fisher families are exemplifications, as perfect as may be, of absolute adherence to a very high, if simple, code of ethics. One can barely conceive of social relations more

366

TO AND FROM THE WHARVES THE SCHOONERS COME AND GO

essentially righteous, of religious convictions more consistently followed, of a more rational or saner observance of hygienic and physiological principles.

And, withal, from cradle to grave it is always the tragic aspect of the fisher's life which is seen to be most heavily underscored, most unmistakably emphasized. Those most familiar in a sympathetic sense with the sea will realize that even in its gayest moods it is inseparable from this hint of melancholy. It is too old, too cruel, with all its kindness, and the custodian of too many terrible memories and awful secrets to be ever less than ominous. And it may almost be said that as the land approaches the sea it comes under this influence, and shows, even in its conformation, a reflection of the lurking grimness before it.

The long swelling sand dunes of Cape Cod, rolling away in majestic emptiness, mile on mile, and the gaunt, grim rocks of Maine, wrinkled, as are the faces of the fisher-folk, with much gazing across the sea — are they not equally suggestive of infinite loneliness, ageless endurance, stupendous power, and, more than all, the pitiable littleness of man?

The fancy could be carried further, down to the blackened and mussel-covered piles of the wharves, whereunder the tide rises and murmurs mystery, and retires as if to seek yet other stories from the informing deeps beyond. Above, the weather-beaten planking is strewn with an infinity of discarded rubbish—spars, anchors, chains, sail-cloth, blocks, and cordage. Where they have been, whence they come, there is no knowing now. Only in two respects are all alike. In their time they have been new, strong, well fitted to their appointed uses. Now they are but mute additional proofs of the impotency of man's device. The omnipotent and everlasting sea has laid hand on one and all, as upon those who made them, and they are as if they had never been. The sea! the sea! the sea! To and from the wharves the schooners come and go. They too are blackened, and bear witness to the eternal struggle and the inevitable end.

So, little by little, is born in the observer not merely a realization of the pervading melancholy inseparable from this environment, but an appreciation of the primary cause, the emotion which lies below. Every most trivial detail of this people's life is instinct with the thought of facing an unknowable and invincible force, wherewith they may struggle for a little, may even seem to master or cajole, but which must inevitably stand victor in the end. Each year the sea claims its tithe, and this comes as no unexpected calamity, but as a duly calculated nemesis.

One catches a trace of its abiding presence, now and again, in the eyes of a mother or a wife or a sweetheart as she watches him who is to her the fisher of all fishers, on his way toward the shore—oftener, even, in a strange, unconscious glance of apprehension toward the sea itself, which, perhaps, has already smitten, and holds yet other blows in store.

All this tends directly, one cannot but think, to the formation and preservation of a very strong, albeit unobtrusive, nobility of character, as it so apparently induces an admirable simplicity of life. Beneath the evidence of these immaculately kept houses, these scrupulously tended nets and boats, these trim gardens, and severe places of worship, and clear-eyed, sturdy children; back of this spirit of fair dealing and clean living, and earnest, consistent endeavor: there lies a marvellous strength of conviction and an appreciation of duty which is not far from being the chief of our national moral sinews.

The fisher-folk are, to a great extent, a people set apart, barred off by the peculiar conditions which surround them from participation in much of what we are wont to say makes life worth living. More than any other class of Americans they are forced into that close intimacy with elemental nature from which it is the tendency of civilization to wean us. They are part and parcel of the great universal system, and so are impelled and controlled, as is nature's self, by magnificently broad and yet singularly simple laws. As a result, we find them unconsciously imbued in thought, word, and deed with nature's own dignity and sanity and force.

From conditions so elemental it would be strange did there not result the poetry and the picturesqueness which invest whatever is supremely natural, and that are lacking in all that smacks of artificiality or design.

Just as there is no trace of intention in the attitude of the fisher himself, so is there nothing resembling studied effect in what, as the logical result of his needs, has come to be in his surroundings. Even the most sequestered inland villages of New England are not free, in these progressive days, from the reproach of atrocious architecture, made worse by glaring combinations of the unspeakable commodity known as enamel paint. Nature is foully wronged in the presence of grottos and rockeries which have not even the redeeming grace of utility, far less that of ornament, and incongruous iron stags profane the even velvet of the lawns.

But of these and kindred crimes the fisher's environment is guiltless before nature and nature's God. The tints of his shingles and sails and wharves are those lent by the fingers of the salt wind and water. Even where the work is that of his own hands it runs on broad unoffending lines of architecture, and in simple blacks and whites and greens and maroons unspeakably grateful to the eye long weary of gaudier hues. His flowers are the simplest, and while trained away from disorderly riot, yet grow naturally and freely, untrammelled by the intention of ornamental borders.

And if he err in angularity of line or blatancy of hue, his omnipresent mentor, the sea, is at hand to correct, gnawing and rounding and moulding with busy teeth and fingers, till the sharp corners are made smooth and the gaudy tints softened and the sea's great aim is once more attained—the reduction of all with which it comes in contact to a gray in color and to a curve in form.

Let us leave it as we found it, this modest little cluster of gray and white cottages nestling in a curve of wooded shore, and staring ingenuously from square, green-shuttered windows at the blackened wharves, eloquent of the comings and goings of the simple, brave men who go down to the sea in ships.

Half-tone plate engraved by Frank E. Pettit

THESE IMMACULATELY KEPT HOUSES

YOUR FISHER OF GLOUCESTER OR CAPE COD

Let us leave it with twilight settling down upon the gables, for this is of all hours the best. The schooners are in; the daily work is done; smoke from a score of chimneys spires skyward;—and there, beyond the laughter of the ripples on the peaceful shore, beyond the smooth gray stretch of harbor water, beyond the white foam of surf on the bar—there lies a wide, unruffled calm. There is peace, and there is a truce declared between the fisher and the sea.

24
The Story of the Isles of Shoals

THE

New England Magazine.

JULY, 1898.

THE STORY OF THE ISLES OF SHOALS.

By Aubertine Woodward Moore.

A DELIGHTFUL mystery surrounds the story of the Isles of Shoals. Whoever attempts to penetrate it yields to its spell. It wholly captures the fancy of the favored mortal, who is personally brought under the subtile charm of the atmosphere, outline, coloring and music of these jagged, wind and wave-swept rocks. They are Enchanted Islands, whose origin is unknown, whose period of usefulness to man cannot be computed, and whose complete cycle of romance will ever remain untold.

Since the silence shrouding their past was broken they have found many appreciative annalists, and have afforded inspiration to some of our best writers. Hawthorne felt their witchery when he visited them in 1852, and made the acquaintance of Celia Thaxter, then a young wife of seventeen, living with her husband in their Appledore cottage. In his *American Note Books* he styles her the pretty Miranda of the lonely island, and presents a fine bit of word painting in his description of the locality.

"It is quite impossible," he writes, "to give an idea of these rocky shores —how confusedly they are tossed together, what solid ledges, what great fragments thrown out from the rest. Often the rocks are broken, square and angular, so as to form a kind of staircase, though for the most part such as would require a giant stride to ascend them. Sometimes a black trap-rock runs through the bed of granite; sometimes the sea has eaten this away, leaving a long, irregular fissure. In some places there is a great hollow excavated into the ledge and forming a harbor, into which the sea flows; and while there is foam and fury at the entrance, it is comparatively calm within. Some parts of the crag are as much as fifty feet of perpendicular height. * * * It seems as if some of the massive materials of the world remained superfluous, after the Creator had finished, and were carelessly thrown down here, where the millionth part of them emerge from the sea."

Wherever you walk or drive on the sea-coast within several miles of the mouth of the Piscataqua, you are confronted, with more or less distinctness and from the most unexpected points of view, by the Isles of Shoals. In clear weather no vessel can skirt the coast without sighting them, and they cannot have failed to attract the attention of all early navigators in the vicinity. Like the tips of sunken mountains, they bristle with danger for mariners approaching them at night or in a fog. At the same time they so emerge from the sea as to form a harbor in the midst of the

THE LANDING AT APPLEDORE.

called also Hog Island, from its supposed resemblance to a hog's back rising from the water, or possibly from the swine that once roamed at large on its surface. Haley's Island, christened by early sailors Smutty Nose, because of a long black rock stretching to the southeast, comes next, and is a mile long. Two small islands, Malaga and Cedar, are connected with it at low tide, the first named permanently by a breakwater. A quarter of a mile to the southwest is Star, so named from its star-shaped outline, three-fourths of a mile long and half a mile wide. West of this is Londoner's, an irregular rock, on which perchance some London ship of old was wrecked, with a bit of beach where all the shells belonging to the cluster are tossed. Last comes picturesque White Island, with its warning lighthouse, not quite a mile southwest of Star, and forming with Seavey's Island at low water a double island. Shag and Mingo Rocks, isolated by a narrow channel from Duck,

ocean, and this, combined with their climatic advantages, affords a natural cause for their importance in history.

They lie to the southeast of Portsmouth harbor, with nine miles of Atlantic Ocean between them and the nearest point of the New Hampshire coast. The most northerly of the group is Duck Island, a dangerous reef of rocks, seven-eighths of a mile in length, a mile farther out in the ocean than the rest, and a favorite resort of the shy sea-gull. Two miles southwest of this is Appledore, a mile long and five-eighths of a mile wide,—

THE APPLEDORE.

a round rock west of Londoner's called Square, and Anderson's Rock, off the south-east end of Haley's Island complete the list.

Some authorities maintain that the islands were named from the reefs or shoals lurking about them. Others suppose that a shoal, or multitude of islands was meant. Still others attribute the designation to the shoaling or schooling of fish about the rocky shores. The first theory is strengthened by an extensive shoal, called Jef-

retreat. She was but five years old when her father, Thomas B. Laighton, a friend of Franklin Pierce, disappointed in obtaining some coveted political preferment, accepted the position of lighthouse-keeper at White Island, that he might forever withdraw from worldly turmoil. His faithful wife followed him unmurmuringly, with their three children, Oscar, Cedric and Celia, who grew up like seabirds on the rocks, cared for by "the sweetest mother in the world."

WHITE ISLAND, FROM APPLEDORE.

frey's Ledge, stretching to the southward of the islands, which confirms the supposition that the group once formed part of the mainland. In the earliest recorded mention, the term Isle of Shoals was applied to the island on which the population concentrated. As soon as others of the cluster became inhabited, each must have an individual appellation, and Isles of Shoals was affixed to the entire group. The spelling has been variously Shoals, Shoulds and Sholes.

The high-priestess of these isles was Celia Thaxter. No one can ever equal her poetic pen pictures of her beloved

On stormy days the little ones played in the long covered walk bridging the gorge between the lighthouse tower and the quaint stone cottage that was for six years their dwelling. The winters seemed like a whole year to the merry trio, who delighted in watching the vessels scudding over the blue sea and the sea fowl soaring aloft or tossing in the waves. In calm weather they saw the stealthy Star Islander paddling among the ledges or stretched out on the wet sea-weed seeking wild fowl. The bullet head of a seal appearing amid the rocks varied the monotony.

Mr. Laighton was a man of books. He had with him his library, and the Portsmouth pilot boat brought him letters, papers and magazines, with all the news of the day. There was much reading aloud of events then transpiring, as well as records of former times; but the children cared more for the fate of little Red Riding Hood than for that of any historic hero that occupied the attention of their elders.

Unspeakable bliss crowned the advent of spring, with its growing grass, budding flowers, birds, insects, soft skies and softer winds, and the "everlasting beauty of the thousand tints that clothed the world." During the first warm days the little ones built sand-hills on the beach, and made the acquaintance of burgomaster gull, of kittiwakes, sand-pipers, gannets, loons and the blue heron. They played with empty limpet shells, launched fleets of purple mussels in still pools left by the tide on the rocks, cut from the brown leaves of the slippery varnished kelps grotesque shapes of man, bird and beast, and manned with a weird crew of "kelpies" their rude boats of driftwood which they sent floating away on the deep.

CELIA THAXTER IN HER GARDEN.

Baby as she was when she left Portsmouth, the gifted Celia was drawn with a vague longing seaward, as she and her brothers sat perched on the household goods with which the boat bearing the family to its destination was laden. She well remembered seeing the first lamps lighted in the tower and swinging rich, red and golden in mid-air. She recalled her pride when she was thought old enough occasionally to light them herself, and realized that even so small a creature as she could be of service to the great world.

She early longed to voice the impressions made on her by winds, clouds, birds, sea and all that sweetened her life, although at times wondering if it were not better to "bless one's self with silence." There came moments, amid the matchless glory of the sunshine or the awful sublimity of the tempest, when she felt compelled to mingle her voice with the myriad voices of nature.

After six years of arduous lighthouse duties, her father removed with his family to Appledore, whose proprietor he became. Here she developed rapidly. The sights and sounds encompassing her enriched her knowledge. She grew familiar

CELIA THAXTER'S COTTAGE.

came in the season of bloom "lovelier than sky or sea or distant sails, or graceful gull's wings reddened with the dawn," and which she has made famous. Her "Among the Isles of Shoals," her poems, her "Island Garden," proved irresistible loadstones to turn the tide of summer travel Shoalwards. She herself often wondered how travellers could wish to go elsewhere. The wonderful noise of the

with the language of birds and flowers. She was seen on the rocks surrounded by the feathery friends who came at her call. Among her finest descriptions are those of her garden, where from scanty soil she conjured up a luxuriant growth that "fairly ran mad with color."

An odd freak of fortune finally compelled the recluse to open a house of entertainment; and among his guests came Mr. Levi Thaxter, who captured the scarcely fifteen years old lover of birds and flowers. Finding

sea among the rocks was to her the most suggestive of all the sounds of nature. Each island, each isolated rock, she declared, had its own note, that could be distinguished by ears sharpened through listening, and might clearly indicate to the islander his whereabouts, though shrouding mists were mocking him.

During more than thirty summers she presided with matchless grace over her Appledore cottage, where distinguished men and women engaged with her in brilliant discourse, and

that his young wife did not thrive elsewhere, he passed much time with her, in the summers of their early married life, on the islands; and here came to them in the summer of 1852, their eldest child, Karl, the first infant born at the Shoals since the Revolution.

Her recently published letters add fresh testimony to Mrs. Thaxter's love for these bare, bleak rocks, which be-

A CORNER OF MRS. THAXTER'S PARLOR.

MRS. THAXTER AT HER PAINTING TABLE.

From " Letters of Celia Thaxter."

Published by Messrs. Houghton, Mifflin & Co.

day spent amid music and flowers. Her son declared that his grandmother had come and called her. She had dreaded lingering illness, and it was sweet to those who loved her that she was spared it. She had often said that if Karl, who was her inseparable companion and needed her more than her other children, could go with her, she would be glad to die.

Cedric and Oscar Laighton are the present genial hosts of the Appledore hotel, owners too of the other great hotel, the Oceanic, on Star Island. If you find them in talkative mood, you can learn much from them regarding the traditions of the island. You will discover how thoroughly they are in sympathy with their life-long environments, and how tenderly they cherish their sister's memory. You will turn with fresh interest from a talk with them to Mrs. Thaxter's books. You will read with

whose windows looked out over her sunlit, glowing garden on the breezy, sparkling sea. She even passed some winters here, especially when her mother's health failed after the father's death.

Thomas Laighton died in May, 1865, and was buried on the island. It is said that his lifeless form was seated on a chair carved from stone, in his rocky tomb, with the face turned toward the sea. His wife went to her rest in November, 1877, and was laid by his side. Near them now reposes Celia Thaxter. The sun set on her life, she said, when her mother left her. She passed away in the night of August 26, 1894, after a

VIEW FROM MRS. THAXTER'S GARDEN GATE.

new interest Lowell's "Pictures of Appledore," what Hawthorne has written of the Shoals, the writings of Samuel Adams Drake, Williamson's "Maine," Young's "Chronicles," and the sundry reports in the various historical collections. You will come to think there can exist no greater point of romantic interest in the whole country than the Isles of Shoals.

It being impossible to cruise along the coast without sighting these islands, there is no doubt they were well-known objects to the mariners from many lands who frequented our waters, in oddly rigged vessels, throughout the sixteenth century. In view of the obvious advantages they present for fishing, it is not unlikely that they were the annual resort of adventurous fishermen scores of years before the Pilgrim Fathers landed at Plymouth. The various expeditions from England that attempted colonization or sought adventure, during the first decade of the seventeenth century, on the Maine and New Hampshire coast, then known as Virginia, by virtue of Queen Elizabeth's grant to Sir Walter Raleigh of the territory between Florida and Nova Scotia, must inevitably have been familiar with them.

Martin Pring, who, in 1603, searched the banks of the Piscataqua for sassafras, from which our forefathers hoped to distil the elixir of life, sighted a number of small islands as he approached the coast at a latitude of forty-three degrees, and anchored under the shelter of the largest. His account of the voyage gives no name

THE LAIGHTON BURIAL LOT ON APPLEDORE.
Mrs. Thaxter's grave at the left.

to the islands, but as none others answer his description they are supposed to be the Shoals.

The next recorded mention, and a more clearly defined one, was by Samuel Champlain, in 1605. He sailed, as geographer and chronicler, with Sieur de Monts, that noble gentleman of Henry of Navarre's household, who was empowered to colonize Acadie from the fortieth to the forty-sixth degree. Owing to the New World discoveries, in 1524, of the Florentine navigator, Giovanni Verrazano, under the patronage of Francis I., the French, it will be remembered, had numerous claims in what they were pleased to call New France. The appearance of the English on the scene was followed by frequent struggles for supremacy. Toward sunset, on a July afternoon, De Monts and part of his company, in a fifteen ton pinnace, seeking a milder and more suitable place of habitation than St. Croix, where they had wintered, put out to sea near the Piscataqua harbor to make observations. "On the East, about two leagues distant," writes Champlain, "we saw three or four rather prominent islands." There can be no question what group this was.

Panounias, a young Indian from Acadie, was the interpreter and guide who pointed out the landmarks, and with him on the vessel's prow stood his newly-wedded squaw, "from whom he did not wish to part." On stolen visits to her, whose tribe, the Armouchiquois, was hostile to his own, he had learned all the secrets of the coast. The dusky bride proved "a very halcyon of the seas," and the bark was wafted by soft breezes over smiling seas, while the natives, with every

GLIMPSES OF APPLEDORE.

token of amity, gamboled along the shore, inspired by the reed flageolets of their musicians.

The romance of the Indian bridal pair who assisted in pointing out the islands had a tragic denouement. After two years of wedded bliss, Panounias was treacherously slain by his squaw's jealous kindred. The following summer the warriors of his tribe were summoned to the war-path, and much blood was shed before vengeance was satiated. L'Escarbot, a Frenchman, who witnessed the departure of the avenging expedition, composed a poem on its cause and achievements, the first epic known to have been written in America.

It is a curious and most interesting fact that one of the results of the mighty storm which inspired Shakespeare's "Tempest" was a visit to the Shoals destined to influence the future history of New England. This was the storm that, in 1609, wrecked Sir George Somers on the Bermuda Islands, where he passed the winter, and built the good cedar ship *Patience*, which carried him to his original des-

THE BATHING POND AT APPLEDORE.

tination, Jamestown, the following spring. Finding the colony there perishing for provisions, he undertook to seek supplies in the Bermudas. With him sailed Sir Samuel Argal, on the *Discovery.* Once more there arose "a most vehement storm which was a taile of the West India Horacano"; and for weeks the frail barks were at the mercy of wind and waves. The *Patience* finally found its way to the enchanted spot where it came into being; but Sir Samuel passed the summer cruising up and down the Maine coast. The story of his wanderings in Purchas's "Pilgrims" shows that he frequently harbored at the Shoals.

When Sir George reached England, he published a pamphlet, entitled "A Discovery of the · Bermudas, otherwise called the Isles of Divils." As the "Tempest" is dated by critics not earlier than 1611, it is likely that Shakespeare's fancy was fired by the narration, even though his "still-vexed Bermoothes" may be located, as

Lowell suggests, rather in the soul of man than in the actual Bermudas.

Sir Samuel Argal renewed his acquaintance with the New England coast in 1613, and his exploits at the Saint Saveur settlement on Mount Desert and at Acadie practically ended the power of the French encroachments on English territory. It is no unreasonable supposition that Shakespeare, with his prophetic spirit, grasped the perils to which English interests were exposed in northern waters, and believed the wild waves were put in a roar for some wise purpose. There is a suggestion to this effect in the reply of Prospero when Miranda, troubled at the workings of his magic wand, asks his reasons for raising the sea-storm.

"Know thus far forth—
By accident, most strange, bountiful Fortune,
Now, my dear lady, hath mine enemies
Brought to this shore; and by my prescience
I find my zenith doth depend upon
A most auspicious star; whose influence
If I now court not, but omit, my fortunes
Will ever after droop."

The results of royal letters patent made the England of Shakespeare's time quite familiar with the New novel visitors aroused and the glowing accounts afloat of their native land, whose waters were fairly alive with cod-fish,—the Poor John of fishermen,—colonization received a new impulse. Shakespeare evidently considered the interest manifested in the painted, tattooed children of the wilds an exaggerated one. His Trinculo, the jester, on espying the deformed Caliban, exclaims:

"What have we here? a man or a fish? dead or alive? A fish; * * * a kind of, not the newest Poor John. * * * Were I in England now (as once I was), and had but this fish painted, not a holiday fool there but would give a piece of silver; there would this monster make a man; any

CASWELL'S POINT.

World. Sir Martin Frobisher had brought home from an exploring voyage, as early as 1577, a red man and his squaw, whose likenesses are still preserved in the Canterbury cathedral library. In 1605, Captain George Weymouth kidnapped, on the Maine coast, five natives, who, reluctantly though they followed him, created a most favorable impression in London. They were considered fine specimens of primitive manhood, handsome—albeit a trifle disfigured with paint and tattooing,—brave, social, courteous, and strong in their attachments. Something of European customs and many French words they had learned from French Catholic missionaries, by whom they had been greatly influenced.

Owing to the enthusiasm these strange beast there makes a man; when they will not give a doit to relieve a lame beggar, they will lay out ten to see a dead Indian."

Tradition has it that, one of the Indians exhibited in London having died, a gaping multitude was admitted, by entrance fee, to the place where he lay prepared for burial. The word *lame* has been pronounced a misprint, and the comparison Trinculo offered supposed to be between a live beggar and a dead Indian.

An important rôle was played in the affairs of our islands by Captain John Smith, who became Admiral of New England as well as Governor of Virginia. On a whaling and trading voyage, in 1614, his roving eye lighted on a "heape of rocks," near Cape Cod, which he pronounced "the remarkablest Isles for land-marks, none neare them, against Acco-minticus." Landing on them, he declared himself their lord and proprietor and gave them his own name. On his return to England, he wrote, "with his own hand," the story of his exploits, illustrating it with a chart, and with royal permission called the coast he

MISS UNDERHILL'S CHAIR, STAR ISLAND.

had visited New England, being the first to designate it thus. Later, when numerous patentees were scheming to divide the territory, John Smith chose the wild, picturesque rocks by which he hoped to perpetuate his name. "No lot for me," he protests, "but Smith Isles, which are a many of barren rocks, the most overgrowne with such shrubs and sharp whins you can hardly pass them, without either grass or wood, but three or four short, shrubby old cedars." These cedars, presumably a growth of Cedar Island, attracted the attention of John Winthrop, when he sailed past the Shoals, and misled him to describe them as "woody." Shoalers and Shoal enthusiasts devoutly

believe the ruinous cairn on the summit of Appledore, toward the southern part of the island, to be the work of John Smith. Being a structure that must have required much labor, it is certainly more likely to have been built in honor of what was deemed an interesting discovery than as a mere landmark by any chance sailor. Gallant Admiral John gave more than one indication of wishing to leave his impress upon the rocks. As a recognition of his prowess in taking the heads of three boastful Turks, the German emperor under whose banner he had fought in the Moslem War had given him for his coat of arms, three Turks' heads in a shield. Fortune having finally turned against the Christians, the little giant escaped captivity through the favor of the charming Princess Tragabigzanda, an Oriental Pocahontas, whose unselfish devotion he never forgot. He dubbed the headland facing the islands—our Cape Ann—Cape Tragabigzanda, and the three rocky islets at its point, the

HAULING UP THE BOATS FOR THE WINTER.

STAR ISLAND AND THE "OCEANIC" FROM APPLEDORE.

"Three Turks' Heads." These titles soon fell into disuse, and one little cove alone, at the southwest angle of Appledore, bears the name of Smith. In 1864, on one of the highest eminences of Star, a shaft of marble, surmounting a rough stone pedestal, was erected to the memory of this hero of many adventures. The ravages of Time have sent tumbling down, one by one, the three Turks' heads once crowning the monument, and rendering it difficult to decipher the lengthy eulogium occupying its three sides.

Much interest was manifested in the Isles by the fathers and founders of New Hampshire and Maine, John Mason and Sir Ferdinando Gorges, who first saw them five years later than Smith. They became the owners of the group, annexing the southern half to New Hampshire and the northern half to Maine.

A member of the Grand Council which they organized for the purpose of "planting and ruling New England," Captain Christopher Levett, "His Majesty's Woodward in Somersetshire," crossed the ocean on a Shoals bound vessel, in 1623, and in his "Voyage" presented the most complete description of this excellent fish-

THE LANDING AT STAR ISLAND.

ing-place that had then appeared in English. He found the rocky shores a lively scene of activity and inconveniently crowded with fishing stages. These were floating platforms, roofed by open sheds, and used for splitting and salting fish. They were a valuable part of the island property, their erection on the steep rocks being difficult and expensive.

During the three years' reign of the Laconia Company, an outgrowth of the Grand Council, and the period of daring freedom that followed, the business and wealth of the "heape of rocks materially increased. The month of March, 1634, saw seventeen fishing vessels arrive at their harbor, and their significance as a fishing station became widely recognized. Laborers of all sorts appeared, a magazine was established, which held close intercourse with the emporium on the mainland, dwellings were erected of as comfortable size and as amply furnished as any in New England, and the titles to the wild rocks obtained substantial value. By the middle of the seventeenth century the resident population numbered six hundred souls. There was a court-house and an ordinary, or tavern, on Smutty Nose, a meeting-house and bowling alley as well on Hog, or Appledore, besides "a seminary of such repute that even gentlemen from some of the principal sea-coast towns sent their sons here for literary instruction." Times have changed indeed from that day to this, when the Isles of Shoals are simply a summer resort, with their cottages and

two great hotels,—the only institutions of "repute" known to the happy people upon the little steamer which runs back and forth between Portsmouth and the Shoals being the "Appledore" and the "Oceanic."

Early settlers located on the northern half of the group, Hog attracting the largest number, partly because of its good spring water. Straggling up the rocks on its southerly slope, a thriving village came into being. The spot is even now eloquent with reminders of a vanished race. In some places ancient graves undermine the

THE OLD CHURCH ON STAR ISLAND.

ground, and ruined cellars, tenderly covered with luxuriant growth, are distinctly outlined. Voyagers, refugees, adventurers and fishermen sought the Shoals, and it became a centre for foreign news. Gorges wrote Governor Winthrop from Gorgeanna (now York): "I cannot send you news from England, because the contrariety of winds hath hindered it from coming from the Isles of Shoals." Tidings of the outbreak of the English rebellion and news of the execution of King Charles, in 1649, reached New England through a Shoals vessel. Ships sailing from these busy islets bore prisoners of state to England. An early victim of Puritan intolerance, transported from their harbor in 1628, was Thomas Morton of Merry Mount, one of whose most grievous offences was dancing and singing with his merry men around the Maypole. He enjoyed the full sympathy of the Shoalers, who themselves indulged in this hearty old English custom. They were arrayed with the New Hampshire planters on the side of the English Established Church, whose genial patronage of gaiety and merriment commended itself to their free spirits.

Intense antipathy existed between Massachusetts Bay and the eastern improvident folk. Their virtues lay, as has been said, in the rugged domain of daring, fortitude, frank honesty and generosity of heart, robust traits which developed into extravagant forms, yet ever retained a spicy flavor. What religious aspirations they had were satisfied by the liturgy and ordinances of the Church of England.

Some curious laws were made for this people in the early day. One of those enacted prior to 1635, prohibited women from inhabiting the Shoals. On the establishment of permanent residences, married men brought with them their wives, in de-

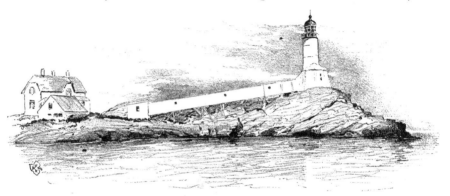

WHITE ISLAND LIGHT.

settlements. The Puritans regarded the Episcopal conformists at the Shoals and on the mainland as utterly irreligious and desperately wicked. The eastern settlers, on their part, deemed the Puritans "not worthy to live on God's earth." The austerity, bigotry and uncharitableness of many of the long faced people farther south who trampled on so much that made life bright and beautiful, was especially obnoxious to the Shoalers.

What manner of men were these rude toilers by the sea? An oft-repeated tradition has characterized them as God-fearing, industrious, temperate and decent in their religious observances. This is scarcely consistent with their record, which is rather that of a brave, yet reckless and fiance of the law. An attempt was made to revive it, in 1647, and the court of Maine was petitioned to order one John Reynolds to remove his great stock of goats and hogs, which "doth spoile the spring of water," and his wife, whose presence was contrary to an Act of Court. It is pleasant to note that, although the removal of the goats and swine was promptly ordered, the court decided as to the wife that "if no further complaint come up against her, she may as yet enjoy the company of her husband." The ungallant petition was doubtless a retaliation for certain taunts and flings of the good wife and others of her sex on the island, who delighted in giving vent,—with singular volubility of tongue, we are told,—to the free spirit rife in the place. They were prone to use biting language to aid their husbands in resisting obnoxious laws. We read of one Joane Forde, convicted for calling the constable a rogue, one Grace Tucker, presented for railing speeches, and other similar offenders. Various humiliating punishments were submitted to by the unruly women; but they rose in a body when an attempt was made to introduce among them the *cucking stool.* This was a chair suspended by a crane over water, in which scolds and termagants might have their irritability moderated. Its establishment on the breezy rocks was successfully resisted, and the liberty of speech so highly prized by the goodies and gammers of the Shoals was never afterward assailed.

When the islands were brought under nominal obedience to the Bay, the General Court was petitioned to erect them into a separate township. The modest request, to which every signer wrote his name in a good fair hand, was long denied, presumably because the residents were inimical to Puritan ideals. Not until 1661 was the group allowed to be a township, called Appledore, after the ancient hamlet of that name in North Devonshire.

On the erection of New Hampshire into a Royal Province, the original division of the islands was restored. The township was dissolved, and the name Appledore left to Hog Island. At this period, 1679, there was a complete exodus to Star Island, where prosperity reigned for nearly a century. It was created into the township of Gosport or Gosper, whose activity and wealth are shown by its carefully kept town records.

During the war with the French and Indians, a small fort had been erected on an eminence near the western point of Star. Its ruins alone remain. The Revolution saw it dismantled, its four nine-pounders shipped to Newburyport, and the people for whose defence it was meant commanded by government to quit the Islands for affording "sustenance and recruits to the enemy." When the war was over, the population began to recover, but through a new race. Few former residents returned to the dilapidated dwellings. The Gosport records of 1800 show 112 inhabitants mostly in a "state of great poverty and wretchedness."

The Appledore Church enjoyed occasional ministrations from the Episcopal clergy, even after Massachusetts authority made it possible to arraign Rev. Richard Gibson for marrying and baptizing at the Shoals according to the discipline of the Church of England. In 1652, a long line of Congregational divines began with the Rev. John Brock, of whom Cotton Mather said: "He dwelt as near Heaven as any man on Earth." When this most excellent man, after twelve years of faithful service, had gone to his rest, the ancient structure that had weathered the storms of half a century was permitted to fall to decay, and in 1685 the northern islands were presented at court for "not maintaining a sufficient meeting-house for the worship of God."

The denizens of Star were not slow in erecting a substantial church, twenty-eight by forty-eight feet, of timber from the wreck of a Spanish ship. It was situated on the loftiest height of the island, that it might serve as a landmark to mariners. The warning light gleamed from its belfry on dark, tempestuous nights, while its friendly bell served as a guide amid the perils of the fog.

"About the year 1790," say the Gosport records, "some people of the baser sort, not having the fear of God before their eyes, pulled down and burnt the meeting-house." That the inhabitants might not "burn it for fuel," the new place of worship constructed on its site was of rough native granite. It stands, a picturesque object, to the present day. An entry of 1859 reads: "At a considerable expense, the inhabitants of these Isles have put up a *beautiful vane* on our

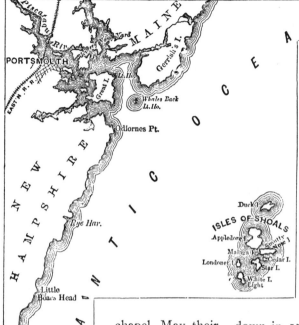

disposition, of g r e a t
piety and integrity, giv-
en to hospitality, dili-
gent and faithful in his
pastoral office, w e l l
learned in History and
Geography, as well as
General Science and a
careful Physician both
to the bodies and the
souls of his People."

East of the church
stands the parsonage, a
two-story building, re-
duced apparently to a
temporary resort f o r
fishermen. A tablet on
its side states that it was
built in 1732 by Rev.
J o h n Tucke, taken
down in 1780 by his son-in-law, and
carried to York, Me., and rebuilt in
1802 for Rev. Josiah Stephens.

Zealous missionaries and their wives
continued to live and labor in the
stony vineyard for half a century, and
certain brave, self-sacrificing women
appeared from time to time as teachers
of the children. It proved no easy
task to make an impression on a people who from all accounts must have
fallen into some pretty bad ways.
Gosport became little more than a
name. Graves, monuments and ruins
alone recalled past glory. The life
of Star now centres in its hotel and
summer visitors.

One of the interesting sights shown
to strangers on this island is a platform called Miss Underhill's Chair,
in a high cliff on the eastern shore,
about whose base the billows dash
with resistless power. Here Miss
Nancy Underhill, a Gosport teacher
of fifty years ago, was wont to repair
for reading and contemplation. A
tidal wave rising fifty feet swept
her from the rock and bore her
to the mainland, where her lifeless
form was found, the shawl pinned

chapel. May their
own hearts yield
to the breathings
o f t h e Divine
Spirit, as t h a t
vane does to the
w i n d." T h e
church was used
as a school-house
or for town meet-
ings during the
week, and when
not otherwise employed was utilized
for storing fish.

The old burial ground adds little to
the town annals, the head-stones being mostly without trace of lettering.
Two horizontal slabs alone possess interest. One of these is to the memory
of Rev. Josiah Stephens, "a faithful
Instructor of Youth and pious Minister of Jesus Christ," who died in 1804,
and "Mrs. Susannah Stephens, his
beloved wife." The other was erected
about the same time, in memory of Rev. John Tucke, who died in
1773, aged 72 years, after a valuable
ministry of two score years. The inscription pronounces him "affable and
polite in his manner, amiable in his

across the breast, the bonnet on the head.

Not far from the fatal spot is a deep cavern, formed by the lodgment of rock over one of the gulches common to the place, and known as Betty Moody's Hole. Betty was a woman of the island at the time of King Philip's War, who concealed herself here with her two children when the Indians appeared and bore away many female captives. The little ones began to wail, it is said, and the mother, in a frenzy of terror, strangled them and then drowned herself. As a rule the Shoals were free from savage depredations.

Another place of interest on Star Island is Caswell's Point, which took its name from Joe Caswell, an eccentric fisherman, who was town clerk when Hawthorne visited Gosport. It is reached by following the harbor side from the old fort.

William Pepperell, father of William Pepperell, the conqueror of Louisburg, carried on a large fishery for twenty years at Gosport. John Cutt, first royal president of the province of New Hampshire, long did business in that ancient town.

A most attractive figure among early Shoals settlers was Mistress Rebecca Sherburne. She was the first white child brought to New Hampshire, where her father, Ambrose Gibbins, was an official of the Laconia Company, and is often mentioned in the records as "little Becke." As a bride of seventeen, she went in 1647, with her husband, Henry Sherburne, to his home on Appledore, and seems to have led a prosperous and happy life. Some of her descendants to-day occupy the oldest brick house in Portsmouth.

The Shoals are known to have been frequented by pirates, and have their traditions of hidden treasures in three-legged black pots and other weird receptacles. Much fruitless search has been made for these valuables. Mr. Samuel Haley, who owned Smutty Nose from Revolutionary times until

his death, in 1811, is reported to have found four bars of silver beneath a stone, and to have used them in defraying the expense of the safe harbor he made "for seamen in distress of weather." This man, by whose name his island is now chiefly known, was quite a person, possessing industry, ingenuity and honesty. He erected salt-works, which manufactured excellent salt for curing fish, set up wind-mills to grind the corn and wheat he managed to raise on his few arable acres, started a bake-house, a brewery, a distillery, and a blacksmith's shop, and planted an orchard. His prostrate tombstone, setting forth his many virtues, and his homestead, shorn of sundry adornments, recall his life and achievements.

The Islands are rich in ghost stories. A favorite apparition is Old Babb, supposed to haunt a certain shingly beach of Appledore, and to be the shade of a wealthy citizen of the island's prosperous days, who was so desperately wicked in life that the grave has no rest for him. The spectre wears a coarse striped butcher's frock with a leather belt, and has a countenance dreadful to behold. He carries a ghostly knife, sharp and glittering, which he delights to brandish in the face of terrified humanity.

White Island boasts the shade of a pirate's lady, who was left by her lord in charge of a treasure from which he was compelled to flee. She was made to swear a fearful oath that she would guard from mortal ken the spot where it lay hidden until his return, were it not until the last trump should sound. She is represented as a lady of tall, shapely form, wrapped in a dark sea-cloak, with head and neck uncovered save by a profusion of golden hair, and with an exquisitely-rounded face as white and still as marble. She has been seen on the rocks gazing fixedly out on the ocean, in an attitude of intense expectancy, her young face wearing the look of infinite age. The wailing sound through the gorges of Appledore before a tempest is supposed to be her Banshee-like lament.

Among other objects that haunt the islands in winter are the snowy white owls. When disturbed, they utter a shrill cry like that of a human being in despair; but it is in silence that they are the most ghostly. With outstretched wings, during flight, they present an imposing appearance. The artist who adorned Trinity Church, New York, with sculpture, during the fifties, used the wings of a Shoals white owl as a model for his cherubim wings.

Half the wonders of the Enchanted Isles of our story must remain untold. Make the acquaintance of the "heape of bare and splintery crags," and you will exclaim with Lowell that:

"Till now you dreamed not what could be done
With a bit of rock and a ray of sun."

25

Decadence of the New England Deep-sea Fisheries

DECADENCE OF THE NEW ENGLAND DEEP-SEA FISHERIES.

BY JOSEPH WILLIAM COLLINS.

TO one familiar with the New England coast for the past forty years or so, nothing is more painfully apparent than the change that has occurred in its deep-sea fisheries. Four or five decades ago nearly every cove or harbor on mainland or isle from Connecticut to eastern Maine was a site for curing fish, or for "fitting out" vessels for the mackerel fishery, or for voyages to the ocean banks in pursuit of cod or halibut.

Harbor rivalled harbor in fleets of sturdy, trim-built, and gayly painted fishing-vessels, and the wealth and consequence of many coast towns were dependent on their piscatorial navies. While modern "sharp-shooters," with their low hulls, long raking masts, and gilded filigree-work, rather ostentatiously elbowed the older types out of the way on Long Island Sound and in the larger Massachusetts ports, many a veteran sea-toiler was still content to sail his round-bowed "jigger" or pinky, and even the "Chebacco-boat" was occasionally in evidence in some of the out-of-the-way coves "down East." Indeed, though these coves could not compete with the larger ports, many of them claimed distinction for what had been accomplished in their restricted limits. Through thrift and adventurous enterprise not a few of them had attained marked success. In unsuspected nooks, lying cozily quiet under a declining summer sun, that threw shadows of wooded heights and rocky points upon the placid water, one came upon little piers, storehouses, and flake-yards, redolent of the odors that characterize the industry to which they were devoted, and it scarcely required further evidence to convey the information that here fares of fish were received, and cured by careful and experienced hands. If the vessels were not there, one instinctively knew that they were away at sea collecting finny treasures, and erelong the eyes of watching women—mothers, wives, sweethearts, and daughters—would be gladdened by returning sails, that swept gracefully into the home port and came to rest at the pier, while the hardy fishers disappeared through many devious paths—winding among bowlders and beneath balsam-scented firs and pines—toward their cottage homes in the near vicinity.

The tragedies of the sea, that occasionally brought mourning and distress to those whose loved ones had gone forth to exact tribute from old ocean's living wealth, were the dark shades of the picture. Nevertheless, these threw into

393

stronger light the general happiness, as well as the value of an industry that utilized nearly every vantage-point, maintained a hardy coast population, built and navigated fleets of ocean-going vessels, boldly dared storm and calm, and contributed largely to the food-supply of the nation.

From early spring until the flying snowflakes of latest autumn surely indicated the departure of migratory species of fishes, the white wings of swift smacks were seen on every fishing-ground from Montauk to distant Labrador — on the dread George's, the great bank of Newfoundland, in the Gulf of St. Lawrence, usually called "The Bay," and off the shores of New England from Grand Manan to Cape Cod. Fleets followed the migrations of the mackerel with unwearied ardor; not infrequently the vessels gathered in immense numbers, covering the sea for miles, as they lay close together, drifting slowly to leeward while engaged in fishing. It was something to be long remembered to see a fleet varying from three hundred to eight hundred sail of schooners thus assembled, the majority of them nearly motionless, but a considerable number always on the move, driving along under full speed, seeking more favorable positions.

But it was vastly more exciting to see them when a rising storm compelled all to seek shelter in harbor. Think of a regatta in an on-coming gale, with hundreds of vessels racing for a given point! What rivalry! What seamanship was displayed! How sails were reefed and set in haste! How lee rails were buried, and lines of creamy foam streamed astern! And then came the critical moment, when scudding schooners crowded so closely in the narrow entrance to the haven that the most skilful management could not always avert collision. Broken spars, torn canvas, and crushed bulwarks were not infrequent mishaps on such occasions. Words can scarcely convey an adequate idea of such an experience. It was often like a battle, so great was the excitement in some sections of the fleet; but even the participants thought little of their hairbreadth escapes from danger when once they were safely anchored in port, for greater peril to those outside the harbor's friendly shelter was presaged in the fierce blasts of the rising tempest.

It is impossible to picture the awful-

ness of the situation when such a fleet is caught in a sudden gale at night on a long lee shore where harbors are inaccessible—when the rush of the storm-demon intensifies the blackness, filling the air with mist and driving sea-spume; when death stares each fisher in the face, and nothing can be done except to courageously meet the conditions and make a desperate attempt to work to windward, away from the dangerous breakers and foaming reefs that stretch along the lee beam for miles and miles—a nearly hopeless task, as too often has been proved. Neither pen nor tongue can tell the horrors of such an experience, when the long struggle for life is perhaps successfully maintained for many weary, sleepless hours, and then, even while hope is in the ascendant, the rending of canvas, the snapping of a bolt, or the breaking of an overstrained spar makes further effort unavailing, and the

DOWN-EAST FISHING-SCHOONER, OR PINKY.

fishermen are cast helpless on the merciless coast, with all the dread uncertainties which it involves.

Unfortunately truth is stranger and more horrible than fiction. To fully appreciate this, one has but to recall the dreadful disaster that attended the "Yankee Gale" of 1851, when the northern shores of Prince Edward Island were strewn with broken wrecks and drowned or maimed fishermen.

Nevertheless, while such dread tragedies came occasionally, almost with paralyzing power, and though peril and loss of life have ever attended the prosecution of the winter fishery, for many years no other industry had so great an attraction for the young men of the New England coast as the fisheries.

Catching mackerel was the poetry of fishing. Ordinarily there was only danger enough to give zest to its prosecution, while the rivalry between vessels, and even between different individuals of a crew, had all the elements of sport, not to speak of the daily contests between competitors in speed among the clippers, with all the attendant manœuvres for advantage which prove so enchantingly attractive to the yachtsman.

Each cove had its clipper that could outstrip others, at least in the opinion of its local champions, and each of the larger ports usually had several claimants to the honor of being the swiftest of the fleet. The fame of the more noted of these spread from end to end of the coast. The names of swift fishing-schooners became household words among the seafarers, and at many a fireside and grocery, from Eastport to New London, discussions of their respective merits divided attention with tales of big catches of fish.

Evidently there was a pride in the vessels and a reliance upon the industry, and though the returns sometimes failed to meet expectation—for the sea-harvest is an uncertain one at best—reasonable prosperity prevailed, and there were happy and contented homes along the shores of the Northeastern States, where in many cases fishermen spent their winters with their families, and some even deferred going to sea in spring until after "the planting was in." Then these farmer-fishermen devoted the remainder of the season to the sea, leaving the "gardening at home" to be attended to by the "women folks," or by boys too young to pull an oar or haul a line, unless perchance the sea-toiler had the opportunity between trips to hoe the potato-patch.

If Dame Fortune was chary of her smiles during the summer months, if a "Jonah" in the crew (always an unknown but suspected pariah) threw the shadow of his dread presence over the vessel, and "luck" deserted her in consequence, then the fisherman sought employment elsewhere in winter. Perhaps he shipped on a coaster or West-Indiaman, or went to Gloucester to brave the dangers of winter trips to the George's Bank for cod; or possibly he formed one of the crew of a schooner that, having followed the mackerel during its season, was now engaged in transporting oysters from the Chesapeake Bay region to ports north of Cape Cod. Many avenues were open for employment, and actual want seldom confronted the thrifty and energetic fisher, even though he might meet with temporary ill fortune.

Such was the condition of the New England deep-sea fisheries at the middle of the present century, and immediately thereafter, when they had reached their highest degree of development, as the result of more than two centuries of effort, during which they had been subject to many perils and vicissitudes.

Naturally it might have been expected that they would continue to increase with the general growth of the country. But the opposite is true, and instead of progress, signs of decadence are too evident. With the exception of a few of the larger ports, where the industry of deep-sea fishing has gradually become centralized, industrial paralysis is nearly everywhere apparent, for it has fallen like a blight upon the small fishing-towns along the coast.

In coves from which formerly sailed brave fleets of schooners on their cruises to the distant banks or mackerel-grounds, little or nothing now remains to tell of their one-time consequence. Tumble-down store-houses that may still shelter a few lobster-pots; decaying piers, alongside of which perhaps one sees the superannuated hulk of a fish-freighter leaning against this last support, while incoming and outgoing tides run riotously through its gaping seams; or an old-time clipper, once the proud queen of the fleet, lazily reclining on the mud at the head of the cove, her bare leaning masts silhouetted against the sky — are some of the object-lessons that tell of departed glories and ruined industries. They are like the crumbling ruins of antiquity, which, in some measure, tell the history of the decadence of industries that prospered in other years.

It is true that occasionally one still meets with a remnant of former activity. Fishy odors sometimes float on the mid-

A QUIET COVE WHERE OYSTER-MEN ARE FOUND.

summer air, as schooners discharge their fares of cod in quiet nooks, where the wharves of other years still suffice, and the renovated flake - yard is filled with wide-spreading, salt-encrusted fish, which now lie drying in the sun. And we know that erelong these products from distant banks will appear in many a far-away grocery as "boneless cod."

More commonly no one remains except lobster-men and perhaps a few pound-net fishermen, though sheltered behind some point and quite hidden from view one may come upon a "pogy-factory," where fish, supplied by steamers, are converted into oil and fertilizer, the wealth of the sea thus being drawn upon to enrich the soil.

But the rule is that these fishing-hamlets have been invaded by "rusticators," who seek rest and recreation in summer along the coast, where their pretty cottages and pretentious hotels confront the less imposing homes of the fishermen, and constantly encroach upon territory once devoted to other purposes.

Fishermen often find profitable employment in catering to the wants of these summer visitants. And it is among the interesting phases of the change which has come to see bronzed skippers, who have dared every peril, now engaged in boat-building, or in "running" a cat-boat for the accommodation of pleasure-seekers. He whose word was once law on the quarter-deck, who has rounded Cape Horn, and hunted whales in the icy North or among the palm-covered isles of the tropics, is now obsequiously solicitous for patronage. And the same is true of the rugged cod-fisher or other brine-hardened sons of the ocean, who in earlier days sought fortune in many seas, and led a life of self-reliance and independence.

What has wrought this change? Why has the deep-sea fishery industry fallen into such decay all along the New England coast, until it is no longer vigorously pursued except at a few ports? Why have erstwhile clippers been allowed to decay, or disappear sometimes, while yet sea-

AN OLD-TIME CLIPPER.

historical facts bearing on the development of the deep-sea fisheries.

Fishing was the earliest industry of New England. Years before the advent of the Pilgrims, ships came to its shores, and temporary settlements were effected in its sheltered coves and harbors, for no other purpose than to engage in the fisheries. The fame of its marine resources had reached Europe, and glowing accounts were spread abroad of the wealth to be gained from the waters that washed its coasts. The exiled Pilgrims, then residing in Holland, saw in this industry commercial possibilities that might make emigration to the New World a prosperous undertaking. History indicates that when the delegation from Leyden appeared before King James to solicit a charter, this thought was uppermost in the minds of the Pilgrim leaders. For when the King asked, "What profit may arise?" they laconically replied, "Fishing." In a few years after they settled in Massachusetts they despatched ships to England loaded with fish. Thus it is evident that the Pilgrim was disposed to improve the opportunities open to him.

worthy, being left to lie deserted beside wharves? Why have their places been unfilled by other craft? And why is it that this industry, which is such a great nursery of American seamen—a training-school of inestimable importance to a nation that aspires to commercial or naval greatness—has been left to such a fate?

These and many other similar questions may appropriately be asked. And it will be found far easier to make inquiries than to give correct and satisfactory answers. Most writers find in a temporary scarcity of certain species of fish the sole cause of all changes, and much that is misleading concerning fish and fishing has been published. But it is evident to the well-informed that the trouble lies deeper, and that there must be other reasons for a decline that is permanent, and which has been most noticeable in recent years, despite the most determined efforts to combat it. It is the purpose of the writer to invite attention to some of these causes of decadence, for he believes there are many. But in order to present the subject more clearly, brief reference will be made to certain

Certain it is that of all sections of the colonies which subsequently became the United States, New England was early noted for its prominence in sea fishery. Not only did it supply a large percentage of the fish food eaten in America, but cargoes of fish, chiefly dried cod, were sent to southern Europe. Its fleets grew apace. Before the Revolutionary war Massachusetts had more than five hundred fishing-vessels, and Marblehead alone had one hundred and fifty sea-going schooners engaged in fishing. As early as 1701 Gloucester had a fleet of seventy vessels employed in the cod-fishery on the Grand Bank. In winter some of the largest schooners carried the products of their summer's fishing to Bilbao, Spain, and returned laden with European goods, that found a ready sale in the colonies. Thus a spirit of enterprise and adventure was stimulated, and many fishermen became expert traders, as well as skilful navigators.

In the mean time the schooner rig had been invented at Gloucester, Massachusetts, by a builder of fishing-vessels. History records that "Captain Robinson built and rigged a *ketch*, as they were then called, masted and rigged it in a peculiar manner; when launched the peculiar motion she made as she glided into the water from the stocks caused one of the bystanders to exclaim, 'Oh, how she scoons!' Robinson instantly dashed a bottle of rum against her bow and exclaimed, 'A scooner let her be!' And thus the schooner originated." This event happened in 1713, and three years later mention is made of the employment of a "scooner" in the fisheries off Cape Sable, Nova Scotia.

The invention of the schooner was an important event to the New England fisheries, for its rig has been found, after nearly two centuries of trial, well adapted to fishing-vessels employed in the western Atlantic. It has been materially improved, however, since its adoption, and the lofty, yachtlike fishing-clipper of to-day bears little resemblance to its ancient prototype, even though the rig remains the same in principle.

The American sea fisheries suffered much in the four decades from 1775 to 1815, during which time occurred the war of the Revolution, the embargo act, and the second war with Great Britain. This was a period noted for wars and rumors of wars. The larger fishing-vessels, which had formerly sailed to distant banks, were forced to lie idle, and the brave men who had composed their crews were chiefly employed in the army or navy while the struggles were in progress for the establishment of liberty and the maintenance of the principle of "free trade and sailors' rights" on the sea. Impoverished by the long contest for independence, the fishermen were generally unable, after the peace of 1783, to provide themselves with large vessels; therefore they built smaller craft, on which they cruised to comparatively near-by grounds along the New England coast.

The impoverished condition of the fishermen at that time may be judged from the following reference to them in a speech made by Fisher Ames, a Representative in Congress from Massachusetts:

"When gentlemen contemplate the fishery, they admit its importance, and the necessity we are under of encouraging and protecting it. . . . In short, unless some extraordinary measures are taken to support our fisheries, I do not see what is to prevent their inevitable ruin. If, instead of protection, we extend to them oppression, I shudder for the consequences. It is supposed that the fishermen must be poor if they are not able to bear the tax proposed. I contend they are very poor: they are in a sinking state; they carry on the business in despair. But gentlemen will ask us, 'Why, then, do they not quit the profession?' I answer, in the words that are often used in the eastern country respecting the inhabitants of Cape Cod—they are too poor to live there, and are too poor to remove."

Immediately after the Revolutionary war the adoption of the "Chebacco boat" became quite general, especially along the north shore of Massachusetts. These diminutive craft, at first ranging from about five to ten tons, derived their specific name from Chebacco, now a part of the town of Essex, Massachusetts, where they originated. Cat-rigged, with two masts, they were "handy" boats, and became so popular that they could be met with on almost all of the inshore grounds. In later years, when some were as large as from fifteen to twenty tons, they grew more venturesome, and not infrequently their cruises were extended to the off-shore banks.

Indeed, tradition tells of some going as far as the West Indies during the embargo period, carrying out cargoes of fish, and returning with rum, sugar, or molasses. The difficulty of intercourse at that time often made these ventures profitable, and apparently less risk was taken in these diminutive vessels than would have attended similar enterprises in larger craft.

Although the peace of 1783 continued to Americans the right to fish in waters bordering the British North American provinces, the conditions that environed our fishermen for many years thereafter were such as to render them unable, in a large measure, to take advantage of this right.

Soon after the peace of 1815, and the general pacification of Europe, as a result of the close of the Napoleonic wars, the New England fisheries began to improve. After 1820 they advanced rapidly in prosperity. The bounty given by the government to vessels engaged in the cod-fishery had a most encouraging and beneficial effect; the remarkable and growing popularity of the mackerel as an article of food led to the establishment and rapid development of the fishery for this species; and last, but not least, there was little competition from the British

North American provinces until after 1850. Prior to 1830, the British colonial policy, which prevented the colonists from trading with foreign countries, completely prevented exportation of provincial fish to the United States. And even later, trade in fish grew slowly, partly owing to the undeveloped condition of provincial fisheries, and partly to our tariff laws, which were quite sufficient to preserve to Americans control of the home market, and to protect them from foreign competition.

It is true that the transportation facilities were crude and undeveloped. Nevertheless, small freighters carried the cured products of the deep-sea fisheries from every nook and corner of the coast to Boston and New York, whence they were sent to the remotest sections of the country. Dried cod, pickled mackerel, and herring, smoked or salted in brine, were admirably adapted to the transportation facilities of the period and the conditions of trade; for they could be carried without deterioration by the slow process of travel then in vogue, while the dealer rarely found them otherwise than "in order" when they were called for. The luxury of having fresh fish whenever wanted was then practically unknown. The most important requirement was to have products that would "keep." And so the well-preserved food treasures of the Atlantic found a ready sale and increasing appreciation. The fleets of fishing-craft along the New England coast not only augmented in numbers, but also in the size of the vessels, while material improvement was noticeable in the form and rig.

As early as 1820 the pinky began to supersede the Chebacco boat. This was similar in form to the latter, being a sharp-sterned craft, but it was larger, and carried a bowsprit and jib, thus having a full schooner rig. It was most generally in use north of Cape Cod until about 1840. In the mean time, square-stern schooners, usually with low quarter-decks (thus distinguished from the old-fashioned high quarter-deck craft of the Marblehead type), were built, and for some years after the last-mentioned date they were generally preferred to all others. Prosperity led to continued improvement, and about the middle of the century a material change was made in the introduction of clipper schooners.

Nevertheless, it is true that the fisheries were confronted with certain difficulties that seriously handicapped their development; but possibly the dark shadows of adversity, which were sometimes rather heavy, will throw into stronger light the general success, and suggest the underlying causes of it.

A source of discouragement was found in the scarcity of the mackerel for nearly a score of years after the marvellous abundance of 1831. But during the recurring seasons it was pursued as eagerly as usual, with ever-varying success, until Nature, in her own good time, again cheered the fishermen with increased abundance, while the product of their labor, skill, and daring found a ready demand and remunerative market. It will probably not be denied that the decade from 1850 to 1860 was the period of greatest development of the New England sea fisheries, though it must be conceded that the unusual demand and high prices of the war period — 1861 to 1865 — gave a material impetus to the industry. This was a temporary boom that probably would not have occurred under peaceful and normal conditions.

Various things have contributed to check the advance that was patent to every one up to the period named. But while these differ as to time, location, and character, they can, with few exceptions, all be summed up under the single generalization of competition. This competition has, in some measure, been due to governmental action, but it has always been so keen as to prove an unsurmountable obstacle to the prosperous continuance of the New England fishery industries on the basis of former years. It may be accounted somewhat remarkable that there should have been a combination of circumstances, such as will be mentioned, which were detrimental to the New England fisheries; for perhaps it rarely happens that industrial progress is hampered by so many untoward conditions due to changes occurring about the same time.

Probably the most important event, in its influence upon New England fisheries, was the conclusion with Great Britain of the "Reciprocity Treaty" of 1854, by the terms of which Canadian-caught fish came into our markets free, in direct and untrammelled competition with the products of our own fisheries. Canadian vessels sailing under the British flag had the same rights in our markets, and on the fishing-grounds off our shores, which were frequented by New England schooners, as the vessels carrying the flag of the United States. In return, Americans were permitted to fish within the three-mile limit along the shores of Canada, to purchase bait or other supplies in its harbors, and to transship cargoes.

This treaty was the result of the development of the American mackerel - fishery, and the troubles consequent upon the harsh enforcement by the British of their interpretation of the fishery clauses of the treaty of 1818.

The presence in the Gulf of St. Lawrence and elsewhere off the Canadian coasts of large fleets of American fishing-vessels led to captures for alleged or actual trespass on the part of the latter. Even when this did not occur, the constant pursuit of the Americans by the British or Canadian cruisers, and the not infrequent imposition of indignities upon our fishermen, caused a general feeling of irritation, which it was expected the treaty would allay.

It is not necessary to enter upon a discussion here of the right or wrong of the conditions prevailing prior to the treaty of 1854. It may suffice to say that it was generally believed this settlement would prove mutually beneficial, and probably few, if any, foresaw the baneful effects it would have. Indeed, it is but just to say these were not immediately apparent, for certain reasons, some of which have been specified. Nevertheless, the treaty did not prove satisfactory to Americans, and was discontinued in 1866, in compliance with announcement made by the United States. After a few years, however, during which time our fishermen suffered much abuse and hardship in Canadian ports and waters, the Treaty of Washington was negotiated—in 1872. This was essentially like its predecessor, so far as the fisheries were concerned, and, like the former, was limited to ten years' duration, with a proviso that after the expiration of that time either party to the contract could ask for its annulment. However, it would not cease to be effective until two years after notification was given. Thus the fishery clauses of this treaty were in force until 1885, when they were abrogated by request of the United States.

But the free access to our markets by the Canadian fishermen for upwards of twenty-four years, during the period between 1854 and 1885, together with other conditions, gave a great impetus to the fisheries across the border.

Not only had the Canadians the freedom of our markets, but in recent years they have enjoyed the benefit of a bounty which comes from the $5,500,000 paid by the United States as a result of the "Halifax award." And thus the government of this country, which in 1866 deprived our own deep-sea fishermen of the bounty they had previously enjoyed, and which was then more than ever necessary to the successful continuance of their business, actually furnished the money, through this award, to subsidize the Canadian competitors of American citizens.

But our fishermen uncomplainingly bore the loss when their bounty was taken from them. Many of them had braved death on sea and land in the struggle for the perpetuity of the government, and they were loyally willing to assist in meeting its obligations, even when it was evident that the withholding of the little subsidy they had formerly received meant abandonment of ocean fishery. And so there was never a murmur, even though the *Little Polly* and the schooner *Julia Ann* must be laid up to rest and rot in the cove, or else be sold to provincials, who could know little of the memories that clung around these fishing-boats.

What wonder that the harbors of Nova Scotia, Prince Edward Island, and other British provinces were alive with the bustle of prosperity and enterprise, while throttled industry shrivelled and died along the New England coast! Is it remarkable that the fisheries of our Eastern States suffered materially from the keen rivalry of foreigners; that indications of decay were manifest on every hand, and that grass grew in New England shipyards, where the building of fishing-vessels had formerly been actively pursued?

In the mean time other influences were at work not favorable to the prosperity of the deep-sea fisheries. Among these the most prominent perhaps were the introduction of the present methods of canning aquatic products, the improvement in transportation, making possible the rapid carriage of material, and the general adoption of various methods of refrigeration, through the use of which fish or other aquatic products can be sent in a fresh condition to the markets from the most distant sections of the United States. To these may be added the recent remarkable development of the shore fisheries, resulting from the last-mentioned causes, and especially the growth of the pound-net fishery. Millions of pounds of fresh fish, of the choicest varieties, are caught in pound-nets, and are sent to compete with the salted products that come from distant deep-sea fishing-grounds.

Although the process of canning was first introduced at Eastport, Maine, about 1840, for the purpose of packing lobsters, the enterprise developed rather slowly, and there were only three canneries in the United States as late as 1850. Thereafter a more rapid advance was made; canneries were built along the coast of northern New England, and many fishermen found employment in supplying these, and in furnishing cargoes to the smacks which carried lobsters alive to Portland, Boston, or New York. The influence of this new branch of fishery on the vessel fisheries was very considerable; for not only did the lobsters—canned or fresh—come into direct competition with other sea products, but many of the best fishermen preferred to stay at home and catch lobsters rather than to incur the discomfort of separation from their families, and expose themselves to the greater peril and uncertainty that attend fishing on distant grounds. Besides, lobster-fishing generally gave larger returns to the average fisherman, while each man became a small capitalist, being the owner of his equipment of boat, cars, pots, etc.

Thus it was that difficulty was sometimes met with in obtaining crews at the small fishing-stations, more especially as many of the young and more adventurous men were attracted to Gloucester or some other of the larger fishing-ports.

The industry of salmon-canning was begun on the Sacramento River, California, in 1864, and on the Columbia River two years later. Although limited in its scope at the start, it soon grew to immense proportions, and during the seventies the pack rose to hundreds of thousands of cases, with a value of millions of dollars. At first the products were chiefly, if not wholly, exported to foreign countries, but for many years the west-coast salmon has been in nearly every grocery in the country; and whether in near or remote markets it contends for supremacy with the mackerel, the cod, the herring, or oth-er food species that are products of our Eastern sea fisheries.

Nor should mention be omitted of the fact that car-loads of fresh salmon and sturgeon are now shipped east from the Columbia River and Puget Sound, while car-loads of fresh halibut are sent from Seattle to New York, and even to Gloucester, the headquarters of the New England deep-sea fishery.

Starting in the seventies, the sardine-canning industry of eastern Maine has reached large proportions, and great quantities of young herring, formerly of little or no commercial value, are now put upon the market in an attractive form for food. They do something more than to compete with imported sardines, for they are cheap as well as wholesome, and it is not difficult to believe that they supply in some measure the demand for salt mackerel and salt herring that formerly was such a well-recognized feature of our fish-market. Thousands of mackerel taken in pound-nets are canned annually.

The foregoing shows some of the obstacles that have confronted the deep-sea fisheries, and which alone might be considered sufficient to cause the conditions now prevailing. But it is only just to say that the recent great development of the shore fisheries in various parts of the country, and the consequent increase in the supply of fresh fish placed upon the market, due to causes already alluded to, have had a material influence on the demand for salt fish.

From the beginning salted cod, hake, pollock, cusk, mackerel, and herring have been the chief products of our ocean vessel fishery, and any marked change in the demand for these must necessarily be felt by the industry.

It is true that welled smacks in southern New England formerly found profitable employment in carrying live fish and lobsters to New York. Connecticut sloops of moderate tonnage were often seen, forty or fifty years ago, on the spring mackerel-grounds from off Sandy Hook to Block Island. Their crews angled with lines attached to poles, and when mackerel were caught they were deftly swung on board and dropped into the well of the vessel, where they were easily kept alive until the smack completed her fare and reached her destination at the great metropolis. But the catch so disposed of was comparatively insignificant, and bore small proportion to the immense quantities of salted mackerel. It is only in recent years, since the use of ice for preservation is better understood, that hundreds of barrels of this delicious fish have been marketed fresh in a single day, and distributed throughout the country. Nor is it longer necessary for vessels to always seek the larger markets. A morning's catch of fish taken off Montauk, Block Island, or Gay Head can soon be landed at Newport or New Bedford; on a flying train or swift steamer they reach Boston or New York in a few hours, and the dawning of the following day sees these sea treasures, bright and fresh, being used at T Wharf or Fulton Market to fill customers' orders—and perhaps whirled away again on the swift steam-driven express to meet the demand of the hour, whether it come from near-by points or distant Chicago or Omaha.

The fresh-halibut fishery, which was begun in the most primitive manner sixty years ago, ultimately developed into a large industry; and though it encountered many vicissitudes, it sometimes employed as many as forty or fifty of the finest schooners. Lately it has fallen off somewhat, and its relative importance is less now than formerly, though the character of the vessels engaged in it and the fact that it is vigorously pursued throughout the year give it a consequence it otherwise might not have.

Fishing on the inshore grounds for cod and haddock — chiefly for the latter—which were carried fresh to market, began in a limited way about fifty or sixty years ago. The small vessels supplying the demand at Boston and vicinity fished largely in Massachusetts Bay, while those sailing from ports on Long Island Sound generally frequented grounds near home, and carried their catch to New York.

It was not, however, until after 1870 that this branch of sea fishery grew to large dimensions. Until that time, and shortly subsequent thereto, the haddock-fishery was pursued on the inshore grounds, the vessels rarely going more than twenty-five or thirty miles from land. But competition led to greater ventures, and about 1873 the trips were extended to George's Bank. Since then more distant banks have been visited; the fishery has been pursued with the utmost courage and diligence; the swift-

est and most seaworthy vessels constitute the large fleet employed in winter, and the catches arriving at Boston in a single day often aggregate upward of a million pounds, and sometimes reach a total approximating double that amount.

In southern New England, however, this market fishery is comparatively unimportant. A few vessels fish for cod in winter to supply New York, but at other seasons catch blue-fish and other species from off Cape Hatteras to Nantucket Shoals.

Reference is made to these phases of the deep-sea market fishery to indicate the growing demand for fresh fish, and the means adopted by the vessel fishermen in recent periods to meet that demand, and to sustain their prestige and prosperity by improving every opportunity that came to them.

Allusion need only be made to the frozen-herring trade, which employs a number of New England vessels in winter, and besides supplying bait for the market and cod-fishing fleets, furnishes hundreds of thousands of pounds of cheap fresh fish for food.

While, however, all these fresh products lessen the demand for salt fish, and to that extent limit the branches of fishery that must depend on preservation of fish by salting, it will be seen that this is practically only a change from one method of preservation to another, and therefore not a material interference with the general prosperity of the ocean fishery.

But the great competitor of the deep-sea fishing-vessel, whether engaged in the salt or market fisheries, is the pound-net, the increased employment of which in recent years has been one of the most remarkable phases of the fisheries of the United States. The introduction of this has led to almost phenomenal conditions in some sections, notably in Chesapeake Bay and its tributaries.

An attempt was made in 1858 to introduce pound-nets in this region, but much prejudice was encountered, and the occurrence of the war shortly after delayed the employment of this form of apparatus. The fisheries of the Chesapeake were of little importance prior to 1870; they were engaged in only for a few weeks in spring and fall, and the catch was chiefly obtained with hand-lines and drag-seines. Even as late as 1880 it was historically recorded that only "162 pound-nets were fished in Virginia waters, with two others located at Crisfield, Maryland, just above the Virginia line." When it is stated that, ten years later, in the two States of Virginia and Maryland there were 1670 pound-nets, and the total catch of food fish in those States for that year, in all forms of apparatus, reached the vast aggregate of 67,656,041 pounds, the effect of this coast fishery on the markets will be apparent, especially when it is known that practically all of this immense product — that would load a fleet of three hundred large fishing-vessels, and about half of which is taken in pound-nets — is sold fresh, and includes the choicest species, such as shad, Spanish-mackerel, striped bass, blue-fish, sheep's-head, etc. When delicious Potomac shad sell for less than ten cents each, as during the present year (1896), it is easy to understand the difficulty of successfully competing with them. And this was more than paralleled by conditions in 1893, when many tons of living weakfish — one of the best of our food fishes—were turned out into the open sea from the retaining-pounds of Rhode Island, because over-supply of fish was so great that the price for them at Fulton Market was not sufficiently high to pay the cost of transportation and leave any balance to the fishermen.

Similar and only less startling statistical statements might be made concerning New Jersey, so conveniently near the large cities of New York and Philadelphia. The great fisheries of the North Carolina sounds, and the catches obtained in pound-nets on Long Island, or in certain sections of southern New England, are also far too important factors in influencing the supply of food fish to be omitted, if a detailed discussion were possible.

But while we may be content with only the slightest reference to these localities, which contribute their millions of pounds of fish to the general supply, we must not neglect to notice the fisheries of the Gulf States, which have recently experienced a phenomenal advance, from Florida to Texas.

Between sixty and seventy years ago Connecticut fishermen began supplying the Havana market with fish taken in the Gulf of Mexico, chiefly on the grounds off the shores of Florida. Their catches of red-snappers, groupers, etc., were taken alive to Havana in welled smacks, and disposed of at remunerative prices. In time this business fell largely into the hands of resident Key West fishermen. Finally it had to be practically abandoned, because of the prohibitory duties levied in Cuba. Attention was then turned to supplying to the markets of the North the large variety of fine fish which are taken in Gulf waters, and especially the red-snapper. About 1874 parties at Pensacola made attempts to organize the red-snapper fishery on an improved commercial basis. The success met with led to the subsequent participation of other firms, and ultimately to the spread of the business to other points.

Shipping fish from the Gulf shores rapidly developed, and soon extended so as to embrace nearly every favorably situated locality touched by the railroad, and to include many of the choice varieties of fish taken in that region.

Although it has not been found practicable to operate pound-nets, the catch by lines, seines, and gill-nets is large, the food fish reaching a total, for the region, in 1890, of 37,980,434 pounds. As in other cases, this excludes oysters and other shell-fish, as well as crustaceans and edible reptiles, which constitute a large percentage of the food taken from the waters of this section.

But the Great Lakes have a still more important influence. Lack of transportation facilities, the sparsely settled condition of most of the lake region, and general ignorance of modern methods of refrigeration made it impossible to fully develop the fishery resources until recently. Consequently the fisheries of this section exerted comparatively little influence half a century ago. Practically all the fish taken in the early days, except those locally eaten, were salted. Thus, while the settlers along the lake shores could obtain supplies for family use or for local distribution, the industry of fishing did not attain marked distinction until after 1850. This will be evidenced by the fact that the largest annual shipment of lake fish by canal — then the chief transportation agency for such products — from Cleveland, Toledo, and Maumee, prior to 1850, was only 17,792 half-barrels. The adoption of other methods of preparation, a few years later, and the utilization of swifter transportation, caused a marked increase in the distribution of lake fish.

The pound-net was introduced on Lake Erie about 1850, and a few years subsequently its use developed rapidly. The adoption of the pound-net was followed in about fifteen years by the inauguration at Sandusky of the process of artificially freezing fish, so that they could be kept in a frozen condition from fall until the next summer. This made possible the distribution of lake fish, in a thoroughly fresh condition, to the most distant parts of the United States. Subsequently freezing-houses were established at the leading fishing centres on the lakes, and they increased in number at Sandusky, some having a capacity of from ten to twenty tons per day. Steamers were also built to operate immense gangs of gill-nets, and for some years the development in this branch of lake fishery kept pace with progress in other directions.

The result is easy to anticipate. Not only do iced fresh fish from the Great Lakes meet those of the East in spring and summer, but the frozen products of these "brothers of the ocean" stoutly contest for control of the markets in winter, and force their way even into New England. The energy and commercial enterprise exhibited by the lake dealers are most remarkable, and if these were supported by such unfailing sources of supply as can be drawn upon by those engaged in deep-sea fishing, it is evident the latter would meet even sharper competition in the future than in the past. But the limit to which the lakes can be safely drawn upon for fish food has long ago been reached, and the well-recognized falling off in abundance of the most desirable species indicates that, even with the utmost fish-culture can do to assist in maintaining the supply, no greater competition can be expected from this region than exists now. But this has a marked influence, as will be easily understood when it is stated that the total production of the lakes in the last census year amounted to 117,085,568 pounds of food fish—enough to load about six hundred fishing-vessels larger than the average sailing from New England.

Nor should we lose sight of the river fisheries, which, under the same impulses that have caused the conditions on the coast and in the lake region, have recently been actively pursued. As a consequence, many thousand pounds of fish are shipped from points in the Mississippi River basin, where no commercial fishery existed a few years ago. The product of this river fishery will aggregate millions of pounds annually. It not only takes the place locally of salted sea-fish, but competes with the latter for supremacy in the great markets of the Mississippi Valley.

Thus it will be seen that whereas to a large extent the products of the New England deep-sea fisheries had a monopoly of the markets of this country prior to 1850, the conditions then existing have changed radically. Consequently these products of the Atlantic fishery must now meet and compete with the salmon, sturgeon, cod, and halibut of the Pacific; the white-fish, trout, pike, perch, and cisco, or herring, from the Great Lake region; the catfish, buffalo-fish, and other species from the rivers; the red-snapper, pompano, and many other choice varieties from the Gulf coast; the shad, Spanish-mackerel, striped bass, and blue-fish from the region extending from North Carolina to New York; and also frozen smelts, herring, and fresh salmon from Canada, not to speak of Canadian-caught cod and mackerel, which are so extensively marketed in this country.

When it is remembered that practically all these numerous varieties of fishes, excepting a portion of those coming from Canada, and the Pacific cod, are put upon the market fresh, generally in the most attractive form, and usually at prices which indicate that the supply is more than ample for the needs of the people, is it remarkable that difficulty is found in competing with them, when the success of our deep-sea fisheries must depend chiefly upon marketing salt fish, which can be obtained only by the employment of costly and expensively fitted sea-going vessels? When the extent and character of this competition of coast and interior fisheries are considered, when also we find that the New England fisher had for many years to wage a sharp fight with Canadians for even a share in the home market, and when we see the American fishing bounty taken off, while a subsidy is given to foreign fishermen, is it any wonder that even New England courage, thrift, and enterprise have proved insufficient to successfully continue the contest? In view of all this, it is believed surprise will be felt that Gloucester and a few other ports still pursue the business with unfaltering courage and devotion, and, by unexampled daring and determination, continue to exact tribute from the sea, and to maintain a stubborn fight for the existence of an industry which means more to this nation than the mere obtainment of food or dollars.

Impressive as this is, it is not all. For, while depressing influences have confronted the fisheries, New England has been developing her manufactures to a remarkable degree since 1850. And as these industries have grown they have become active competitors for the control of American labor. It is not therefore strange that the fisherman has often found remunerative and satisfactory employment at home, and that he has been disposed to accept a condition which not only attracts him to new fields of labor, but invites capital to build and operate manufactories instead of fleets of fishing-vessels. Thus Marblehead, the quaint old port, whose fishermen performed such important services on sea and land during the Revolutionary war, is now a town of shoemakers. It is true a few old fishermen, with salt-hardened and deeply bronzed faces, still go dory-fishing, or act as bumboat-men to the many yachtsmen who go there in summer. But, nevertheless, there is an odor of leather about the place; the talk is of the price per case for making foot-wear, and yarns of famous fishing voyages, of wrecks, and of miraculous escapes are now rarely told, for they are as ancient history as Whittier's story of "Skipper Ireson's Ride."

Newburyport, once celebrated for its mackerel fleet and its cod-fishers who went to Labrador, is now a city of spindles, and the hum of cotton-mills is the industrial music of the hour.

New Bedford, too, is now a great manufacturing centre. While it still has a fleet of whalers, which rendezvous at San Francisco, and rarely "round the Horn" for the home port, the whale-fishery is a decadent industry, and receives comparatively little consideration, except from those directly interested in its prosecution. Partially dismantled "blubber-hunters" —as the old ships are called—lie contentedly alongside the wharves, where they seem to be kept rather as reminders of other days for the curious to gaze at than for any present or prospective utility.

A few months ago the writer saw a lusty eighteen-months-old babe in the arms of its proud grandmother, and he was told that this son of a New England whaling skipper had never been seen by his father, who had passed the previous winter near the mouth of the Mackenzie River, and at that moment was probably hunting whales among the ice-floes that fill the ocean along the northern shores of this continent. Such separation of husband and father from wife and children is hard to bear, and when satisfactory employment can be found on shore, which will admit of a united family, it is usually accepted. And to that extent the fisheries are deprived of the skill and hardihood necessary to their successful continuance.

It may be incidentally mentioned that in addition to the growing scarcity of whales, and the rivalry of other industries, the whale-fishery has suffered from a remarkable decline in the price of oil, due to the competition of mineral oils and other materials which take its place. The influence of this is such that whales are now often hunted for their bone alone, since in some cases the oil is not thought sufficiently valuable to warrant saving the blubber and trying it out.

The menhaden fishermen have also keenly felt the result of this change, for the success of their industry depends chiefly on the price of oil. Thus, though the average catch of fish per vessel in recent years is larger than it was in former periods, the business is frequently unremunerative. Therefore this comparatively new branch of sea fishery, in which New England is largely interested, seems to be suffering almost as much as any other from the strangulation caused by competition.

Various minor causes have contributed to the decay noticeable in many coast fishing-towns. Mr. F. W. True makes the following reference to one of them in *The Fishery Industries of the United States* (vol. i., section v., page 599):

"The restless waters of Massachusetts Bay have caused many changes in the configuration of the northern shore of Cape Cod. Moved by their power, the sand has spread itself in an even plain, extending from high-water mark a half-mile seaward, and but little inclined to the plane of the horizon. Relentlessly it has filled the old-time harbors, and thereby stifled the activity of the north-shore fishing-towns of former days. But while the vessel fishery

DRYING FISH, GLOUCESTER.

has forever disappeared from many of the towns, the weir fishery has taken its place to a considerable extent."

The scarcity of certain important ocean fishes has had a somewhat dejecting influence on those fishermen who relied chiefly upon the pursuit of these species. For some years decrease in abundance of the halibut on the grounds where it is chiefly sought has been one of the marked features of the Atlantic fisheries. However, this has not so far caused any material loss in financial receipts, since there has been an enhancement of price when

halibut-fishery has never had any special importance except at Gloucester.

The present scarcity of mackerel, which there is reason for believing is only temporary—a repetition of history so far as relates to this species—is a far more important matter. Probably no other branch of the New England sea fishery was so much relied on by the fishermen of the smaller coast towns as that which had the mackerel as the object of pursuit. Although the cost of prosecuting this fishery was materially advanced by the general adoption of the purse-seine as an appara-

BAITING TRAWLS.

the supply temporarily failed to equal the demand. Also, the discovery of new halibut banks or areas from time to time has generally enabled the fishermen to supply the demand, while this changing from one locality to another may possibly enable the fallow grounds, which are at least temporarily depleted, to regain something of their old-time fertility. If so, no serious inconvenience may be anticipated, but only time can answer this question. The most that can be said of it now is that it needs no consideration, so far as the general decadence of the New England fishing-towns is concerned, since the

tus of capture, and the disparity of catches between vessels was increased, there was still a reasonable average of success in seasons of abundance. Consequently a show of prosperity was maintained at some of the fishing coves and harbors, even after the grip of financial disaster had been felt in most of them. For it must be conceded that the decadence, which began shortly after the middle of the century, continued more or less uninterruptedly, and even the phenomenal abundance of mackerel in the early eighties, culminating in 1884, when the catch exceeded any ever made, scarcely arrest-

UNLOADING FISH FROM A GRAND BANKS FISHERMAN.

ed the downward progress. Indeed, in 1879 and 1880, when mackerel were normally plentiful, schooners lay deserted in the harbors of Maine, and crews could not be found to go on them. Nevertheless, matters grew worse when the mackerel catch fell off, and many who had until then courageously faced the conditions which confronted them, were compelled to succumb to the inevitable, and sell their vessels or employ them in some other trade.

In many cases this was due not only to scarcity of fish or condition of markets, but to the difficulty in obtaining skilful and trained fishermen, without whom it was folly to send vessels to sea.

Reference has already been made to the influences which conflicted with the deep-sea fisheries in this regard. It remains to be added that those still inclined to follow the sea fishery naturally preferred to sail on the swiftest and most expensive vessels, which also were usually commanded by the most skilful or "luckiest" skippers. Few fishing-ports have been able to successfully compete in the matter of vessels with Gloucester, where new and costly clippers are added to the fleet each year. This, together with other advantages, led large numbers of the best fishermen to go there from Cape Cod and Maine, the result being, of course, beneficial to the port they sailed from, but correspondingly detrimental to the development or continuance of home fisheries.

But, whatever influence this may have had, it is probable nothing could have arrested the progress of decay, for it is well known that the most determined efforts were made at certain points: the best vessels and the most skilful men

CLEANING AND SORTING FISH.

were employed, everything that intelligence and business sagacity could suggest was done, and ruin came in spite of it.

It may be true that the increased cost of vessels, the additional expense of running them, together with the enhancement of the cost of living which now confronts the fishermen — and this depends more on change in the methods of living than the purchasing power of a dollar — have had a disheartening influence, and have reached a point where it may not reasonably be expected the returns from fishing, as conducted from the smaller ports, will give the necessary income to meet expenditures and leave a profit. But, however serious these obstacles may now appear, it is probable they would be found of small moment, and it may fairly be assumed that the sea fisheries might still prosper, as in earlier years, except for the fierce competition that comes from foreign countries and from all sections of the United States.

It is highly probable that there will always be demand for salt cod, mackerel, and other fish that come from distant Northern seas. But the question of cheapening the product by increasing the catch per man or per vessel will ever be a vital one in this competitive battle, where sentiment is not a factor; and a problem scarcely second in importance is the introduction of new or improved methods of preservation.

The limit of human possibility seems to have been reached in the matter of capture of sea fish; for it is difficult to conceive of more exertion being made or of greater risks being taken. The use of steam-vessels may increase the catch of fresh fish, as well as the scope of the market fishery. But even now the supply often exceeds the demand, and steamers are not available to the salt-fish industry, and scarcely can be expected to build up the waste places in the coves and small harbors along the New England coast.

However, cargoes of herring have arrived from Newfoundland that were artificially frozen on board the vessels, and the question arises as to what extent, if any, this method may be applied to the cod or mackerel taken in summer on remote fishing-grounds. Canning the products on board the vessels may also receive consideration in the not distant future.

It is undoubtedly true that the cure of salt herring is susceptible of improvement in this country, and there seems no reason why our markets should be filled with European herring when it is quite possible for our own fishermen to furnish as good an article if intelligent care in preparation is observed.

To what extent, if any, the sea fisheries may hereafter be profited by exportation of salted products remains to be seen. At present, however, the prospect of any material benefit from foreign trade is not encouraging. For not only are sea fish now imported in large quantities from British North American provinces, but salt mackerel come to us from Norway and Ireland, and herring from various European countries. It is therefore evident that more favorable conditions than now exist are required to create an extensive demand for our salted sea fish in other countries. Until there is material change in this regard, the balance of fish trade will not favor our deep-sea fisheries, and the home market must be relied on for any improvement that may come.

Much has been done recently to render more attractive the salted sea products, and to this as much as to anything else is due the continued prosperity of Gloucester, or of other fishing-ports that may still thrive. The intelligence that has brought these and other improvements may reasonably be relied upon to meet the exigencies of the hour, so far as human skill and business activity can meet them. Never-

theless, the fact remains that (even though the present importance of the New England fisheries, including those termed "shore fisheries," may be maintained in the aggregate) the same forces are now at work that caused the decadence in the vessel fisheries along our northeastern coast, and their future influence may well prove an interesting subject for observation by all who are concerned in the continuance of industries which train seamen for commerce or for manning our navies in time of war.

Time may again bring piscatorial prosperity to New England; fleets of fishing-clippers may once more sail from its many green isles and quiet coves; a hardy race of native-born seamen may be bred along its shores and schooled in its sea fisheries; for circumstances now unforeseen may bring these changes. However, the present outlook is not promising for the immediate realization of these hoped-for conditions. Nevertheless, they may come in the future, when an immense population requires a larger supply of fish food, and when a great nation more fully appreciates the importance of encouraging a self-sustaining militia of the sea, which, as history shows, embodies professional skill, brawn and brain, courage and hardihood, to a degree not to be found elsewhere.

A MODERN FAST-SAILING FISHING-SCHOONER.

26

Pilgrim Ports
in Old England

NEW ENGLAND MAGAZINE

DECEMBER

Pilgrim Ports in Old England

By Edwin D. Mead

FROM the top of the high tower of St. Botolph's Church, in old Boston in England, I imagine that one can see, in a clear day, the scenes of both of the two unfortunate attempts of the Pilgrim Fathers to escape from England to Holland. The first attempt was at Boston itself, almost at the very foot of the tower on which the spectator would be standing, perhaps at the very point on the little river Witham from which Turner's beautiful picture of old Boston and its church was painted. The second attempt was at a point on the river Humber, between Hull and Grimsby, and so about fifty miles from Boston, away at the very northern border of flat Lincolnshire. Here, at "a large common, a good way distant from any town," the Dutch captain was to meet them with his ship. One can read the story of both unhappy ventures in Bradford's Journal. At Boston their shipmaster betrayed them; and they were seized and brought back, Brewster and six others being thrown into prison. At Grimsby only a single boat-load had been taken to the ship, when they were surprised by the authorities, and their endeavor once more thwarted. But in this "first boat-load" was Bradford himself, who tells us the story. Fourteen days he and his companions were tossed on the North Sea, driven by a tempest to the very coast of Norway; for seven days "they saw neither sun, moon nor stars;" but at last they arrived safely in Holland, and were able to act in Amsterdam as pioneers for their brethren, who escaped from England one by one, as best they could. "In ye end," says Bradford, "notwithstanding all these storms of

413

opposition, they all gatt over at length, some at one time & some at another, and some in one place & some in another, and mette togeather againe according to their desires, with no small rejoicing."

Scrooby, Boston and Grimsby,—all in a country overlooked by Lincoln cathedral, and all at equal distances from the cathedral,—those are the three places to remember in connection with the Pilgrim Fathers before their exile. Amsterdam, Leyden and Delft-Haven,—those are the three places with which they were connected in Holland. In Amsterdam they spent the first year; Leyden was their home for eleven years; from Delft-Haven, on the Maas, just below Rotterdam, they embarked on the "Speedwell," in July, 1620. The stirring lines in Dr. Holmes's poem on Robinson's farewell to them will be remembered:

"He spake: with lingering, long embrace,
  With tears of love and partings fond,
They floated down the creeping Maas,
  Along the isle of Ysselmond.

They passed the frowning towers of Briel,
  The 'Hook of Holland's' shelf of sand,
And grated soon with lifting keel
  The sullen shores of Fatherland.

No home for these!—too well they knew
  The mitred king behind the throne;
The sails were set, the pennons flew,
  And westward ho! for worlds unknown."

Southampton, Dartmouth and Plymouth were the three old English ports in which the Pilgrim Fathers took refuge for a little, in that summer of 1620, on their way from Holland to New England. Southampton has a double interest to us; for it was from there that Winthrop and the Massachusetts colonists also sailed,

in 1630. Winthrop's Journal, it will be remembered, opens with the author "riding at the Cowes, near the Isle of Wight, in the Arbella"; and at Southampton, John Cotton, coming down from old Boston, had just before preached the farewell sermon to the colonists, "God's Promise to His Plantation." Winthrop does not tell of the sermon, which indeed has been strangely overlooked by the historians; but it was for Winthrop's company what John Robinson's farewell sermon at Delft-Haven was for the Pilgrims.*

Southampton is directly opposite the Isle of Wight, a score of miles up Southampton Water, in the very middle of the south coast of England. Plymouth is one hundred and fifty miles farther west, in beautiful Devon, far on toward Land's End. In the channel directly over against it, fourteen miles from the citadel, is the famous Eddystone light-house. Dartmouth, too, is in Devon, east of Plymouth, nearer Tor Bay, where William III., coming from Holland, landed in 1688, to take possession of England. Dartmouth is only a little town, of perhaps six thousand people, —a little town that looks as though it went to sleep there by the river about 1620. Plymouth and Southampton are two of the greatest ports of England; and Plymouth and Portsmouth, which latter lies so close beside Southampton that we always think of them together, are England's two greatest naval stations. American travelers and merchants know Plymouth and Southampton as the two English ports where the German steamers call.

*The sermon is printed among the Old South Leaflets—No. 53.

SOUTHAMPTON BARGAT

which sail from New York. The English themselves think oftener perhaps of the steamers sailing thence for Gibraltar and the Mediterranean, for Egypt and India, for Australia and New Zealand, the West Indies and Brazil. "The perpetual arrival and departure of passengers," says one of the Southampton books, "gives an animation and interest to the town

415

not readily to be found elsewhere. The arrival or departure of the Indian mail packets presents a scene that will not easily be forgotten. The mail for India is contained in variously colored boxes, sometimes reaching to a weight of twenty tons. The American mails are packed in India rubber sacks; the West Indian, in canvas bags. Notabilities of all sorts—foreign monarchs, royal Bengal tigers, Indian, African and Egyptian princes, great monkeys, distinguished ambassadors, hippopotamuses, alligators, generals, admirals, illustrious exiles, California bears, colonial governors, etc., are constantly arriving by the various steamers, and afford infinite amusement and occupation to the loungers and gossip-retailers of the town. When a couple of large mail steamers arrive on the same day, which often happens, the windows of the hotels are to be seen crowded with foreign merchants, West India and American planters, East Indian, Australian and Californian nabobs, military or naval officers, and foreign officials, with their families, dressed in every variety of costume,—all besieged vigorously in all their hotels by English, Italian and German street bands."

So Southampton to-day; and Plymouth is hardly less busy and bustling. Very different was it two hundred and eighty years ago, when the "Speedwell" came sailing up Southampton Water from Holland, when the "Mayflower" went sailing out of Plymouth Harbor for New England.

It was about the 20th of July, 1620, that the "Speedwell" sailed from Delft-Haven. "Thus hoysing saile," says Bradford, "with a prosperous

416

winde they came in short time to Southampton, where they found the bigger ship [the "Mayflower"] come from London, lying ready, with all the rest of their company. After a joyfull wellcome, and mutual congratulations, with other friendly entertainments, they fell to parley aboute their bussines, how to dispatch with ye best expedition." They had trouble with their agents; and they were forced to sell sixty or eighty firkins of butter from their stock of provisions, in order to raise money necessary before clearing the harbor. "We put ourselves upon great extremities," they wrote from Southampton to the merchants and adventurers, "scarce having any butter, no oil, not a sole to mend a shoe, nor every man a sword to his side—wanting many muskets, much armor, etc. And yet we are willing to expose ourselves to such eminent dangers as are like to ensue, and trust to the good providence of God, rather than his name and truth be evil spoken of for us."

It seems that the "Speedwell" and the "Mayflower" arrived at Southampton, the one from Delft-Haven and the other from London, on the same day, July 22, and remained until about August 5, a fortnight. Tradition has it that it was at the West Quay that they lay.

It was at Southampton that John Alden, then a youth of twenty-three, joined the Pilgrim company. Governor Bradford writes in his notes at Plymouth, long afterward: "John Alden was hired for a cooper, at Southampton, wher the ship victuled; and being a hopfull yong man, was much desired, but left to his owne liking to go or stay when he came here; but he stayed, and maryed here." This was the John Alden of Longfellow's poem—the John Alden who married Priscilla. "Mr. William Mullines, and his wife, and 2 children, Joseph & Priscilla; and a servant, Robart Carter,"—that is the way that Bradford describes Priscilla's family, as it came in the "Mayflower.'

WESTGATE, SOUTHAMPTON.

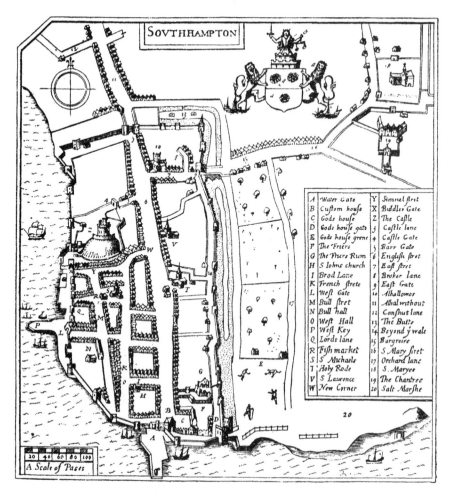

A	Water Gate	Y	Simnel firet
B	Cuftom houfe	X	Biddles Gate
C	Gods houfe	Z	The Cafle
D	Gods houfe gate	3	Cafle lane
E	Gode houfe grene	4	Cafle Gate
F	The Friers	5	Barr Gate
G	The Friers Rum	6	Englifh firet
H	S Iohns church	7	Eaft firet
I	Brod Lane	8	Broker lane
K	French ftrete	9	Eaft Gate
L	Weft Gate	10	Alhallowos
M	Bull firet	11	Alhal wthout
N	Bull hall	12	Canfhut lane
O	Weft Hall	13	The Butts
P	Weft Key	14	Beyond y wale
Q	Lords lane	15	Bargreive
R	Fifh market	16	S Mary firet
S	S Michaels	17	Orchard lane
T	Holy Rode	18	S. Maryes
V	S Laurence	19	The Chantree
W	New Corner	20	Salt Marfhe

FACSIMILE OF A MAP OF SOUTHAMPTON, DATED 1611

With all their troubles at Southampton, the Pilgrims wasted no time there. In little more than a week their accounts were all settled, the freight and passengers were properly placed, and the "Mayflower" and the "Speedwell" sailed from Southampton Water, through the Solent. Before they sailed, however, they received a farewell letter from their pastor, who was left behind at Leyden,—a letter full of wisdom. "The company was caled togeather," says Bradford, "and this letter read amongst them, which had good acceptation with all, and after fruit with many. Then they ordered and distributed their company for either shipe, as they conceived for ye best. And chose a Govr. & 2 or 3 assistants for each shipe, to order ye people by ye way, and see to ye disposing of there provisions, and shuch like affairs. All which was not only with ye liking of ye maisters of ye ships, but according to their desires. Which being done, they sett sail from thence

418

aboute ye 5. of August." (August 15, N. S.)

All men have read the old story about King Canute, the Dane,—how one day, disgusted with the flattery of his courtiers, who went so far as to declare in his presence that nothing in nature dared disobey him, he ordered them to place his chair on the sea shore when the tide was rising; how, as the waters approached he commanded them to retire, and not to wet the edge of his robe; how the tide came on, regardless of his word; and how, retiring, he rebuked his courtiers, saying how weak was every earthly creature, even though a king, and that power resides alone with Him who can say to the ocean, "Thus far shalt thou go, and no farther." It is said to have been on the shore at Southampton that this famous rebuke was given. It would be pleasant to believe that it was at the very spot where the Pilgrim Fathers embarked on the "Mayflower," flying from the fitful tyranny of England's king, but strong in the strength of the great King of Kings, to lay the corner-stone of a nation.

It was six hundred years before the time of the Pilgrims that Canute lived. In those six hundred years, many kings had stood on the shore at Southampton. The town began to grow great from the very time of the Conquest, because there was a ready transit hence to Normandy. Here Henry II., with his queen, landed, on his return from France, immediately before his penance at the tomb of Becket. Here Henry's son, Richard the Lion-Heart, gathered part of his fleet before sailing for Palestine to join the crusade. Here, too, John came frequently, once remaining three months in the

Isle of Wight, expecting succor from the Pope against the barons. On the 4th of July, 1345, Edward III. and the Black Prince embarked here with the army which was presently to win the great victory at Cressy. The army consisted of 4,000 men at arms, 10,000 archers, 12,000 Welsh footmen, and 6,000 Irish; and we read that the number of vessels employed was 1,600. A grand spectacle it must have been, as that great fleet moved down Southampton Water. It would have been hard for the men at the docks in 1620, seeing the "Mayflower" and the "Speedwell" sail, to realize that they were the witnesses of a more important scene.

In 1415, Henry V.'s great expedition for the conquest of France set sail from Southampton. As the ships passed out, we read that swans floated about the mouth of Southampton Water; and the old chroniclers regard these as foretokens of the great victory at Agincourt, which was destined to crown the expedition. Henry VIII. used to come to Southampton; and when Leland, the famous antiquary, visited it in 1548, he saw in the great dock at Portsmouth the ribs of the "Harry Grace de Dieu," the great ship built at Erith, which had conveyed Henry from Dover to the "Field of the Cloth of Gold." In 1522, the Emperor Charles V. embarked at Southampton, on his return to Spain from his visit to Henry. Catharine of Aragon was now Henry's wife. The unfortunate Catherine was the daughter of Ferdinand and Isabella of Spain, who equipped Columbus for America. I speak of her here, because I wish to say that when she came to England from Spain, a girl of sixteen, she landed at Plymouth, the other Pilgrim port. This was in 1501; and she came not to marry Henry, but his brother Arthur, marrying Henry after Arthur's death. When Emperor Charles, her nephew, sailed back to Spain from Southampton harbor, a hundred years before the "Mayflower," she had been Henry's wife a dozen years and more; and her daughter Mary, afterward Queen Mary, was six years old. Thirty-two years later, Friday, July 20, 1554, Philip II., Charles's son, landed at Southampton, to marry Queen Mary. We read that he remained at Southampton till the Monday, when he left to join his longing bride at Winchester, on a gray gelding, in a violent storm of wind and rain, wrapped in a long scarlet cloak.

These things, or some of them, we may suppose that John Alden, who ought to have known all about Southampton, told Priscilla, as they stood by the railings, while the "Mayflower" dropped down Southampton Water. If it had been a century later, he might have told her of a rather important business which subsisted at Southampton,—the business of runaway marriages; for in the last century, and until comparatively recent times, we read that there were always vessels at Southampton ready to carry parties over to Guernsey, at five guineas per couple, where weddings were managed as easily as at Gretna Green.

But I do not suppose that John Alden and Priscilla were thinking of marriages in August, 1620. They were thinking more of good friends whom, I doubt not, they left in Southampton, and some of whom, I hope, came to the dock to see the "Mayflower" sail. Among them, perhaps,

were men and women from Holland, exiles like themselves,—men and women who had fled from the persecutions of Philip and the bloody Duke of Alva and taken refuge here; for Southampton was one of the places where Elizabeth gave these Dutch pilgrims leave to settle; and the chapel in "God's House," which she appointed them, remains to this day. And I do not doubt that there were many English Puritans in Southampton in 1620; for long before the century was over there was much persecution of dissenters there. Isaac Watts, whose hymns were to be sung so much by the children of the Pilgrim Fathers, was born at Southampton in 1674, while perhaps a score of the old "Mayflower" passengers were still alive at Plymouth, and he had begun to write religious verses before John Alden died; and while Isaac Watts was still a babe, his mother was known to sit, with him in her arms, on a stone by the door of the prison where his father was in bonds for non-conformity.

Many things remain in Southampton much as they were three hundred years ago. The High Street is still said to be, as it was in Leland's time, "one of the fairest streets that is in England." "Few of our towns," says one of the English books, "present so many relics of our ancient domestic and military architecture." There are churches on whose towers the Pilgrim Fathers looked that busy week; in St. Michael's Square, they show an ancient house said to have been occupied by Henry VIII. and Anne Boleyn; by the Arundel Tower, they show remains of the old castle first mentioned in the reign of John; and three of the an-

·cient gates and many remains of the old town walls still linger. "Coming out on the shore of the estuary of the Test, the long line of massive gray wall stretches itself out, very little changed since it assisted in repelling the French atta⌐' in 1377, or since it witnessesd t!· departure of King Edward's soldiers for Cressy, or of King Henry's for Agincourt."

Yet if John Alden could come back to Southampton to-day, I do not suppose that he would know where he was. I do not suppose that he would know where he was if he should sail down Southampton Water, with the New Forest, where William Rufus was killed, still on the right, with the ruins of Netley Abbey still on the left, and with the Isle of Wight still in front. Portsmouth, at the mouth of Southampton Water, was, when John Alden knew it, only a small town, its harbor perhaps defended, as in Leyland's time, by a "mighty chain of iron" stretched between two round towers, as was then the case also at Dartmouth and at Plymouth. Now, Portsmouth is a city of nearly two hundred thousand people, with its great docks full of men-of-war, and with batteries and ramparts innumerable grown up about Southsea Castle, which John Alden knew, and whence Nelson sailed for Trafalgar. John Alden probably knew men who had seen the great ship, "Mary Rose," go down off Portsmouth harbor, with her commander and six hundred men; but the boy, Charles Dickens, who was born at Portsmouth, doubtless heard men talk who, in the very harbor itself, had seen the "Royal George" go down, carrying the gallant Admiral Kempenfeldt and "twice four hundred men"; and in our own time men have witnessed here in Spithead the similar sad fate of the "Eurydice." Tragical indeed is the spirit which has brooded over these beautiful waters.

But the tragical fate of the "Mary Rose" and the "Royal George" and the "Eurydice" is remembered on very few of the gayly decorated boats with which the Solent is brilliant on a summer day, carrying merry people to and fro between the Isle of Wight and Portsmouth or Southampton. Perhaps it is the wedding day, a dozen or fifteen years ago, of the Princess Beatrice. Osborne House, the royal residence, and Whippingham church, in which the princess is married,—more interesting to some of us because near it Arnold of Rugby was born, and within it his father sleeps,—are in the very northernmost part of the Isle of Wight, the part which lay stretched before the Pilgrim Fathers as they sailed down Southampton Water in the "Mayflower" and the "Speedwell." If we would have a picture, therefore, of the scene of the first section of the "Mayflower's" voyage, as it is to-day, we have only to read the London papers of that morning; for all of them are full of descriptions of Osborne and the Isle of Wight. From such a paper is cut the following, on the coming of the German bridegroom:

"If a bridegroom's thoughts could by any possibility be deflected from the object of his adoration, Prince Henry, as he approached the shore at East Cowes on Monday afternoon, might have admired the gentle beauty of the spot where the Queen's sea palace stands. To some, at least, of his princely party, the scene would, no doubt, be new; and these cannot fail to have been impressed with the blending of sylvan and marine charms which the Solent exhibits all the way from Egypt Point to the Medina. There is, indeed, no gayer or pleasanter strip of inland waters anywhere to be traversed than that which winds like a broad, green ribbon between Ryde and the Needles. Its lightsome waves, thronged at this season of the year with the pleasure craft of a score of yacht clubs, and shadowed on the southern side by the foliage which overhangs the coast of the Isle of Wight almost all the way, present a succession of maritime pictures scarcely to be equaled in any part of the world for placid beauty. Mingling with the ever graceful schooners and cutters, there are grim men-of-war, picturesque old hulks, busy and burly trading ships, fishing smacks and lighters, vessels of all kinds and sizes, perpetually lending variety to the land-locked but never stagnant surface of the inlet. Nowhere does it exhibit more attractions than at the point where the towers of Osborne rise with stateliness, if not magnificence, above the lawns and woodlands of her Majesty's marine domain. The *ensemble* of the prospect hereabouts is, indeed, perfect for the seaside residence of a British sovereign. From the terraces of Osborne, the spectator can look upon the distant masts and buildings of Portsmouth dockyard on the one hand, and away on the other to the Needles and those broad sea-gates by which the ships of the Empire come home 'to their haven under the hill.' Close beneath the royal residence, the quiet wavelets of the Solent glitter, and reflect the white sails of the summer fleet which has its headquarters round the verdant foreland where the Medina's small but useful channel opens a lively harbor under the walls of Whippingham Church. A prettier place to be married in could not be discovered."

But to-day we think less of a wedding procession in the Solent than of a funeral procession. It was at Osborne House that Queen Victoria died; and on one of the days of the last January her body was borne, in the draped yacht, over these historic waters, amid the booming of guns from the long lines of war-ships, on

PLYMOUTH HARBOR.

WHERE THE MAYFLOWER LAY.

the first stage of the journey to the final resting-place at Windsor.

It was as the "Mayflower" passed into these fair waters of the Solent, shadowed then as now by the foliage of the Isle of Wight, though then there was no Osborne House, that John Alden, with his new Pilgrim friends, had his last look back toward Southampton. The last point of the Isle of Wight which they would see would be the Needles, by which to-day is Farringford, the former home of Tennyson,

"Close to the ridge of a noble down.

"Groves of pine on either hand,
To break the blast of winter stand;
And, further on, the hoary channel
Tumbles a breaker on chalk and sand."

As the Needles faded from their sight, they supposed that they were fairly and finally launched on their voyage for New England. But here comes a chapter in Bradford's Journal on "The Troubls that befell them on the coaste," which begins as follows :

"Being thus put to sea, they had not gone farr, but Mr. Reynolds ye mr. of ye leser ship complained that he found his ship so leak as he durst not put further to sea till she was mended. So ye mr. of ye biger ship (caled Mr. Joans) being consulted with, they both resolved to put into Dartmouth & have her ther searched & mended, which accordingly was done, to their great charg and losse of time and a faire winde. She was here thorowly searcht from stem to sterne, some leaks were found & mended, and now it was conceived by the workmen & all, that she was sufficiente, & they might proceede without either fear or danger. So with good hopes from hence, they put to sea againe, conceiving they should goe comfortably on, not looking for any more lets of this kind; but it fell out otherwise, for after they were gone

THE MAYFLOWER STONE.

THE BARBICAN, PLYMOUTH

to sea againe above 100 leagues without the Lands End, houlding company togeather all this while, the mr. of ye small ship complained his ship was so leake as he must beare up or sinke at sea, for they could scarce free her with much pumping. So they came to consultation againe, and resolved both ships to bear up backe againe & put into Plimouth."

Again, therefore, they turned back; and all know how, at Plymouth, the "Speedwell" was discharged as unfit for the voyage, and twenty of the passengers were left behind, including Cushman, whose melancholy letter from Dartmouth to his friend in London Bradford gives. "Friend," writes the discouraged Cushman in this letter, "if ever we make a plantation, God works a miracle; especially considering how scante we shall be of victualls, and most of all ununited amongst our selves, & devoyd of good tutors and regimente. Violence will break all.

Wher is ye meek & humble spirite of Moyses? & of Nehemiah who reedified ye walls of Jerusalem, & ye state of Israell? Is not ye sound of Rehoboams braggs daly hear amongst us? Have not ye philosiphers and all wise men observed that even in setled comonewelths, violente governours bring either them selves, or people, or boath, to ruine; how much more in ye raising of comonewealths, when ye mortar is yet scarce tempered that should bind ye wales."

Finally, a full month after the departure from Southampton, the "Mayflower" set sail alone from Plymouth for her sixty-six days' voyage across the Atlantic, with one hundred and two passengers. "Thus," says Bradford, "like Gideon's army, this small number was divided, as if the Lord by this work of his providence thought these few too many for the great work he had to do."

Six years before the "Mayflower"

425

furled her sails in the harbor of Plymouth, in New England, Captain John Smith had named that harbor Plymouth; and so it stood on the map which the Pilgrims carried with them. But Morton says, in speaking of the naming of the colony, "This name of Plymouth was so called, not only for the reason here named, but also because Plymouth in Old England was the last town they left in their native country; and for that they received many kindnesses from some Christians there." The Pilgrims, too, must have remembered their relations to the Plymouth Council, in whose domain they were. When King James parceled out America, in 1606, it was to two corporations, or Virginia companies, one established in London, the other at Plymouth; and, in 1620, the king gave a new charter, whereby henceforth the region which had been called "the North Parts of Virginia," extending from the forty-first degree of north latitude to the forty-fifth, was to be the domain of "the council established at Plymouth in the county of Devon, for the planting, ruling, ordering, and governing of New England in America."

Great numbers of men went from Devon to New England in that first half of the seventeenth century. At Dorchester, in the neighboring county of Dorset, lived Rev. John White, whose work in promoting the settlement of Massachusetts was so important. There is no county in England which is, to me, so beautiful as Devon. There is no seaport in England which is more beautiful or has had a greater history than Plymouth. Devon is full of pretty little rivers flowing through the greenest of valleys to the sea,—the Sid, the Ex, the Teign, the Dart, the

Plym, — each river giving its name to the town that lies at its mouth. Thus, Sidmouth is the town at the mouth of the Sid; and so of Exmouth, Teignmouth, Dartmouth and Plymouth. One beautiful summer afternoon, I took the steamer

PLYMOUTH GUILDHALL

at Dartmouth, that first Devon port in which the Pilgrims took refuge, and sailed up the pretty river Dart to Totness. More like an old French town than like an English town little Dartmouth seems, there at the foot of the steep hills by the mouth of the river. I said it seemed like a town that had gone to sleep; and yet, on this sunny summer afternoon, the river was full of boats, sailors and midshipmen rowing back and forth between the "Britannia," the great train-

ing ship, and the two gunboats which had just come into port.

In a few minutes, as you sail up the Dart, you come to Greenway, once the home of Sir Walter Raleigh, opposite which, in the middle of the stream, is a rock called the Anchor stone, where, according to the local legend, Raleigh smoked his first English pipe of tobacco. Further up is Sandridge, the birthplace of John Davis, the famous navigator, who in the reign of Elizabeth sailed from Dartmouth to Greenland, and after whom Davis Strait was named. And a little further still is Totness, where you take the train for Plymouth, regretting that you have not time for a visit to old Modbury, the seat for centuries of the famous family of the

ST. ANDREW'S CHURCH, PLYMOUTH

IVY BRIDGE

Champernownes, of whom a daughter married Otho Gilbert, a Devonshire gentleman, and became the mother of Sir John, Sir Humphrey, and Sir Adrian Gilbert, and next married Walter Raleigh of Fardell, and bore to him the great Sir Walter. An illustrious mother indeed, was this daughter of the Champernownes,—the mother of four of the greatest of the great Elizabethan worthies.

It is with no ordinary interest that the New Englander finds himself in old Plymouth, so closely associated with the history of the Pilgrim Fathers. He is glad to find that they are proudly remembered there. His heart beats fast when he goes to the great Town-hall to see its painted windows, and there, among the emblazoned scenes from Plymouth history,— scenes from the time of the great siege,

when Plymouth and Dartmouth were faithful to the Parliament, though all the Devon country sided with the King,—scenes from the time of Drake and the Armada,—looks on the picture of the Pilgrim Fathers embarking from the Barbican. He walks in the old Barbican, scarcely hearing the noisy men and women crying their fish. The spot where the "Mayflower" actually lay by the Barbican is now marked by a stone tablet bearing the simple inscription: "Mayflower, 1620"; and upon the adjacent wall is a memorial tablet with these words:

"On the 6th of September, 1620, in the Mayoralty of Thomas Fownes, after being 'kindly entertained and courteously used by divers Friends there dwelling,' the Pilgrim Fathers sailed from Plymouth in the Mayflower, in the Providence of God to settle in New Plymouth, and to lay the foundations of the New England States. The ancient causey whence they embarked was destroyed

428

PLYMOUTH

not many days afterwards, but the site of their Embarkation is marked by the Stone bearing the name of the Mayflower in the pavement of the adjacent Pier. This Tablet was erected in the Mayoralty of J. T. Bond, 1891, to commemorate their Departure, and the visit to Plymouth in July of that Year of a number of their Descendants and representatives."

The visitor climbs to the Hoe and to the Citadel. He looks beyond Drake's Island to the beautiful Mount Edgcumbe; he looks upon the ships-of-war and yonder great New Zealand steamer; he hears, perhaps, the sound of the mighty hammers in the dockyard, round the point. He thinks that he has looked on few scenes so fair. But his thoughts chiefly run back into the past,—to the time when Earl Hugh sailed out with the men of Devon against the French pirates; to the time of the great Elizabeth, when Plymouth was the rendezvous of those daring navigators who then did so much to extend the power and glory of England. Drake, Hawkins, Gilbert, Raleigh,—all these sailed from Plymouth, and all were Devon men. He thinks of Humphrey Gilbert sailing, in 1583, for Newfoundland, on the voyage from which he never should return: he thinks of Drake's voyage round the world, and how his ships sailed out of Plymouth to destroy the great Spanish Armada, filling all the sea outside: and he thinks of Raleigh arriving in Plymouth from his unfortunate Guiana expedition, and going up to London to meet his tragic end, two years before the "Mayflower" sailed. If he is a student of the English Commonwealth and the struggles which led up to it, he thinks of Sir John Eliot, the first of that heroic group—Pym, Hampden, Cromwell, Vane, Milton and the rest—who stood for the rights of Parliament, and remembers that Port Eliot, close by, a few miles up the St. Germans river, was his home, and that he may well have seen the "Mayflower" as she lay in Plymouth harbor. But he thinks chiefly of that little "Mayflower," and that, among all the great days in the great history of old Plymouth, there was none greater, there was none so great, as that when she sailed thence to found New England "in the name of God. Amen."

27
The
King Philip
Country

MOUNT HOPE, FROM TIVERTON.

THE KING PHILIP COUNTRY.

By William Adams Slade.

IN the upper Narragansett waters, where the expanse of blue is broadened by the outflowing tides of the two arms of the bay which reach back to Providence and Fall River, there is a neck of land whose eastern extension is a fair green hill, which gently slopes down to the waves which lap its base. This hill, noticeable for its beauty, is still oftener pointed out as Mount Hope, the home of the famous Indian king, Philip, and the headquarters of the Wampanoags, the most powerful of the tribes in the Pokanoket confederation. In the neighboring bays and rivers, these aboriginal inhabitants fished, in the surrounding country they hunted, and here they long held sway until the end of the terrible and bloody King Philip's war, when the dominion of the whites was established beyond question. Back from the hill, at the extension of the point, runs Mount Hope Neck, about nine miles, into the pleasant farming region of Swansea, which, even yet, retains much of its primitive character. Two

rivers narrow the Neck at the Swansea end, one the Warren River, which flows into Narragansett Bay, and the other the Kickemuit River, which seeks an outlet in Mount Hope Bay. In this region beside the Kickemuit Spring, which still wells forth its cool water, Massasoit, the father of King Philip, lived and ruled over his people, constantly maintaining friendly relations with the Plymouth colonists. For its aboriginal history alone the story of the King Philip country would attract the antiquarian, but still more is offered in its traditions, perhaps mingled with fact; for to it or the neighborhood the explorer, Verrazano, is reputed to have come, and, before him, the Northmen.

There is a fascination in following the adventures of the hardy Northmen in their supposed visit to this region. It was in the year 1000 that Leif, the son of Erik the Red, of Brattahlid, and his thirty-five companions made their famous voyage. Their first landing in their expedition from the North was at a place of bar-

433

DIGHTON ROCK.

high, and thence the ship was floated into the lake. This body of water has been identified by some as Mount Hope Bay, and the river as the Sakonnet.

The explorers, having reached the lake, cast anchor and went ashore. After taking counsel, they decided to remain there for the winter. Shelters were then erected, it being recorded that large houses were built. Food was abundant. The salmon in the river, which were larger than any they had seen, existed in great plenty. The nature of the country seemed so good that cattle would not require house feeding in winter, for there was no frost and the grass withered but little. But the fruitful region was as yet without a name. An incident soon occurred to make this deficiency good.

ren aspect, believed now to be Newfoundland, but which they called Hellaland (land of flat stones). Next, they put ashore at what is thought to be Nova Scotia, but which they named Markland (woodland). Sailing on, they came to an island which pleased them much, for they happened to touch the dew upon the grass and raise their fingers to the mouth, "and they thought that they had never before tasted anything so sweet." This voyage of discovery was continued

It happened one evening that a member of the company, Tyrker, a German, was missing. This grieved Leif much, for Tyrker had been long with his father and loved the son greatly. So he headed a party of twelve and went out to find the lost one. When the searchers had got a short way from the house, he was seen coming towards them. The man was highly excited, rolling his eyes, twisting his mouth, and

A NORSE BOAT.

along the coast until they came to "a place where a river flows out of a lake." Entrance to the river was made when the tide was

NORSEMAN'S ROCK, BRISTOL.

at first being wholly unable to speak the Northern tongue, talking only in German. Finally he found his senses. "I have not been much further off, but still have something to tell of," he said; "I found vines and grapes!" Then Leif asked: "But is that true, my fosterer?" And Tyrker answered, "Surely it is true, for I was bred up in a land where there is no want of either vines or grapes." This discovery by the wanderer from the icy fastnesses of the North of the product of the warmth and sun of his Southern home not only overcame him, but excited all the others. The next day they saw the vines and grapes with their own eyes, and Leif called the country Vinland. When they sailed away a cargo of the purple clusters was taken with them.

In 1002 Thowald, brother of Leif, headed the Northmen's second expedition to Vinland. The land was safely reached, and three winters were passed in the dwellings which Leif had erected. These they called Leifsbudr or Leifsbooths. The account of this expedition is not very complete, for in an exploring trip to the regions north of Cape Cod Thowald was shot and killed by the Skraelings, as they called the natives.

Several years later, in 1007, a third and important voyage was made to Vinland, Thorfinn Karlsefne setting out with three ships and 160 men. Hellaland was visited, and then Mark-

KING PHILIP.

From the cut originally published in Church's History.*

land. Landings were also made at other places. At one of these landings a member of the exploring band, Thorhall, taking eight men, left the others and traveled along the coast northward. Karlsefne and his companions meanwhile continued to the south, and during their voyage came to the river flowing through the lake, which Leif had described. As he had been, so they, too, were detained by the shallowness of the passage, but with the high water they made an entrance to the river and sailed into the mouth. They called the latter place Hóp. What significance can be attached to this name is a question, and an interesting one. It has been asserted that Hóp is the origin of the Indian name Haup or Monthaup, from which the present name, Mount Hope, is derived. The explanation of the use of the name among the Indians is that some of the explorers from the North quite likely married native women, and the names which were bestowed upon places in the vicinity were handed down long after the traces of the Northmen's blood had disappeared. This, however, is more likely conjecture than fact. It remains to be said, however, that Hóp, in Icelandic, may denote either a small recess or bay, formed by a river from the interior fall-

*See the discussion of the authenticity of this portrait and that of Colonel Church, by Dr. Dexter, in his edition of Church's History. They have very slight historical value. They were engraved by Paul Revere.

IN THE TIME OF PHILIP'S WAR.

ing into an inlet from the sea, or the land bordering upon such a bay. To this Mount Hope Bay or the shore which it washes very well corresponds. It was at this Hóp that Leif erected his dwellings and that Karlsefne, on the elevation that rises from the water, did the same.

One morning the men from the North were visited by the natives, who came in canoes. The strangers were sallow and, to Karlsefne and his followers, ill looking, having great heads of hair, large eyes and broad cheeks. This visit was at rather long range, for the natives held aloof in their canoes, looking upon the men whom they saw with great astonishment. Early in the next year they returned, and this time commenced bartering, showing considerable preference for red cloth, and giving furs and squirrel skins in exchange for it. They would have bought swords and spears, but the owners were forbidden selling

noteworthy incident of the engagement was the courage of a woman, Freydisa, a natural daughter of Erik the Red, whose bravery won the day for the Northmen. When, at the first onslaught, the latter were driven back, she sprang to the front, seized the sword of one of the men whom the enemy had killed, and struck it against her naked bosom. The natives became terrified at this apparition and fled.

Karlsefne's people decided after this

THE CLIFFS AT MOUNT HOPE.

them. Suddenly the trading was stopped by a bull which Karlsefne had brought with him, and which came out of the wood and bellowed loudly. This was too much for the natives, who rushed to their canoes and rowed away to the south. At the beginning of the succeeding winter they came back again in large numbers and made manifestations of hostility. Karlsefne caused a red shield to be borne against them, whereupon the Northmen and the natives advanced towards each other, and the first recorded battle between white men and American savages began. A

battle that their strength was not sufficient to hold out against any repeated attacks, and they returned to their home in Greenland. From this time on a number of expeditions were made to Vinland, and it is probable that a colony was established there. But it is centuries since all this occurred, and with the lapse all but a meagre account of the land of vines and grapes has disappeared. Even this account has been questioned, and the identification of the Old Stone Mill at Newport and the rock carvings at Dighton, with the remains of Northmen, is derided. Nevertheless, some

KING PHILIP'S SEAT.

investigators have brought forward a third piece of evidence to assist in proving that the bold sea rovers actually did come from their remote northern home to the Mount Hope lands. This evidence is derived from a curiously inscribed rock in Bristol, Rhode Island. This rock is of "graywacke," oblong, about ten and a half long, six and a half feet wide, and twenty-one inches thick, with a surface nearly flat. The inscriptions, now hardly visible, are strange, suggestive of those on the rock at Dighton, and certainly bear marks of great antiquity. By itself, the Bristol rock would, of course, be insufficient testimony of an early visit to the land, but, with what else has been ascribed to the Northmen, it is not without a certain value as cumulative evidence.

Without, however, going into the wearisome detail of an examination of the Vinland narrative, but passing on, it is found that the next account of this region and its aboriginal inhabitants is contained in the letter of Giovanni da Verrazano to Francis I., king of France. Verrazano commanded the

first French expedition to America sent out under royal auspices. He was, like Columbus, an Italian, having been born in Florence. In 1521 he appears as a French corsair, preying upon the commerce between Spain and America, in which capacity he is supposed to have won the notice and favor of Francis. Three years later he started on his voyage across the Atlantic in the *Dauphine*, his object being to reach Cathay by a westward route. In the spring of 1524 he discovered the American coast, sighting it off what is now North Carolina. Then he turned the *Dauphine* northward, and sailed as far as Newfoundland, then returning to France. Writing to the king from Dieppe, July 8, 1524, he tells of entering a body of water, which has been identified as Narragansett Bay, and of the natives who came to meet him. The traits which he describes as possessed by them may be taken as those of a tribe of Indians nearly related to that of Massasoit and Philip about three generations before the arrival of the *Mayflower* at Plymouth. Verrazano's account is a very early one, but how accurate it is hard to tell.

"Weighing anchor," Verrazano wrote, "we sailed fifty leagues towards the east, as the coast stretched in that direction,

KING PHILIP'S SPRING.

THE DEATH OF KING PHILIP.

and always in sight of it; at length we discovered an island [Block Island] of a triangular form, about ten leagues from the mainland, in size about equal to the island of Rhodes, having many hills covered with trees, and well peopled, judging from the great number of fires which we saw all around its shores; we gave it the name of your Majesty's illustrious mother [Louisa]. We did not land then, as the weather was unfavorable, but proceeded to another place, fifteen leagues distant from the island, where we found a very excellent harbor [Newport Harbor]. Before entering it, we saw about twenty small boats full of people, who came about our ship, uttering many cries of astonishment, but they would not approach nearer than within fifty paces; stopping, they looked at the structure of our ship, our persons and dress; afterwards they all raised a loud shout together, signifying that they were pleased. By imitating their signs, we inspired them in some measure with confidence, so that they came near enough for us to toss to them

COL. BENJAMIN CHURCH.

From the portrait originally published in Church's History

some little bells and glasses and many toys, which they took and looked at, laughing, and then came on board without fear. Among them were two kings more beautiful in form and stature than can possibly be described; one was about forty years old, the other about twenty-four, and they were dressed in the following manner: The oldest had a deer's skin about his body, artificially wrought in damask figures, his head was without covering, his hair was tied back in v a r i o u s k n o t s, around his head he wore a large chain ornamented w i t h many stones of different colors. The young man was similar in general appearance. This is the finest looking tribe and the handsomest in t h e i r costumes, that we have found in our voyage. They exceed us in size and are of a very fair complexion (?); some of them incline more to a white, and others to a tawny color; their faces are sharp, their hair long and black, upon the

adorning of which they bestow great pains; their eyes are black and sharp, their expression mild and pleasant, greatly resembling the antique. I say nothing to your Majesty of the other parts of the body, which are all in good proportion, and such as belong to well-formed men. Their women are of the same form and beauty, very graceful, of fine countenances and pleasing appearance in manners and modesty; they wear no clothing except a deer skin, ornamented like those worn by the men; some wear very rich lynx skins upon their arms, and various ornaments upon their heads, composed of braids of hair, which also hang down upon their breasts on each side. Others wear different ornaments, such as the women of Egypt and Syria use. The older and the married people, both men and women, wear many ornaments in their ears, hanging down in the oriental manner. We saw upon them several pieces of wrought copper, which is more esteemed by them than gold, as this is not valued on account of its color, but is considered by them as the most ordinary of metals — yellow being the color especially disliked by them; azure and red are those in highest estimation by them."

Verrazano stayed fifteen days among these people, being treated with the greatest hospitality. Their simple friendship, which was even exhibited with signs of joy, is similar to that which Massasoit later exhibited, but in remarkable contrast to the bloody Indian wars of the seventeenth

THE PLACE WHERE PHILIP FELL.

THE ROAD TO MOUNT HOPE.

century, which so devastated New England. Nothing was too much for Verrazano to have, and when his men were ashore for supplies the natives would willingly assist in procuring them. The voyagers went into the interior a number of times, perhaps even to Mount Hope, finding the country as pleasant as is possible to conceive, "adapted to cultivation of every kind," Verrazano wrote,

"whether of corn, wine, or oil; there are open plains twenty-five or thirty leagues in extent, entirely free from trees or other hindrances, and of so great fertility that whatsoever is sown there will yield an excellent crop. On entering the woods we observed that they might all be traversed by an army ever so numerous; the trees of which they were composed were oaks, cypresses, and others unknown in Europe. We found also apples, plums, filberts and many other fruits, but all of a different kind from ours. The animals, which are in great numbers, as stags, deer, lynxes and many other species, are taken by snares and by bows, the latter being their chief implement; their arrows are wrought with great beauty, and for the heads of them they use emery, jasper, hard marble and other sharp stones in place of iron. They also use the same kind of sharp stone in cutting down trees, and with them they construct their boats of single logs, hollowed out with admirable skill and sufficiently commodious to contain ten or twelve persons; their oars are short and broad at the end, and are managed in rowing by force of the arms alone, with perfect security, and as nimbly as they choose. We saw their dwellings,

which are of a circular form of about ten or twelve paces in circumference, made of logs split in halves, without any regularity of architecture, and covered with roofs of straw, nicely put on, which protect them from wind and rain. . . . The father and the whole family dwell together in one house in great numbers; in some we saw twenty-five or thirty persons. Their food is pulse, as with other tribes, which is here better than elsewhere, and more carefully cultivated; in the time of sowing they are governed by the moon, the sprouting of grain, and many other ancient usages. They live by

IN THE MOUNT HOPE WOODS.

LOOKING TOWARD BRISTOL FROM MOUNT HOPE.

hunting and fishing, and are long-lived. If they fall sick they cure themselves without medicine, by the heat of the fire, and their death at last comes from extreme old age. We judge them to be very affectionate and charitable towards their relatives — making loud lamentations in their adversity, and in their misery calling to mind all their good fortune. At their departure out of life, their relatives mutually join in weeping mingled with singing for a long time. This is all we could learn of them. Their region is situated in the parallel of Rome, being 41° 40' of north latitude."

On May 5, 1524, Verrazano spread his sails and left the wondering natives, perhaps, thinking that it was a god who had appeared to them. Quite ninety years afterwards another white man explored these waters in which the Florentine had so pleasantly lin-

gered, Adrian Block, the Dutch navigator, following his predecessor, giving the island which had been called Louisa his own name, and then entering Narragansett Bay. The country which here met his eyes he is said to have named Roodt Eylandt (Red Island), because of the red clay in some portions of its shores. From this name Rhode Island was easily transposed. It is thought quite likely that Block explored the bay and anchored beneath Mount Hope; but this cannot be affirmed, for no complete narrative of his voyage can now be found.

Interesting as the Mount Hope lands are for their possible associations with these early voyages, they will be much longer remembered for their Indian history. In this, as has

LOOKING TOWARD TIVERTON FROM MOUNT HOPE.

LOOKING TOWARD FALL RIVER FROM MOUNT HOPE.

been hinted, the region is abundantly rich. Here the good Massasoit held his sway, here his two sons came to the succession, wielding their influence far and wide, here the younger struck the first blow in King Philip's war, and here he died, killed by a countryman, beneath the trees which had sheltered his ancestors for generations. The history of these aboriginal inhabitants of the land is pathetically attractive, for in it is found the story of a dying race. Its great chieftain, the hero of that terrible war which bears his name, is now justly considered not as the heartless and bloodthirsty wretch which the early historians believed him to be, but as the patriotic defender of his people, his land and his religion against the encroachments of the white men from the lands across the sea.

The first of those who came to the Massachusetts shores found that all the native tribes who inhabited the region comprised within the jurisdiction of New Plymouth, Cape-wack or Nope (Martha's Vineyard) and Nantucket were known by the general name of Pokanokets in their totality made up of a number of small tribes. The most important of these were the Wampanoags, who inhabited what are now Bristol, Warren and Barrington, in Rhode Island, and a part of Rehoboth, in Massachusetts. Massasoit was their sachem, Wamsitta or Wamsutta (Alexander) succeeding him, and Metacomet or Pometacom (Philip) becoming sachem upon Wam-

LOOKING TOWARD SWANSEA FROM MOUNT HOPE.

sitta's death. Adjacent to the Wampanoags were the Pocassets, whose territory included the present Swansea, Somerset, Fall River and Tiverton. Corbitant was their sachem, and when he died his successor was Weetamore, sometimes written Weetamoe, probably his daughter, and altogether an interesting character. In Tiverton were the Sakonnets, who in Philip's war were also governed by a female sachem, Awashonks. Other neighboring tribes were the Namaskets, seated at Middleborough; the Nausites, at Eastham, on Cape Cod; the Mattachees, at Barnstable; the Monamoys, at Chatham; the Saukatucketts, at Mashpee; and the Nobsquassetts, at Yarmouth. It was, indeed, no inconsiderable confederacy which had Massasoit for its head; his rule extended even to the Nipmuck country. Previous to 1612 the Pokanokets were a powerful people; but in that year a pestilence made such deadly ravages among them that their warriors were reduced to a band of only five hundred.

The chief sachem, Massasoit, had his headquarters at this time at Sowams or Sowamset, now Warren, Rhode Island. This was one of four Indian villages on Mount Hope Neck, the other three being at Mount Hope, Bristol and Kickemuit. It was from Sowams that Massasoit went forth one day in the early spring of 1621 and appeared at Plymouth with sixty armed and painted warriors. No hostilities were attempted, for this was farthest from the sachem's mind. His only desire was to cement a strong tie of friendship between the Pokanokets and the stranger people. The result was a treaty, proposed by Governor Carver and signed by Massasoit. It is the oldest act of diplomacy recorded in New England, and the treaty was kept for over fifty years. In text it is simple, reading as follows:

"That neither he (Massasoit), nor any of his, should injure or do hurt to any of their people (*i. e.*, the settlers at Plymouth).

"That if any of his did any hurt to any of theirs, he should send the offender, that they might punish him.

"That if anything were taken away from any of theirs, he should cause it to be restored; and they should do the like to his.

"That if any did unjustly war against him, they would aid him; and if any did war against them, he should aid them.

"That he should send to his neighbor confederates to inform them of this, that they might not wrong them, but might likewise be comprised in these conditions of peace.

"That when his men came to them upon any occasion, they should leave their arms behind them.

"Lastly, that so doing, their sovereign lord, King James, would esteem him as his friend and ally."

At the same time that this treaty

MOUNT HOPE AND THE BAY, FROM FALL RIVER.

MOUNT HOPE AND THE BAY, FROM TIVERTON.

was concluded, Massasoit gave to the whites all the lands adjacent "to them and their heirs forever." It is recorded that in these transactions Massasoit was under alarm, which was shown by his trembling. This suggests the question whether the simple chieftain did not believe it his duty to give way before the newcomers as he would before any manifestation of sacred beings. Had his eyes been opened, his sensibilities sharpened, as in the case of his son a half century later, he might have pursued the same course. If he had, how quick and ruthless would have been the destruction of the colony at Plymouth!

But Massasoit was a kind and trusting man, proving always a good friend of the English. He was renowned for his honest speech, for his gentleness, and for the esteem in which he was held by those under him. Did he ever give way to anger or passion, it was only a transitory burst. He governed his people well, and was venerated by them. Twice he was visited by Edward Winslow, as the representative of the Plymouth colony. On one of these occasions he was reclaimed to life by Winslow's superior medical

skill; and on the other occasion, "John Hamden, a gentleman of London," who was wintering at Plymouth, and who has been believed by some to be the great English patriot,[*] accompanied Winslow on his visit. Roger Williams, also, is numbered among the Englishmen who acknowledged Massasoit as their benefactor.

Far different from this noble-spirited chieftain is the petty sachem of the Pocassets, Corbitant, who owed the Wampanoags allegiance, and who had his seat at Mattapoisett, but a few miles from Mount Hope. He was a crafty Indian and opposed to the whites, whom he viewed as intruders. On one occasion Captain Miles Standish had to lead out a force in order to subdue him. Corbitant was intimidated and accepted the good offices of Massasoit to reconcile him to the English. Later, he came to Plymouth with several other chiefs, all of whom subscribed to a paper and acknowledged themselves as subjects of King James. Where or how Corbitant died is not known. It has been suggested that the skeleton in armor found at

[*] See article, "Did John Hampden come to New England?" by Edwin D. Mead, in the *New England Magazine*, September and October, 1889.

Fall River and which the poet Longfellow associated with the Old Stone Mill at Newport was that of the Pocassets' sachem. This skeleton was buried in a sitting posture, and the body was found to be enveloped in a covering of coarse bark under which, on the breast, was a plate of brass, and below this a belt of brass tubes, encircling the body and enclosing arrows of brass. The brass plate was so corroded that it was impossible to tell whether or not anything was engraved upon it.

Weetamore, when she came to rule over the Pocassets upon Corbitant's death, was easily inspired to harbor the same ill will towards the whites. She married Wamsitta and, upon

his death, Petananuet, who was better known as Peter Nunnuit. In Philip's war she was a faithful ally to that doughty chieftain, and patiently suffered every reverse with him. She was an intelligent woman, and "as potent a sachem as any round about her, * * * having as much corn, land, and men at her command." Mrs. Rowlandson describes her in the narrative of her own captivity among the Indians as follows: "A severe and proud dame she was; bestowing

GLIMPSES OF SWANSEA.

every day in dressing herself near as much time as any gentry in the land, powdering her hair and painting her face, going with her necklaces, with jewels in her ears, and bracelets upon her hands. When she had dressed herself, her work was to make girdles of wampum and beads." But there came a time when her work was cut short. One night in August, in the second year of Philip's war, the camp of Weetamore and her followers was betrayed to the English. The Indian princess attempted to escape across the Titicut (Taunton) River on a raft, but was drowned in the passage. Her body was afterwards found on the Swansea shore, and her head was cut off and set on a pole at the neighboring settlement at Taunton. Here many of her subjects were held as prisoners, and the gruesome spectacle presented to them was the cause of great outcries of grief.

What little is known of Weetamore's short-lived husband, Wamsitta, has its own part in the interesting history of the time. Wamsitta was Massasoit's elder son, and Metacomet his younger. These two, while at Plymouth, after the death of their father, professed great friendship for the whites, and asked for English names. Governor Prince accordingly called the elder Alexander, and the younger Philip, probably from the famous Macedonian rulers. Alexander succeeded his father as chief sachem of the Pokanokets, but had not served

THE MYLES GARRISON HOUSE, SWANSEA.

long before rumors came to Plymouth that he was plotting rebellion against the English. Major Josiah Winslow was sent out with an armed force to arrest him and bring him back to answer to the charge. At this time all was at peace between the Indians and the English, and so the approach of the men from Plymouth occasioned no surprise among the red men. But when Alexander was informed what their mission was, his passion knew no bounds. Brooding over the insult, as he was escorted towards his place of trial, he fell into a fever, and as he steadily grew worse, his Indian companions begged the whites that they might take him home, promising that they would return with him when he had recovered. Permission was granted, and the chieftain, broken in spirit and body, was placed on a litter and tenderly carried through the woods and clearings towards Mount Hope. The party reached the Titicut safely and embarked in canoes. Alex-

ander, however, had become much weaker, and it was deemed best to go ashore and give him rest on the cool, green banks, beneath the shade of the spreading trees. This was done, and there, on the banks of the beautiful river which before long was to claim his ministering wife, the proud sachem joined his father, Massasoit, in the red man's paradise.

The Wampanoags now looked to Philip as their chieftain, and a chieftain in spirit and in deed he truly proved to be. His principal habitation and that of his followers was made at Mount Hope; and thenceforth that was the centre of his operations. For some time there was no disturbing incident to mar the relations between the savages and the whites, Massasoit's treaty being renewed by Philip; and this is the period for one to investigate if he would inform himself as to the nature and condition of this famous Wampanoag tribe before their great uprising. A visitor from the communities to the east would have found the larger portion of them inhabiting a village situated in the open on a slope of the hill. Near by is a spring of clear water, to which the squaws are accustomed to resort for their daily supply. Not all of the year

ON GARDNER'S NECK, SWANSEA.

do the whole number live here, as hunting and fishing trips are frequently made for considerable distances to the north and northwest; but this is the tribe's headquarters, and its own territory is chiefly confined to Mount Hope and the immediately adjacent lands. The houses of the village are built with a frame of poles, placed in circular form, the tops being bound

wind blows. The fire is kindled in the house in the middle of the floor, and lodgings are made on skins about the fire. Near to the houses are the magazines, which are dug in the earth and used for storing provisions. Corn is always laid away in quantities, and fish and meats are preserved by salting, an art not long since learned of the English.

The visitor would find the people

PAINTING OF AWASHONKS ON THE HOUSE OF CHARLES E. WILBOUR, LITTLE COMPTON, R. I.

COL. CHURCH'S GRAVE AT LITTLE COMPTON.

SITE OF COL. CHURCH'S HOUSE, LITTLE COMPTON.

"TREATY ROCK," LITTLE COMPTON.

hospitable, generous with their food, and offering the best lodgings at their command. Their clothing he would notice to be varied; some wore the skins of native animals, and others those of animals of other regions, secured by barter with friendly tribes. There was a certain ingenuity in the use of the skins, the hairy side being worn next to the body in winter, and reversed in summer. Sometimes very striking coats were made of turkey feathers, which were fastened together with twine. Shoes were made of

together with the tough bark of the walnut tree. This frame is covered with mats, some made of reeds and others of flags, sewed together with threads of Indian hemp. Places are left for doors, which are also covered with mats, and left opened or closed according to the direction in which the

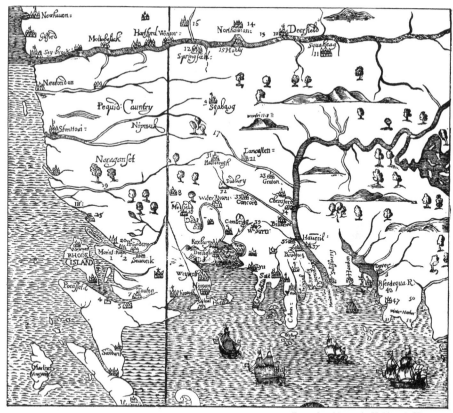

From the old map in Hubbard's History.

THE THEATRE OF PHILIP'S WAR.

moose skins, and stockings of deer skins. The habits of life were simple, and little occurred to break the monotony. Not far away were numbers of "praying Indians," converted by John Eliot and the Mayhews; but Philip and most of his tribe professed with pride the religion of their fathers, and scorned the teachers from across the great water. As was common among the New England Indians, they were probably not without knowledge of God, a Great Spirit who, tradition said, had made one man and one woman, commanded them to live together, beget children, kill deer, beasts, birds, fish and fowl, and do their pleasure in all things. But their posterity was evil, and so the sea was let in upon them, and the greater part, who were wrong-doers were drowned. The latter went to Sanaconquam,

where the devil reigns supreme. The others populated the earth, and, as they have died from time to time, they have gone to the house of Kytan, which is in the neighborhood of the setting sun. This being, according to the accepted belief, makes the corn and the trees to grow, and the good Indians whom he calls to him are always well cared for. A good man is one who does not lie or steal, and when he dies he will live with Kytan forever. Such was the thought in regard to immortality, and it was potent in regulating Indian conduct.

Once, when Eliot had tried to convert Philip, the latter took him by the button and said he cared no more for his gospel than he did for the button. Despite this assertion, Philip could but have seen how strong in number the praying Indians were. At an early

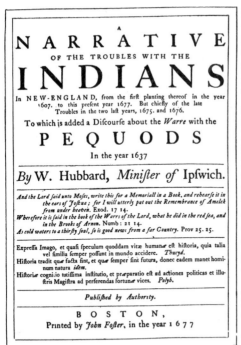

A

NARRATIVE

OF THE TROUBLES WITH THE

INDIANS

In NEW-ENGLAND, from the firſt planting thereof in the year
1607. to this preſent year 1677. But chiefly of the late
Troubles in the two laſt years, 1675. and 1676.

To which is added a Diſcourſe about the *Warre* with the

P E Q U O D S

In the year 1637

By W. Hubbard, *Miniſter of* Ipſwich.

*And the Lord ſaid unto Moſes, write this for a Memoriall in a Book, and rehearſe it in
the ears of Joſhua; for I will utterly put out the Remembrance of Amelek
from under heaven.* Exod. 17 14.
*Wherefore it is ſaid in the book of the Warrs of the Lord, what he did in the red ſea, and
in the Brooks of Arnon.* Numb : 21 14.
As cold waters to a thirſty ſoul, ſo is good news from a far Country. Prov 25. 25.

Expreſſa Imago, et quaſi ſpeculum quoddam vitæ humanæ eſt hiſtoria, quia talia
vel ſimilia ſemper poſſunt in mundo accidere. *Thucyd.*
Hiſtoria tradit quæ facta ſint, et quæ ſemper ſint futura, donec eadem manet homi-
num natura *idem.*
Hiſtoriæ cognitio tutiſſima inſtitutio, et præparatio eſt ad actiones politicas et illu-
ſtris Magiſtra ad perferendas fortunæ vices. *Polyb.*

Publiſhed by Authority.

B O S T O N ,
Printed by *John Foſter*, in the year 1 6 7 7

FAC-SIMILE OF THE TITLE-PAGE OF HUBBARD'S
HISTORY.

date there were some twenty Indian churches on Cape Cod, no small number of converts to Christianity upon the islands of Nantucket, Martha's Vineyard, and seven villages or towns of the praying Indians in Massachusetts, in which the English had established ecclesiastical and civil government. These Indians had pastors, elders, and deacons, and generally schoolmasters of their own race, and also rulers and constables. Still more, the labors of Eliot had borne fruit in the Nipmuck country, where there were also seven villages of praying Indians. Philip, stern adherent as he was to the religion which had been handed down in his tribe from a time to which their minds could not reach back, must have viewed all this with a silent opposition which boded no good will and which finally made itself a potent cause for war against the English.

It is not safe, however, to give too large a place to resistance to the Chris-

tian religion as the cause of Philip's war. One wrong after another had been heaped upon the red men by the whites, whether consciously or through lack of tact and failure to understand the true condition of affairs. The Indians had been constantly made amenable to the laws of the English, forbidden to perform acts which they had always looked upon as their natural rights; and in other ways collisions had been occasioned between the two races. The simple nature of the Indians doubtless caused them to believe that when they parted with their lands it was not for good, and their wonder must have been great that, instead of receiving them back again, fresh shiploads of people continually arrived at the coast settlements and kept pushing on into the heart of their best hunting territories. Philip's proud and fiery nature could not brook this accumulation of wrongs; and he had besides a personal grief in the loss of his brother Alexander. His feelings were exhibited in a speech of true eloquence which he is reported to have made when he was approached in the interests of peace. Said he:

"The English who first came to this country were but a handful of people, forlorn, poor and distressed. My father was the sachem. He relieved their distress in the most kind and hospitable manner. He gave them land to build and plant upon. He did all in his power to serve them. Others of their own countrymen came and joined them. Their numbers rapidly increased. My father's counsellors became uneasy and alarmed lest, as they were possessed with firearms, which was not the case with the Indians, they should finally undertake to give law to the Indians, and take from them their country. They therefore advised to destroy them before they should become too strong, and it should be too late. My father was also the father of the English. He represented to his counsellors and warriors that the English knew many sciences which the Indians did not; that they improved and cultivated the earth, and raised cattle and fruits, and that there was sufficient room in the country for both the English and the Indians. His advice prevailed. It was concluded to give victuals to the English. They flourished and increased. Experience taught that the advice of my father's counsellors was right. By various means the English got possessed of a great part of his territory. But he still remained their friend till he died. My elder brother became sachem. They pretended to suspect him of evil designs against them. He was seized and confined, and thereby thrown into sickness and died. Soon after I became sachem they disarmed all my people. They tried my people by their own laws, and assessed damages against them which they could not pay. Their land was taken. At length a line of division was agreed upon between the English (and my people, and I myself was to be responsible. Sometimes the cattle of the English would come into the cornfields of my people, for they did not make fences like the English. I must then be seized and confined till I sold another tract of my country for satisfaction of all damages and costs. Thus tract after tract is gone. But a small part of the dominion of my ancestors now remains. I am determined not to live till I have no country."

summated war was precipitated, in June, 1675. The Indians were excited over the execution at Plymouth of three of their companions, who were believed to be guilty of the murder of Sausaman, a praying Indian, who had served as an informant to the English. Philip's restraint could control his men no longer. They emerged from their village at Mount Hope, reinforced by accessions from other tribes, and began to rob houses and kill cattle in the border town of Swansea. This was on June 20, and four days later the massacre began. Nine of the inhabitants of Swansea were slain and seven wounded. The alarm of war spread throughout the colonies; and scarcely were the people aroused when the fearful wrath of the savages was made known far and wide. Houses were

Such a speech as this truly shows a patriotic man, a genuine leader, and the careful guardian of his people's rights. If it is so, as it has been said, that he was called King Philip in mockery, a true king he turned out to be, keen in understanding, wise in counsel, politic in action, and altogether one to command respect. His plottings against the English were his last resource, and it is even recorded that he wept when the first bloodshed occurred. This interpretation of the great Indian's character is the one most commonly accepted; but how vastly different is it from that of contemporaneous writers! Colonel Church called the dead Philip "a doleful, great, naked, dirty beast."

Philip had been planning to annihilate the English for some time; but before his arrangements were con-

Entertaining Paſſages

Relating to

Philip's WAR

WHICH

Began in the Month of June, 1 6 7 5.

AS ALSO OF

EXPEDITIONS

More lately made

Againſt the Common Enemy, and Indian Rebels, in the Eaſtern Parts of New=England:

WITH

Some Account of the Divine Providence

TOWARDS

Benj. Church Eſqr;

By T. C.

B O S T O N: Printed by *B. Green*, in the Year, 1 7 1 6.

FAC-SIMILE OF THE TITLE-PAGE OF CHURCH'S HISTORY.

ANNAWAN ROCK, REHOBOTH.

formidable appearance, with their painted faces, their hair done up like a cock's comb, and with their powder-horns and shot-bags on their backs. But Church, nothing daunted, called them wretches and said they thirsted for their neighbors' blood. He even told Awashonks the best thing she could do would be to knock the six Mount Hopes in the head, and he advised her not only to refrain from joining Philip, but to apply to the governor of Plymouth for protection. Church then hastened to Pocasset, where he found Peter Nunnuit and Weetamore. They, too, confirmed the report that war was soon to break out. These statements were sufficient to take Church to Plymouth, where he told all he knew. He then returned to Swansea, where soldiers were sent and stationed, some at Bourn's garrison at Mattapoisett, some at Brown's garrison at Wannamoiset, and still others at Myles' garrison on New Meadow Neck. All of these garrisons were within a comparatively short distance of Mount Hope. As the troops prepared to occupy them, the full danger confronting them dawned upon the inhabitants of New England, and there was an outbreak of superstitious fear. An unusual black spot upon the surface of the moon was interpreted by some as an Indian's scalp. Others thought that not long before the disc had borne the form of an Indian bow. Omens there were in plenty, and they were all read for their bearing upon the pending conflict.

The soldiers in the garrisons, however, had more important things to at-

sacked, towns burned, men, women and children tomahawked or carried off into captivity, and vengeance for real or fancied wrongs wrought everywhere with merciless fury.[*]

The English were first made aware of the fact of their close proximity to war through the famous Benjamin Church. Philip had sent six of his men to Awashonks, the squaw sachem of the Sakonnets, to enlist her sympathies and those of her tribe in the projected outbreak. The men had crossed over from Mount Hope and had gained an attentive ear. But before proceeding, Awashonks planned a great dance, at which the matter was to be decided, and invited Church to it, in order that his advice might be heard. When the latter arrived, he found Awashonks in a foaming sweat, leading the dance. This affair was quickly stopped when he was seen, and he was told that the Mount Hope Indians reported that the Uupame men (the English) were making preparations for war. The Mount Hopes were summoned; and they made a

* See "King Philip's War," an Old South Lecture, by Caroline C. Stecker, in the *New England Magazine*, December, 1890; also the passage upon Philip's War in Rufus Choate's address in "The Romance of New England History," reprinted in the *New England Magazine*, November, 1897. The Editor's Table of the last (June) number of the *New England Magazine* was entirely devoted to the subject of Philip's War and the King Philip Country, occasioned by the Old South historical pilgrimage to Mount Hope. Considerable attention was given to the literature of the subject.

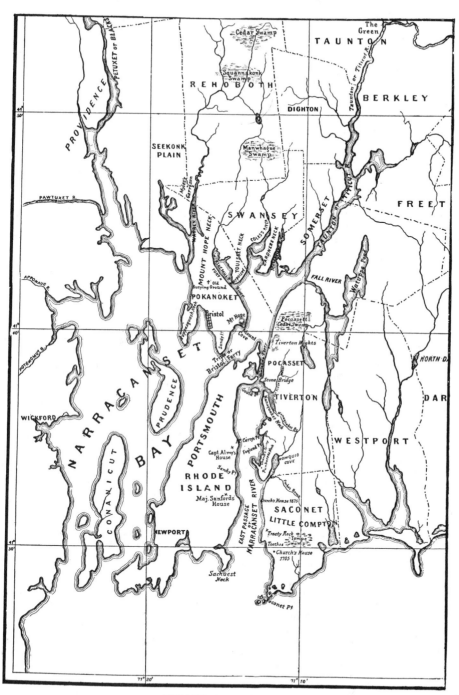

THE KING PHILIP COUNTRY.

tend to than omens. The main body of the men were at Myles' garrison house, that of the good pastor of the Baptist church in Swansea, which was the first of the denomination in Massachusetts. Some of the Indians, flushed by their recent exploits, drew near enough to the garrison to shoot down two of the sentinels. Thus provoked to action, a sally was made by the English, and the company crossed the bridge by the house, known as Myles' Bridge, only to be dispersed by an ambuscade of about a dozen of the enemy. Church was one of the attacking party, and his conduct was characterized by the same coolness that he displayed throughout the war. On the next day the temporary discomfiture of the English was made good by a sortie upon the Indians, who lost five or six of their number. This was on Tuesday, June 29; and that night Philip and his forces abandoned Mount Hope, crossing the river to Pocasset,—for had they remained they would have been caught in a veritable *cul de sac* and compelled to fight a decisive battle. It was this escape which enabled them to prosecute the war with such vigor and with such terrible results.

On Wednesday morning the whole English force marched down Mount Hope Neck. About a mile and a half from Myles' Bridge they came upon some houses recently burned, and near by, as Hubbard writes, "a Bible newly torn, and the leaves scattered about by the enemy, in hatred of our religion therein revealed." Some distance further on, in Kickemuit, they saw the heads of eight Englishmen, killed near the head of Mattapoisett Neck, stuck up on poles near the highway. Continuing, they came to Philip's camp, where a few prowling dogs were the only signs of life. The Indians had gone from Mount Hope, "where," to quote Hubbard once more, "Philip was never seen after till the next year, when he was by a divine mandate sent back, there to receive the reward of his wickedness, where he first began

his mischief." Church and a small band of volunteers determined to cross the river and seek out the enemy. This was accordingly done, and on the shore the trail was found after a first night passed in a vain ambush. This trail was followed towards Sakonnet for some distance, when fresh tracks were discovered, and a little later the party were attacked by a band of Indians outnumbering it fifteen to one. This heroic encounter was waged for six hours in a peas-field, whence it gets its name, "the peas-field fight." Aside from the courage of the men, the inspiring confidence of their leader is to be noted. He told his comrades that he had hitherto observed so much of the remarkable and wonderful providence of God in preserving them, that it encouraged him to believe, with much assurance, that God would continue to keep them safe and that not a hair of their head should fall to the ground. He bade them be patient, courageous, and prudent, sparing of their ammunition, and he had no doubt that they would yet come well off. His men withstood the strong Indian force valiantly, and made use of what shelter they could find beneath stones heaped into piles. Finally a sloop was seen on the river, and quickly bore to their relief. The deliverance Church characteristically ascribed "to the glory of God and his protecting providence."

Another of the early battles of this war followed ten days after, when Philip, now joined by Weetamore, fortified himself in the great Pocasset swamp, a little south of the present city of Fall River. The army of the English penetrated the swamp, and a sharp contest ensued, with the final result of the flight of the Indians, who escaped across the Titicut. The English sustained the loss of sixteen men. Philip, while crossing the Seekonk plain in his westward flight, was discovered by the people of Rehoboth, who, headed by the Rev. Samuel Newman, their minister, gave pursuit and killed a number of his men without losing any of their own. Philip, however, succeeded in effecting a junction with the Nipmucks, who were already in arms, and henceforth Mount Hope was at a considerable distance from the theatre of the terrible scenes which ensued.

The war was carried on with relentless fury. There was no fighting on open ground, but all was a matter of ambushes and surprises, of sudden attacks and as sudden disappearances. One town after another was kindled by the incendiary's torch. Brookfield, Deerfield, Springfield, Hadley, Lancaster, Medfield, Weymouth, Groton, Marlborough, Rehoboth, Warwick and Providence all were burned. Alliances were made with different tribes, and the contest was widely extended. Once during this time Philip came in the neighborhood of his old haunts at Mount Hope, being present when Rehoboth was burned. There is still preserved the chair which he sat in as he watched the houses being consumed, and which was partly fired itself when he arose to go. In more peaceful times it is told that Philip used to visit the owner of the chair, and the latter was brought out as a kind of throne of state for the Indian potentate. Now all was different. War was continued with unabated vigor. Captain Wadsworth and fifty men marching to the relief of Sudbury had been overwhelmed by a large body of Indians, and every man slain. The same fate had attended Captain Pierce with a like number of English and some friendly Indians. The Narragansetts, while defeated in the great Kingstown fight, were still strong and doing great damage; and, all told, it was an extremely dark time for the English.

During the second summer of the war, however, the tide of affairs began to turn. The Indians were defeated in a number of successive battles, large numbers were either taken or slain, and Philip in each of these ways lost some of his most valiant captains. The contest between the English under

A BRIEF
HISTORY
OF THE
VVAR
WITH THE
INDIANS
IN
NEW-ENGLAND.

From *June* 24. 1675. (when the firſt *Engliſhman* was Murdered by the *Indians*) to *Auguſt* 12. 1676. when *Philip*, alias *Metacomet*, the principal Author and Beginner of the War was ſlain.

Wherein the Grounds, Beginning, and Progreſs of the War, is ſummarily expreſſed. Together with a ſerious EXHORTATION to the Inhabitants of that Land.

By *INCREASE MATHER*, Teacher of a Church of Chriſt in *Boſton* in *New-England*.

Lev. 26. 25. *I will bring a Sword upon you, that ſhall avenge the quarrel of the Covenant.*
Pſal. 107. 43. *Whoſo is wiſe and will obſerve theſe things, even they ſhall underſtand the loving Ki-dneſs of the Lord.*
Jer. 22..15. *Did not thy Father do Judgment and Juſtice, and it was well with him?*

Segnius irritant animos demiſſa per aures,
Quam quæ ſunt oculis commiſſa fidelibus.   *Horat.*
Lege Hiſtoriam ne fias Hiſtoria.   *Cic.*

London, Printed for *Richard Chiſwell*, at the Roſe and Crown in St. *Pauls* Church-Yard, according to the Original Copy Printed in New-England. 1676.

FAC-SIMILE OF THE TITLE PAGE OF MATHER'S HISTORY.

Captain Church, and Philip and his warriors, at a point between Taunton and Bridgewater, on July 31, 1676, marks the beginning of the end. In this engagement the Indians had to retreat hastily, and the English captured a number of their women and children, among them Philip's wife and nine-year-old son. Six days afterwards Weetamore was drowned in her effort to escape from the English.

Philip at length, worn out by the rigor of the campaigns he had undertaken, and sick at heart, resolved to return to his ancestral home at Mount Hope. The loss of his wife and son overcame him. "My heart breaks," he said, "now I am ready to die." Nevertheless, while there was life in him he was ready to fight. Upon reaching the Mount he encamped in a swamp for a brief wait before continuing hostilities. One of the accompanying Indians, believing that the reverses suffered were sufficient, to cause the consideration of peace with the English, proposed the matter to Philip, and was shot on the spot. This incident was reported to Captain Church by the murdered Indian's brother, Alderman, who offered to guide the soldiers to Philip's camp. This proposal was accepted, and at daybreak, August 12, 1676, the place was surrounded by the whites, who now had the Wampanoag chieftain safely entrapped. A friendly Indian and a white man were placed behind every available shelter, and each one was charged to use extreme care not to injure those on his own side. After all the preliminaries had been arranged and the men warned, Captain Church turned to his companion, Major Sandford, and said: "Sir, I have so placed them that it is scarce possible Philip can escape." The same moment a gun was discharged, and a moment later it was followed by a volley from the English. The Indians were wholly surprised, and started to run. Philip was one of the foremost, and started directly upon two of the ambush. The latter let their man come within a fair distance, when the Englishman's gun missed fire, but his ally, who was none other than Alderman, taking careful aim, put one bullet into the great leader's heart and another about two inches from it. Philip fell upon his face in the mud and water of the swamp. And here died the most famous Indian of colonial times within the shadow of his favorite home.

Old Annawan, Philip's great captain, restored confidence to the dismayed Indians, crying out, "Iootash! Iootash!" (Stand to it! Fight stoutly!) But a successful stand could not be made, and there was a general flight, Annawan being among those who escaped.

Philip's head was cut off and his body quartered, Captain Church forbidding a burial. The head and one hand were given to Alderman as a reward for shooting him, and the renegade Indian afterwards gained at least a partial livelihood by putting them on exhibition.

Sixteen days after Philip was slain, on August 28, Annawan was taken. His capture was effected by Captain Church, and was accomplished without the firing of a gun or the loss of a single man. The whole affair has well been said to furnish one of the most astonishing instances of daring intrepidity recorded in history. Annawan was securely encamped in the great Squannakonk swamp in Rehoboth, and was accompanied by a considerable band of Philip's most resolute warriors. The particular fastness chosen was beneath a great rock some seventy or eighty feet long and twenty-five or thirty feet high, and which is pointed out to this day as Annawan's rock. While Church was at Plymouth, whence he had gone after Philip's death, a messenger came from Rehoboth, saying that Annawan was scouring the woods and doing much harm, both there and in Swansea. Church and a number of men, both English and friendly Indians, immediately set out after him. At Mount Hope Neck, Church learned of Annawan's whereabouts from an Indian and a young squaw who had just come from his camp. This knowledge obtained, the Englishman with one white companion and a small number of Indians started out to seize the famous captain that very night, the captured savages acting as guides. When the camp was neared, Church found that the only entrance to it was to be gained by letting one's self down the big rock from bush to bush and crag to crag; and this meant complete exposure to the enemy. The two guides were thereupon ordered to go down into the camp with baskets upon their backs, that no intrigue might be suspected. This order was obeyed, and in the shadow of the two, while a squaw below was making considerable noise pounding corn, Church and a few men descended and approached

Annawan. The old Indian was completely surprised and quickly forced to surrender. In acknowledgment of his obeisance, he later gave Church Philip's wampum belts, two horns of glazed powder and a red blanket, which he said were Philip's regalia, and in which he appeared whenever he sat in state. A few days after Annawan was beheaded at Plymouth. With him, Tispaquin, or Tuspaquin, a chief of the Narragansetts, whose capture had immediately succeeded his own, was also executed in a like manner. The other royal prisoners at Plymouth, Philip's wife and son, were sold into slavery, probably in one of the West India Islands.

The war virtually closed with Annawan's capture. It had been indeed a baptism of fire and of blood for the colonists of New England. At least six hundred of the English were killed, either in battle or by open murder, and an equal number of buildings were destroyed by fire. In addition, more than one hundred pounds sterling were expended by the colonies to make reparation for losses sustained besides those occasioned by the destruction of goods and cattle. Such was the war which Philip directed from Mount Hope and which, sanguinary and destructive as it was, all but crushed out the early settlements in New England.

Yet this Mount and the lands which bear its name are worthy of note for more than the story of the terrible war and the narrative of early voyages. They have tales to tell of peaceful days and even of other wars. Of the settlements established in the locality, several grew to considerable proportions and prospered as headquarters of trade with the Indies and with other lands. Not only did commerce in silks and spices increase, but also, be it recorded, a considerable slave trade sprang up, and many were the slavers which were sent out of the port of Bristol. Yet the inhabitants of these lands were lovers of freedom, loyal to their country, and fought vigorously for independence from British rule; and in the first and second wars against Great Britain some of the most feared and most successful of the Yankee privateers sailed from this region. Until recent years the section retained many of its early characteristics, everything about it savoring of age and history. But changes are now gradually taking place. Rehoboth, which hitherto has never been cut by a steel rail of any kind, is soon to be invaded by the modern trolley car, and from its windows Annawan's rock can be pointed out. And Mount Hope, the most interesting place in the whole neighborhood, is to be the situation of a pleasure-making enterprise. Yet, should greater changes than these occur, they can never destroy the thrilling history and interesting associations of the King Philip Country.

28
Yachting Around Cape Cod

YACHTING AROUND CAPE COD.

THE schooner yacht Idler, with a cabin party of eight on board, had sailed from Boston on a pleasant June forenoon, and with an ebbing tide and gentle southerly breeze had come past Point Allerton, and now, in the early afternoon, on the calmest of summer seas, was passing Minot's-Ledge light.

We of that party were invited to pass a month on board, cruising around Cape Cod and in Long Island Sound, loitering here and there as we liked. Some of us — the two Wellesley-College girls and a Yale man, beside Dick (the boy of the party, and my son) — were having their first sea experience; but the owner, Doctor Bell, and his wife had often cruised this way, while Colonel Graham, a cousin of the doctor's, and I had only now and then travelled by steamer; so that to all the cabin guests a cruise on a large yacht was a novel adventure, and we were prepared to see and enjoy all, —

"Cold, heat, and moist and dry,"

as the hymn says.

How delightful it all seemed to us! The air from the heated land behind us rose quiveringly, but we were enjoying a cool, bracing breeze. Nearing the tall granite monument, which defies the storms on the outer Cohasset ledges, we were all interested in watching a little boat that was moored at its foot, and seeing ladies and gentlemen, one by one, hoisted in a chair by a rope to an opening in the tower, when they were swung in to visit the keepers, who are very glad to see visitors when the sea is quiet enough to permit the approach of

MINOT'S LEDGE LIGHT.

461

The breeze continued to drop and the air grew chillier. We all sought our wraps. Presently a wisp of gray fog came drifting by, and then our sails began to slat, and finally filled on the other side. We had passed into an easterly wind and a fog-bank was before us.

"Now I

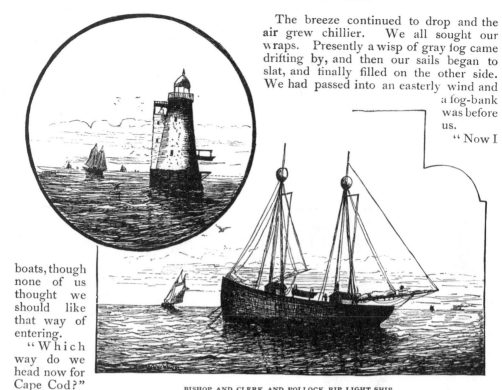

BISHOP AND CLERK AND POLLOCK RIP LIGHT SHIP.

boats, though none of us thought we should like that way of entering.

"Which way do we head now for Cape Cod?" asked Dick, as we left the light tower astern.

"Just about south-east," answered Dr. Bell; "and Race Point is about twenty-six miles from here."

"Shall we get there before dark?" asked one.

"I hardly think so," said the doctor. "Probably it will be moonlight when we get to Provincetown."

"Oh, how charming that will be!" we all exclaimed.

So chatting, we gayly sailed on. The wind fell a little, and the air grew cooler. The captain took his glass and scanned the horizon, and then said quietly to the doctor, "The vessels coming round the cape have the wind the other way;" who replied, "Yes, I have noticed."

The shore was now well astern, and the high lands of Marshfield lay low in the horizon. "It is as far to return as it would be to go on," said the captain.

"What became of that distant schooner?" suddenly asked the Yale man. "A minute ago I saw her, and now I can't find her."

"Nothing unusual, I guess," said the doctor, cheerfully. "Vessels frequently pass suddenly out of sight that way at sea."

know what became of the vessel," said the student.

"Shall we be lost?" asked Dick, anxiously.

"Oh, no!" said Captain Blake. "This may hold on, or it may blow away; but we have plenty of sea-room. We will keep right on. We shall hear fog-signals before we come near any land."

A silence settled down over us all. The sun still shone two hours high, and the sky was bright and blue behind and over us, but at intervals we were enveloped in the gray mists driving by, great ragged masses which the wind had detached from the heavy cloud-bank which lay on the sea, and had sent on as *avant-couriers*.

The look-out forward had brought up a great horn, and now and then sounded a hoarse blast. Once we heard an answering horn, and then we blew ours at regular intervals, till the other sound grew fainter, and was lost.

The fog was all around us; no more blue sea or blazing sun, only a cold, cheerless gloom. No one felt like talking. The chill had penetrated even our spirits. Unconsciously we grouped ourselves as we might have done in an hour of danger. My boy had crept to my side. The Wellesley girls were looking appealingly at the Yale man. We were all thinking how helpless we were to combat some of the simplest and most frequent operations of nature. We may even in some degree make the dreadful lightning our servant, and we may ride exultingly on the wings of the strong winds; but when or how may we ever obtain any mastery over this silent, shapeless enemy, the fog? How arrest its coming or hasten its going?

As we came on deck again we were delighted to find that the fog was thinner. Now and then, as it drifted by, we could see, through rifts in it, the clear blue sky above. All at once we came into a clear air. The white sand-hills of the cape were bathed in the last rays of the now setting sun. Race Point was just ahead. The fog still hung over the sea behind us, but the hot air from the land had dissipated it here.

PROVINCETOWN BY MOONLIGHT: IN THE FOG.

> "'Twere all as well to bid a cloud to stand,
> Or hold a running river with the hand."

And still we sailed on. How strange it seemed! The veil opened to let us pass, and closed behind us as we advanced. Our vessel seemed to typify human life: a steady, onward-going into the unseen; the ever-closing past, and the ever-opening future.

The steward's voice, calling us to supper, broke the long reverie, and, though it was hardly in consonance with our mood to obey his summons, we all did so.

"What has become of the fog?" asked Dick.

"That's all safe," said the captain. "We are lucky now to see our way into Provincetown. I think that by to-morrow morning you will not need to ask where the fog is."

"What do you mean," asked Mabel Wellesley, as Dick had christened the older of the girls.

"Why, later," said the doctor, "the land will become cooled, and will not dry up the fog. If this east wind keeps on all night we sha'n't see land to-morrow morning."

Changing our course, we now followed the trend of the coast-line to pass around the long hook which encloses the fine harbor of Provincetown. What a dreary prospect lay before us! A long white sand-beach, backed by brown sand-hills, sloping steeply to the shore at the place where the Race-Point light tower stands, and the life-saving station, — a solitary cluster of buildings in the sandy desolation, — and then a long, steep, white beach, backed by innumerable white sand-hillocks, here and there scrubbily wooded, and beyond all the tops of several church-spires of the town.

Soon after we changed our course the lamp was lighted in the tower, for it must burn from the moment of sun-setting to that of sun-rising; and with a prosperous breeze we were, in less than half an hour, off the end of the long waste of sand, and ready to turn north-easterly to pass inside the sheltering hook of the cape. Here we could see behind us the Race-Point light, burning white, but intensified at intervals by flashes; while Wood End, near by, sent its frequent red gleams over the water, and the light on Long Point, at the very extremity of the hook, shone steadily white. Six miles away, seen over the land, blazed with unvarying radiance from its lofty situation the noble Highland light, the first to greet the incoming mariner approaching Cape Cod. We were deeply interested in watching these lights, as one after another they came into view, until at last they were all in sight at one time.

"Now you can understand," said Dr. Bell, "that it is no easy matter to locate a light-house properly, so that it shall be seen from all the needed directions, yet not in a confusing way; and, besides, each, by day and night, must have a perfectly distinctive character. The keeper cannot alter the shape of his house, or choose its color. The government makes all these matters invariable."

"How far does a light show over the water?" asked Dick.

"That depends on the height and power of the light," answered the captain. "The Highland light can be seen for twenty miles, but these others for only about twelve each; for while that is a first-order light, Race Point is only a fourth-order, and these others fifth-order lights."

We were now well abreast of Long Point and had come about to go up into the harbor. The twilight was fast dying out, and the moon shone only dimly in a dull, heavy sky as we came to anchor in this spacious basin, now dotted here and there with the twinkling vessel lights on a large fleet of coasters and fishermen, who, rounding the cape, preferred, like ourselves, a safe anchorage to a night outside in a fog. The air grew momently chillier on deck, and we were glad to gather by the pleasant cabin light.

"Was it only to-day that we started?" asked Mabel. "It seems a long time ago that we left Boston."

And to this feeling we all assented. Perhaps none of us had realized how deeply the new and strange impressions of our first day on the sea had moved us. Certain it was that all were glad to retire early, and in a short time all was quiet; but I did not find it easy to sleep. The faint creaking of the boom as the vessel gently rocked in the slightly-heaving tide, or the footfall of the anchor-watch as he paced the forward deck, waked strange fancies in my brain, and my sleep was fitful and unrefreshing.

A loud ringing of our vessel bell roused me in affright; but my room-mate, Mrs. Bell, still slept undisturbed. I could not be calm, and woke her to ask what could be the trouble.

"Nothing, poor soul!" she said, listening a moment. "Don't you hear that distant bell striking twice, and then, after a bit, once, and then again twice, and so on? That is the fog signal at Wood End. Now hear that far-off, deep-toned, long-held sound! That is the trumpet at the Highland light. The fog must have settled down again, as we expected. Now hear that horn blowing! Some vessel is trying to work her way into the harbor. Now we answer with our bell, because we are at anchor, and that is both a guide and a warning to her. Go to sleep again. We are all right," she said, and in a moment more returned to sweet unconsciousness.

But not so I. The light-house bell kept up its solemn tolling, and if I fell into a light sleep my dreams continued the vein of my thoughts, and now I was lost at sea, and again dashed on reefs, and then floated for days helpless on a dismasted hulk.

My night was one of misery, and I ignominiously resolved to avail myself of the first opportunity to abandon the trip. But, as we gathered at breakfast, all were so bright and had slept so soundly that I was ashamed to tell of my fears.

"We're out of sight of land!" shouted

Dick, who, now that he felt safe, thought the fog quite a joke.

Presently we heard a call: " On board the schooner!" Dr. Bell, and in fact we all. hurried on deck. Alongside was a man rowing a dory, who asked us to give him the direction of the town, which we did after glancing at our compass, and he rowed away and was soon lost to sight. About half an hour later the same call roused us again, and we hurried again on deck to see — to our surprise and the chagrin of the rower — the same man asking the same question. We started him again, and watched him wearily pull away into the mist and disappear. Not long after the same call from the same man roused us the third time. Twice he had rowed in so complete a circle as to bring him again to his starting-point. When he recognized us he looked for an instant disheartened, then relieved his mind in a vehement soliloquy, which so amused the young people that the Yale man called for cheers, which, being heartily given, the angered man turned away. We called to him to come back and come aboard for a lunch ; but he surlily rowed on, nor indeed, to our satisfaction, and undoubtedly to his, did we see him again.

" Why didn't he carry a little compass in his dory?" asked Dick, as Captain Blake was telling him that it was in that same way that many fishermen, overtaken by fogs, are bewildered and lost on the Grand Banks each year.

" The motions of small boats are too quick ; the compass never has time to adjust itself," answered the captain.

We returned to the cabin and resumed our books or letter-writing.

" The fog-signal has stopped," said Dr. Bell ; and we all followed him on deck, delighted to see the mists rolling off and the sun breaking through, though it was now about noon.

" Let's be all ready," continued he, " and after dinner we will go ashore and take a drive to the Highland Lighthouse."

" Yes," said Mrs. Bell ; " this drive is quite the approved thing for visitors to Provincetown. They have three-seated vehicles here, which carry nine, which is just our party and a driver, and a pair of good horses will take us there and back easily this afternoon."

" We needn't take a driver," said Colonel Graham. " I think I could manage any horses that this town could bring on."

" You might manage the horses, but you couldn't for your life find the right road," answered the doctor. " I've been there before. We'll take a driver."

By the time we were all ready the sun was bright and the horizon clear. We secured a carriage and driver without delay, and were soon out of the streets of the thrifty little town.

Our horses began to labor in the sandy way and the big vehicle creaked dolefully.

" How much of this sort of riding do we have?" asked the colonel, dejectedly.

" It's the same all the way, except where it's coarse," answered our charioteer, and we soon came to be of his mind. Such a dreary outlook! There were wide marshes, crossed by a great causeway built by the State to prevent the sea from making a channel for itself across the land, if one could call that land where the tide flowed in and out among the tall reeds ; then banks of sand. clean and white, now and then overspread with a tangle of wild roses blossoming deeply red in the sea wind they

NAUSET LIGHTS.

love so well; some tufty beach-grass here and there; more wretched scrub-oaks; and at length young pines growing in long, straight rows as if they had been planted.

"And so they had been," our driver told us.

"Who by, and for what!" exclaimed we all, for not a vestige of a habitation was in sight anywhere.

"To keep the land from blowing all away into the sea," said the doctor. "History tells us that when this land was first visited by the Pilgrims it was covered with a growth of pine trees; but, once cut away, the forests never sprang again, and then the sand began to blow about and drift into hills, and in storms to whirl over the sea till it became plain that something must be done to keep Cape Cod at home. Some years ago a good minister settled here, interested the towns about in replanting these sands, and the State gave some favorable assistance by way of remitting taxes and otherwise, till now you see the result in these hundreds or thousands of acres more or less covered with these young pines. You can see about how much they plant each year by the height of the trees in the different plantations. There, some are as much as ten feet high, while this growth here is not more than three inches tall."

"But why do they plant only pines?" asked Helen.

"Because pines live almost wholly on the air, and you can see that there is hardly any soil-food here. Then, too, for this location, they possess the very great advantage of being evergreens, and so they serve also as a wind-screen for any unhappy creature who may have to travel these roads in winter."

"Roads!" said Dick, "I don't call these cart-ruts roads."

"You see, now, why we needed a driver," went on the doctor, as the man turned the horses in another direction and whipped them up a little sandy rise. Various wagon-tracks ran in devious ways through the pine growths, but nothing was in sight to indicate our way.

"A hermit lives there," presently said our driver, pointing out to us a wretched shanty with an adjacent wood-pile and hen-coop, though none of us could imagine why he should confine the poor hens, till the Yale man suggested the old joke, — that it might be to prevent them from getting out and starving.

A mockery of a corn-field was also near by. We wished to stop and visit the recluse; but our informer assured us that we would see no one, though he had spent several years in this seclusion, and that his name and history were unknown.

As we kept on we began to find better grass, and here and there little patches of corn were growing well. At last, almost before we were aware, we came to some grassy slopes, and before us, on a rise of ground, stood the tower and buildings of Highland light. Here, too, were a few pleasant country homes, and evident tokens of the ubiquitous summer visitor. We were much amused at an old dismantled and abandoned wind-mill of a by-gone time, which stood in a field near by, bearing the incongruous legend of "Ice cream," in new paint, on its time-worn face.

At the gate of the keeper's ground we alighted, and, as we crossed a field, came at length to a view of the sea that thrilled us with emotion. From the high bluff we looked directly down a hundred and fifty feet to where the gentle waves were rippling up the sand-beach that skirts the base of the long sand bluff, and then over the sea, the vast open ocean. We thought we could imagine how Xenophon's army felt as the blue Euxine came suddenly into their sight from a hill-top, and, embracing each other, they cried, "Thalassa! Thalassa! The sea! The sea!"

From north to south along this great highway of the coasting fleets vessels were coming and going. Below us, passing, so belittled by the distance, they seemed like some miniature fairy fleet. The effect upon the mind was startling.

Ordinarily we look at the sea from its own level or, perhaps, from a hill with intervening slopes. But here is the ocean, its wide expanse unbroken by a single island, lying far below us at our feet, only sea and sky before us, as if we were floating in the air. Some of us grew dizzy and had to draw back from the face of the cliff; but it was a glorious prospect, many times repaying for the hot and dusty drive over the eight miles of sand.

"To-morrow," said the doctor, "some visitor here will be looking at us passing by."

"I wish we were there now," said Dick.

Returning to the tower, we took a hurried look at the lantern, and peered into the trumpet of the Great Siren — the fog-signal — and then, not being able to escape the attraction of the place, visited the ice-cream

OLD WINDMILL.

incetown has the reputation of having the largest average wealth of any place in the State ; and we wonder at this as we think that now, and from its location, it must always draw all its wealth from the sea.

After leaving our vehicle we climbed the steep hill, which stands directly back of the tower, sheltering it in wintry storms, and forming an important landmark. A large school-house stood formerly on the crest of this sand-heap, but, having been destroyed by fire, was never rebuilt. Now bunchy beach grass is planted carefully here, so that its roots may hold the sand against high winds, and wild roses bloom profusely over the neglected ruins. The

rooms in the old windmill, and at length, as our driver was growing impatient, we reëntered our vehicle and started homeward.

Returning by another road we came through the quaint little village of North Truro, and then over the same weary sands, back to the thriving seaport, many of whose neat houses boasted very pretty door-yards, although we were told what, we are sure, must be true, that every flowerpot full of soil has been brought many miles, much of it on vessels. Prov-

harbor lay like a map before us, — a pleasant view. At length we came down and returned by the narrow streets, with their board walks, by the fish-houses and wharves, to the long pier, where our tender was awaiting us, and then on board the Idler, which already had come to seem homelike to us.

Next morning, soon after sunrise, we were all astir. The anchor was weighed, and with a fair breeze we left the harbor and came out beyond Wood-end, and retraced our way to Race Point. Here our breeze began to fail us, and before we were hardly well by the dangerous Peaked-Hill bars it fell entirely, and we lay becalmed in a lazy ground swell, our sails idly slatting as the yacht rolled slowly. We all gathered in the shade of the sail as a protection from the hot sun, and then we drifted about till the middle of the afternoon, when a light air stirred, and with all our sails set we slowly worked along; but by night-fall all was again calm, and we were still only a little past the Highland light, and it became very evident that here we were to pass the night, — a fact which occasioned no regret, for the sea was remarkably quiet, the air bland, and the moon was almost at its full. We hung out our side-lights, and not far away could see the red or green lights of other vessels lying, like ourselves, becalmed on this summer sea.

"Just about here I had a dreadful experience many years ago," said Captain Blake, who sat at the wheel, and we all stopped our conversation to listen to his story. "It was near the close of the war, and the high price of cotton had made sail-cloth very expensive. Vessels used their old sails and patched and re-patched them till they were sights to see, and masters had to sail very cautiously because the sails were too old and worn to bear the strain of heavy winds.

One winter day I was coming up along the cape, with the wind blowing very fresh from the north-west all day, and about nightfall came along to a fleet of vessels anchored off here, making a lee of these high sand-bluffs. I joined them, and was the twenty-fourth and last vessel of that company, of which one was quite a large brig.

Soon after anchoring the wind fell, and not long after all was quiet. Now I had always noticed that, after such a sudden lull in the wind, it was very apt to come on again suddenly and strong from another direction, and so, as my sails were very old, I thought I had best get under way and leave that place; and so, although the last to come, I was the first to go. About eleven at night I hoisted sail, though my men were very unwilling to do so, and we had slowly worked only a mile or two away, when the wind suddenly struck in from the north-east, and in a few minutes the returned storm was upon us in redoubled strength. The other vessels, still riding at their anchors, thus driven on a lee-shore, struggled to get away, but before they could make any headway, five of them, including the brig, were driven upon the sand-beach, and pounded to pieces; and of the rest some more were lost between here and Race Point, the Peaked-Hill bars catching several of them. That was a terrible night."

"How did you manage to get away, captain?" we all eagerly asked.

"Well, I was far enough from shore to have some sea-room, and so I tried to work around to Provincetown. I got safely by Race Point, and then, finding myself likely to lose my sails at any moment, and the air being then full of blinding snow, I decided to drop my anchor and try to hold my vessel on the other side of the cape. There were twenty-seven fathoms of water there, but my anchor held, though I feared each moment that the cable would part, for the vessel labored terribly in the strong gale and heavy sea. The day at last came, and finally went without any lessening of the storm. I did not dare to start again, because I was sure my sails could not serve me; and yet I knew that if my cable should part, or my anchor drag, I should be helplessly adrift. But the next night the storm abated, and in the morning we went into Provincetown to get some rest. When we heard what became of the rest of the fleet we were very thankful that our case had been no worse. Everything then depended on our anchor holding on. You see we were in unusually deep water for anchoring, and in an almost open sea. I hope never to have to repeat that experiment."

From the Highland to Nauset lights, twelve miles below, the shore has the same unvarying character, — a long sand bluff, gradually lowering in height, with a narrow strip of beach at the base. At Nauset three beacons of equal height send their rays over the water, forming a beautiful sight, and, as far as I know, a singular instance of triple lights on the coast. Up to this place we had really only drifted on a favoring tide; but here, at Nauset, the tidal currents divide as the incoming waters meet the land, some flowing northward and some southward, so that now we came into an opposing tide. The night was absolutely perfect. The unsentimental sailors were asleep below; but the Yale man and the girls had long been sitting in the bow, conversing in low tones.

At midnight, after some remonstrance, we all obeyed the doctor's advice to retire; but in the early morning we were again astir, eager not to lose anything that was to be seen. Nor, indeed, had we lost much, for we were then only abreast the two Chatham lights, nine miles below Nauset.

Here a dear little yellow bird, weary of his flight, lighted on our rigging; but a sailor instantly rose and shook the shrouds, so that he flew away. The girls were quite indignant, but Captain Blake told us that all seamen thought it a very bad sign for a bird to rest on a ship.

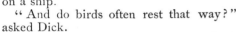
WOOD END LIGHT

"And do birds often rest that way?" asked Dick.

"Oh, yes! Sometimes a whole flock of swallows, or other birds, especially in the migratory seasons, will light on a vessel; but the sailors never allow it if they can prevent it."

Passing Chatham, we still drifted southerly by the long, low sand-strip of Monomay Point, toward the light-ship anchored out at sea, where the shifting, sandy bottom rendered tower-building impracticable, on Pollock Rip shoal, some nine miles away; a two-masted, red-painted vessel, with its name in great white letters on its sides, and some red iron day-marks at the mast-head,—a curious sight to us who were unfamiliar with sea-travel. Then, with the same calm sea, and a brightly shining sun, we worked on westerly a few miles to another light-ship, this one painted green, but bearing in the same huge white letters its name, — The Shovelful; — and then slowly on to the straw-colored hull of a third light-ship, whose mast-head day-marks and lettering were black, — The Handkerchief, — past which we were fairly inside Nantucket Sound; but we had come so slowly that it was now noon.

A scorching sun poured down from a hazy sky, and the many vessels in sight began to take on strange shapes. The hull of one would seem to lift itself high above the water, while that of another would disappear as if below the surface. The sails would appear to contract or to lengthen, now stretching upward on towering masts, now shrinking on shortened spars; each form constantly changing as the bent lines of light came to us through the distorting medium of the hot air. The mirage — or loom, as the sailors call it — now suddenly brought the almost invisible island of Nantucket boldly into view, and then, again, suddenly let it sink from sight. It was all very curious and novel to us. The tide being now in our favor, with all our kites set, we were trying to work along to the north-westward to the singular-looking tower called the Bishop and Clerk, which stands on the half-uncovered reef of the same name; but it was the middle of the afternoon before we got abreast of it.

Hot puffs of air now began to reach us from off the land, and a general murkiness prevailed. We determined to try to get into Hyannis, and so kept on toward the large red bell-buoy, now solemnly sounding as it swayed in the sea. About two miles away a stretch of breakwater made a sheltered harbor.

"Was that thunder?" suddenly asked Helen; but there was no need for a reply, for, from a heavy black cloud now rising fast, we saw a vivid flash of lightning fall.

"Is that rain or wind?" asked the doctor of the captain, who had long been watching the weather.

"Both, I think. I hardly know whether we shall catch it before we get inside, but I think it will be as well to clew up our topsails and take in our balloon-jib," said the captain, as he went below and got his oil-clothes, then looked about to see that all was snug and in order on the deck. One man began to lay out some anchor chain, ready to let it run when needed.

"We might as well lower our flies," said the doctor. "They will only whip out in the wind."

Meanwhile Mrs. Bell had picked up the

wraps lying on the deck-house, and the steward was screwing up the side-lights in the cabin.

" I don't like to take a squall here," muttered the captain. " There isn't sea-room enough."

The air grew rapidly thicker and darker, and little puffs of wind came now from one direction, then another. We took in all but our three lower sails. " I guess we will try to get in," said the captain. " Those vessels yonder are still carrying all sail." But as we looked we saw them suddenly stagger, and then lay away down as the first heavy blast struck them.

" Down the foresail ! Stand by the main-sheet ! " shouted Captain Blake.

" Everybody in the cabin ! " called Doctor Bell, and we hastened to obey. The captain put on his tarpaulin, and carefully took his compass-bearings. The cloud looked grandly terrible. It came rolling over and over, headlong upon us, and the rain under it was like a dark wall on the water, which itself took on an inky hue. On came the wind, and as the first strong blast struck us our vessel quivered in every part. Her masts bent and cracked. The wind howled in the rigging. " Lower the peak ! " cried the captain, and the vessel eased herself somewhat, though she still rushed through the sea, which now was lashed by the wind.

Shut down in the cabin, we could hear the orders above the pounding of the rain or the crashing of the thunder, and we could hear the hasty foot-falls on the deck. Dick crept into his berth and drew the curtains. The girls covered their faces, and were white with terror.

" We shall be lost," moaned Helen, by whose side the Yale man sat, regarding her with mute pity. I felt as if I should stifle, and rose and pushed open the doors in the companion-way. A dash of water greeted me, but I looked out. We were heeled down in an alarming degree.

" I can't help it," said the captain. " I must not let her up here," and he firmly held the wheel. Through the pouring rain I saw a great black mass of rock near by, past which we rushed, and then all in an instant, as it seemed, the vessel was brought around head into the wind, and righted herself, while the jib was let go, and then we heard the anchor-chain noisily running out of the hawse-hole.

" Oh, dear ! " groaned Mabel. " I knew we should hit something."

" What nonsense ! " said the colonel.

" The anchor is the only part that has hit anything."

We were, indeed, safe behind the break-water. The squall had struck us in a way to drive us along as we wished, and now, with plenty of scope to our anchor, we could and did ride out the tempest with comfort and safety.

In an hour all was again quiet, and the declining sun shone brightly on the retreating cloud, where a glorious rainbow was painted.

A pleasant evening followed the rain, but the wind had raised quite a sea, and we made no effort to go ashore till the next day. Finding the town pleasant, we spent two days here, taking some long drives ; and the third, with a prosperous easterly wind, we left Hyannis, and, re-passing the bell-buoy, sailed directly for the Succonesset light-ship, — a curious-looking craft, with its hull painted like a checker-board, in alternate red and buff squares, and its own long name in big letters over all, — by which we sailed so closely that we spoke easily with the light-keepers, and even threw over to them a big bundle of newspapers that we had accumulated on board.

About nine miles more in a southerly way brought us to the harbor and old town of Edgartown, where we lay another night. We were greatly pleased with this fine village, which stands as quietly among its trees as if it had never heard of its crowded, bustling neighbor, Cottage City. The one suggests age and repose as much as the other does youth and activity ; but seen at a little distance, and from the sea, nothing could be more picturesque than these oak bluffs, with the endless variety of cottages, large and small, vine-hung among the oak groves. As we left Edgartown we came up along the shore in front of the bluff, and then around the East Chop into Vineyard Sound, intending to enter Vineyard Haven ; but the sailing was so fine that we decided to keep on as far as the highlands of Gay Head, and then, having traversed the entire length of the Nantucket and Vineyard Sounds, to return, and after delaying at Tarpaulin Cove return to the Haven for the next night.

These sounds, through which so many vessels pass daily, several hundred being sometimes in sight at once, are admirably lighted and buoyed ; and it would seem that, except for the presence of fog or a snow-storm, they should always be crossed with safety ; but this is far from the case. Vessels are not infrequently run directly upon some one of the many shoals, and in beating, collisions often occur, so great is the carelessness of the masters. What the navigation of the shoals must have been before government located all these marks we can hardly imagine, but we know that the almost sole reliance then was that now-too-much-neglected article, the sounding-line; for in winter, not only these many buoys, but even the light vessels themselves, are sometimes carried from their proper places by drifting masses of ice, and so cannot be blindly depended upon; of course the amount of obstructing ice varies with the winters, some years there being hardly any, while in others it opposes an almost constant barrier. Indeed, in the winter of '75 the sound was closed entirely for about six weeks. Then, too, among these many shoals the tidal currents run very strong, and set in a very bewildering way, although the entire rise of the tide is only from two to four feet.

From Gay Head we could easily see the Vineyard Sound light vessel off the Sow and Pigs reef, indicating the other side of the westerly entrance of the sound, and we marvelled that men could be found willing to live in such places as these light-ships; for, indeed, so strangely careless are some coasters that these very vessels are occasionally run into, thus needlessly adding to the unavoidable dangers incident to the sea.

On Gay Head stands a conspicuous light tower, another of the few first-order lights alongshore; and yet here, as we all well remember, on a clear night, with several other lights in full view, the City of Columbus was run directly on to the ragged outlying rocks and lost,—another sad illustration of the carelessness of some masters of vessels.

" How many first-order lights are there alongshore?" asked Dick.

" Not many," said the captain; " off the New England coast there are only eight; or rather nine, for there are two together on Cape Ann. Then there is one at Seguin, off the mouth of the Kennebec, the Highland light, and this at Gay Head. Beside, there is one on Block Island, one at Montauk Point, and two on the seaward side of Long Island, — one of them at Shinnecock Bay, and the other at Fire Island. All of these lights can be seen at a distance of twenty miles."

Coming about at Gay Head, we sailed back through the sound, between the green fields of the Vineyard and the wooded, but desolate, shores of the islands on the other side separating us from Buzzard's Bay, to Tarpaulin Cove, where we entered, and, letting go only one jib, dropped anchor to wait while we all went ashore for a walk. Here we found a welcome from the light-keeper, who told us much about the island called Nanshou, upon which we were. It is almost wholly the property of Mr. Forbes, of Boston, who keeps it for a hunting-preserve, many native wild deer still living on the island. This seemed very romantic to us, but the keeper quite destroyed the illusion by telling us that these deer are a great plague to the farmer, who has his solitary house near by. He told us that they were so fond of potatoes that they would destroy his entire crop, if he had not found that by chaining his dog in the middle of the potato-field, the poor, cold, homesick animal would bark and howl so dreadfully to get loose that he frightened off the deer. He said that one could frequently see them in the moonlight, kicking at the potato-hills.

Such conduct on the part of the deer seemed to us very reprehensible and unpoetic, and we tried to fancy Landseer painting a group of these monarchs of the glen digging potatoes. The idea was so absurd that, on the whole, we regretted that the keeper had enlightened us as to the habits of the animals. We should have preferred a pleasing ignorance.

Back of the keeper's dwelling we had to cross a wonderful growth of what we decided to be rose mallows, hundreds of whose large red blossoms were open to the sun, — to us a very remarkable sight.

Again leaving this pleasant cove we crossed to the Vineyard shore, and entered the Haven, the favorite resort of the coasting fleet. Here, in this deep indentation, several hundred vessels at a time sometimes find a refuge in stormy periods; but as it is open and unprotected to the north, it is sometimes a very uneasy anchorage, and vessels often drag their anchors and pull back on each other, and occasionally go high and dry ashore. In the morning we visited the village, and drove over to Cottage City, and then, returning, lingered about an old wreck, which some fierce tempest had stranded here. The day was hot, and finding the sea water comfortable the girls took off their shoes and stockings, and waded and paddled about, while the gentlemen all went to the village to negotiate for a vehicle to take us over the island to Gay Head. Throughout the trip, each day brought its own fill of new experiences and scenes! It seemed to us all as if we had opened some other world, this life was so unlike that we had left behind us. And, as we re-turned at last to our yacht, we congratulated ourselves that our cruise was as yet only well begun, and that we were still to pass several more weeks in the waters beyond.

Sarah Leslie.